JUREK BECKER

JUREK BECKER

A LIFE
IN FIVE
WORLDS

SANDER L. GILMAN

THE UNIVERSITY OF CHICAGO PRESS
CHICAGO AND LONDON

SANDER L. GILMAN is Distinguished Professor of the Liberal Arts and Sciences and of Medicine and director of the Humanities Laboratory as well as the Program in Jewish Studies, University of Illinois at Chicago. He is the author or editor of more than sixty books, including most recently *Jewish Frontiers* (2003).

The University of Chicago Press, Chicago 60637
The University of Chicago Press, Ltd., London
© 2003 by The University of Chicago
All rights reserved. Published 2003
Printed in the United States of America

12 11 10 09 08 07 06 05 04 03   1 2 3 4 5

ISBN: 0-226-29393-9 (cloth)

Library of Congress Cataloging-in-Publication Data

Gilman, Sander L.
    Jurek Becker : a life in five worlds / Sander L. Gilman.
      p.   cm.
    Includes bibliographical references and index.
    ISBN 0-226-29393-9 (alk. paper)
    1. Becker, Jurek, 1937–   2. German literature—Jewish authors—Biography.
3. Holocaust, Jewish (1939–1945)   I. Title.

    PT2662.E294 Z675   2003
    833'.914—dc21   2003010002

To Stanley Fish,
who does not trust biographies

Contents

Introduction

Beginnings are always difficult. To write a biography of someone you knew and liked is complex. I hosted Jurek Becker during his stay at Cornell University in 1984 and taught his works jointly with him for a month. I had known him since the late 1960s, when he was the darling of young writers in East Berlin. He later wrote that he felt that the tasks of the critic and those of the writer were very different. The metaphor he often employed for this difference was that of the ornithologist and the bird. I was the ornithologist; he was the bird.

But my task as a critic was never scientific; it was, rather, empathetic. I was and am a bird watcher rather than an ornithologist. I like to watch and speculate rather than to label and classify. And Jurek Becker was a *rara avis*. He was a Jewish child-survivor author. He was an Eastern European Jew who held a major position in the culture of both Germanys. He was, in part, the abandoned child in Jerzy Kosinski's *The Painted Bird* (1965), Kosinski's metaphor for the mindless torture that marked human relationships in the Shoah. But he was also a completely secular Polish Jew transformed into a good if critical German by his upbringing in the German Democratic Republic. After 1977, he was a well-known figure in the literary and media scene in West Berlin, and after 1991 he was at home as much as he could be anywhere in the new, reunited Germany.

As a cultural critic and a literary historian, I had already written about Becker and his work, among other places in my study *Jewish Self Hatred* (1982), which was published in German a decade later by the Jüdischer Verlag in Frankfurt (1992). After his death, however, I wanted to capture his life as well as understand his writing in all the registers in which he wrote. The importance of his writing rests on a trilogy of novels about the Shoah that are unique in postwar German writing. For present-day Germany, his reputation rests primarily on his authorship of one of the most successful and intellectually challenging television series ever seen in Germany. His biography—as Jew, Pole, and East German, as oppositional writer and spokesman for a united Germany, as novelist and scriptwriter—is unusual enough to encompass many of the questions about identity and culture in Central Europe from the 1930s to the 1990s. To explore them, I thought it necessary to make sense of his life as well as his texts. This was something he truly feared. He did not want his works to be reduced to the "biographical sources" that critics love to find.[1] In this biography I have tried to point out aspects of his life that are incorporated in the novels, but only as reference points. Each is adapted and changed in the narratives that Jurek created in his novels, his films, and his television shows. I have not pointed to any of Jurek's works and said: here is a truth about Jurek's life. What I hope I have done is to illustrate the stories he told about his life and to show how they too became part of his creative world.

One way of doing this was to create a set of various "worlds" for Becker's life. The conceit I have used throughout this book is to use the names he was given, from his actual name Jerzy, to his "German" name Georg, to the name with which he signed his books, Jurek. The shift of names signifies a restructuring of an identity, but it was also a restructuring of emotions and attitudes that were shaped in his earliest childhood and reinforced over the rest of his life. This is a not a crude attempt at a psychoanalytic reduction of all experience to the events of earliest childhood. I believe strongly that all the experiences of our life shape what we are. Each experience is layered upon earlier experiences and beliefs, shaping and forming them, giving them meaning. This critical approach to an understanding of whole life experience is the view espoused by Erich Fromm and Karen Horney. I have used this approach, not in a rigid or dogmatic way, to explore the events and experiences of Jurek's life as I have been able to reconstruct them. This reconstruction is often tentative.

Jurek had reason to fear people rummaging about in his life. His childhood was a mystery to him. No exploration would leave the scars he bore untouched. The records of his early life are not only fragmentary but inherently contradictory. As an adult he became the object of quite the opposite fascination. As one of the most articulate spokesmen for reform within the German Democratic Republic, he had the attention of the Stasi (Ministerium der Staatssicherheit, or Ministry of State Security), which shadowed him for over two decades. The West German intelligence service did the same. Their secrets are still well kept; their state still exists, and no "Freedom of Information Act" allows access their files.

The moral problem is that the initial shadowing of Jurek Becker provided constant intrusion into his private life and into his psyche. I found myself exploring the complex life of a man I admire often through the very eyes of those who were shadowing him. To use the earliest documents about Jurek's life, I had to create a context; to use the Stasi documents, I had to make sure that they actually reflected the sense and the texture of Jurek's life. I therefore undertook extensive interviews with virtually all of those quoted in the Stasi documents, including some of those who wrote reports as "unofficial agents" of the Stasi. Jurek had provided a key to their names. I was not interested in reports of his sexual affairs unless they shed light on his creative work. Only when these relationships became part of the fabric of his creative work did I need to recount the stories I have been told.

The many reports cited and read that appear in this biography are open to interpretation. The evidentiary status of the Stasi reports, always problematic, beg the following question: are they "true" in the sense that they provide accurate information about real events recorded in close proximity to these events? While this may generally be the case, the reasons why any given report was actually written are almost impossible to determine. Does a report exist because the subject was the primary or, as early in Becker's career, only secondary to the prime individual being shadowed? Did Jurek "know" he was being shadowed, as was clearly the case in the mid-1970s when he was overtly being followed just to frighten him? He even used the fact that he knew his phone was bugged to get responses from the authorities. On one occasion in 1976, Jurek encouraged a West German who was having difficulty arranging an interview with Hermann Kant, then vice-president of the Writers' Union, simply to call him, Jurek, and ask for an interview to substitute for the one with Kant. Two days later the journalist got his interview with Kant.[2] The "truth" value of this material must also be tempered by knowing who the reporters were. Virtually all of the Stasi files are coded, but Becker provided a rather complete list of those individuals he assumed to have made the reports. I have not used this information unless I could verify the identification. It would also be necessary to check the motivation of the reporters. I often use this material to show attitudes rather than facts. Having been one of the first to file under the Freedom of Information Act for the FBI files in my work on Bertolt Brecht, I know how poor such material can be as sources.[3] They must be confirmed by other sources, including interviews with those quoted in the files, and even then they are suspect.

I have also benefited from undisputed sources of Jurek's opinions over time, for he gave a large number of interviews that were subsequently published. Many of these were edited by him or were, in fact, written responses to questions. Richard Zipser's long interview with him in 1977 was actually a set of written responses to questions that were put to Jurek.[4] In other cases, we have the heavily edited transcripts of interviews with him, as in the long interview with Wolfram Schütte and Axel Vornbäumen of the *Frankfurter Rundschau* on August 28, 1995, that is reprinted at the close of his collected essays.[5] One of Jurek's greatest gifts was his ability to craft dialogue that looked and sounded spoken—an essential gift for a scriptwriter and a major advantage for a novelist. What is striking about these interviews is that they often present responses both carefully thought out and beautifully phrased. The artist Willi Moese, a friend of Jurek's, once told me that Jurek was one of the few people he knew who spoke in paragraphs. He tended to do this either because he had said much the same thing over and over again or because he planned what he said very, very carefully. Using interview materials means taking all of this into consideration. I became aware of that fact years ago when I interviewed I. B. Singer.[6] Singer's answers were brilliant, but it turned out that they were part of a mental archive of responses that he used when he gave interviews. They were texts, and they also needed interpretation. I use the interviews with Jurek in much the same way, often to indicate the contradictions over time in his own accounts of his life, work, and beliefs.

I had access to a wide range of people who were willing to be interviewed about Jurek's work and life. Many of my conversations are with them are part of the "deep background" of my research. I have not listed those persons in this volume; nor have I, for the most part, annotated the information they provided. In almost all cases I was able to find either documentary accounts or multiple oral histories to confirm what I have written. The archival sources are listed in the notes. The end result is my interpretation of Jurek's life.

The "Becker Papers" were deposited in the Akademie der Künste (Academy of Arts) in Berlin after I was done with my work on them. I was able to use all of them—including correspondence, reports, Jurek's Stasi file, and family documents—as well as archival holdings at numerous institutions in Germany. All the members of the Becker families and most of his colleagues and friends were more than generous with their time in answering endless and, sometimes, contradictory questions. Jurek's widow, Christine Becker, was willing to read drafts of this volume and comment on them. François Guesnet lent me his support as I reconstructed the Polish aspects of Jurek's life. All errors or misinterpretations remain mine. My wife, Marina Gilman, the daughter of German and German Jewish immigrants in the 1930s, read and commented on the volume from her own critical perspective. With this biography I pay a debt to both the memory of Jurek Becker and to my friends and colleagues in Germany and the United States who have begun the serious study of

Jewish culture in present-day Germany. Jewish life in all its complexity
continued in Germany after the Shoah. Jurek Becker is a representative
of the youngest survivor authors. As I was writing this introduction, the
first German-language volume of literature by a member of the youngest
generation of Russian Jews to come to Germany after 1989 appeared. In
his book *Russian Disco*, Wladamir Kaminer describes how he became
a German after his immigration from the Soviet Union in 1989 and,
through that process, a Jew.[7] The story continues.

An early draft of this book was given as the annual Mertes Prize Lecture
at the German Historical Institute, Washington, D.C., in 1997 and the
inaugural Heinz Bluhm Memorial Lecture at Boston College. I continued
to write the book while a Humboldt Foundation Prize fellow, working
with Hartmut Steinecke, and completed it while holding a Berlin Prize
fellowship at the American Academy in Berlin in 2000–2001. I thank the
academy and, especially, Gary Smith for their hospitality. Anke Pinkert,
Astrid Kurth, Robyn Schiffman, and Dana Rovang assisted me on this
volume. My German editor, Krista Maria Schädlich, of the Ullstein Verlag
in Berlin, provided immeasurable help. A member of the oppositional
literary circle in Berlin in the 1970s, Schädlich brought a deep knowledge
of the nuances of the period to the German edition. Eagle-eyed readers
who take the time to read both the German and the English editions
will find the German version more compact, in part because German
readers are more familiar than most English-speaking readers with the
background and content of Jurek's books and films. The Becker family
allowed me to use the photographs of Jurek that appear in this volume.
Finally, I wish to thank Margaret Mahan for her sensitive editing of this
book.

Berlin June 2001/Chicago June 2002

Chapter 1

JUREK IN LODZ, 1937–1939

Jurek Becker—at first named Jerzy Bekker (sometimes spelled Beker); later, in the German Democratic Republic, to be called Georg Becker or as Georg Jurek Becker; and still later to be known again as Jurek, his childhood Polish nickname—was born in Lodz, Poland, in September 1937.[1] As with much about his childhood, even this date has been called into question. Yet little Jurek was born into a time and a place that we can try to capture, if only in its contradictions. He was born a Jew and a Pole in a city that was at once the most modern and the most Jewish city in Poland.

Whether for good or for ill, Lodz was a city that defined its inhabitants and was in turn defined by them. Lodz was the "Jerusalem of Poland," according to the great Polish Yiddish novelist, Israel Joshua Singer, writing in the late 1930s.[2] Yet its ironic nickname, "the Promised Land," captured the double face of modern Poland. *The Promised Land* was the title of the 1924 Polish Nobel Prize–winner Wladyslaw Reymont's novel that appeared in 1898. In it he bemoaned the inexorable course of industrialization in Lodz and the resultant destruction of the Polish peasantry. According to contemporary historians, Lodz was considered the "Manchester of Poland" because of its status as a center of textile production. Like Manchester, the home of Friedrich Engels, Lodz was also a center for revolutionary activities, especially among the Jewish socialists. In summary it was the *zle miasto*, the bad city, for Jurek's Polish contemporaries: too new, too modern, too capitalist, too revolutionary, too Jewish.

Not that everyone benefited from the fruits of industry. There was poverty among the Polish workers and the Jewish weavers at one end of the economic spectrum. By the 1930s the Bekkers were very much at the other end. Sródmeijska (Central) Street, where they lived, was a relatively upscale area inhabited by Jews and Poles and Jews who were becoming Poles.[3] The Bekkers—a good Yiddish name, by the way, *bekker* meaning "baker"—had moved there from 189 Piotrkowska Street before their only child's birth. Piotrkowska Street was the main street in Lodz, running from the Market Square in the north for a number of miles to the southern part of the city, where many of the large textile mills where located. Before World War I, the upper reach of the street was the finest in the city; expensive shops and major hotels existed alongside the apartment houses where the Lodz bourgeoisie, both Jews and Christians, lived.[4] The Bekkers' new apartment on Sródmeijska Street was somewhat grander, even more solidly middle-class.

The world economic crisis of 1929 had affected the Jews of Lodz as it had everyone else in Poland, but by the late 1930s Lodz had rebounded. As one young Jewish child wrote about middle-class Lodz: "We lived in a new apartment complex that was very nice . . . It was two bedrooms and a kitchen."[5] Another noted that "the buildings were four floors, huge buildings. Like here, four floors would be here about twenty-four apartments, and over there were maybe ten or eight."[6] The one-year-old Jurek Bekker (Jurek is the standard Polish nickname for Jerzy) was oblivious to all this. In his short pants and sailor shirt, this was his world, the very comfortable world of the Jewish middle class in an independent Poland.

Jurek was the apple of his parents' eye. He was their firstborn, their *Kaddish*, the male child who would remember them yearly after their deaths with the Jewish prayer of sanctification. His thoroughly modern parents, the thirty-seven-year-old Mieczyslaw (his good Polish nickname was Mjetek) and his thirty-five-year-old wife with the elegant Polish name of Anette, (née Lewin), were still very much Jews.[7] They were secular Jews in the conflicted world of modern Poland, modern Lodz. Jurek Bekker's birth was a promise to his somewhat older parents of the continuation of their very bourgeois life into the next generation. Part of Jurek's legacy would be his command of Polish.

Mieczyslaw and Anette were well established in Lodz before Jurek was born. Their own *mame loschen* (mother tongue) was Yiddish, but by the time of Jurek's birth the language of the household was Polish. In a fit of exasperation, however, Anette described her newborn son, in Yiddish, as *essen, pissen, kaken, trinken* ("eating, pissing, shitting, drinking") after the sole activities that occupied him. Mieczyslaw and Anette were going to raise their child in the most modern manner, for as a Polish-speaking Jew one had a certain invisibility, they believed, in Polish society. They spoke Polish to him, even though it was their second language, as more and more middle-class Jews in urban Poland did. Indeed, Barbara Góra, an older Jewish contemporary of Jurek Bekker's in Poland who was born in 1932, remembered her Polish upbringing. A decade later she commented: "I was born into a Polonized family that never denied its Jewish roots and its Jewish members, who on my mother's side were more or less orthodox Jews. In spite of that, I knew nothing about Jewish rituals, nor did I know any Yiddish."[8] Katarzyna Meloch, who too was seven years older than Jurek, recalled: "My father and his cousin, who were his same age, attended the Polish schools, spoke Polish at home, but one celebrated the Jewish holidays, one did not abandon one's tradition."[9] In Poland, the acceptance of Polish as the primary language to be spoken by Jews who still thought of themselves as Jews was something relatively new.

Mieczyslaw and Anette had every intention of giving Jurek the best of their world—a world that was Jewish and Polish, but not too much of either. They had chosen to name him Jerzy and gave him a Polish nickname. A good Polish name for a beautiful Jewish child. At work, as the assistant manager of his uncle's textile mill, Mieczyslaw would often lapse into Yiddish when he spoke with his Jewish colleagues.[10] Speaking Polish was a sign of being part of the new Poland. Most importantly, it was modern. Jewish ritual was an ever less important part of their lives. Jurek had been circumcised eight days after his birth, but Mieczyslaw himself went to the synagogue only sporadically and often just to meet his colleagues from the other mills. His generation of urbanized, Polonized Jews were "three-day Jews." On the days of Rosh Hashanah and Yom Kippur he went to remember the dead and to honor the memory of his parents. His life was more that of a white-collar Pole than that of the stereotyped Jews of Warsaw, living in a self-imposed ghetto with their miracle rabbis. They were not modern, not modern at all. He later said to his adult son: "If it had not been for anti-Semitism, do you think that I would have felt myself to be a Jew for an instant?"[11]

Anette had been a seamstress in one of the numerous clothing factories until her marriage. Money was to be made in textile mills in Lodz. Even after the severe depression that followed World War I and the virtual collapse of the textile industry that had been a central part of the war effort, money was still to be made in cloth. Jewish entrepreneurs had shaped this industry. Indeed, it was Abraham Prussak who had introduced the steam engine to Lodz in 1859, which made possible great steam-driven plants that by the 1890s had replaced the hand weavers.

The world of Lodz was the world of these Jewish manufacturers. Even the small children remembered "in the 1930s the Jewish people building up big manufacture from cloth. Israel Poznanski was building up a big factory where he employed 26,000 people."[12] Poznanski had died in 1902, but his myth (and his family) lived on. Just up the street from Sródmiejska Street, where the Bekkers lived, was the second of the three Poznanski palaces, a sign of how vital the Jewish entrepreneurs, manufacturers, and even workers were to the city.[13] Another child recalled the international world of the textile magnets and their employees: "My father was a wealthy man. He made cloth, different kinds. We had a factory outside Lodz, and in town we had a place where the cloth came . . . We even had contracts with England, with companies, and after the war I wrote to them."[14] The industry in which Mieczyslaw worked for his uncle, who operated a medium-sized textile mill, was a world in which Polish goods were manufactured by Jewish mill owners and sold throughout Europe by their multilingual sales force.

Written in the late 1970s, one of Jurek Becker's most amusing and most often read short stories, "The Best-Loved Family Story" ("Die beliebteste Familiengeschichte"), is the tale of a Jew within this world of textile manufacturing in pre–World War I Poland.[15] It is the story of the narrator's Uncle Gideon, who was an "old man when they took him to Majdanek" (42). The narrator places himself as a survivor of a huge (*unüberschaubar*) extended Jewish family from Lublin, a Polish manufacturing city in eastern Poland with a Jewish (prewar) population of 40,000; the Majdanek death camp was a few miles outside of the city. For the adult Jurek Becker, Poland was the place where Jews lived well before the war and were murdered during the Shoah.

Set in the pre–World War I period, Gideon's story was the one always requested at the family gatherings that took place to celebrate the birth of new members. It ran as follows: Uncle Gideon does not like to travel. Indeed, he has only traveled in the immediate neighborhood, to Lemberg and Krakow on business and to Zopot on vacation. Suddenly he has to go to London to buy two knitting machines for his stocking factory (43). After checking into the hotel, he looks for a kosher restaurant; not finding one, he lives on coffee and cake (45). Having concluded his business, he is invited by his British counterpart to a party. Gideon gets the impression that this is to be a costume ball and dresses as a sad, white-faced clown. After he arrives, it is clear that he is the only one in costume. They must imagine, he thinks, that all the poor Jews in Galicia dress this way. He sneaks away, returns to his hotel, and then goes home.

The short story is the adult Jurek Becker's fantasy of Jewish life in pre–World War I Poland. The Jews are seen as wealthy, religious, and fertile. Jurek's use of the manager of a textile mill and his "English" trip draws from his knowledge of Lodz and the world of his father. This clearly historical tale ends with the Shoah and the destruction of this world. Jurek's story evokes the trajectory of Polish Jewry as he imagined it in the 1970s. Of equal importance for us, his fantasy of middle-class Polish Jewry centers on the telling of stories, such as the story told by Uncle Gideon. Jurek wrote his story in German, but his readers are never clear whether the German of his tale is supposed to represent Polish or Yiddish or, indeed, German itself, the language of educated Jews in Poland. For it is in German that Uncle Gideon, not knowing any English, makes himself understood in London (56). Becker's fantasy of a secular Polish Jewry world became part of the stories he tells about telling stories. This is the legacy that the adult writer saw himself as receiving from the lost world of Polish-speaking Jewry.

In 1937, Lodz was an intensely Jewish city. Of the 700,000 people who lived there, about 233,000, or one in three, were Jews. But understanding oneself as Jewish did not mean being part of a monolithic culture. There were conflicts even among the "Jews" of Lodz. The secular Jews were condemned by the religious Jews; the traditional orthodox Jews from Lithuania by the pious Hassidic Jews of Poland. As I. J. Singer ironically noted in *The Brothers Ashkenazi*, his great novel about the Jews of Lodz: "They are not over fond, these Jews from other parts, of the Polish Jews, with their long gabardines, their drawling Yiddish, their fanatical piety; and the Polish Jews return the dislike with interest, calling their visitors heathens, unbelievers, blasphemers, and pigs."[16] Lodz was a city in which all the various streams of European Jewry met.[17]

Secular Jews played a major economic and political role in this most modern of Polish cities, an industrial nineteenth-century city in a primarily agrarian part of the Russian Empire. Until 1915, Lodz was a Polish city that was politically part of the Russian Empire. During World War I the German army defeated the Russians not far from Lodz and turned it into a "German" city. It had had a German-speaking majority well into the 1870s, and German culture remained the litmus test for being modern, as Uncle Gideon showed. Indeed, with its large German-speaking minority, Lodz retained the patina of German culture even under the Russian Empire.

In Poland the twentieth-century model of Jewish emancipation and secularization was built on an eighteenth-century German model. The

Haskalah, the Jewish Enlightenment of the eighteenth-century thinker and philosopher Moses Mendelssohn, had argued for the integration of Jews into the German petty states of the eighteenth century. Mendelssohn maintained that religion was a private matter, not a public one, and should be left to the individual citizen, a view that Thomas Jefferson fought for in colonial Virginia. Poland had been divided between Imperial Germany and Imperial Russia, the latter being the most aggressively anti-Semitic nation in Europe at the end of the nineteenth century. Civic emancipation of the Jews and their integration into a modern Polish world took much longer in coming than elsewhere in central Europe. Jews who desired to be integrated into the more general culture opted to become "Germans" or, if they could, "Russians," speaking German or Russian as their primary language. It was industrialization and the establishment of a democratic Polish constitution immediately after World War I that made possible the idea of a Polish Jewish identity, parallel to that of a German Jewish secular identity. No longer was "being Jewish" a religious identity. In postwar Poland, "being Jewish" could be a political (Zionist) or even an ethnic designation (analogous to that of Lithuanians, who wrote and spoke Polish in the new state).

The cultural world that Jurek was born into was polyglot. Before World War I, German culture defined culture for central Europe. Educated Jews spoke German or Russian—rarely Polish, the language of peasants and dreamers. I. J. Singer wisely observed that "in the heart of Poland Russian and German were spoken, and one hardly heard a word of Polish. The Russian officers looked down on the conquered race. The Jewish bankers despised the pretentiousness of officials and officers and aristocracy. The German industrialists smiled ironically at the Russians, Poles, and Jews."[18] But after the conference at Versailles that reshaped Europe after the war, the Polish state was once again established. A new, democratic Poland was created, and it defined itself against the Russian state that had ruled it, the Germany army that had occupied it, and the millions of Jews who lived in it. The echoes of the "Song of the Crocus" sung by the Polish legionnaires on their way to massacre the Jews of Lemberg in 1919 still echoed through the streets of Poland during the 1930s:

General Roya on his horse!
Behind him comes the Crocus band!
Song on tongue and sword in hand!
We'll drive the foeman from our land!
We'll clean them out, the dirty crews,
The Russians first and then the Jews![19]

Anti-Semitism was an ancient factor in Polish life. In conformity with the church's attitude toward the Jews, the Poles simply believed that the Jews represented an unassimilable population that stood for everything that the ideal of Poland did not. The movement toward Jewish integration into the surrounding culture that had occurred rather quickly in the German-speaking states or in Hungary during the nineteenth century was only beginning in Poland at the start of the twentieth century. Young Jews in the new Poland spoke Polish in spite of, or maybe even because of, the presence of anti-Semitism—an anti-Semitism aimed, they believed, at those Jews who were "different," who spoke Yiddish. "I spoke Polish quite often because of my sisters. They all went to public schools, and one went to the gymnasium, which was like a university. My mother and father spoke Yiddish. They knew Polish, but their Polish was not too fluent. They spoke some Russian," said one young man who grew up in Lodz during the 1930s.[20]

As a manager dealing with salesmen across central Europe, Mieczyslaw Bekker spoke Yiddish, Polish, Russian, and, rather more poorly, German. Even though, when Jurek was born, a third of the population of Lodz was Jewish and was still primarily Yiddish-speaking, his close contemporaries saw themselves as Jews in Poland, not as Polish Jews, because of the anti-Semitism that permeated the new Polish state from its creation in 1919. Many of the secular Jews of Lodz felt trapped. They wanted to become Polish nationals if just to escape Polish anti-Semitism. They did not want to embrace utopian solutions such as Zionism, which urged them to go to Palestine, or Jewish socialism, which argued for a new communist state in which all anti-Semitism would vanish. Thus, many of the Jews of Lodz would have agreed with I. J. Singer: "Side by side with the resurgence of Polish nationalism [after World War I] there was a tremendous wave of hatred against the Jews, who were everywhere denounced as the friends of Germany, as spies and traitors in her pay."[21] Yiddish writers such as Singer saw anti-Semitism as a defining aspect of a Polish national identity in that period.

After World War I Poland was only nominally democratic and even that for a very short time.[22] The state quickly came under the authoritarian rule of General Josef Pilsudski, who seized dictatorial power in 1926. Pilsudski argued for an older tradition of Polish religious toleration, which ran against the grain of most Poles. It was seen as the result of special pleading on his part and was quickly attributed to the "fact" of having a Jewish wife. In 1930 Pilsudski suspended the Sejm (the Polish legislature), arrested opposition leaders throughout the country, and instituted what was to become a pattern in Austria, Germany, Spain, and

Portugal: the authoritarian state. Anti-Semitism had been long recognized by the National Democrats and other parties of the far right as a tool to manipulate the masses. Pilsudski himself seemed not to believe the conspiracy theories concerning the Jews as a threat to the Polish state. His Poland was quite comfortable in espousing a strong anti-Semitic policy in its campaign against national minorities such as the Ukrainians. Yet in 1931 it lifted many of the legal restrictions against the Jews. Under Pilsudski's authoritarian regime there had been self-conscious attempts to secure the civil rights of the Jews of Poland, especially Polish-speaking Jews such as Mieczyslaw. These attempts were thwarted, however, by the deeply engrained religious anti-Judaism that marked Polish identity in the new post-WWI world.

Mieczyslaw Bekker saw how the growing violence directed against Jews on the street was undoing the "normal" nature of his life in Poland during the 1930s. When Polish-speaking Jews were granted some of the same civil and economic rights that other Poles enjoyed, the response was a strong wave of anti-Semitism, especially among Polish intellectuals. In October 1931, riots broke out at the university of Krakow against the Jews. By 1934, concentration camps had been created, such as the one at Bereza, to house those who "were a menace to public order, anarchic elements, mostly of Jewish origin."[23] During the 1930s, Jews were increasingly regarded as an enemy, if not *the* enemy, of all that was Polish. This view took root even as more and more Polish Jews, like the Bekkers, came slowly but surely (at least through their children) to identify with the Polish language and its national claims. Could one be Jewish and Polish in spite of anti-Semitism? Certainly the Dreyfus affair and other manifestations of French anti-Semitism had not prevented Jews in France from identifying with French culture and, especially, the French language.

Pilsudski's death in May of 1935 led to an explosion of anti-Semitic actions in Poland. Poland was transformed into a fascist state, paralleling the world of pre-Nazi Austro-fascism (1934–38). Even working-class Jews in Lodz sensed the change. "After [Pilsudski] died, a very anti-Semitic government came, which forced the people to work on Saturdays, because you could not make a living from a five-day week."[24] Jews felt ever more alienated. A new national constitution in May 1935 established a dictatorial, elitist system, which abolished the sham democracy that Pilsudski had suspended. Anti-Semitic riots rocked the nation in 1936. Anti-Semitism became part of the ideology of the major party, which simply parroted Nazism. The Polish politicians advocated that Jews have their civil rights removed, be isolated from any economic activity and cultural life, and eventually be physically removed from Poland.

In January of 1937, Jozef Beck, the Polish foreign minister, addressed the Sejm, claiming that Poland could not house more than half a million Jews. Three million had to leave the country. Poland had argued for an expansion of the quotas to Palestine and wanted to create a Jewish state. Thus the Zionists and the Polish nationalists seemed to have much the same goal. Yet the idea of a forced expatriation was anathema to Zionists in Poland and throughout the world. Stephen Wise of the American Jewish Congress vehemently opposed the forced expatriation of Poland's Jews.[25] The twelfth congress of the Zionist Organization in Poland, held in March of 1937 likewise opposed the expulsion of the Jews of Poland. The Bundists (Jewish socialists) also condemned the idea, noting that the government had embraced Nazi ideology.

Shortly after Jurek's birth, Adam Koc, the founder of a new fascist party OZON (Obóz Zjednozczcnia Narodowego, "Camp of National Unity") in 1937, told the Polish peasantry that the only way to resolve their problems was to seize the industry in the towns and to drive out the Jews. Violence became part of the daily experience of the Jews in the large urban areas of Poland, just as it had been in Vienna and Berlin. On January 30, 1937, a "Jew-free day" was proclaimed at the University of Warsaw. It was announced in a broadside that included these words: "Whenever you see a Jew, knock out his teeth. Don't waver even if it is a woman. Don't fear anything. The only thing to be regretted is that you did not hit hard enough."[26] In Poland well before the German invasion of 1939 (as in France before the fall of France) anti-Semitism was rife. No doubt it encouraged many to become less visible by becoming/speaking Polish and abandoning their Jewish religious identity.

As an adult in the German Democratic Republic and, later, in the Federal Republic of Germany, Jurek Becker came to understand himself as the child of Jews, but he never felt himself to be a Pole. For his father, Polish anti-Semitism world colored his sense of what it meant to be a Pole. Mieczyslaw was a Jew *from* Poland, not a Polish Jew. Over time, Jurek Becker's new German identity was created as the antithesis of a Polish Jewish identity that had failed the Polish-speaking Jews of Poland.[27] Even in the German Democratic Republic after 1949, Jurek kept his distance: this was a world where a compulsory "friendship" bound communist Germans and communist Poles. It was also a world where one of the rewards for success was recognition in the Eastern bloc. Jurek never for a moment, either in his fiction or in his private life, felt himself to be Polish. For him, as for his father, a secular Jewish Polish identity was the God that failed: "My father never felt himself to be a Pole and did not speak well of them."[28] And neither did his son.

The city of Lodz was a city in turmoil from 1937 to 1939. As his world was small, confined to his parents and the apartment, young Jurek noticed none of this. Indeed, like all infants, he was the unabashed center of his world. The trauma of anti-Semitism on the streets made his parents ever more conscious of the need to protect their child. The social transformation of Polish Jews into Jewish Poles failed to become part of Jurek's legacy. Poland would soon vanish again after less than two decades as an independent state, and the city of Lodz too would vanish, absorbed into the world of terror inherited by the Jews of Europe.

Chapter 2

RUMKOWSKI, THE GHETTO KING, AND JERZY, THE JEWISH CHILD, 1939–1945

Lodz moved from peace to war before Jurek Bekker's second birthday. The summer of 1939 was one of increasing tension. In April 1939, the Polish-German nonaggression treaty was signed. No one in Lodz believed the treaty would end the countless demands the Germans had been making both for territory and for their nationals in Poland as well as in the Free City of Danzig. Given German anti-Semitism and anti-Polish feelings, young Polonized Jews in Lodz, as elsewhere in the country, identified strongly with the Polish government's new slogan: "We are strong, united, and ready!" On hearing this slogan, thousands of Jews in Lodz contributed to the National Defense Fund. Poland, which had the largest Jewish population of any state in the world, was about to be invaded by a government whose anti-Semitism was now part of its legal code and had already been exported without much difficulty to Bohemia and Austria. The Poles were neither strong nor united nor ready.

On September 1, 1939, the Germans, dressed in Polish military garb, attacked across the German-Polish border. The Nazi state—which had seized the Rhineland, partitioned Czechoslovakia, and occupied a willing Austria—"defended itself" and marched into Poland. On August 23, 1939, Joachim von Ribbentrop, the German foreign minister, and Vyacheslav Molotov, his Soviet counterpart, signed a nonaggression pact between their two countries and divided Poland between them. The

Soviet Union helped the Nazis dismember Poland, Soviet troops invading it on September 19, 1939.

For two-year-old Jerzy Bekker and the other Jews in Lodz, occupied Poland quickly became the Poland of ghettos and camps. It made no difference to the Germans that you were a middle-class Polish-speaking Jew; you were rounded up and forced into the ghettos. Such Jews shared a common experience of acculturated Jews in Germany, Bohemia, and Austria.[1] As we have seen, the assumption that a strong religious identity provided Polish Jews with an autonomous "Jewish" identity was false, certainly among acculturated Jews such as Mieczyslaw Bekker. Polish and, later, German anti-Semitism came to define what "being Jewish" meant for Jews such as Jurek's father.

Moving rapidly into Poland after the September 1 attack, the German army occupied Lodz by September 8. During those few weeks at the beginning of September, many young Jews, like their non-Jewish Polish counterparts, volunteered to fight the Germans. But it was a disaster in the making, one that the Poles, with some of the best intelligence agents in Europe, had foreseen. During this first example of Hitler's Blitzkrieg, Lodz was overwhelmed with air power supporting massive movements of troops and tanks across multiple fronts. The children, especially, were traumatized. Krystyna Chudy, born in 1931, wrote: "My first impression of the war was the continuous sirens that woke me. I had to get dressed and go into the basement. Those were the first bombings and the outbreak of the tragic war. As a little girl of eight I did not understand why the adults were so excited and frightened. The first bombs, flack, no food, and lines in front of the stores."[2] All at once, this most modern of Polish cities, this city of textile mills and small industry, was no longer Polish but German again. It was included in the Reichsgau Wartheland, a new unit of the Third Reich that compensated for the "German" territory that had been returned to the Poles after World War I. Lodz, now needing a new name, became Litzmannstadt after April 11, 1940, in honor of Karl Litzmann (1850–1936), the German general who had fought a successful battle near Lodz in 1915.[3]

The Germans' initial intent was to clear the Reichsgau Wartheland of all Jews, ironically following the Polish suggestion of stripping the Jews of civil rights and eventually expatriating them. Many Jews fled or, as late as February 1940, were deported to the Generalgouvernment, the rump part of Poland, which remained under German military occupation and was controlled by the brutal anti-Semite Hans Franck. There they became nonpersons, without any rights or, eventually, life. This policy was consistent with the revocation of the civil status of the Jews that had begun in Germany with the Nuremberg laws in 1935.

The ghettoization of the Jews in Lodz began on September 21, 1939, two weeks after the German occupation of the city. The Germans had demanded that all the Jews in Lodz wear the *Judenstern* (Jewish star, or Star of David), beginning in November 1939. As one young inhabitant recalled: "The days ahead were so difficult that I couldn't go to work any more. When you went out on the streets you had to wear an armband with the Star of David. Any German could hold you up and take you to work any place he wanted to. You had no right to resist."[4] By April 30, 1940, more and more Jews were forced into a ghetto, which was hermetically sealed off from the rest of the city. Soon there were 160,000 Jews in a ghetto with no sewage system. Reeking carts roamed the streets daily to take human waste to Marischin, the cemetery of the ghetto as well as its waste pit. Most of the "houses" were wooden shanties, prone to fires. Only 757 of the 30,000 buildings had running water.

Jews in the ghetto had, or were given, "Jewish" names. Mieczyslaw reverted to Mordeha (Mordechai), his Yiddish name, and Anette again became Chana. Jerzy, little Jurek, retained his Polish name. In the ghetto census he was listed as Bekker, Jerzy, with his occupation stated as "child." On March 7, 1940, the three Bekkers were forced to move from their light, airy apartment on Sródmeijska Street to a one-room apartment with neither kitchen nor toilet at 27 Hansenaten Street, which they had to share with two other people. They had been given space in this building as it was down the street from the headquarters of the tailors' organization in the ghetto at number 45, where Mordeha worked. In November 1940, the Bekkers managed to improve their situation. They moved from this overcrowded space to a one-room apartment in the same building, which, at least, they occupied by themselves.[5] They were also allotted a small piece of ground with two other families, where they grew potatoes and vegetables, a luxury in the ghetto. Later, they lived at 1 Dworska Street (renamed by the Germans the Matrosengasse, Seamen's Lane), which was right around the corner from the Jewish police office and virtually at the heart of the Jewish ghetto.[6]

The Litzmannstadt ghetto was an odd, even a remarkable, institution. It was ostensibly self-governed by the *Judenrat* (Jewish council), a system organized under Reinhard Heydrich to give the illusion of autonomy. In reality, the ghetto was completely dependent on the whims of the German authorities. The visible face of the *Judenrat* was that of the "king of the ghetto," Mordechai Chaim Rumkowski, an insurance agent and the former director of the Jewish orphanage in Lodz. He was an older, distinguished-looking man who strongly believed his mission was to rescue as many Jews as possible.[7] To do this he converted the ghetto into a source of "productive work." If the Jews in the ghetto worked, he argued, they would counteract the Nazi (and Polish) stereotype of the Jew as never producing anything of value. According to this myth of nonproductivity, Jews avoided work at all costs, whether it was physical labor in the fields or factories or war service. While completely untrue, it provided an image of a Jew who could be removed from the economic world without damaging (indeed, by improving) the lot of everyone else. The reality had been quite different in Lodz, where a very large number of Jews were involved in the cloth or garment industries. Rumkowski played on the image of the unproductive Jew and argued that the ghetto had to be seen as valuable to the German war effort.[8]

In the Litzmannstadt ghetto, everyone had to work according to Rumkowski's "survival through work" strategy.[9] His model was the textile industry, and Lodz became the center for war manufacture in this area, producing, for example, the uniforms for General Rommel's Afrika corps. Much of the other work fell onto the shoulders of the children. Despite the productivity of this ghetto, the mortality rate in Lodz almost doubled between 1941 and 1942, without counting the tens of thousands regularly deported to the east to be murdered.[10]

By April 1940, Rumkowski's mottoes were plastered all over the walls of the ghetto and could be read in the ghetto newspaper, the Yiddish *Getto-Zeitung*. The mottoes parroted the German demands for Jewish productivity: *Unser einzige Weg ist Arbeit* (Our only way is work); *Gute Arbeit wird überall geachtet* (Good work is universally respected); *Das Ghetto Litzmannstadt ist ein Produktionsbetrieb* (The Litzmannstadt ghetto is a factory); *Alle Arbeitsfähigen müßen arbeiten* (Everyone who can work, must work); *Die Arbeit ist unser Ruhepaß* (Work is our road to rest). The latter was closer to the truth than Rumkowski knew. Those last inhabitants of the Litzmannstadt ghetto deported to Auschwitz in 1944 read on the gate, as they arrived: *Arbeit macht frei* (Work frees).[11]

Rumkowski was simultaneously an ironic and a mythic figure in the ghetto, accorded extraordinary powers over life and death even by those who did not believe he could exert them. Despite Rumkowski's faintly comic air, his parodying of prewar Polish society, his chauffeured car, and the self-aggrandizing statements in his own newspaper, most knew he was not truly in control. Yet the jokes and stories barely concealed a desire to become a member of the *Sonder*, the "special service" under Rumkowski's direction. For it was the *Sonder* that distributed food and medicine and gave thousands access to goods and services rarely made available to the entire ghetto.

The Bekkers worked in order to prove their value to the Germans (and to Rumkowski). Chana was given a job as one of the 10,000 Jews employed by the *Judenrat* in one of their many offices. Mordeha tried to continue in textiles, now servicing the German war effort as well as the civilian front. Over time, the family's situation became more and more hazardous; and one of the sources of their anxiety was Jerzy. Children under the age of ten were seen as nonproductive, partly because they ate more than the value of the work they produced. So Jerzy was set to work stuffing cigarettes in a small, dank apartment. He tapped tobacco into the cigarettes and carefully stacked them, a simple task even for a three-year-old. The primary memory he retained was of the monotony of life in the ghetto. Yet every cigarette brought three marks into the family, and for ten marks you could buy a kilo of potatoes (if any were available). The images on the marks that circulated in the ghetto were Jewish stars and menorahs.[12] Life was very different from the way it used to be.[13] As an adult, looking at Mendel Grossmann's photographs from the Litzmannstadt ghetto at that time, Jurek noticed that that almost all the children in the photographs were boys: "Only boys, how come?" he wondered.[14] But little boys and girls were virtually identical in the photographs—ragged clothes, emaciated faces, cropped heads. Jurek saw himself in the photographs, the son protected by his parents.

On July 16, 1941, shortly before the Nazis launched their surprise attack on their Soviet allies, it became clear to the German authorities in the ghetto that they had a supply problem. Irene Hauser, a forty-one-year-old Viennese Jew, had been deported to Litzmanstadt with her six-year-old son, Eric. She discovered that there was no food available. "Nothing to eat. Have to stay in bed. He has to bring me soup from the store for the child. God should spare us from such hunger but not through suicide. We wait for a miracle . . . Leo didn't bring any soup, and we have not eaten for 24 hours. The child sleeps out of exhaustion, and many flies settle on his mouth. I am afraid when he awakes, for I have nothing to give him."[15] There was simply not enough food for the winter, and the Germans' response was to "dispatch [the inhabitants] expeditiously as the most humane solution."[16] Beginning in December 1941, there were "shipments" of 20,000 people "for work outside of the ghetto," which meant being sent to the death camp at Kulmhof (Chelmno), about fifty-five kilometers north of the city. And more and more of those sent were children. In Rumkowski's speech of September 4, 1942, he stated that

25,000 Jews under the age of ten and over the age of sixty-five had to be "resettled."[17] All it took was to be too small or to have too many gray hairs. In the summer of 1942, 20,517 children were sent to Kulmhof and murdered.[18]

The Litzmannstadt ghetto teamed with unrest. Rumkowski's ghetto police had to control the various forms of opposition to the Germans, as did the German authorities. Opposition took the form of labor strikes, hunger strikes, and, more radically, the circulation of news or, rather, rumors.[19] Rumors were the daily bread of the ghetto. They were considered in those very terms: "From mouth to mouth fantastic information spreads. This warms and feeds the harried people."[20] Rumors enabled the inhabitants of the ghetto to make adjustments to ever-changing circumstances.[21]

The rumors were of two types. With dark rumors, "everywhere one hears the same; one looks for comfort in another and finds it not. This has enveloped everyone with apathy and boundless pessimism." "Happy" ones also circulated, such as the rumor that Jews from Litzmannstadt were being exchanged for Germans from America.[22] Rumors also took the form of satire, criticism, and even humor, directed against both the Germans and the ghetto authorities.[23] The source of "real" news was the *Getto-Zeitung*, which espoused the official views of Rumkowski's administration. But the Jews in the ghetto found the *Litzmannstädter Zeitung*, which they were forbidden to read, a more accurate source of information, since it was intended for the German inhabitants of the city. Yet everyone knew that it too was suspect.

Radio provided the best link to the outside world; it was therefore strictly forbidden by the German authorities. Owning and using a radio had serious consequences. Operators were regularly hunted down, and other inhabitants of the ghetto hid them at great personal risk. It was through people with a radio, such as Chaim Widowsky, that the fate of the Jews deported east from Lodz was learned. So efficient was this system that news heard on the radio often circulated to the far ends of the ghetto within a day.[24] Most often listened to was the underground Polish radio *Swit*. It was based in England, but its news was so accurate that the Germans believed it broadcast from Poland. When news of the defection of Hitler's confidant Rudolf Hess was broadcast, a man named Weksler heard it on the radio, and the news quickly spread throughout the ghetto. "The news appeared to suddenly implant a new soul into the Jews of the ghetto. In all the workshops, workers began to work more slowly, and whispering ensued: 'perhaps after all, perhaps the time has come for us to be freed?' It is simply impossible for me to describe the happiness which existed."[25] Contemporary letters and documents buried in 1943 and uncovered after the war reveal that this medium of communication, so often mentioned, was a source of hope rather than of information, since most of the radio reports turned out to be false.[26] Mordeha Bekker later said he was one of those who listened to the radio. He had somehow acquired a radio in the ghetto and listened to the British and Polish news. He passed on bits of information to the people with whom he worked in the mills, who in turn passed them on to others. He became part of a network that spread hope at the same time as news, no matter whether it was true or not. This was why, he claimed, he was wrenched from his family in the winter of 1944 and deported to Auschwitz.

In 1944, trainloads of 10,000–20,000 Jews were regularly being sent to Kulmhof. By May, the decision had been made to eliminate the ghetto. On June 16, Rumkowski issued a proclamation for "voluntary registration for labor outside of the ghetto." The staff of volunteer historians in the ghetto wrote in their *Chronicle of the Lodz Ghetto* that the "actual goal is multiple, large-scale shipments of workers outside of the ghetto."[27] From month to month, from day to day, things grew worse. Food was always lacking, working made no difference. By May of 1944 the situation in the ghetto was catastrophic.

Holding families together was difficult if not impossible. The Bekkers were constantly concerned that Jerzy should get enough to eat in order to survive. Having a child survive meant that some adult had taken care to assure that the child received food, shelter, and succor. "I was terribly hungry," wrote a boy from another family in his diary entry for May 5, 1944. "I had the prospect of living only from the *ressort* soups [the soup ladled out to forced laborers], which consisted of three little bits of potato and two decagrams [three-quarters of an ounce] of flour. I was lying on Monday morning quite dejected in my bed, and there was my dear little sister's half-loaf of bread . . . I could not resist the temptation and ate it all up . . . I was overcome by terrible remorse and by a still greater worry about what my little sister would eat for the next five days. I felt like a miserable, helpless criminal . . . I have told people that it must have been stolen by a reckless, pitiless thief, and to keep up appearances I have to curse and condemn the imaginary thief: 'I would hang him with my own hands if I came across him.' "[28] Duplicity, horror, and inhumanity drove families apart, but also there was a need, a desire, to rise above the circumstances.

On June 23, 1944, the final deportations to Kulmhof took place. Jews deported from Litzmannstadt were thereafter sent to Auschwitz to be gassed and burned. Between August 3 and August 6, 1944, the German boss of the ghetto, Hans Biebow, asked the *Judenrat* to persuade the last 68,000 Jews to be sent, unresisting, to "work in the Reich," a veiled reference to Auschwitz. Eventually 65,000 were sent to Auschwitz-Birkenau. Smaller transports were sent to the concentration camps near Berlin, the Germans describing such treatment as "a great privilege." These were not death camps like Auschwitz; so being sent there meant a chance to live a little longer.

While the ghetto was being dissolved, someone had denounced Mordeha to the Nazi authorities. One evening, he vanished with his radio, leaving his wife and son alone.[29] He was transported to Auschwitz and, when Auschwitz was emptied, to the Sachsenhausen concentration camp (near Oranienburg), where again he was greeted by the motto "Works frees."[30] At the end of August 1944, Rumkowski himself, "the king of the ghetto," was shipped off to Auschwitz with a special letter of protection from the Germans. The rumor back in Litzmannstadt was that the Germans did not even bother to gas him. They threw him alive into the ovens.

In February 1944, Chana and Jerzy were shipped in a cattle car to the "women's" concentration camp at Ravensbrück,[31] just fifty kilometers from the camp at Sachsenhausen and ninety kilometers from Berlin. They had been permitted to pack a small bundle of clothing and no more than 25 kilograms of food.[32] Mother and child, now separated from Mordeha, may have had what the Nazis called the "privilege" of going to Ravensbrück because of Chana's work in the *Judenrat*'s office. Mordeha had not been so privileged.

Ravensbrück was one of the original German concentration camps, designed to house those who were suspected of being—or who were—opposed to the Nazis. The first had been built outside the Bavarian town of Dachau in 1933. Created in 1938, Ravensbrück was different from the other camps because women could bring their children with them. In addition to children like Jerzy, who arrived with their mothers, about 870 children were born in Ravensbrück, almost all of whom died. Each group transported to the camp had children: The Dutch Jewish women in Ravensbrück, for example, brought 140 children with them, including infants.[33] The children had to adjust to new norms, new surroundings, and the ubiquitous presence of death. They also learned the *Lagersprache*, the language of the camps.

What was Jerzy's mother tongue? Was it really the Polish he spoke as a child? Was it the Yiddish, also spoken by his parents, which was widely spoken in the ghetto? Or was it the *Lagersprache*, which became the lingua franca of the camps, spoken by the child perhaps as his primary language, and lost after the death of his mother. Polish is what he remembers speaking, not the language of the camps, the composite language with its overlay of the guards' German. What he retained from the *Lagersprache* were the first German words he heard, necessary words for existence: "Nothing left," "Formation—Count off!" and "Hurry-hurry" (*Alles alle, Antreten—Zählappell!* and *Dalli-dalli*).[34] The very word *Lagersprache* evokes the problems of a Jew who, after the Shoah, sought to speak German. The adult Jurek Becker commented that when his father found him in 1945, he spoke Polish like a four-year-old rather than an eight-year-old, "for it was at this age that I was exposed to circumstances that made language superfluous." No language would have been sufficient, yet for the inmates of the camp and the ghetto a command of the *Lagersprache* was necessary for daily existence.

Those who arrived in Ravensbrück in 1944 were severely maltreated. After the camp at Auschwitz was liquidated in January 1944, a young Hungarian girl, Magda Somogyi, was forced to march with her sister to Ravensbrück. "We lay on the floor [of the block] the whole day. We were so sick, so weak, and our skin was covered with lice and boils. Every day, early in the morning, we stood *Zählappell*, and then the SS whipped us back to our bunks." Her sister, who was even weaker than she, weighing only about 50 pounds, died in mid-April, just two weeks before the liberation on April 30, 1945.[35]

Many others were shipped from Litzmannstadt to Ravensbrück about the time Chana and Jerzy arrived. One of the other children recalls: "We lived thus until the summer of 1944 when my mother and I were deported to the concentration camp at Ravensbrück. Here I spent the first days in the notorious tent camp ... My mother worked very hard, often outside of the camp in Waldroden. Starved and sick, she was put in the camp 'hospital' for a while. Now I was alone, but not for much longer. In December of 1944 at Christmas, we children were gathered in the youth camp. I saw a wonderful full table, which seemed to strain under the weight of the food. I took an apple for mamma, which I later ate myself. It was the only apple I had during the entire war."[36] The Christmas "feast" was put on for the observers from the International Red Cross. At liberation, only 500 children at Ravensbrück were still alive.[37] Most of them were desperately ill with epidemic diseases and malnutrition.

In late March 1945, Ravensbrück had been evacuated. In an attempt on the part of the SS to cover up the mass murders but which, in fact, only added to them, 24,500 prisoners, men and women, were put on the road on a death march. To salvage his political situation, Fritz Suhren, the camp commander of Ravensbrück, had in early April turned 500 women prisoners over to the Swedish and Danish Red Cross, and 2,500 German women prisoners were set free. On the night of April 29–30, troops from the 49th Soviet Army reached Ravensbrück, where they found about 3,000 sick female prisoners being cared for by other prisoners.[38] The 47th Soviet Army had liberated Sachsenhausen on April 22, 1945, and parts of it were turned into a hospital for those in greatest need. In late April and early May of 1945, the Soviet army moved some 300 desperately ill inmates from Ravensbrück to Sachsenhausen. Among those evacuated were Chana and Jerzy Bekker.

Chana Bekker died of tuberculosis, having sheltered and succored her son to the very end. She was buried at the cemetery at Sachsenhausen on June 2, 1945, a few weeks after the camp was liberated by the Russians.[39] During early June, the final inmates were moved out and the camp closed. Jerzy always felt that he had survived at the expense of his mother's life, having been given "the bit of food she had in the camp. She starved to death, I didn't."[40] As an adult, he learned of this when he stopped on the Kurfurstendamm one day to buy a newspaper. The woman behind the counter recognized him as a celebrity and said that she had known his mother and him in Ravensbrück. She asked him, did he know how his mother had died? She gave the answer herself: from starvation. But do you know why? she continued. His silence was followed by her answer: in order to feed you.

Chana Bekker remained a vague memory. "I remember someone from my childhood, a woman with two small hands, which she held before her and calmed me through gentle movements to and fro, when I was upset: 'Quiet, my dear, it's all right.' "[41] He remembered this in German, the language he heard his mother speak in his dreams. The absence of his mother was central to his experience of the post-Shoah world. But it was also the loss of the language associated with the mother, Polish, and its replacement by the language of the camps, German. Jerzy survived the camps with a veneer of German as part of his legacy of the camps. Learning German correctly afterward meant forgetting the *Lagersprache*.

The tedium of life in the ghetto and the camps for a child between the ages of two and eight left few detailed memories.[42] Becker claimed that his loss of memory was complete. "When I was two, I went into the ghetto, and at five I left for the camps. I cannot remember anything. I was told about it, it is in my papers, so it must have been my childhood. Sometimes I think: too bad, that something else is not written there. In any case I know of the ghetto only from what I was told."[43] To have survived as a child meant that he had had a very special place in the emotional lives of his parents. In this sense he was a privileged child, odd as it may seem. He had been privileged as a small child in Lodz, the only son of older parents; he was privileged in the camps, shielded to the best of their ability by his parents. The very proof of this special status was his survival. The reality of his survival and the fact of his rescue after the war only added to this sense of privilege. The death of his mother signaled a type of emotional abandonment that could never be made good, and it is echoed through his all of his writing.[44] She left him, but his father sought him out.

After his liberation, Mordeha desperately looked for his family through the offices of the Joint, the American Jewish Joint Distribution Organization, who located his son for him. UNRRA (the United Nations Relief and Rehabilitation Administration) had taken control of the camp at Sachsenhauen after it was liberated, and distributed food and medicine. Mordeha was told that his wife had died but that his son was still alive and in the makeshift hospital that had been created out of one of the barracks at Sachsenhausen. He entered the hospital where his son lay. Jerzy was seven but was tiny for his age and so weak that he could no longer walk. The hospital beds had been made from the lower bunks in the camp, the upper ones sawn off. When Mordeha came into the room, a nurse lifted Jerzy out of bed to give him to his father. The boy's leg caught on the jagged edge of the bed, and his skin was torn. He screamed, and Mordeha yelled at the nurse, "Why are you torturing the child!"[45] The child did not recognize his father because he was severely emaciated and his hair had turned white. He too had difficulty recognizing his tiny, undernourished son. Finally he stroked the boy's forehead, pushing his hair back, and saw a distinctive pattern of freckles. Only then did he know it was Jerzy. It took Jerzy somewhat longer to be convinced that this old man was his father.

Mordeha's presence was associated not with Jerzy's early-childhood world of comfort and then loss but with the day-to-day reality of a Jew raising a son alone in the post-Shoah world of Germany. Adolescent conflict and the very sense of his father's difference colored his memories, as did his father's silence about their shared experience in the ghetto and the camps. Mordeha's silence, as well as the GDR's silence, about the Shoah provided the subject matter for much of Jerzy's work and filtered his memories of the past. It was a silence he desired, for he never asked his father to elaborate on his experiences in the camps. Only after his father's death did he realized that Mordeha too needed that silence. Jerzy did not remember his experiences or the language in which they were cast; but his literary work remembered them for him.

Chapter 3

GEORG IN THE SOVIET ZONE, 1945–1949

When the war was over, Mordeha and Jerzy had survived—not so much by intelligence or skill or connections than by luck. All the Jews in Europe would have been murdered had the Third Reich continued to exist. Its goal, to kill as many Jews as possible, was accomplished in as many brutal ways as could be imagined—from starvation to overwork to shootings and gassings to forced marches through the winter snows.

The Bekkers, father and son, were part of the *She'erit Hapleyta*, the remnant of the saved, around 200,000 Jews who remained from the Jewish communities of central Europe. Before the beginning of the death marches west from the camps, about 500,000 were still in the various camps and ghettos; 60 percent died on the marches.[1] By 1946, the remaining fragment of the once flourishing Jewish life of central Europe had all but vanished among throngs of "displaced persons" (DPs), perhaps as many as nine million. These included ethnic Germans from Poland and Bohemia, forced laborers from all over Europe, Russian soldiers who had fought for the Germans, and people simply displaced by war and moving west before the Soviet army.[2] (Officially there were no DPs in the Soviet zone of occupation; officials there used the term only of those in the Western zones.[3] The reality, though, was quite different.)

Anti-Semitism was a constant presence among the DPs in Germany, resulting quite often in physical confrontation and even death.[4] After 1945, some fragments of Polish Jewry arrived in Berlin through the Brichah movement, which attempted to rescue all the Jews left in Poland and eventually to settle them in Palestine, then under the British mandate.[5] Being a Polish Jew in Germany meant that one was stateless, just as those Polish Jews in Germany had been in 1938 after the *Kristallnacht*, when they were loaded onto a train and shipped east. As a way of becoming less visible in Berlin, Mordeha Bekker became more "German" and changed his name to Max Becker. His Polish Jewish friends in East Berlin continued to call him Mjetek. Jerzy Bekker quickly became Georg Becker. (Even the deceased Chana became Annette Lewin in Georg's 1953 application for his pension as a survivor, and Anja in his 1955 application for admission to university.[6] The names in Georg's youthful account of his family's history shift as they need to.)

When Max arrived in Berlin in 1945, he found only temporary accommodations. There were a few private hostels that provided a bed and a marginal life.[7] Each DP got 300 grams of bread and half a liter of soup daily; a tomato and a thimbleful of margarine once a week. At the UNRRA camp on Teltowerdamm, things were not much better, but there, as in Sachsenhausen, child-care facilities for Max's sick son were available.[8]

On December 4, 1945, Max applied to the Berlin Jewish Community for living quarters for himself and Georg. The child remained in the makeshift hospital at Sachsenhausen until the end of the year, when he was moved to Berlin for treatment. Max and Georg were assigned a furnished room at 226 Prenzlaueralle, a street-front building. Prenzlauer Berg, one of the poorest parts of Berlin with a population of more than 1,170,000, was in the Soviet sector. Because the city had been thoroughly bombed, just finding a space to live was difficult. Jews were given some priority, however, and being in the Russian sector had certain benefits for the Beckers. Max, as his son later reported, said that it was "the fascists who tortured him and put him in a concentration camp and murdered his family; and it was the communists who freed him."[9] But it was not Max's political decision to live in the Russian sector; that was merely where an apartment happened to be found for them. Father and son remained there while Georg began his convalescence.

Relatively few Jewish children had survived. Of the 25,000 Jews in Germany in the summer of 1945, fewer than 4 percent were under the age of sixteen.[10] After Max had rescued him from Sachsenhausen, Georg recuperated until January 7, 1946, in the children's home of the Berlin Jewish Community; the home was on Moltke Street, in the Niederschönhausen section of Berlin. He had been officially designated a "victim of the Nazi regime" (*Verfolgter des Naziregimes*) in Sachsenhausen, which meant that he received immediate medical care and somewhat better rations. His health remained precarious, and the medications he received ameliorated but did not cure his general weakness.

As Georg slowly grew stronger, Max began to transform himself into a different person. The dates of his life slid somewhat. He was suddenly six years younger; according to a statement he made in 1946, he was born on November 3, 1906. His hair dyed, he was now only forty, making up for the six years lost in the ghetto and the camps.

No one looked very carefully at Max's and Georg's identities. When Max, on December 28, 1945, had registered with the city of Berlin as a "victim of the Nazi regime," he did so as a new person.[11] How fluid the facts were at that moment can be judged by Max's seemingly random change of Georg's birth date. When a birth certificate was needed for Georg, Max simply claimed that Georg was born on September 30, 1937. Later, Georg dutifully wrote, "I hereby declare under oath that according to my father's account I was born on September 30, 1937, in Lodz. My mother died in a concentration camp."[12] The document was stamped and became a part of the public record.

Max not only was suddenly younger; he just as suddenly was a German. Now he claimed that he was born in Fürth in Bavaria, and thus was no longer a Pole (and a Jew) but now a German (and a Jew). Fürth, near Nuremberg—and, incidentally, the birthplace of Henry Kissinger in 1923—was selected because Max, along with other DPs, had heard a rumor that the city hall there had been totally destroyed when the city was bombed. His claim of German identity meant that Georg too had a new birth date and a new identity—as the son of a German and therefore German himself. The *lex sanguinis* (law of blood) promulgated in the German Empire in 1913 defined both father and son as Germans. A further advantage was that most of the officials in the newly reconstructed Berlin Jewish Community were German Jews, as only a minority of the residents were Eastern Jews (*Ostjuden*). The pre–World War II competition (and condescension) felt between the groups was once again noticeable in Berlin. After 1945, Eastern Jews accounted for only 30 percent of the total Jewish population in Berlin, while overall in Germany they made up close to 50 percent of the total number. (In Bavaria they constituted more than 90 percent of the Jewish population.)[13] Max straddled both communities: now as an ethnic German he belonged to the political majority in the Jewish community; as a Yiddish and Polish speaker he was also a member of the visible minority.

To survive under such circumstances you had to tell stories, especially in response to the kinds of questions asked of Max: Who are you? What is your name? Where are you from? What are you still doing here? Telling stories became an obsession with Max after his arrival in Berlin, much like Uncle Gideon in Jurek's tale of prewar Poland. Storytelling was a necessity. It was through stories that you told who the enemy was, where danger lay, where safety could be found. Max had to explain who he was to a hostile world and to himself. And he began to train Georg to do the same thing.

As his son noted later, he entered a world that was a "contest in storytelling. When I was uninterested [in telling stories], everyone knew it . . . I did not belong to any larger group with this need [for storytelling]. But when my father and his friends came home to our apartment, they did the same thing. Oral narrative had played a role for me ever since I was a child. And I can remember that I once told a story and was unhappy with the reception it got. I thought about why it had not been successful: it was not the story's fault. It is a good story that I know well. It must have been how I told it."[14] In a television interview in the 1990s, Becker noted that as a child his father never praised him for his storytelling but would say, "You call that a story?" So Georg felt impelled to keep polishing his tales until his father listened and believed.[15]

In October 10, 1945, the Allies had encouraged the creation of a Jewish community organization in Berlin to provide temporary aide to DPs "in transition" through Berlin. From 1945 to 1949, 11,139 cards bearing the names of DPs were on file in the Jewish Community office in Berlin, including those of Max and Georg Becker. In the whole of Germany in the fall of 1946, there were about 112,000 Jews in DP camps and 45,000 elsewhere.[16]

Max became "officially" Jewish when he joined the Berlin Jewish Community. He joined it not for religious reasons but to seek out those with a common past. He met with them in the synagogue in the Soviet sector at 28 Oranienburger Street, which gathered in the ruins of the great nineteenth-century Neue Synagogue. In his application to join the community, Max noted that he was born and remained a Jew. In reality, he remained among Jews because he was comfortable with people who shared his experiences of the Holocaust. He felt much more comfortable with them than with the non-Jewish Germans in his neighborhood,[17] whom he saw as the cause of his wife's death and of the torments that he and his son had experienced.

In Max's file, archived by the Berlin Jewish Community, his deportation from Lodz is attributed to his having owned a radio and having spread "oral propaganda" (read: rumors) against the Germans. How accurate this claim was is open to question. After the war, virtually everyone, including those who had undertaken real acts of resistance, wanted to be seen as opponents to the Nazis—whether they were in the camps, the ghettos, or on the home front. Elie Wiesel, an Auschwitz survivor, noted in a conversation with the former resistance leader Jorge Semprum, a Buchenwald survivor, that "members of the resistance were loved, those who had been deported were shunned . . . No one wanted us, we caused shame, we disturbed."[18] Having owned a radio was a sign of resistance. In the GDR this assumed even greater importance since the state denied the very existence of a Jewish resistance to the Nazis; communist resistance was what was stressed.

Outfitted with a new identity as part of the ghetto resistance, Max managed gradually to gain more leverage with the Berlin Jewish Community. On February 13, 1946, the Beckers moved to a more spacious apartment at 5 Lippehner Street, now making the conscious choice to remain in the Soviet sector. There had been a major addition to Max's own life. He developed a relationship with a non-Jewish woman by the name of Irma Kautsch, who had two sons a little older than Georg. Irma and her sons moved into an apartment just above Max and Georg. They were the siblings Georg had never had and a mother who was clearly not his own. Since Georg was still badly undernourished, Irma persuaded Max to send him, along with her sons, to her parents in the country outside Berlin to be fattened up (*aufgepäppelt*). Georg was separated from Max for the first time since they had been reunited. But, even more of a jolt, he was thrown into a world that was evocative of his life in the ghetto and the camps. In his eyes, Irma's father was a huge, scary German whose crude sense of humor he could not fathom.

Everything away from Max was new and frightening. One day, for example, Georg saw a pet dog for the first time. The only dogs he had ever known were the vicious guard dogs in the camps and the ghetto. Assured that the pet dog would not harm him, he pulled its tail, whereupon the dog took a chunk out of his thigh. He bore the scar for the rest of his life. He found he could neither understand nor control the world without his father. By the time he returned to Berlin, he had put on a little weight, but there were aspects of this new world that were incomprehensible to him. Irma's father and his dog epitomized the terrifying Germans from whom he had been rescued. His privileged status as the focus of Max's life was restored only when, soon afterward, Max and Irma ended their relationship.

On June 18, 1948, a currency reform was introduced into the Western zones of Germany that had the effect of creating a new and separate economic entity. The Soviets responded by introducing their new currency into the Eastern zone on June 24. At almost the same time, beginning on June 23, 1948, the Soviets attempted to force the Western Allies out of the zones of control by means of a land boycott. The Western Allies, however, built an "air bridge" into Tempelhof Airport to supply the city by air. It must have been clear to Max that the Soviets held a strong hand in the East. The beginning of the cold war made it imperative to chose between a Western presence that could help Berliners survive and a clear, antifascist Soviet presence that would maintain control over day-to-day life. Having initially settled in the Soviet zone by happenstance, Max now placed his trust in the Soviets. In doing so, he decided to become a "German," but one defined by the new situation in the Soviet zone.

Over and over, Max told his young son that he was more comfortable in a defeated and divided Germany, occupied by the Red Army. Like the tattoo from Auschwitz on his arm, he felt that shame was inscribed on the national body of Germany by its division into zones of occupation: "It wasn't the Polish anti-Semites who lost the war."[19] He was speaking from experience. Until 1945, Poland could not see enough Jews killed, even if it meant Poles murdering their Jewish neighbors.[20] In Kielce, south of Warsaw, a town with a population of 50,000, including 350 Jews (down from 25,000 in 1939), a pogrom took place in July 1946. Inflamed by the spreading of the ancient myth that Jews had slaughtered Christian children, Poles murdered forty-two Jews, including women and children. By April 1946, more than a thousand Jews had been murdered in postwar Poland. A Jewish doctor who fled Lodz stated: "The government is 100 percent for us; the people 100 percent against us."[21] Gitta Guttmann returned to a small town near Lodz in 1946: "It was a horrible experience. The only good thing was that I found my mother . . . It was a huge cemetery. I grew very sick. Not that I had any physical symptoms like fever. I was psychologically sick. I was ill for weeks. Simply could not understand what had happened."[22] The idea of returning to Poland was inconceivable to Max. It has been suggested that Max decided to stay in Germany simply because he was too tired to leave.[23] But Max, like so many DPs, was not merely "stuck" in a defeated Germany. The land occupied by the Allies provided a refuge from both the past and the present.

Other than returning to Poland, few options remained for Max and Georg. For many of the DPs, Palestine was not an option because of the British opposition to Jewish migration to the Middle East. You could only go illegally, at some personal risk. With a small, sick child, that did not seem a possibility. After the ending of the British mandate in Palestine on May 14, 1948, many DPs did go there. The United States seemed an ideal destination, but it was complicated for the Beckers. The

Displaced Persons Act (passed only in 1948) would have allowed Max to enter the USA, but it precluded Georg because American immigration laws since the beginning of the century demanded that all immigrants be healthy, which Georg certainly was not. The pull of America, however, remained strong in Georg's memory. Later he would invent an aunt who had survived the Shoah and lived in the United States. Along with the Russians, the British, and the French, the Americans were guarantors of safety.

The Soviet soldiers did not have as positive an image as the Americans, who handed out cigarettes and chocolate bars, but their presence in the Soviet zone reassured Max and Georg that pogroms such as those in Poland would not take place. The Soviets tried to stop the movement of Polish Jews into their zone, arguing that Jews came west for purely economic reasons and had thus come illegally to Berlin.[24] But Max had made himself over into a German Jew and was not affected by this decree. The real constraints on his leaving seem to have been primarily the state of Georg's health. Why he decided to stay in the Soviet zone and, then, in the GDR was a more complex story.

The Beckers' situation was only marginally improved by their priority in getting homes and some access to food and clothing. Jews, like others in Berlin, lived very much on the economic edge. Virtually everyone functioned on the black market, trading goods for goods in a time when all currency, whether coins or bills, was unstable or unwanted. Just as Polish Jews had been viewed with suspicion by the Soviet authority, Jews in Germany were seen as taking special advantage of the economic instability of the immediate postwar period. Even more than other DPs, the Jews were seen as the source of the unwholesome and un-German black market. Indeed the very abbreviation "DP" was translated in one case as *Deutschlands Parasiten*, Germany's parasites, bringing back the Nazis' image of Jews as parasites because of their unwillingness to work.[25] In February 1946, the Berlin newspaper *Der Tagesspiegel* warned Jews that anti-Semitism in Berlin was a result of the black market: "We are all poor. If our Jewish fellow citizens act like every one else, the anti-Semitism in Berlin will cease, insofar as it exists at all."[26] The Jews imagined by the editorial writer were the "foreign" Jews, mainly from eastern Europe, who "occupied" Berlin.[27] This perception was a powerful reason Max wanted Georg to become "German."

Certainly the black market was illegal, as Max was well aware. Like many of the DPs in Berlin, Max thought of himself as a "sojourner," a person permanently in transition. He felt no obligation to any set of communal ethical standards, especially in the light of his experiences in the ghetto and the camps. To compensate for the horror of Georg's experience, Max sought out things to give the boy pleasure. These things could only be found on the black market. One day he came home with a bicycle for Georg. With transportation at a standstill, having a bicycle was a sign of affluence. Although it was much too big for him and he was unable to ride it, Georg pushed it around the neighborhood as a sign of his father's ability to provide for him.

In order to become a German, the first thing was to learn to speak German. When Georg was eight, Max suddenly stopped speaking Polish to him, assuming that the boy would learn German immediately. What happened was that Georg forgot Polish more quickly than he learned the new language. For a time he was almost literally between two languages.[28] As Polish vanished, so did his association of German with the *Lagersprache*. Language and memory were lost simultaneously.[29]

In an uncanny incident during the 1980s, Georg's Polish returned. While visiting a German newspaperman whose wife was Polish, he pulled a familiar book out of a box of Polish children's books. He could not have read it, he thought, for there were almost no books in the ghetto and the camps. So it must be something from before the war, from his childhood in Lodz. Having been unable to read the book at that time, he now assumed that one or both of his parents had read it to him. "And suddenly I managed to recite a long poem from that book in Polish. I had no idea what it meant, I only knew the sounds . . . I was myself moved by this experience, for the words simply flowed out of me."[30] The Polish language had stuck with Georg only in relation to his earliest childhood memories, the memories of being comforted and read to in the family's apartment on Srodmeijska Street.

German for Georg was a "father tongue." It was the language his father wanted him to speak.[31] Max taught him to read and write a language that Max himself did not truly command.[32] Max's accent always betrayed him. For him, Yiddish was "bad German" and Polish was the language of anti-Semites.[33] Georg was to become as good a German by speaking German as he would have become a good Pole by speaking Polish, had the times and circumstances been different. Consequently, Georg developed a strong emotional attachment to German, which he later labeled as a "perversion."[34] As an adult he was well aware of the implications of the shift in language for his role as a "German" author.

The German language itself bore the scars of Nazi abuse. The East Berlin–Jewish philologist Victor Klemperer elegantly illustrated the corruption of German in his study of Nazi language, published in 1947. That Klemperer, then a professor at Humboldt University in the Soviet zone, was able to publish his study (which was culled from his then un-published diaries) highlighted the need to cleanse the very German that Georg was learning.[35] A new literary and cultural language was evolving in the Soviet zone as a response to the corruption that scholars such as Klemperer revealed.

Listening to good German meant listening to the radio. The radio hidden in the ghetto had figured in Max's creation of his identity in 1946. Radio also figured in Georg's slow process of becoming a German. He spent his childhood listening to radio and imagining the world.[36] In 1948, Max made a deal with him: Move up into the next grade, and I will get you anything you want! This extraordinary promise could only be redeemed by Max's connections in the black market. What Georg asked for and received was his first radio. He listened to broadcasts about Roald Amundsen at the North Pole and about Max Schmeling boxing; he listened to science fiction by Jules Verne, to radio plays of the kind he himself tried to write in the late 1970s.[37] In the late 1940s, radio was his first window to a German-speaking culture.

In his talks as the annual poetry lecturer in Frankfurt in 1989, the adult Jurek Becker began to imagine a different scenario for himself (and, by extension, for other child survivors who shift languages and write creatively). He saw learning the new language as indicating a desire to please, a need not to make errors. He described the game his father played with him: Max would give him fifty pfennig for a cleanly written page but subtract five for each error.[38] One of the myths of anti-Semitism in central Europe, often internalized by Jews themselves, was the belief that no matter how well they learned a language "not their own"—German, or French, or Polish—there was always something "Jewish" about the way they used language that betrayed them as Jews.[39] Even Jews who spoke only one language, who could not speak a word of Yiddish or Hebrew, suffered under this view, for it suggested a cultural difference in Jews even where no such difference existed. For Georg, such a difference did exist. He did speak a language associated with Jews (as "victims of fascism"), the *Lagersprache*. His fear of people drawing conclusions about him from the way he spoke German was a fear of being seen as Jewish.

Belonging was now a major goal for Georg and Max, and mastering German was the only way to achieve it. At ten years of age, Georg was fi-nally sent to school, where he entered in fourth grade. He was taller than most of the children in his grade. He still spoke very broken German. His fellow students clearly regarded these two characteristics as a sign of mental retardation, and they treated him in the brutal way children treat those who are different.[40] He quickly learned what all children know:

any difference from the group makes you a target. He had to improve his German. The quicker he erased the errors, the more rarely others would note that he was a stranger. "And when the mistakes ceased completely, they would take me, even if falsely, for one of their own."[41] Language became a way of belonging to the peer group. Georg did not want to be marked as a "foreigner" or a "Jew." So speaking good German became a passion for him. While other children his age were interested in bugs or racing cars, he played with words and sentences. This intensive preoccupation with language he saw as the only means to avoid the mockery of his peers and those disadvantages attendant on his being the only child his age in the school who could not speak correctly.[42]

Writing German was substantially more work than speaking and listening, and Georg never wrote a line more than was required.[43] He gradually conformed to what his peers expected of him. Conforming became a topic for him when as an adult he turned to writing. The roots of conforming, the grounds for conforming, the results of conforming all shape his later literary work.[44] As a child he conformed, but not without some resistance.

In 1949, when Georg was twelve, the various zones of occupation that had provisionally divided the remnants of the Third Reich transformed themselves into two German states. The Soviet zone was transformed into the German Democratic Republic (GDR) on October 7, 1949. The GDR disavowed any relationship with the old German nationalist tradition. It was a new Germany and would contain new Germans. The Western (American, British, and French) zones had united on May 24, 1948, as the Federal Republic of Germany (FRG). Unlike the FRG, where any type of overt patriotism was automatically linked to the Nazi past, the GDR, in its new status as the first German socialist state, encouraged traditional patriotic fervor among its youth.

Georg was a citizen of the new state. But he was also a "victim of fascism," a label he found burdensome. It set him off as an object of pity or derision. In his mind it was another way of saying that he was a Jew. His victim status was checked by the officials with whom his father had to deal. When an Office for the Victims of Fascism was eventually established in the GDR, a staff member wrote to the official "Ravensbrück" committee on March 3, 1950, to check whether "Georg Becker with his mother had been transported from Lodz to Ravensbrück in February of 1944."[45] An answer was received on March 16, 1950, from Herbert Rosenberg of the Auschwitz Committee, stating that he personally knew this to be a fact. Max's deportation to Auschwitz was proof of his son's story. Georg received a pension as his father's dependent until August 1953, when he was given his own pension as a "victim of the Nazi regime." It amounted to 30 percent of the full pension for an adult, or about 45 marks a month in 1953.

Georg also acquired a new surrogate mother. Max moved in with his longtime companion "Dorchen," Dora Großpietsch, whom Max's grandsons came to call Oma (Grandma). Like Irma, she was a non-Jewish woman, and the couple never married. She was, however, a permanent part of Max's life. As he struggled with alcoholism and depression, she became his buffer against the world. She outlived Max and remained very close to his grandchildren even after their father left the GDR in 1977. The relationship between Max and his two women friends served as one of the models for Aron's failed relationships with women in *The Boxer* (1976), Jurek's novel about a Holocaust survivor in the GDR. Yet Max's long-term, if difficult, relationship with Dorchen indicated a somewhat greater ability to form lasting relationships than Jurek is willing to ascribe to his fictional character.[46]

Max's economic status was reasonably good. He engaged in small-time commercial activities, buying and selling whatever he could lay his hands on. Max's great passion, in addition to playing billiards, was sports. He had become an obsessive soccer fan.[47] Georg too discovered sports at school and, like his father, adored soccer. It was something immediate that they could talk about. It engaged both of them completely without their needing to think about their past or even present lives. Georg became more and more involved in school sports activities. At first he showed no great talent, and received poor grades in gymnastics. He persisted, however, and in 1950 he joined the official (East) German Sports Committee (*Deutscher Sportausschuss*) to improve his boxing skills. But it was at table tennis that he excelled, winning local and regional championships. He even noted that fact on his applications for university.

Like his increasing command of German, sports were a sign of belonging to the dominant group, of conforming to the model of what a young German in the GDR should be. Max and Georg were hardly unique. In both East and West Germany, DPs were enthusiastically rediscovering sports; Jewish sports clubs had sprung up all over the place.[48] Sports provided outlets for the real anger that existed among these marginal groups. And often this type of symbolic warfare degenerated into physical conflict, as in a soccer match between Polish and Jewish teams at the DP camp at Dachau that ended in a knife fight.[49]

The obsession with sports was part of a German tradition rooted in a nineteenth-century belief in the link between national identity and physical health. At the beginning of the twentieth century, early Zionists such as Max Nordau had advocated reshaping the sick Jewish body, which was the result of "2,000 years in the ghetto," into that of a healthy "muscle Jew." This was the Jew who would become the new citizen of Zion. In the Weimar Republic the interest in self-improvement had blossomed with the formation of Jewish sports organizations with a wide range of political affiliations. Later, in the young GDR, involvement in sports, like speaking German, became part of what it meant to belong to the new state. In becoming a German, young Georg came to excel in both.

Chapter 4

GEORG AS A YOUNG COMMUNIST IN THE
GERMAN DEMOCRATIC REPUBLIC,
1949–1960

What Is a "Victim of Fascism"?

Georg Becker became a young communist in 1951. He joined the Free German Youth (Freie Deutsche Jugend, or FDJ), the official youth organization of the German Democratic Republic, before he had completed the eighth grade. Decades later he noted that he had joined not out of conviction but only at the insistence of his father. Max had carefully explained to Georg how important it was for a young man to take part in the life of the new nation. Without quite believing him, Georg did as his father wished.[1]

The new state was already developing its own rituals to symbolize becoming a new German. Being a German, more than anything, was what the young Georg sought: "I wanted to stop being different, which was hard...I wanted to develop average practices and reactions, to be as inconspicuous as possible."[2] After March 1955, rites of passage such as bar mitzvah or confirmation were replaced by a new one: at the age of thirteen, young German-speaking citizens of the German Democratic Republic entered into the socialist community through the "youth initiation" (*Jugendweihe*) with its communal oath to the state, to socialism, and to eternal friendship with the USSR.

Even as a young communist, Georg did not make friends easily. He missed school periodically for fairly long periods to undergo treatment for his still fragile body. So the other students knew he had been in the camps. Georg tried hard not to be labeled a Jew but, rather, to be a "citizen of Jewish ancestry," the official designation in the GDR. (Later in life he altered the wording somewhat, speaking about his Jewish parentage, rather than being a Jew.) Yet his status as a victim of fascism and his small pension from the state signaled that he would remain different. He discovered that the harder he tried to be like everyone else, the more different he became.[3] To become a "good" German like the other students at the Käthe Kollwitz School, Georg needed to change his body, his language, and his attitude. "Victim of the Nazi regime" was written on his fragile body even as he trained as a boxer. Sports became his way of becoming a German.

Max had provided Georg with food, more food, and even more food, hard won on the black market. From the emaciated child in the UNRRA orphanage, a rather fat little schoolboy emerged. Indeed, tubby Georg came to be nicknamed Paffi by his school friends in grade school after a pig so named in one of their English readers. It was a name he detested, but one that his schoolmates continued to use, especially when he achieved some celebrity.

By 1953, Max had become active in "the interzone business," buying things in the West unavailable in the East and reselling them to those who wanted them. He had done the same sort of thing on the black market. Many of the goods, such as gold and silver, could not legally be resold in the GDR. Max spent most of his free time in a bar on Danziger Street playing billiards with his Jewish friends. As we have seen, he was a great storyteller. His accented German lent him a certain exoticism. The more he drank, the funnier he was—to everyone except Georg, who was distressed by his father's growing dependence on alcohol. Georg was afraid his father was losing control over his life.

Becoming a new German also meant retaining some sense of one's own difference. Georg saw Max's overprotection of him as a comment on Max's own failure to function well in the world. He stifled his son with material things rather than speaking to him frankly about his past and about his feelings. Georg saw himself as a "monster." "My father, who was a simple man, had difficulty keeping up with me. In his eyes I was somewhere between a protégé and a child. It must be because of the way he raised me that I insisted on my opinions, that my greatest joy was winning an argument, that I loved to argue."[4] In the eleventh grade, Georg's teacher noted that his "behavior gives reason for complaint. He has a sense of superiority, which has its roots in a certain immaturity."[5] The more Georg became a German, the better he learned the language; and the more he tried to become like everyone else, the greater was his sense of his own value. Max, with his heavily accented German and bouts of drunkenness, was clearly different from the Germans (or, at least, from their idealized self-image). Georg learned that he could consciously become like "them," whereas "they" were condemned to being only themselves. He was thus an even better German than they were. The beloved infant, the ghetto and concentration camp survivor, the fat boy with the oversized bicycle, so used to being the center of a loving parent's attention, grew certain of his place in this new world through his fantasy of controlling it.

Georg always seemed to have pocket money. He had a piano at home and a very expensive camera with a telephoto lens, but most importantly he had a typewriter. When asked as a child what he wanted to be when he was grown up, he always answered "a writer."[6] He could reshape himself as a young German, a young socialist, and be better at it than anyone else. He would write his way into belonging to this new society. Still, he was a "passive member" of the FDJ. Like Max, he thought rules were made to be broken. As a high school student he became a passionate fan of Western films and would sneak across the open border into the American zone. This was against the express directives of the FDJ leadership, which forbade its members to be exposed to Western culture.[7]

Georg's GDR was being created by a cadre of returning citizens. The leaders of the Soviet zone and the GDR were returnees—from Moscow, from Mexico City, from Los Angeles. All were communists; some were secular Jews.[8] For most of the latter, being Jewish was an insignificant part of their identity—though a real one in postwar Germany. Everyone "knew" who was Jewish in the GDR. It made little difference whether they were individuals such as Hermann Axen, a hard-line member of the Politburo of the ruling party (the SED, Socialist Unity Party of Germany), or intellectuals of various political shades such as the novelist Stefan Heym or the historian Jürgen Kuczynski. Among Georg's younger compatriots were those such as Wolf Biermann, and Thomas Brasch, whose sense of Jewish identity in the GDR was minimal or nonexistent but who remained visible as Jews. Others, such as Peter Kirchner, had religious identities as Jews, which precluded any political or ethnic identity.

While Georg was in high school, the meaning of Jewish visibility had begun to change. In the same way that McCarthyism identified foreigners in the United States with communism during the 1950s, in the new socialist states the Jews were becoming more and more identified as the fifth column, threatening to undermine the new regime. While the leading political voices of the GDR, including Paul Merker, who had returned from Mexican exile, heralded the founding of the state of Israel in 1948, they did so in the light of Soviet support. By the 1950s, the tune had changed remarkably.[9] In 1952, all the tiny Jewish communities in the GDR (initially with the exception of the four-power city of Berlin) were formally associated with one another in the Organization of Jewish Communities, which allowed the GDR to have control over them.

The early 1950s saw the show trial of the "Zionist agent" Rudolph Slansky, who was convicted in Prague in 1952 as part of a purge of "anti-Stalinist" elements in the Communist Party. The so-called Jewish doctors' plot against Stalin was one of the underlying factors in the purge.[10] Being Jewish or even of Jewish ancestry was not necessarily seen as positive in the GDR. The trial of Paul Merker, himself not a Jew, before the Supreme Court in East Berlin in March 1955 paralleled those in Prague and Moscow, compromising the very idea of a Jewish identity in the GDR.[11] Well publicized, Merker's trial marked a clear rejection of a GDR obligation to the political memory of the Shoah. Merker had returned from Mexican exile convinced that the struggle against anti-Semitism and the memory of the Shoah had to be central to shaping a new socialist state in Germany. The GDR government under its first prime minister, Walter Ulbricht, disagreed. Merker was arrested and accused of being an agent of the Americans and the Zionists, a "German Slansky." Ironically, he was tried and convicted under a law that was designed to thwart the revival of Nazism in postwar Germany. On March 30, 1955, the judges of the GDR's highest court sentenced him to eight years in prison. Merker's conviction was the clearest sign that any public identity as a Jew in the light of the new state of Israel would be difficult if not impossible in the GDR.

Being Jewish was a public and political sign of a "dual loyalty" in a world in which the claims for a "universal" Marxist identity only allowed identification with the new state. The establishment of a new socialist German identity in the GDR was, at least after the beginning of the anti-Zionist campaign of the 1950s, incompatible with a "Zionist" or a nonreligious "Jewish" identity. After Stalin's death, the Jewish doctors were "rehabilitated" in April 1953, and some of the pressure on the Jews in the GDR was lifted. The GDR had "cleansed" itself of all of the "destructive" and "cosmopolitan" forces within and beyond the SED.[12] It had "organized" the Jewish communities in such a way as to make them extensions of state and party ideology and, in doing so, had clearly isolated them from their Western compatriots. Introducing anti-Zionism as an acceptable way of talking about Jews provided a justification to those who still believed in an "international Jewish conspiracy." Needless to say, it made being Jewish in the GDR, no matter how defined, uncomfortable and dangerous.[13] It also provided an alternative means for Jews or people "of Jewish descent" to distance themselves from a Jewish identity. Jews had to be anti-Zionist if they were to be true internationalists. A case in point was the Jewish poet Stephan Hermlin, who was born in Chemnitz in 1915. A major cultural figure in the GDR, he carefully removed from his biography the fact that his family had been active Zionists in the Weimar Republic. Indeed, his brother and sister had emigrated to Palestine after the Nazis came to power, and he had joined them there before leaving for France in 1937.[14] In the GDR, anti-Semitism simply transformed itself into anti-Zionism, and even Jews such as young Georg became actively anti-Zionist. Thus there was some truth in the often-heard statement that there was little or no anti-Semitism in the GDR. Anti-Zionism took its place, becoming a requirement for a Jewish secular identity.

Between the death of Stalin in 1953 and the early 1960s, the emphasis of anti-Semitic rhetoric in the GDR shifted from Stalinist attacks on Jews as "cosmopolitans" to attacks on Zionists as the representatives of capitalism writ large.[15] Georg's impression that there was no anti-Semitism in the Berlin of his youth was based on the sense that a clear line could be drawn between those who were Jewish by the accident of birth and those who chose to highlight their Jewishness.[16] The latter may have seen themselves as religious Jews, but they were officially regarded as "tools of Zionism." Dual loyalty was not permissible. The official anti-Zionist rhetoric became an acceptable mask for anti-Semitism. Being anti-Israel seemed to be a reflex of foreign policy, but it was aimed just as much at Jews within the GDR. As a young member of the FDJ, Georg could not allow himself to recognize this veiled anti-Semitism, for it cast doubt on the stories he was telling to shape his own identity.

In 1953, Georg visited a friend in Hamburg. He reported later that all he saw was the "horrible poverty," not the "promised fine houses." In the harbor he saw communist slogans plastered all over the docks. When he returned to Berlin, he determined "to counter the lies about the West . . . and enable the good to conquer."[17] Recalling this trip two years later, he had to recount it in a more heroic mode: he had heard the attacks on the GDR that were circulated in the West and felt a need to "fight with my entire being for the victory of justice."[18] Young Georg told stories about his experiences in the West precisely in order to claim membership in the new state and to show his conversion from a passive to an active membership. Both versions of these stories were written as part of his application to the prestigious Humboldt University. Georg knew that telling stories about his role as an activist precluded any parochial identity as a victim of the Nazis or as a Jew. In this way he was as able to blind himself to the problems of his own tenuous Jewish identity.

In his final years in high school, Georg tried to become a better student and a good citizen. His grades, especially in German, history, and social sciences, improved radically. While at the Käthe Kollwitz School, he was even elected to the central committee of the FDJ. He became a model leader for the younger students, serving as organizer for their political activities. Desperately trying to be like his fellow students, Georg knew that his experience in the Shoah, the accented German of his father, and his own circumcised body could betray him at any moment.

Georg's teachers still saw him as too "impulsive" and considered that his "good political consciousness" needed to be strengthened and "made more consistent." His application to study literature at the university was approved in part because of his victim status. "His lack of concentration can be explained by his unusually difficult childhood, which he spent in the ghetto and the camps. He has developed positively in spite of his poor health. One must note that Georg has attended school only since he was ten and yet has been able to integrate himself well."[19] Although Georg maintained he had forgotten all the details of his early life, his teachers always kept his victim status in mind when evaluating him.

Max was never as convinced of the merits of state socialism as his son was.[20] He never attended any of the "official" meetings that were constantly required in the GDR, pleading his poor command of German.[21] Max's accent branded him as a Jew. Georg, on the other hand, a tabula rasa with no remembered past, transformed himself into a member of the first generation of young citizens of the GDR. Yet his role as a young communist was seen as only a mask. He was still was regarded as a victim, a survivor, a Jew.

What Is a Jew?

It was only much later that Georg comprehended the difference between his father's life in "Germany" and his own in the GDR. As a student he began to distance himself from the label "Jewish," seeing it as something belonging only to Max. After 1949, Max spoke only of the *Germans*. He would ask Georg: "How do the *Germans* treat you in school?"[22] Both father and son were officially "returnees" since Max had claimed a German birthplace. This invented ancestry never mitigated Georg's sense of being an outsider, because he had had to learn a new language. The more German he became, the more Max wanted him to understand his difference from his classmates: "Let them know you don't belong to them."[23]

This sense of belonging but not belonging, of being a German but inexorably different because the loss of his past, marked the mature Jurek Becker as a German writer. Being "Jewish" was negatively weighted for Georg.

The negative quality ascribed to being Jewish haunted Jurek Becker's literary work. "What is a Jew?" asks the protagonist in Becker's novel *The Boxer* (1976), and the question was a recurring theme in all his work. In his great first novel, *Jacob the Liar* (*Jakob der Lügner*, 1969), he introduced a Polish Jewish figure, Dr. Kirschbaum from Krakow, whose identity was clearly more Polish than Jewish: "He was a surgeon, not a Jew: What does it mean, of Jewish origin? They force you to be a Jew while you yourself have no idea what it really is. Now he is surrounded only by Jews, for the first time in his life nothing but Jews. He has racked his brain about them, wanting to find out what they all have in common, in vain. They have nothing recognizably in common, and he most certainly nothing with them."[24] Later, in *The Boxer*, the author describes how a survivor father discovers his seven-year-old son in an orphanage and takes him to Berlin, where he is raised as a young German. The father changes his name from the very Jewish Aron to the very German Arno. The father's inability to speak to his son about his experiences in the camps means that the son, as he matures, lacks any sense of who he is and what he can do. During the Six-Day War, this young communist goes to Israel to defend the Jewish state. He dies there. The father, numb with grief, can only speculate what might have made his son into a Jew.

The final section of the Jurek Becker's most commercially successful novel, *Amanda Heartless* (*Amanda Herzlos*, 1992), deals with the attempts of the protagonist, Amanda, to leave the GDR, so she can marry her Western lover. Unbeknownst to both of them, the GDR is about to collapse. The couple turns to a lawyer named Colombier, who is well placed to help them leave. Amanda asks the lawyer's wife whether her husband was a Huguenot, since their name sounds French:

> Oh no, we are not Huguenots, we are Jews. We are not Jews, we are of Jewish descent, you know the difference? We don't keep kosher, we have no knowledge of prayers, our two youngest sons are not even circumcised. If you are a Catholic and leave the church, then you aren't a Catholic any more. With the Jews, unfortunately, it's different. So for simplicity sake I told them: we are Jews. It's immaterial that our name was Tauber until our emigration to France.[25]

And so on: they chose a new name, new ancestry, but remained Jews—or at least of Jewish ancestry—even in the GDR after their return. It is implied that the more hidden one's identity as a Jew is thought to be, the more public it actually is. And that is especially true in the GDR.[26]

The view that the invisibility of a Jewish identity actually makes it more visible is captured in an anecdote from 1986. Jurek Becker's second wife, Christine, suggested the name Aron Becker for their future child. His uncensored response was that it would be as if he were running around with his fly open.[27]

Young Georg took part in the constitution of a Jewish identity whether he wanted to or not. He neither sought nor avoided other Jews. "Whether one was or was not a Jew was something I experienced haphazardly, if at all. If someone drew my attention to it, I always asked myself: Why is he telling me this? I may even have been a bit alienated. Because I thought that after an admission of one's Jewishness the person would expect me to relate to him differently than I would have normally."[28] He is referring to the sense of being and not being, of the desire to pass as merely a human being, not as a human being who is also a Jew.

Over time, Jurek Becker acknowledged the sense of a "common mental construction," to use Sigmund Freud's definition of the salient quality of the Jew.[29] He almost paraphrased Freud in a television interview he gave in 1996, noting that he had been exposed to myriad influences and that their combination was what he understood as Jewish. If asked, he reported, he always said that his parents were Jewish, never that "I am a Jew."[30] And yet in his last interview, given when he was dying of cancer, he said: "I would argue with you about the question of whether I am or am not a Jew . . . I am also aware that what you call "being Jewish," that is, Jewish culture, has played a role for me in a hundred different ways."[31] During his lifetime, the meaning of "being Jewish" gradually ceased to be a negative label for something the young Georg needed to abandon in order to become a good citizen of the GDR, and became an inexorable part of who the dying Jurek Becker saw himself to be.

What Is a German?

Between 1949 and 1955, Georg had become a "German." After graduating from high school in 1955 and being admitted to Humboldt University in February of that year, he volunteered for two years' service in the KVP (*Kasernierte Volkspolizei*, People's Barracked Police), a new unit of the German police that had been created only in October 1952. Max was very unhappy with his son's decision and appealed to Georg's teachers and principal, who tried to talk the young man out of it. Georg had been admitted to the university to study literature, which Max thought a much more appropriate choice for his son than service in a quasi-military unit. Since the beginning of 1955, Max had been at home full time, having been officially declared unable to work because of the effects of his time in the camps.[32]

Georg's decision was not completely free of external pressure. It had been made clear to him that after gaining his high school diploma (*Abitur*), joining the KVP would be seen as fulfilling his obligation to serve the state.[33] Georg also became a "candidate" member of the Socialist Unity Party in June 1955. It provided a place where his ideological beliefs could be rewarded by increased status.

Enlisting in the KVP allowed Georg to escape from Max's day-to-day control, since Max now spent ever more time at home. Georg joined his unit for basic training on September 1, 1955. His life at Ludwigsfeld consisted of three months' strenuous physical training, weapons training, and sports, which demanded "even more" than all of his strength.[34] During this time, he lived quite independently of Max, who was delighted when his son returned home after the three months.

He was then assigned to the Watch Guard (*Wachschutz*), which was reserved for party members. While most KVP units were stationed in barracks and were on full-time service, members of the Watch Guard worked only shifts and lived at home. Georg wore a black uniform and guarded a building at the Schönhauser Tor that, at least initially, was empty. One afternoon, some West German trucks pulled up and unloaded files and furniture belonging to the West German Communist Party, which had just been banned in the FRG. Georg, like everyone else, spent his shift reading.[35] On one occasion his school friend Helge Braune visited him while he was "guarding" the Central Committee of the SED. Georg told him that he read as much on duty there as he did anywhere else.

Life in the KVP, like life in the concentration camps, was regimented and boring. According to Georg, each day consisted of a long series of useless tasks. It was during this time that he developed an aversion to "blind obedience." He contended that it was his time in the KVP that taught him to think, for thinking was the only way to overcome boredom. It was there too that he felt the first inclination to write, or at least the desire to formulate thoughts as precisely as possible.[36] His supervisors judged him to be "punctual and responsible . . . Comrade Becker consistently represents the goals of the party and is open and honest in his demeanor."[37] He was rewarded with a three-week "study trip" to the Soviet Union in July and August 1956.[38] What seemed to be adherence to the rules of the game was also good training in how to manipulate them.

The works that Georg read during this time, as well those he had read as earlier in his life, shaped his sense of the kind of writer he wanted to become. Books could be found in large numbers in Max's apartment, even though material goods may have been lacking.[39] Max read, and encouraged his son to read, both "important" books and popular literature of the sort his contemporaries were reading. Georg's reading ranged from the socialist realism of his school textbooks to the world of German culture from before the war and from the other side of the political divide. In his father's bookcase he found classic Russian works by Nikolai Gogol, Fyodor Dostoevsky, and Maxim Gorki; the Wild West novels of Karl May; the murder mysteries of Edgar Wallace and Rex Stout. He read Jean-Paul Sartre's *The Flies* as well as the novels of Ernest Hemingway. He bragged about reading literature that was banned in the GDR.[40] But it was Max Frisch, especially in his novel *Stiller* (1954), who taught Georg that the serious and the comic were closely related and that "tragedy doesn't always have to wear a dark suit, and comedy a T-shirt."[41] Of Jewish writers who wrote in German, only Franz Kafka captured his attention when Georg was still at high school. Kafka had self-consciously stripped his texts of any Jewish references.[42] Georg appreciated Kafka's accuracy in depicting the details of life, a more important accuracy than that of mere representation. Kafka was then banned in the socialist countries and came to hold a special position in the pantheon of "banned writers." As a Jew and a modernist, Kafka became one of the writers most feared and most suspected in the GDR, especially after the "Prague Spring" of 1968.[43] Literature became the medium by which a new role and a new identity could be crafted. Like Kafka, Georg started to see his identity as mirrored both in the books he read and in the way he read—against the grain.

While still in the KVP, Georg first met the young Manfred Krug in 1956 in a bar, the Young Artists' Club. Both were still in their late teens. (The club was the "alternative" scene in East Berlin. At the end of the 1950s it was raided and closed down by a group of FDJ members led by the later reform politician Hans Modrow.)[44] After leaving the club, the two young men wandered through the night, talking and telling each other stories. Krug, lacking a scrap of paper, wrote Georg's address on the wall of a ruined building with the stub of a pencil. He went back the next day, made a note the address, and got in touch with Georg.[45]

Krug would become Georg's best friend and artistic collaborator over the next four decades. Almost exactly the same age as Georg, he was born in February 1937 in Duisburg, which after 1945 was in the American zone. His father was an engineer, his mother a secretary. After his parents divorced, Krug followed his father to the GDR in 1949. There he began an apprenticeship as a steelworker and then was employed as the youngest craftsman in the steelworks in Brandenburg while studying in night school. He entered the army about the same time as Georg had joined the KVP, and they became fast friends. In 1954, Krug enrolled in the state acting school in East Berlin but was expelled after a year and a half for "disciplinary difficulties." More than a head taller than Georg, Krug's huge, bearlike physique was in striking contrast to Georg's slight, wiry body.

Krug passed his state examination as an actor in 1955 and was given small roles as a member of Bertolt Brecht's repertoire theater, the Berliner Ensemble. By 1956 he had acquired his first role in a film, *The Mazurka of Love*, a musical based on the classic operetta *The Beggar Student*, and in 1957 he was given his first television role, as a juvenile delinquent in the FRG in Karl-Heinz Bieber's *Dangerous Truths*. All the while, his friendship with Georg grew closer. By 1959 they had decided to share an "apartment," actually an abandoned spice store on Cantian Street, smelling strongly of vanilla and lacking any real conveniences. (Georg described it in his censored novel *Sleepless Days*[46] [1978] as the living quarters of the protagonist and his girlfriend.)

The apartment was the site of so many raucous parties, labeled "orgies" by the police, that on one occasion Georg was fined 50 marks because of excessive noise.[47] The relationship between Krug and Georg was so emotionally intense that at one point they were reported to be homosexual lovers.[48] Later, Becker used a similar image to describe his friendship with Krug. "No sooner did we meet than we moved in together. Had we been man and woman, it would have been called love at first sight."[49] One complication was Krug's growing relationship to Max, as Krug became a surrogate son to him. Alienated from his own father, Krug spent hours listening to Max talk about his life before and after the war. Indeed, as George became more independent and strove for his own identity, Max and Krug grew closer.

Georg's friendship with Krug led to a friendship with the poet Wolf Biermann, a little older than both of them and known to Krug from the theater world of Berlin. Biermann's father had worked on the docks in Hamburg and had been part of the communist underground before he was murdered at Auschwitz in 1943. Biermann's Jewish grandmother raised him. He was one of the few workers' children to attend high school in Hamburg. He then enrolled at Humboldt University, where he studied mathematics and philosophy from 1959 to 1963. From 1957 to 1959 he was a directorial assistant at Brecht's Berliner Ensemble. Growing up as a Jew in the GDR, he did not experience anti-Semitism per se but was constantly aware that it was not necessarily a positive thing to be seen as Jewish.[50] Like Jurek, he found it easier to become a good socialist than to struggle with the label of "Jewish." Biermann would come to play an important role in Georg's life.

In February 1955, before his service in the KVP, Georg had been admitted to Humboldt University to study literature, his professional goal stated as "writer." He reapplied in 1957, but when he arrived at the university, it was not literature but philosophy that he studied, along with some courses in law. His stated professional goal was to be a diplomat or an editor, but he still wanted to become a writer. There were only about thirty students admitted to study philosophy in Georg's class. When asked later why he did not study literature, he answered that he did not want to become a literary historian; he wanted to become a writer. Studying philosophy seemed, for various reasons, the most useful way to achieve this ambition. He thought it would somehow sharpen his mind, his capacity to think clearly. Equally important, it was a means of joining the central intellectual current of his society. Philosophy was, of course, Marxist-Leninist philosophy. It was the official system of thought in the GDR, providing the rules of argumentation that were acceptable to the society in which Georg lived. Becoming a Marxist meant learning those rules, internalizing them, and shaping oneself in their terms. Argue like me, the society says, and you will belong.[51] This choice of an academic major shows up again in his novel *Bronstein's Children* (1986). Its protagonist states that he wants to study philosophy rather than medicine because philosophy will provide him with guidelines for his life.

Georg was one of the more noticeable figures on campus. Always well dressed, he sported a leather jacket at a time when this was clearly a mark of someone with "Western" sources of income. The money, however, came from his pension and from Max's largesse. By his own account, he was not a good student. If a subject did not interest him (and there seem to have been quite a few of those), he did no work at it.[52] He claimed that he attended classes more or less at his own whim. When he left the GDR a decade later, he took very little with him. He did, however, take a sheaf of papers he had written as a philosophy student at Humboldt University.

Among these papers are studies of Marx's views on Hegel's philosophy of law, a study of the rise of Cartesian philosophy (written in his fourth semester), a detailed paper on the essence of physical idealism, and a study of the reactionary content of Plato's theory. All show a young, serious student working within the limits of the Marxist-Leninist educational system.[53] During the three years when he was studying philosophy and law at the university—from September 2, 1957, to December 9,

1960—he was enthusiastically involved in sports. He learned how to combine membership of the social world with that of the intellectual world. After the 1956 Hungarian revolt, the authorities in the GDR were extremely worried that the universities might become, or indeed had become, centers of resistance to the system. Georg seemed to be an ideal student. He learned to use the system from within while believing in the abstract values advocated by the theories he studied. He became a good German. Yet his fellow students immediately labeled him a "ghetto child."[54] That he was still a "victim of the Nazi regime" was clear to everyone around him.

Georg's unspoken visibility was shared by a number of his professors. Everyone knew who among them were Jews. But there was a code of silence concerning them. Two of Georg's professors during his first year— Marie Simon, professor of the history of philosophy, and Peter Alfons Steininger, who taught the theory of law—were Jews. They had been forced to abandon their career plans by the Nazi Nuremberg laws and were able to return to an academic career only after the reconstitution of Humboldt University after 1946. One of Georg's close friends at the university was Hans Bergmann, the illegitimate son of Ernst Fischer, a well-known Jewish communist theoretician from Austria.

In *Misleading the Authorities* (1973), Becker's fictional account of being a student at the university, he describes one of his law professors. "Until the Third Reich he had been a defense lawyer with a future; then they stuck him in a concentration camp because his descent did not approximate that which was necessary."[55] The euphemism reflects the unspoken awareness present in Georg's world. The model for the Jewish lawyer was most probably Klaus Zweiling, who had given Georg his oral examination before he was admitted to study philosophy.

Georg started to write poetry—or, at least, doggerel—for the student cabaret at Humboldt. Through his connections with Krug and Biermann, he soon started writing for the leading political cabaret in East Berlin, the Thistle (*Distel*). The Thistle had been founded on October 2, 1953, by Erich Brehm to counter such well-financed West Berlin cabarets as the Porcupine (*Stachelschwein*). As a citizen of the "workers' and farmers' state," Georg recognized that the ability to write for a broad public meant accepting the limitations of what even "political satire" meant in a socialist state.

Hanging out at the Pressecafé, which was in the same building as the cabaret, Georg met a number of the performers as well as Georg Honigmann, the Thistle's director. They were sufficiently impressed with him that he came to write extensively for the shows. In addition to the public visibility that such writing generated, each of his contributions brought him between 80 and 150 marks, money a student could well use. Over twenty sketches and poems are preserved among the few papers he brought with him when he left East Berlin. They consist almost exclusively of short comic or satiric scenes that reflect the daily language in the GDR, not only by the use of dialect but, even more telling, by the use of the political jargon of both East and West.[56]

As a student in the 1950s, Georg had been a compulsive moviegoer. That meant going to the American, French, and British cinemas in the Western sectors of Berlin. Students from the GDR, showing their IDs, could buy movie tickets in the Western zones with their GDR money at par. It was one of the most effective ways used by the Western democracies to seduce the youth in the East. Georg also went to theaters in East Berlin that showed the official DEFA films. DEFA (Deutsche Film-Aktiengesellschaft) was the state-owned studio of the GDR, which between 1946 and 1992 produced more than 750 feature films and countless documentaries and shorts. Over the years, major directors such as Slatan Dudow, Wolfgang Staudte, Kurt Maetzig, Konrad Wolf, and Frank Beyer worked for DEFA. And Georg regularly saw films from the "brother socialist countries" as they appeared in the East Berlin cinemas.

In 1956, Humboldt University students started publishing a magazine, which they distributed in the Western sectors. It was called *Tua res,* after a quotation from Horace, implying that it is your concern when your neighbor's wall is burning. Until 1959, the magazine was edited by Hermann Kant, who later became a major literary figure in the GDR and a serious political advocate of the regime. Georg wrote film criticism under a pseudonym Hermann Kant had given him, "Lola Ramon," which he disliked.[57] Along with many other students, Georg also distributed the magazine at the West Berlin universities. It was during one of these "Western actions" (*Westeinsätze*) that the West Berlin police arrested Georg.[58] The fictionalized account of this incident in *Misleading the Authorities* has him defend himself against a young West Berlin policeman by simply knocking him down. The protagonist thus frees himself to "escape" back to the safety of "Berlin—the capital of the GDR," amazed at the way this act mirrors those in the movies he has seen.[59] Acting as if he were in the movies becomes part of the way Georg understands himself.

What Georg chose to write about in *Tua res* was the film politics of West Berlin. Georg's position at that time was clearly socialist and antagonistic to the public film policies of the West German government. Following the official Marxist position, Georg saw criticism not as negative but as constructive, reeducative. He perceived those West German voices as vacuous. "There is something comic about opinions. One needs only to repeat them exactly in order to destroy them."[60] That to accurately reproduce specious arguments is the best criticism was a view espoused by earlier critics, such as the turn-of-century Austrian Jewish critic Karl Kraus.

Georg saw the artistic as well as the creative process as rooted in individual vision and commitment to the state. "The true artist must look for a way to achieve his individual monomania. In other words, the collective should be the means to hide his schizophrenia. But it is precisely in the collective that this appears most clearly."[61] It is the voice of the artist that articulates the desires of the collective. But for which collective can the artist speak? The socialist state, in which all art perceived as being equal, or only in older collectives, such as the one to which history has assigned him? Later, Georg dismissed these early critical attempts as more concerned with my "own views than with the films that were being discussed."[62] Film criticism and script writing for cabaret became a passion, and his university studies suffered noticeably.

In 1960, Georg was suspended from the university well before he was to take his final examinations because of what both he and the authorities saw as clearly unacceptable activities. He was granted a two-year leave. In spite of his desire to become a "good" student, he had had a number of run-ins with the university administration. He had been sent into the countryside, as many students were, to help with the harvest. One day, after loading sacks of potatoes at the train station in Buch, he wanted to ride back from the field in the cab of a truck since it was pouring rain. The driver ordered him out. When asked why, the driver said, "Because I said so!" Georg responded with an expletive, and when he refused to budge, the driver pushed him out of the cab. Cursing him, Georg crawled into the back of the open truck. Arriving at the depot, the driver informed the authorities. Georg warned him to watch what he said. When the driver called him a "bum," Georg swung at him. He was restrained, and the driver then gave him a black eye. In his public admission, Georg acknowledged his error, stating that he now understood that he represented all students as well as the university in his actions and recognized that his punishment was just.[63] Yet his own sense of justice had been violated by both the farmer's and the university's actions.

In another instance, when Georg was in the countryside in Zechin, he saw firsthand the repressive measures taken against those farmers who resisted collectivization. So he quit working on the farms "because our actions had nothing to do with what I felt was just."[64] Georg knew that in his philosophy examination Professor Walter Besenbruch would ask why farmers would join a collective. In a long and detailed written answer, which he preserved among his university papers, Georg focused on the pros and cons of this question.[65] Then, in his orals, the examiner asked him why, if he knew the theory, he didn't know how to put the theory into practice. Georg glanced at the list of thirty required questions and answered that the question he had been asked was not on the list. Understandably, Besenbruch considered this an impudent answer, and Georg barely passed the exam. It should be noted, however, that Besenbruch himself had been warned officially in 1958 that he seemed to give the best grades to students who were "partially enemies of socialist construction and revisionists" and that he tolerated a "separation between politics and philosophy." [66] This was not to be the case in Georg's exam. But in May 1960 he passed his preliminary exam in historical materialism with a C (*befriedigend*, satisfactory).

In leaving the university, Georg had been found wanting by the official evaluations. The associate chair of the Department of Philosophy noted for the record that he had often violated the disciplinary rules of the department and showed an "attitude that was not compatible with that of a student at a socialist university."[67] He was officially accused of "vanity and pretentiousness" as well as lack of ideological clarity in his role as a citizen of the GDR.[68] The reason given was Georg's "incomplete working through of his past." Georg's angry, "choleric" nature, a term he himself later used to describe himself, was read as symptomatic of a Nazi victim, too damaged to become part of the community.[69] In complicated ways this was not far from the mark. Georg's sense of being different became part of his attitude toward all authority. For him, this difference meant that he was superior to those who branded him as deviant. Being asked to leave the university allowed him to turn to the cinema, something that had always fascinated him.

Chapter 5

JUREK BECKER, AS GEORG NIKOLAUS, WRITES FOR THE MOVIES, 1960–1974

Learning the Craft

On June 29, 1960, Georg was granted the two-year leave from Humboldt University he had requested. Whether or not he would be readmitted depended on his conduct, for he had quickly asked for the leave when about to be expelled.[1] The university administration strongly suggested that he be assigned for at least a year to assemble television sets in the university's own electronics factory.[2] Instead, he took a six-month course in 1960 as a screenwriter at the state Film and Television College at Babelsberg.[3] This course had been created to fill the need for competent screenwriters in the GDR. The sketches he wrote for the cabaret had been exercises in writing for actors in a public medium. Among them are draft scenarios that he clearly wrote with an eye toward film writing. They are witty. They are condensed. And they are all political in that they all comment on the relationship of individuals to daily life in—though unspoken—a socialist state. All bear the name "Jurek Becker."

Screenwriting in the GDR was, if not a completely respectable, at least a lucrative occupation. Jurek would much later refer to himself as "an author and a screenwriter." The latter, he would say, was no less significant than the former. Once he had written his first novel, for which he received critical approval both nationally and internationally, Jurek felt himself to be a "writer," and that meant a writer of serious novels and essays. Other "serious" writers such as Günter Kunert, Gerhard Wolf, and Ulrich

Plenzdorf, all to become leading "oppositional" writers during the 1970s, also wrote for DEFA, the state film studio.[4]

Still, there was some suspicion about those who wrote for the films at a time when such activities were still seen as in their rudimentary phase in the GDR. It was only later in his life that Jurek became secure with this role. In his novel *Misleading the Authorities* (1973), he portrays the collapse of the moral authority of a would-be writer, Gregor Bienek, who agrees to the compromises demanded by the GDR film industry. Screenwriting was an attractive way of earning a living—in the GDR as well as in the FRG. Yet the desire was always to become a "real" writer. Jurek's protagonist "wants to write a novel, because . . . he wants to be his own director, his own main actor, his own cameraman, because he doesn't want to remain dependent on the abilities of others."[5] Jurek was able to parody writers who scorned writing for television while doing it themselves. In his final TV miniseries in 1994, on the problems of the reunification of Germany, *We Are Also One People* (*Wir sind auch nur ein Volk*), one of the central characters is the "famous" West German author Anton Steinheim, who is persuaded to write a TV series on German reunification. Jurek took all his writing seriously, whether as a novelist or as a scriptwriter. It would not be a catastrophe, Jurek said about his work for television, if instead of a thousand readers he had a million viewers. The important thing was not to forget what was right.[6]

In an ironic turn, Jurek once noted that the only profession he had actually "learned" was that of a scriptwriter. In 1960, he saw learning to write scripts as a craft,[7] in which the "author always has to know that his product has never been completed but only half finished."[8] It may not have been "a writer's work, but a way of bridging time."[9] Yet Jurek understood that writing for movies made him a "movie man" whether he liked it or not.[10] (This association came to haunt Jurek later in his life. He was never awarded the Büchner Prize, Germany's primary literary prize, because of his reputation as a screenwriter.) Writing screenplays also provided a real income for the first time. DEFA could pay as much as 20,000 marks for a screenplay, a boon for a twenty-three-year-old writer.[11] It was certainly a more interesting craft than assembling television sets!

Like his protagonist Gregor Bienek, Jurek began at the bottom as a screenwriter, but found it immensely satisfying. He wrote "as if gripped by an infection. For the first time I feel I have rewarding work" (165). In 1953, DEFA had begun a loose series of satiric film shorts called "Porcupine" (*Stacheltier*), which ran regularly in the cinemas of the GDR. This experimental series was created by the German Jewish returnee Georg

Honigmann, director of the Berlin cabaret the Thistle, which served as a model for the series. The films were to compete for the audience attracted by the contemporary political satire in the cabarets.[12] In 1961, Jurek began to write satires for the series, and Krug was to sing in some of the shorts.

Jurek had already written a good deal of material for the Thistle, and the transition to the series seemed easy.[13] Only a year after he had been suspended from the university, his first film, *With NATO through the Wall* (*Mit der NATO durch die Wand*, directed by Peter Ulbrich, 1961) was produced for Honigmann's "Porcupine" series.[14] Set in the Lüneburg Heath in West Germany, it recounts the story of a farmer, Schade (played by Siegfried Kilian), whose barn is damaged by a West German tank on maneuvers. He complains to anyone who will listen, from the mayor to the local newspaper. Everyone tells him that we must all make sacrifices in the name of freedom and security. When the representative from the West German army comes to negotiate with him about reimbursing the costs of repairing the barn, he too urges Schade to remember that everyone must sacrifice for the common good. While he is saying this, he sees his own automobile flattened by a tank. The film was proposed for release on November 11, 1961, but permission was denied without stated grounds. It has since vanished.[15] Jurek was, however, being noticed.

Having left the university under a cloud because of his attitude toward authority, Jurek became one of the millions spied upon by the Stasi (Ministerium der Staatssicherheit, the state security service).[16] Created in 1955, the Stasi was headed by Erich Mielke after 1957. At its peak it employed 100,000 full-time spies and almost twice that number of "informal agents" (IMs, *informelle Mitarbeiter*) to report on the activities of about 17 million citizens of the GDR.[17] (Under the Nazis, the Gestapo employed about 45,000 people to spy on a population of 80 million Germans.) Virtually everyone was involved in this reporting as agent or as victim or "object" of interest. Jurek was no exception. Initially they were interested in Jurek because he had left the university and because of the circle of friends he shared with Manfred Krug, including Wolf Biermann and the established poet Heinz Kahlau. Kahlau was one of the major figures in a group of critical writers and actors called the Thursday Circle, which had met since the 1950s. A Stasi operative reported Jurek's meeting with Kahlau on April 14, 1961, in detail. The report mentioned a rather attractive young woman who accompanied Jurek; it garbled her name, however, calling her "Reni." She was "a thin figure, chestnut brown hair; gray dress, brown shoes, three-quarter-length blue poplin coat."[18] Erika Hüttig, nicknamed "Rieke," was soon to become Jurek's wife. She met him after he had moved in with Manfred Krug and was impressed by his various talents, including the fact that he could play boogie-woogie on the piano. He was handsome—his jet-black hair, leather jacket, and Western jeans set him apart from the rank-and-file students. As did his very black eye, the result of his run-in with the farmer during the harvest. Rieke's parents were not excited about her relationship with Jurek. He was too wild and too different for them.

Manfred Krug remained central to Jurek's life. Krug often called Jurek "his little brother," and both played at being related. Their friendship and the "orgies" that took place in their storefront apartment made Jurek even more suspect to the Stasi. In the early 1960s, the GDR was prudish in its mix of Prussian rigidity and Stalinist anxiety. Sex was a major topic in the GDR. Krug was seen as someone with whom upstanding members of the FDJ could not work. The reason was telling: "In the pauses between filming he would disappear behind the scenes to indulge in sexual pleasures with the actresses."[19] This was a powerful accusation, for personal amorality was considered a sign of potential political instability. Jurek's social life as a young man was fully as complicated as Krug's. The charge of amorality reappears regularly in the files of Jurek and Krug's circle. And often it was linked with a not very subtle anti-Semitism. In an official Stasi report from September 9, 1972, an IM called "Riese" informs the Stasi about an outbreak of sexually transmitted diseases among actors and actresses at the Babelsberg studios of DEFA—including Jurek's friend, the actor Armin Müller-Stahl. By implication this group would have included Krug and Jurek. In the same report, "Riese" recounts a public argument Jurek had with Krug about the financing of their planned country house. The report then notes that it would be good if they broke up so that Krug could escape "from under Becker's Zionist influence."[20] Sex, money, and Jews are freely associated in this report, which begins with amorality in personal behavior and ends with political unreliability. Jurek and Krug did not speak for a long time after this public confrontation, but thereafter their friendship seemed even stronger.

The early 1960s were heady years for Jurek, years in which he truly believed he was helping to build socialism and to alter it in new and positive directions through his new role as a writer. Yet he also had a sense of entitlement. It was an odd entitlement, which built on the stigma or his status as a "victim of the Nazi regime," allowing him to pursue his own career, ignoring the "official" directives of party officers to work in the television factory. In these years the GDR, at least from the standpoint of its young intellectuals like Jurek, still had the reputation of being the "good" German state, the "antifascist" German state.[21] It was in the FRG, Jurek believed, that former Nazis still held power. Yet anti-Semitic sentiments on the part of officials and people on the street in the GDR were the unspoken background to Jurek's writing. They were constantly present.

On August 13, 1961, Walter Ulbricht, with the support of the Soviet Union, erected the "antifascist wall of protection" around West Berlin. Although the Berlin Wall was generally seen as the only means of stopping the hemorrhage of East Germans (and others) into the West, the official explanation was that it was a means of protecting the GDR against the infiltration of fascist agents from the West. Berlin had remained the focal point of East-West conflict and tensions. Whenever any cold war event took place in Europe, Berlin trembled. To Jurek, just beginning to build a career in the cinema, the wall seemed to mean little. He was twenty-three when it was built, and until then he had been able to move freely all over Berlin. After the wall was erected, he had limited ability to travel to the West but rarely had the sense of being trapped.[22] His friends felt differently. His school friend Helge Braune left the GDR in 1961 shortly after the wall went up. He appeared one evening at Jurek's apartment with a handful of records he knew Jurek wanted, and silently handed them to him. The next day he crawled through the sewers of East Berlin and made it into West Berlin and from there to West Germany.

The wall had a symbolic value for Jurek. He had internalized Max's sense that the only thing that held the Germans in check was the power exercised over them by the communist state (read: the Soviet Union). In 1993, four years after the wall had been torn down, Jurek told a commission of the (now united) German parliament that "one could not build socialism with people from a test tube, but only with those who existed. And they were the people who, not very long before, had for the most part stood on the sidewalks and screamed: 'Heil Hitler.' They somehow had to be brought under control."[23] The view that the Berlin Wall was an appropriate response to the Nazi past was expressed by a number of Jewish writers writing in German after the 1960s. For many Jewish Berliners, the wall seemed somehow the physical embodiment of the Nazi defilement of the city, a trauma that had been experienced during the 1940s but produced a symptom only in the 1960s.[24]

A major reason the Berlin Wall seemed to have little impact on Jurek was his marriage, just two days after the wall started to go up, to Erika Hüttig, the young woman who had attracted the attention of the Stasi. "Rieke," as she was called, was born on April 13, 1939. She lived with her parents in Jurek's old neighborhood at 6 Lippehner Street and was two classes behind him at the Käthe Kollwitz School. After graduating, she took a job as a decorator at a state store and was working there when she and Jurek were married. Her father had been a member of the NSDAP (Nationalsozialistische Deutsche Arbeiterpartei, the Nazi Party) and had worked until 1945 as a manager in the Friedrichshain section of Berlin. Unemployed after the war, he was outspokenly critical of the GDR. Rieke's mother, Charlotte, supported the family by working illegally in the West and as a seamstress at home.[25] Later, as soon as Rieke's father was eligible for a pension, both parents moved to Hamburg.

When, in the spring of 1961, Rieke informed Jurek that she was pregnant, he moved into the dank storefront apartment that she rented on Hufeland Street, around the corner from Max's apartment on Braunschweiger Street. Rieke was soon calling Max "Papa." She and Jurek were married shortly before the birth of their child. For Rieke this was a radical break, from being in a family ostracized because of its Nazi association to marrying a "victim of fascism." They went to the civil authorities and were told they could get an appointment to be married in two hours or in two weeks. Hastily assembling some friends, they were married two hours later. That was on August 15, 1961, and their son Nikolaus (Nicki) arrived on August 23, 1961. For Jurek, the wall came to represent those forces that would protect him and his new family. Within a year, the new family moved into a house with a garden on Argenauer Street, where Max regularly visited his new grandson. A second son, Leonard (Lonni), followed three and a half years later, on May 24, 1964. Even though Max was a member of the Berlin Jewish Community, there was absolutely no sense of religious identity in his world or Jurek's. He had succeeded in raising his son as a good citizen of the GDR with its stress on internationalism and hatred of particularism. So, as a good citizen, Jurek found the very thought of circumcising his (non-Jewish) sons "repulsive."

As they grew up, Jurek's sons saw their father as totally absorbed in his writing. He had his own room in the house to which the family had moved in the spring of 1968, 25 Wilhelm Blos Street, in the Berlin suburb of Mahlsdorf Süd. Heinz Kahlau noted that Jurek had had to make a living from writing for nearly a decade "and had earned himself a nice house."[26] The money for the house, however, came from the inheritance that Rieke's father had left her after he died in Hamburg. Her mother had exchanged the Western marks at a very favorable rate into Eastern currency and smuggled it across the border to her.

The family took regular vacations in the countryside or at vacation resorts in other Eastern bloc countries, often with the Krugs. Manfred too had married and had started a family. Family life seemed to be limited to such moments. In daily life, working in the house that he shared with his family members, Jurek often felt disturbed by them. Max had not provided a positive model for his role as a father. In his *Misleading the Authorities* (1973), Jurek's protagonist, finally achieving success writing for DEFA, describes himself as "against my will becoming introspective and laconic, [as] life about me plays itself off on tip-toes" (165). The novel reflects Jurek's growing alienation from his wife and sons.

From 1962 to 1976, Jurek wrote a number of scripts for film and television that were produced and for which he received screen credit.[27] Some, written jointly with Klaus Poche, appeared under the pseudonym Georg Nikolaus. Combining Georg, his "old" German name, with that of his German son Nikolaus, Jurek created a pseudonym that he used for the less serious body of his work. It was the final mask. After it disappeared, "Jurek Becker" remained the author's name.

In 1967, "Georg Nikolaus" wrote a multiple-episode comedy for GDR TV about the Nowak family and their grandfathers, *Opa* "Eddy" Günther (played by Walter Lendrich) and *Opa* Paul Kuhnke (played by Walter Richter-Reinick). It concerned the comic adventures of the grandchildren and their grandfathers with the theme: "How young older people can be." The shows were entitled *Always around March* (*Immer um den März herum*); *One Still Dreams at Seventy* (*Mit 70 hat man noch Träume*); and *Vacation* (*Urlaub*). They were reviewed as "entertaining and amusing but without a serious background or deeper meaning."[28] Yet all are "monuments to the German grandfather," that Jurek never had.[29] And Max's growing alcoholism prevented his relating well to his grandchildren as well as to Jurek.

The film world into which Jurek now fitted himself had internal cinematic rules as well as external political rules. The rules were clearly set, and what constituted violations was equally clear. The rewards were great, both financially and in terms of status as a creative artist in the GDR. As with the character Gregor Bienek in *Misleading the Authorities*, life as a screenwriter provided precisely the sort of life that a good member of the world of "real, existing socialism" could want, with few of the difficulties. All of the rules for success were spelled out, even the possibility for transgression.

Jurek, with Kurt Belicke as coauthor, wrote his first full-length screenplay for a DEFA film in 1964, two years after the Berlin Wall was built. It was a comedy of manners, *Without a Passport in Strange Beds* (*Ohne Pass in Fremden Betten*), and was directed by Vladimir Brebera for release in 1965. It was reviewed as "witty—with no claim to moral value."[30] Its central character, Václav Jelínek (played by the Czech actor Miroslav Hornicek), finds himself in East Berlin without his passport, which he has inadvertently left on the train on which he was returning to Prague. His adventures in East Berlin as a "foreigner without a passport" bring him into contact with a bunch of Berlin characters. Among them is Wilhelm Kabuffke (played by Gerhard Bienen), the owner of the Ferris Wheel on which Václav is trapped, causing him to miss his train. Kabuffke, like all the people Václav meets in Berlin, helps him without question. While life is "better when one's papers are in order," as one character notes, Václav Jelínek is indeed, as his friend Kabuffke observes to his wife, a version of Jaroslav Hasek's good solider Schweik. He seems simply to be lucky in his dealings with the world, but in his simplicity he has a clearer vision of the world in which he has accidentally found himself than any of the other characters.

East Berlin, despite the presence of the wall, seems to be the one place where everyone is helpful to the foreigner; indeed, being a "good German" means being helpful. All authority figures are benevolent and positive: there is the conductor who finds his passport and suitcase on the train and rescues it; the traffic police officers who drive him to the station; the criminal police who eventually sort everything out and help him to get a train back to Prague. In reality, East Berlin authorities were instructed to shoot to kill at the wall. The first victim, Peter Fechter, had been left to bleed to death there on August 17, 1962. At one point in the film, the potentially negative power of the state becomes clear: when everything is at the peak of confusion, one of the policemen (played by Werner Lierck) turns to the assembled group and announces that "misleading the authorities is a crime." And the crime will be punished.

"Misleading the authorities," a phrase taken from the legal parlance of the GDR, came to be Jurek's title for his novel about the making of a screenwriter in the GDR. It was a leitmotiv in his understanding of the nature of the state at the time. One has to mislead the authorities, but only within the limits that they themselves permit. It is what writers do, even writers of bedroom farces. It is this awareness of the permitted bounds of critical writing in the GDR that provides the (accepted) critical edge to writing. It is in the genre of the comic that this type of critical voice can most easily be expressed and is most easily accepted.

Jurek maintained his connection to Georg Honigmann's cabaret the Thistle until May, 1965 when his contributions to the show *Find a Bed Partner if You Can* (*Bette sich wer kann*) were condemned as part of a general crackdown on what was seen as "liberal" criticism of the state. Over time, Jurek would learn that while the authorities permitted a window of criticism, the window opened and closed (and changed shape) with remarkable frequency. The partnership between satire and politics so important in the first decade was, by 1965, no longer seen as acceptable. "Is socialism better off without cabarets?"[31] asked the official party documents. For Jurek, the answer was clearly that it was better off without him. By 1965, his interests had shifted elsewhere. He had already moved his allegiance from the cabaret to the cinema, where he could use his ability to write satiric dialogue to a better end and for a much wider audience.

Jurek's one attempt to adapt for the screen a "classic" German text, *Young Woman, She Pleases Me* (*Jungfer, sie gefällt mir*), was written in collaboration with its director Günter Reisch (DEFA, 1968). It is a rewriting of Heinrich von Kleist's comedy *The Broken Jug* (1811). This film is a very good example of how works from the German literary tradition (the "cultural inheritance") came to be reshaped in the GDR as contemporary political documents showing a clear trajectory from the German past to the GDR present.

"At Night All Tomcats Are Gray," ("Nachts sind alle Kater grau"), the working title of the script, moved the action of Kleist's play from a small Dutch village at an undefined historical moment to a Saxon village during the wars against French revolutionaries and German Jacobins after 1789. To the mix of small-town sexual adventures and exploitation, Jurek added an overlay of antifeudal criticism. He wanted to tell the story not from the perspective of the powerful but from that of the peasants, so that it could be enriched by "real, historical references."[32] In Kleist's original, the village judge Adam (here played by Wolfgang Kieling) is simply out for a sexual adventure with Eva Rull (Monika Gabriel). In Jurek's version, Adam becomes a deserter from the Prussian army who, before he assuming the role of village judge, has embezzled his regiment's money.

Jurek also added an odd repetition of the seduction scene in which the jug of the title is broken, reprising it in a way that recalls the close of Mozart's *Marriage of Figaro*. In the second version, Walter, the minister of justice (Horst Schnitzer), again attempts to seduce Eva, and a replacement jug is broken over his head by her beau Ruprecht Tümpel (Jan Spitzer). Rather than finding Eva in the bedroom the second time, Ruprecht discovers that Walter is about to seduce his own wife, who had taken Eva's place in bed. Walter is part of the system of feudal oppression introduced into the play, paralleling Beaumarchais' intent in the original version of *Figaro*. In Kleist's play, Adam has blackmailed Eve into silence by threatening to send her lover into the army and to the East Indies; Walter is the figure who resolves the conflict by suspending Adam from his position. In Jurek's version, Walter defends Adam against the village's accusation that he was responsible for the breaking of the jug by dismissing their charges as attempts to "mislead the authorities."

Jurek's screenplay was a GDR rereading of Heinrich von Kleist, that most "Prussian" of authors, as a voice of class struggle and revolutionary ideals. Jurek's script presented in comic form the historical line that was supposed to have led from the French Revolution to the present GDR. The corrupt German feudal state represented by Adam and Walter in the film is replaced by the GDR, a state with new, revolutionary credentials. Indeed, when Walter leaves the village, he turns to the masses and declares: "You can take care of your shit yourself," ("Macht euern Dreck alleene!") recalling the famous line of Friedrich August III, king of Saxony, when he abdicated his throne after the November Revolution of 1918. The "inheritance" of German culture appears, even in the comic, to be a fruitful place to explore politics. The very right-wing *National-Zeitung* in the FRG bridled at this attempt to present the class difference as the central theme of Kleist's work.[33] But even the *Berliner Zeitung* in the GDR took exception to the potpourri of styles and seeming lack of direction of the plot.[34] It was political entertainment—an odd genre—but one well known in the GDR.

In March 1964, less than a year after the mining disaster at Lengende in West Germany in October 24, 1963, Jurek wrote *Too Many Crosses* (*Zu viele Kreuze*), a docu-drama about the catastrophe directed by Ralph J. Boettner for GDR TV. [35] The script details the conspiracy between capital and the press to falsify the horrors of the mining disaster. The use of documentary footage gives a sense of "realism" to this fairly conventional tale of capitalist exploitation. The conscience of Dr. Wieland (played by Otto Mellies), the head of the board of directors, is presented to the audience in the form of voice-overs revealing Wieland's awareness of his own complicity. When the disaster takes place, he is skiing in Austria. At the opening of the film the narrator observes that 129 miners were trapped in the mine but not a single member of the board of directors. The film documents the miners' struggle to free their comrades as well as reconstructing the horrors of being trapped below the surface. The philosophical debates about God and death that mark this reconstruction simply rang false to the reviewers in the GDR, but the film showed that Jurek could write compelling dialogue about "serious" themes.

The year 1963 was marked by another "catastrophe," another shift of ideological direction in the GDR. In January, the Sixth Meeting of the SED (Socialist Unity Party), which by that point already had 1.5 million members, was held in East Berlin. Its main speaker was Walter Ulbricht, who was by that date the unquestioned strongman of the GDR. He announced the creation of the first formal "party program," in which the model of Soviet communism was to be adopted in the GDR. With the restructuring of the state apparatus, Kurt Hager became even more powerful in his control of the cultural life of the GDR. Born in 1912, Hager had returned from exile in England in 1945 and was a pivotal figure in the reshaping of the cultural landscape in the GDR. Hager was also a professor of philosophy at Humboldt University, where Jurek had attended his lectures on the history of Marxist philosophy in the spring of 1958. Since 1955, Hager had been secretary of the SED Central Committee for Culture and Science and, hence, the leading cultural ideologue of the SED. In 1963 he became a full member of the Politburo of the SED. It was also in 1963 that John Kennedy, on the other side of the Berlin Wall, gave his "Ich bin ein Berliner" speech, which evoked West Berlin as the defining space of the cold war. West Berlin experienced a new role as the cultural "window onto freedom," well funded by the CIA.

Jurek Becker was a very minor player in the cultural landscape of the GDR in 1963. While his output was considerable and well received, he was only one of many younger writers working in films and television in the GDR. Between 1962 and 1976 (the year he left the GDR), he wrote thirteen scripts, seven for TV and six for DEFA, that were actually produced. These were the basis for Jurek's growing reputation among the directors at DEFA as a master of dialogue and plot.[36] Jurek's scripts were very much in line with the demands of the East German media. He was, however, about to turn to a topic that was both taboo in the GDR and very personal: the murder of the Jews of Europe.

Jewish Films

Now with children of his own, Jurek began to wonder about his family background. Max spoke about his experiences only in the most formulaic way, and Jurek was unwilling to push him. In 1961, Jurek made his first trip back to Poland since he had left in 1944. He was looking for whatever scraps he could find of his family's presence there. He found their names in a few of the archival records of the Litzmannstadt ghetto and had these photocopied. An idea for a screenplay began to germinate after he returned from Lodz. In approaching the Holocaust, Jurek wanted to structure his story to satisfy his own needs rather than falling into the GDR pattern of recounting the triumph of the Soviets over fascism.[37]

The story he began to elaborate was the one his father had been telling him again and again since 1946: How Max was shipped off to Auschwitz because someone denounced him for having a radio; how Jurek and Chana were shipped to the camps as a result of the same charge; how the radio had been an emotional lifeline for the ghetto. A script about the Holocaust from the standpoint of the heroic resistance of the Jews had never been attempted in the GDR. Indeed, a film about the Holocaust focusing on the experience of the Jews was ideologically at variance with the official view that anti-Semitism in the Third Reich was the result of its innately capitalist nature rather than being a central manifestation of Nazism. In the GDR, capitalism (read: the West), not anti-Semitism, was the enemy. In 1963, when Jurek turned to this topic, Frank Beyer's *Naked among Wolves* (*Nackt unter Wölfen*), the best known DEFA film dealing with the Shoah in the GDR, was released. The film starred, among others, Erwin Geschonneck, Armin Müller-Stahl, and Gerry Wolff. Based on Bruno Apitz's 1958 novel of the same name, it describes the rescue of a four-year-old Jewish child (played by Jürgen Strauch) by the inmates at Buchenwald.[38] Apitz, himself a survivor of Buchenwald, retold an actual incident of survival in the camps, and his novel caused a furor when it was published in the GDR. Still, the focus of Apitz's novel was the communist resistance; the Jewish child was merely a victim needing to be rescued.

By the mid-1960s a very small number of such representations of the experience of the Jews in the Shoah existed in the culture of the GDR. Like the unspoken but real visibility of the Jews in the GDR as "victims of fascism," so too was the absence of any representation of the Shoah, especially in the East, an open, unspoken wound. Jurek's son Nicki came home one day, when he was six or so, and asked, "Father, is it true that Hitler invaded the GDR?"[39] The collapse of past and present was possible only if the specific nature of the past was misunderstood. In the "land of farmers and workers," the official claim was that the GDR was the true German antifascist state, and that it alone understood the legacy of the Nazis. The power of fascism, it claimed, was still to be found in West Germany. The Holocaust had vanished from this cold war retelling.

In writing about the Shoah, Jurek faced the dilemma of whether to write as a "Jew" or as a "German."[40] Was he a victim of the Nazi Regime or a member of the new cultural elite of the GDR? Each position had its advantages and pitfalls. On October 1, 1963, Jurek submitted his first serious script to DEFA: *Jacob the Liar* (*Jakob der Lügner*),[41] which he later reworked into a novel (1969). The initial draft of the film script was set in the summer of 1944 in an Eastern ghetto guarded by the Germans. While in the office of the German commandant, Jacob Heym, the former owner of a small restaurant that sold potato pancakes, overhears a bit of news on the German radio concerning the position of the Soviet troops.

The character of Heym is a version of the *shlamazel,* the classic hard-luck character who haunted the stories with which Max regaled his friends. (And in a sad way Heym was Max himself.) He has been ordered to the commandant's office on the whim of a German guard for supposedly violating the ghetto curfew. One of the German soldiers, noting that it is not quite time for the curfew, orders him to go home rather than—as Jacob expected—ordering him to be shot. The next day, Jacob whispers the news about the Soviet troops to one of his friends to deter him from making a dash to freedom that would certainly be a suicidal act. His friend simply does not believe Jacob. No one survives going into the German commandant's office. He is finally believed when, in desperation, he says he has a radio. As we have seen, no radios were permitted in the ghetto.

The existence of Jacob's "radio" gives the ghetto dwellers a renewed sense of optimism. Yet it is a false hope. In this early draft, another ghetto inhabitant, Mjetek Frankfurter, who actually has a radio, destroys it because he is afraid to use it when he learns that Jacob has one too. Over the next decade, Jurek changed the character's name. "Mjetek" was Max's nickname, and he actually had claimed to own a radio. The invention of the radio is the counterstory to Max's account of his own bravery and its horrific results. In Jurek's script, Jacob manages, for a short time, to rally the inhabitants of the ghetto. Mjetek Frankfurter feels that he is not a hero like Jacob, who seems to use his radio to find out about the world beyond the ghetto. Frankfurter's daughter, Rosa, is in love with Mischa, a young Jew who, like Jacob, is working in the rail yards. Jacob's tale of the radio has inadvertently rescued Mischa, who was about to commit suicide. The love story of Rosa and Mischa is the secondary plot. Jurek uses it to stress the power of "normal" emotions, such as love, in times of great trauma.

The knowledge of the radio provides a ray of hope in the ghetto, and Jacob becomes the source of this hope in a collapsing world. The suicides in the ghetto suddenly stop when rescue appears to be a possibility. Jacob has taken in Lina, a child abandoned when the Nazis deported her parents to the East. She, like everyone else in the ghetto, asks to hear the radio. Jacob wants to indulge her. In the first draft he presents his version of the "radio" to her, having her hide behind a wall and listen to him recreate a program, which captivates her. In this instance, he becomes the radio.

Jurek's first draft places the Eastern Jews at its very center. This draft is still very much within the GDR rewriting of the history of the Shoah. At the conclusion, it emphasizes the Jew as victim. Jacob is dead; he has killed himself by getting shot in an attempt to escape the ghetto, and Lina is led by the hand of a Soviet solder who has rescued her. This image is a trope in the GDR: the enormous memorial to Soviet soldiers in East Berlin's Treptow Park shows a soldier cradling a rescued infant. The ahistorical nature of this image was clear to Frank Beyer, who was to direct the film. Beyer had taken over from a younger director who had been assigned the film when it became clear that the younger man was not up to the task. The Soviets never freed any ghettos, for the Nazis had emptied them all beforehand.[42] The Jacob story is a fiction, an answer to Max's own heroic claim, but in such a story the historical details have to be plausible. The plot has to work within the viewer's sense of what really could have happened. The false pathos of the end of Jurek's first version robbed Jacob's story of any meaning. Why worry about resistance or sacrifice when the Soviets will eventually come and rescue you?

Two years of rewriting followed. During the fall of 1965 a second version was completed. It was submitted to the studio on December 15, 1965—the day before the Eleventh Plenum of the SED began, which was to return the cultural politics of the GDR to a Stalinist model.[43] Earlier, Jurek had gone to West Berlin to work in the archive of the Jewish Community for further documentation. He stayed with his old school friend Helge Braune, who was now living in West Berlin. The second draft of the script no longer contains any specific historical references. Neither time nor place is mentioned. The Germans, who in the first version are the standard "evil" Nazis of GDR film, have become more and more differentiated. Indeed, one soldier now represents a type of educated German, not merely an ignorant and brutal camp guard. His education, however, does not stop him from doing his duty. Other apparently minor changes show how Jurek is shaping the plot both to use and to distance his own and his father's Polish Jewish identity. Mjetek Frankfurter becomes "Felix." In losing his Polish Jewish label, he is (as Max was) transformed into a German Jew.

The story recounted by Jacob to Lina as if it were coming from his "radio" becomes the core tale of this draft. It is now the fairy tale of the "princess with the Star of David (*Judenstern*)." Lina hears the story of the sick princess who asks for a cloud to cure her ailments. When no one has succeeded in bringing her a cloud, a young garden hand comes to her and asks her what clouds are made of (her answer: "cotton batting") and how big they are ("as big as my pillow"). He then gives the sick princess a "cloud" made of cotton, the size of a pillow. She is cured, and she dances off with him in her nightgown, marked with a Star of David.

The conclusion resembles that of the first draft. Now, however, Jacob's death at the ghetto wall is not without consequences. After the guard shoots him, shots are heard from outside of the ghetto, as if in response. The soldier who murdered Jacob collapses. Jurek is still constrained to provide a noble end. The final scene is the same as in his first version, with the Soviet soldier leading Lina off.

The second version was submitted by DEFA to the deputy minister of culture, Wilfried Maaß, for approval on February 9, 1966, and was approved on February 22.[44] The proposal was accompanied by an evaluation that stated that the script was too "full of a humanistic spirit rather than indicating the specifics of a spirit of socialist humanism."[45] The second evaluation stressed that Jurek should continue to develop the script in the light of "the specifics of a socialist-realist aesthetic" and emphasized that the story should "point to progressive forces."[46] The little girl and the Soviet soldier, who, although mute in his bravery, holds her hand, make the film imaginable, even with its emphasis on the Shoah. This ending, however, was also seen by the DEFA studio director in charge as needing to be checked for "historical correctness and truth."[47]

Frank Beyer had wanted to have as authentic a backdrop for the film as possible. He decided to shoot on location in Krakow, where decades later Steven Spielberg was to film *Schindler's List* (1993). After the script had been accepted for production at the beginning of 1966, Beyer took Jurek on a trip to scout the location, as well as to tease out for himself what was memory and what was fantasy in Jurek's script. In May they visited Kazimierz, the poverty-stricken section of Krakow that had become the Jewish ghetto under the Nazis. No memories were triggered by the trip; *Jacob* remained true to the emotional world of the survivor rather than to Jurek's lost memories of the Shoah. As a German, Beyer now felt himself authorized by Jurek's presence, his Jewish identity if not his memories, to undertake a film about the Shoah.

Another complication in the cultural landscape in 1966 was the change in the official cultural politics of the GDR during the Eleventh Plenum of the SED in mid-December 1965. By the beginning of 1966 the so-called "Rabbit films," named after Kurt Maetzig's *I Am the Rabbit*, became the definition of what film culture in the GDR could *not* be.[48] Dealing with the conflicts in daily life in the GDR, works like the "Rabbit" films were accused of undermining the youth of the GDR by creating doubt, skepticism, and negative thoughts, according to party ideologue Kurt Hager. Hager's return to a more conservative, indeed Stalinist, notion of what should be the appropriate culture for the GDR collided with the opening of one of the most innovative and difficult films ever made in the GDR, Beyer's *Trace of Stones* (*Spur der Steine*, 1966). This film was an extraordinary view of workers' life.

With all its limits, Beyer had made the critically acclaimed film *Naked among Wolves* in 1963 as an alternative version of what came to be seen as the obligatory antifascism of the GDR. His new film was based on Erik Neutsch's best-selling socialist realist novel, *Trace of Stones* (1963), which itself had had a complex and difficult publishing history. Beyer cast Manfred Krug as the ironic worker-antihero Hannes Balla. Balla's rival for the love of the young engineer Kati Klee (Krystyna Sty-pulkowska) is the local party secretary Horrath (Eberhard Esche). Their confrontation is much like that of the heroes in the then fashionable spaghetti westerns of Clint Eastwood and Sergio Leone. Klee becomes pregnant by the married Horrath, and their "case" becomes the subject of a party trial. Greatly anticipated and widely advertised, Beyer's film was screened in 1966, but it was quickly denounced by the newly dominant party hard-liners for its "failure to properly portray the political and moral strength of the party."[49] The film was banned after a number of staged demonstrations.

Jurek, as an intimate member of the circle with Beyer and Krug, was present at the first public showing of the film at the Kino International on June 30, 1966. When members of the "audience," who had been well rehearsed, began to disrupt the premiere, he stood up and shouted that they had been paid, that they were agents of the government. He was coming to see "the government" as a negative force. He later portrayed this staged "outrage" of the government's provocateurs in his banned book *Sleepless Days* (*Schlaflose Tage*, 1978). The protagonist and his wife attend a screening, in which there is "a funny kind of atmosphere in the theater." Suddenly a provocateur shouts out, "asking how long the audience is expected to put up with this." Further voices scattered throughout the theater join the chorus, but the protagonist wonders "why two men so obviously of the same opinion are conversing in such loud voices." The next day a fellow teacher comments on the "outraged rejection [of the film] on the part of the public." Our protagonist "can't pluck up the courage to call him a liar," for it was not the audience but the planted agents who disrupted the film.[50] The passivity and anxiety of the fictional audience in the cinema in face of the disruption is the very opposite of the rage that Jurek felt.

Wolf Biermann, who was present at the event, thought it would be prudent to leave before he got arrested. Jurek's anger was real and very much directed at the blind stupidity of the authorities.[51] Kate Klee's final line in the film, "I want to begin anew," became a motto for the GDR opposition. As a result of the scandal, Beyer was eventually sent for two years to the Dresden State Theater and was then limited to doing work for GDR television. As Jurek remembers it, Beyer simply could not make any more films.[52]

It was not until 1973 that the third incarnation of *Jacob the Liar* was finally produced. Yet the second draft screenplay, as approved by the ministry, seemed to be quite unaffected by the government's new attitude toward Beyer and the "Rabbit" films. With its truly conventional ending, its only problem seemed to be its Jewish subject matter. Neither was it innovative in form, nor (on its surface) did it put into question contemporary life in the GDR. The film was firmly placed in the "year's plan" of DEFA for 1966.

At the beginning of July 1966 the Polish authorities notified DEFA that studio space was available and the film could be scheduled.[53] Three weeks later, however, they informed the DEFA producers that there was no space available because of demand from the Soviet Union for space. What had happened in the interim was that the Polish authorities had seen Jurek's screenplay. As Frank Beyer later commented, a film such as *Jacob the Liar* about Jews in the East was simply inconceivable in communist Poland, a nation that in the 1960s regularly practiced anti-Semitism in the form of anti-Zionism.[54] Evoking the Shoah in the East was unacceptable, even in a film to be released in the GDR.

On July 27, 1966, permission for the film was canceled. Frank Beyer went off to Dresden. Jurek was paid for the script, which was not unusual; he had completed other scripts that were not filmed. But Jurek's need to have control, especially over this story, was unprecedented. He sat down and did what some other writers in the GDR were to do when their scripts were rejected and they felt they had a story to tell. He rewrote the script into a novel. Novels were seen as less "dangerous" than films. Ulrich Plenzdorf, his colleague at DEFA, would later follow his lead and transform his rejected idea for a film script into a radical text about GDR youth culture of the 1970s, *The New Sorrows of Young W.* (1972). Even if novels were read by tens of thousands, they did not have the mass audience of any given film.

Angry but focused, Jurek wrote the novel *Jacob the Liar*—the most important survivor novel written in German—by rethinking and reworking the second draft of his screenplay. Ironically, he wrote it in his home, surrounded by family and friends, able to take a break from scriptwriting because of Rieke's inheritance from her Nazi father. According to an interview at the time, his main alternative reading was the weekly soccer newspaper (*Fußballwoche*).[55] Sports remained Jurek's means of escaping from the conflicts of his world. As he was writing *Jacob the Liar*, this escape seemed ever more necessary.

Jacob the Liar: The Novel

Jurek needed to write the story of Jacob Heym and his radio. He needed to bring this tale of the Shoah to his audience in the GDR, but he also needed to craft it into a tale that would be praised for its narrative quality. Max, whose life he inverted in the novel, had demanded of him that his stories be "good"—that is, uplifting, dealing with heroism in the ghetto and such—but *Jacob the Liar*, Jurek noted at the time, was to be an exception rather than the rule in terms of his treatment of the Shoah. He intended to return to his stable job as a scriptwriter writing about other topics.[56] It is the close link between the mode of telling the story and the story itself that is part of the brilliance of *Jacob the Liar* as a novel. Its strength lies to no small degree in its extraordinary narrative framework,[57] which breaks with the notion of "authenticity" that haunted the earlier discussion of the film plot. The framework puts the very act of storytelling into question. Unlike the first two drafts of the screenplay, in which we meet the characters as their story unfolds, we are gradually introduced to Jacob's story by the narrative voice of a survivor of the ghetto. The voice tells us the story of Jacob and his nonexistent radio as intensely as Max told the story of his own radio.

In a 1974 interview, Jurek described his initial work on another survivor novel, *The Boxer* (1976), as presenting "a man, a Jew, psychologically destroyed by the past, who must come to terms with the present. I have been concerned for a while with the question how people who have experienced suffering demand our tolerance. How much does someone who has suffered have a claim not only on the absence of criticism but also on tolerance? I myself am not at all tolerant, I must admit. But certain circumstances forbid impatience."[58] This statement reflects the emotions buried within the frame to *Jacob the Liar*. At some distance, Jurek can laugh at his "angry, opinionated, hard-nosed" attitude; his sense that "he always has to be right."[59] Does his picture of the survivor reflect only his father's drunken silence and the rote tales he repeated? Or was Jurek afraid that being a survivor in the GDR shaped him too in ways over which he had no control?

In the novel, the unnamed narrator begins by speaking about the trees in his life, the tree under which he made love, the tree under which his wife Chana was executed.[60] Suddenly, as Jurek evokes his mother's name, the voice of Max seems to join that of Jurek in telling the story. Central to this account is the difficulty of telling stories about the past, as no one really listens. "I've tried hundreds of times to unload this blasted story, without success. Either I have tried it with the wrong people, or I made some mistake or other. I mixed up a lot of things, I got names wrong, or, as I said, they were the wrong people. Every time I have a few drinks, it comes up again; I can't help myself" (2–3). This drunken narrator knows that the stories are true—but never accurate—and is compelled to tell them. "Just a few words about doubtful memories, a few words about the carefree life . . . I am alive, there can be no doubt about that. I am alive, and no one can force me to have a drink and remember trees and remember Jacob and everything to do with this story. On the contrary, I am offered some choices" (16). The stories he tells are as emotionally real as Jacob's radio. It is vital for the novel that Jurek uses a complex representation of spoken speech—indeed, what struck most of the reviewers of the first edition was that the narrator seemed so very "Jewish." Jurek's intent was to use the narrative device self-consciously as a means of creating character. It was also, of course, a need to question the sort of heroic account of the Shoah that he himself had evoked at the close of the film script with the Soviet soldier and Lina.

The narrator is hampered in his storytelling by the necessary reinvention of his life after the Shoah. How does one live after such an experience, wanting to become "normal" and yet marked by the experience. According to the novel, our narrator, born in 1921, is forty-six in 1967—halfway between Max and Jurek's actual ages. He is visible to all as a survivor. After he has made love with a woman, she still turns to him and asks: " 'Tell me, is it true that you . . . ' God knows who told her. I can hear pity in her voice and go crazy. I go into the bathroom, sit down in the tub, and start singing, to stop myself from doing what I know I will regret after five steps" (16). His story is inscribed on his face, body, and language, which reveal his status as a victim even when he tries to conceal it.

The survivor as narrator frames the story: "Jacob is dead, and besides, I'm not telling his story but a story. He told me the story, but I am talking to you. That's a big difference because I was there . . . Some things I know from Mischa, but then there is a big gap for which there are simply no witnesses. I tell myself that it must have happened more or less in such and such a way, or that it would be best if it had happened in such and such a way, and then I tell it and pretend that's how it was. And that is how it was; it's not my fault that the witnesses who could confirm it can longer be found" (33). Inscribed here are Max's retelling of the story of the radio, Jurek's understanding of his father's bravery, and also the consequences of the story—the death of his mother, which becomes part of the narrative. What actually happened, no one can know. Yet one needs to tell a story.

Max had wanted Jurek to write of bravery in the ghetto, specifically a tale of a man who hid a radio and was the source of inspiration to his friends. He wanted a story of a man who risked his life in doing so. Jurek decided to do exactly the opposite. He said to Max, "You know, I have already read so much about those heroes, there are so many books about them, that I see no sense in writing yet another story about them."[61] His father's response was: "You can tell the stupid Germans what it was like in the ghetto; you can't tell me, I was there. I was a witness. You can't tell me silly stories. I know it was different."[62] For readers in the GDR (and the rest of the world), Jurek's retelling of the story of the radio seemed an appropriate means of understanding the Shoah. Max, however, needed to see the heroic nature of his act. It defined him as someone who was not merely a victim.

The narrator represents the present in the GDR. His voice is that of a survivor whose identity is defined by his experiences and who deals with this by telling stories about those experiences. In telling stories there are always alternatives, better stories, and now the narrator postulates two possible endings to the tale of Jacob and his radio. The first is a version of the screenplay. Jacob dies or commits suicide to escape the tissue of lies he has generated by attempting to cut through the barbed wire that surrounds the ghetto. People surround his dead body, wondering why he would do such a thing. They murmur, "But he had a radio." The Russians attack, and the remaining ghetto inhabitants are finally rescued. But this "invented ending" is not the "pallid and depressing, the true and unimaginative ending." In the novel's conclusion, the camp is cleared, and the train that takes Lina and Jacob off is headed for "Majdanek or Auschwitz," a fate they thought to escape because of Jacob's promise that they were so close to liberation: "Anyone executed now, so shortly before the end, will have suddenly lost a future" (67). In the final scene, the narrator for the first and only time is present with Jacob. They are crowded into a boxcar with Lina and all the others. The novel ends with Jacob turning to the narrator and asking whether he won't go to sleep. Sleep will not come: "We are heading for wherever we are heading." This is the narrator's final line and the last line of the novel (244). Surviving is not a matter of having or not having a radio, of believing or not believing. Jurek's account stresses a random, not a heroic, scenario. Even the fantasy of Jacob's suicide is one in which the character has some control of his life. The narrator knows that this control was missing and that his survival was happenstance, inscribed on his body and soul forever.

Stories, even the best stories, do not satisfy the narrator in *Jacob the Liar*. The suicide of Dr. Kirschbaum on his way to treat a Nazi commandant who has had a heart attack cannot be reconstructed from any ghetto narratives. For that story the narrator has to search out witnesses among the German guards. As Jurek did after the birth of his first son, "sometime after the war" (177), the narrator returns to the ghetto. There he seeks out the building where Jacob lived, the barracks where he heard the radio. He measures everything carefully with his tape measure (137). On the last day of his trip, he goes to the Russian commander's office and asks about the German soldiers who accompanied Kirschbaum that day. He learns that one has survived and is now living in Berlin, where the narrator now also lives.

> "You didn't leave Germany?" she [the Russian officer] asked in surprise. "Why was that?" "I don't really know," I answered truthfully. "It just happened that way." (178)

Life just happens. Jews just happen to survive or not; just happen to live in Berlin; just happen to be raised as good communists, or not. The Russian officer gives him the address of the former German soldier, warning him not to "plan anything foolish." He looks up this man in West Berlin. When approached, the former soldier takes out his certificate of denazification to show his visitor that he is no longer "like that." He tells the narrator in detail everything he wants to know about Kirschbaum's death. The soldier is horrified that Kirschbaum had offered him one of the poison pills as an antacid and that he could have died. Through this account the narrator discovers that there is yet another witness, the German driver, who now lives in Cologne. Former Nazis always live in the West (179–82). At the end of the conversation, the narrator deliberately scares the former camp guard by mentioning that he found out about him from the British Secret Service. There are no secrets about the past that cannot be uncovered, but only through the agency of the powers that are now dominating the Germans. Jurek focuses this anxiety about the presence of the past on West Germany, but it is at least a part of Max's rationale for living in Germany: never again will the occupying forces allow the Germans to do what they did before. Yet Jurek was writing this at a time when the cold war was *re*writing the meaning of the occupation.

While Jurek was writing *Jacob the Liar*, the implications of state socialism began to change radically for him. Although the building of the Berlin Wall did not mark a break in his relationship to the GDR because of his marriage and the birth of his children as well as his sense that the wall was a necessary means of control, his attitude changed abruptly with the

Prague Spring and the invasion of Czechoslovakia by Warsaw Pact troops on August 21, 1968. From January 5, 1968, to April 17, 1969, Alexander Dubcek, the first secretary of the Communist Party of Czechoslovakia, had been leading a reform movement that was characterized by a surge of cultural freedom unparalleled in the Eastern bloc after World War II. The freedom of expression granted to the Czechoslovak media during the early months of 1968 made the repression in the GDR especially evident. Indeed, it was this cultural freedom that caused Jurek to rethink his relationship to "real, existing socialism" in the GDR. The brutal suppression of the Prague Spring was the catalyst for Jurek's "break in his relationship with the GDR."[63] That GDR troops never actually crossed the border, given the Soviet anxiety about awakening the memories of the Nazi invasion, seemed trivial. Jurek was no longer a loyal citizen of the GDR, a screenwriter employed by the state. He saw himself more and more as an outsider. The GDR was no longer the exemplary antifascist state but was assuming the very image of the Germany he feared.

A report of August 26, 1968, to the Stasi noted that on August 23, Jurek and his wife had discussed the situation in Prague with an "unofficial agent," who reported it in detail.[64] The source was quite surprised about the turn Jurek's politics had taken: "Becker's political opinions appeared surprisingly quickly, because he had always spoken correctly before." Jurek's views as expressed in the report are paralleled by his own later accounts. He stated to anyone who would listen that the invasion of Czechoslovakia marked the beginning of the end for the Warsaw Pact, for he believed it would cause Romania to leave the pact. More than just destroying an alliance of progressive states, the USSR's action had undermined the communist internationalist movement and given credibility to its enemies. Jurek believed that the invasion violated the people's ability to determine their own political direction. The Czechoslovak people truly supported Alexander Dubcek, unlike, he implied, the GDR population's ambivalence toward Ulbricht (who, one might add, had duplicitously met with Dubcek shortly before the invasion). What Jurek sensed as necessary in Germany—the imposition of controls to limit possible negative actions—he condemned in Czechoslovakia.

Even more important was the way this event shaped Jurek's sense of his own identity. Following the anti-Zionist rhetoric of the GDR, he started to question how could one condemn Israel and the Americans in Vietnam when the GDR itself had become an aggressor. Israel was really no different in its relations to the Palestinians, he contended, than the GDR was toward the Prague Spring. His very citizenship had now become difficult, for citizens of the GDR had to disguise themselves when traveling to Czechoslovakia. Throughout his attack, Jurek spoke of the "Russians" not the Soviet Union. It was the Russians who had invaded Czechoslovakia, just as the Germans had done decades before. And Jurek called the Russians SS men. In eliding the past and the present, he began to rethink what the past meant for him.

The themes of *Jacob the Liar* now manifested themselves in Jurek's own life. He laughed at Walter Ulbricht's claim that there was no press censorship in the GDR. He stopped subscribing to the official party newspaper, *Neues Deutschland*. To get news about the world beyond as well as within the GDR, he watched and listened only to Western television and radio. When his son Nicki came home from school, he invited his son to join him in watching and listening to the forbidden broadcasts. He told Nicki that if he were asked about this in the school, he should not lie. Jurek began to rethink what the Berlin Wall really meant. The wall surrounding the ghetto in *Jacob the Liar* created an isolation that was fatal to its inhabitants. Jurek now saw the Berlin Wall as no longer surrounding West Berlin but the whole of the GDR. The GDR was a huge ghetto in which you had to listen to Western broadcasts in order to find out what was happening in your own neighborhood. If you listened, and knew about the world, then you had an obligation not to lie about it. In the novel, Jacob's radio reveals the location of the Soviet troops that promise to free the ghetto. To Jurek and his family, the Western radio revealed the location of those troops in 1968 as they destroyed the Prague Spring.

The medium is the message, the story, and way it is told. The fairy tale that Jacob tells Lina through the medium of his radio had a parallel in the daily experience of Jurek's family. At seven o'clock each evening, competing channels in Western and Eastern television both broadcast *The Sandman*, a program for children, begun in 1958, that told fairy tales. The theme song was known to everyone in the West and the East alike: "I am the sandman, every child knows me. And when I come, I say: 'Into bed, quickly!' " ("Ich bin der liebe Sandmann, mich kennt jedes Kind. Und komm' ich, dann sag' ich: 'Ins Bettchen—geschwind!' ")[65] Even fairy tales were political during the cold war. It was rumored in the West was that kindergarten teachers in the GDR asked children to sing the "sandman song"; then, depending on whether the tune they produced was Eastern or Western, they could report which parents were watching "foreign" television. The media competed for the hearts and minds of the children on each side of the wall. They were assumed to grasp the advantages and deficiencies of both systems by simply flipping the channel (albeit in secret). With Jurek, this became a family activity, and it also underlies the complex account of the perception of reality in *Jacob the Liar.*

Jurek acted openly on his feelings about the Warsaw Pact invasion. At the Czechoslovak embassy he signed a book of condolence for German citizens to show their sympathy. At the end of August, at a meeting of the Central Committee of the German Writers' Union, Jurek was among the very few who attacked the statement of solidarity in support of the Warsaw Pact invasion that was required of members of the Berlin branch of the Writers' Union.[66] His role as a member of the opposition was beginning at the very moment his fame as a writer was about to be established. Among the members of the intellectual opposition, his visibility as a victim of the Nazis would give him a status shared by only a few others in the GDR, such as the Jewish returnees Stephan Hermlin and Paul Wiens.[67] Indeed, some of the most distinguished writers in the GDR, including the German Jewish returnee Anna Seghers, avoided the appearance of supporting the invasion by simply not showing up at the meeting where their support was expected. Jurek, one of the newest members, did attend but refused to sign.

Jurek was gaining political maturity. He was willing to confront the state when he felt it was wrong. His relations with Max grew ever more difficult. The voice of the narrator in *Jacob the Liar* was to no small extent the voice Jurek wanted Max to have, the voice telling him about the past. The reality was different. Max was increasingly unable to talk to him. Jurek raged at his father for his drinking, and often walked out on him if he thought Max was drunk. Alcoholism having ruined his health, Max died of pneumonia on April 3, 1972. He was buried in the huge Jewish cemetery at Weißensee. Jurek, who rarely attended a funeral, accompanied his father's casket to the grave. No rabbi officiated. Max never saw the final version of the film that his story had inspired. Indeed, Jurek noted, Max did not speak to him for a year after the novel was published.[68] Nor did Jurek ever return to visit his father's grave.

Fame

After 1968, the political authority in the GDR had lost much of its legitimacy in Jurek's mind. His relationship to it had evolved since his childhood, when he sensed his own marginality and his strong need to belong. The better a citizen he became in his own estimation, the more the state seemed to disappoint him, resulting in frequent outbreaks of anger. In June 1973, Jurek's mother-in-law came from West Berlin for an extended visit, wanting to be closer to her daughter and family after her husband died. Jurek had to inform the Volkspolizei (the People's Police) that she was staying with them. He was asked for his identity card, which was bedraggled, prompting the policewoman at the desk to claim that it was invalid. Jurek yelled at her, calling her "a stupid cow— weak in the head." The policewoman brought charges of "insulting the state" (*Staatsverleumdung*) against "Georg Becker," the name on the ID. The secretary of the Writers' Union had to promise the police that action would be taken against Jurek and that he would be firmly spoken to about his attitude. On August 16, 1973, he was found "innocent" of the charges by a local court.[69] The incident had no resonance until late in 1974, when Jurek was increasingly identified with "oppositional" causes that angered the authorities. It was indicative, however, of his focus on the inequities of the state after 1968.[70]

In the spring of 1968, Jurek submitted the novel of *Jacob the Liar* to the Aufbau Press, the most prestigious publishing house in the GDR. His anger at having his earlier screenplay refused was soothed by the positive reception of the novel by his editor, Ursula Emmerich. The editorial report began with the biographical "fact" that Jurek had "spent six years of his childhood in an Eastern European ghetto." Jurek was thus seen as writing as a Nazi victim. The report then outlined the plot with and described in detail the narrative voice and the tale of Jacob and his radio.

The report stressed "Jewish individual fates," which Emmerich ex- plained as representing the "question of class." This was a standard Marx- ist reading of what acceptable literature was supposed to be in the GDR at that time. Assimilated Jews are upper-class, Orthodox Jews lower-class. Class interest defined religious identity, not the other way around. Em- merich stressed that individual, positive relationships, such as the love story between Mischa and Rosa, were a sign of normal human values that were not undermined by the experience of the Holocaust. The Germans in the novel were anonymous and not especially brutal, which the editor saw as a positive quality. The Polish small-town milieu was well captured and "selectively used Yiddish words to provide local color." The quality of the spoken language represented in the narrative framework, as well as in the dialogue in the novel, has always been seen as one of the its greatest strengths. For Emmerich, as a German reader, it was a "Jewish" novel that used the appropriate Marxist model of society. That was the stylistic effect Jurek clearly wanted to create.

There had been a critique of the double ending of the novel by an outside reader for the publishing house who thought the suicide and the "utopian" freeing of the camps cast a shadow on the Soviet role and made the "real" conclusion seem too ironic. The first ending was also seen as too long and out of proportion to the second ending. Emmerich argued that the historical problem raised by the first ending, that the Soviets never did free a ghetto, would be dealt with on the jacket copy. Its deliberate antirealism would be lost on most readers. Again the question of authenticity evoked by Jurek's biography is raised, even in a text where storytelling is placed center stage. Whatever the author does to distance this novel from his own experience, he remains a Jew "testifying" about his own experiences in the Shoah.

The very positive response of readers, however, led to Jurek's being nominated for membership in the Writers' Union (*Schriftstellerverband*) in 1968, even before the formal publication date of the novel. The role of the Writers' Union was to facilitate discussions of the SED's decisions on literature, to sponsor public literary events, and to lobby the government on behalf of writers. It also provided funds for writers and facilitated their travel abroad, especially to the West. It defined who was a "real" writer in the GDR and who was not. Jurek's election to the group was an important milestone in his life as a writer. As his literary debut on joining this prestigious club, he contributed a chapter from *Jacob the Liar* to a collected volume sponsored by the Writers' Union.[71]

Jacob the Liar appeared in 1969. It was the first novel since 1945 to represent the Shoah in a comic vein or, at least, not to rely on pathos as a way of understanding those murdered in the Shoah.[72] Retrospectively, Jurek felt that Jacob's story was a good enough topic for a first novel. It enabled him to tell the tale of things as terrible as the ghetto and the persecution of the Jews in a nontragic voice.[73] It was a narrative voice, indebted as much to the GDR Protestant novelist Johannes Bobrowski's novel of nineteenth-century rural Jewry, *Levin's Mill* (*Levins Mühle*, 1964), as to any other work written in the GDR.[74] Both Bobrowski and Becker fascinated the reader with their evocation of the lost world of European Jewry. Jurek's novel presented it from the perspective of a Jewish narrator, Bobrowski's from that of a non-Jewish narrator. Heard in *Jacob the Liar* for the first time in postwar German literature, however, was the voice of a Jew seemingly speaking for himself. Yet it was, of course, a construction of the sound of an Eastern Jew as imagined by a German writer in the GDR.

Wolfgang Werth began his review of *Jacob* in the West German periodical *Der Monat* with a comparison to characters in classic Yiddish fiction. He evoked such figures as Tevye the Milkman, Menachem Mendel, and Fishke the Lame, all protagonists of major novels by twentieth-century Yiddish writers such as Scholem Aleichem, I. J. Peretz, and I. J. Singer.[75] He could have cast his eye a bit closer to home. For the hit of the 1960s in West German theaters was *Fiddler on the Roof,* an evocation of the Eastern Jews, now staged as nostalgia for a lost world. For Germans, the 1964 musical by Jerry Bock, Sheldon Harnick, and Joseph Stein provided a world of Jewry before the Shoah in exotic dress and culture. The destruction of that world was the result not of the Shoah but of the Russian pogroms, and its protagonists were not murdered but emigrated to America.

In 1970, shortly after *Jacob the Liar* was published, Walter Felsenstein produced *Fiddler on the Roof* at the Comic Opera in East Berlin.[76] The remarkable success of this presentation of what passed in East Berlin (as well as in New York City) as "live Jews in their authentic Eastern context" set the stage for Jurek's second attempt to get *Jacob the Liar* produced as a movie. The film of *Fiddler on the Roof* appeared in 1971. Readers of Jurek's novel immediately associated its narrative stance with Scholem Aleichim, the Yiddish author of the tales on which *Fiddler on the Roof* was based. Jurek denied knowing this tradition before he wrote the novel, claiming that he read Scholem Aleichim only after seeing *Fiddler on the Roof* in a theater.[77] *Jacob the Liar's* positive reception, however, was clearly to the benefit of Eastern European Jewry now present in the GDR. The authenticity of Jurek's book was immediately attributed to his Jewish identity and experiences, even though he disavowed the former and possessed none of the latter.

Jurek's novel is a continuation of an East German literary tradition that deals with the fascist past, but in a new and extraordinary way. His book is in a German tradition but is read as a "Jewish" novel about the East. In *Fiddler on the Roof,* the English libretto represented the language of Eastern European Jews. They are all supposedly speaking Yiddish, even Tevye's Russified future son-in-law, when they are actually speaking English. But what language is imagined in the unnamed ghetto described in *Jacob the Liar*? The German soldiers speak German, but so do the Orthodox Herschel Schtamm, the Polonized Dr. Kirschbaum, and the totally assimilated German Jew, Leonard Schmidt. Indeed, so does Jacob, the owner of a small restaurant with his Polish and Yiddish-speaking clients, who can also understand the formal German of the radio without hesitation. What is the common denominator that "German" here represents? It is the *Lagersprache,* making a sudden reappearance. The bits and pieces of German overlying the fragments of all of those languages spoken in the ghettos and the camps was the lingua franca that was necessary to survive. This is the key to understanding the novel as a novel of the Shoah. The fragments of Yiddish are not window dressing but part of a patois that made it possible to understand and simultaneously misunderstand all the languages in the ghetto. (In 1971, Fred Wander, a Jewish survivor of Auschwitz and Buchenwald who lived in the GDR from 1958 to 1983, used abundant Yiddish in his profound concentration-camp novel *The Seventh Spring* [*Der siebente Brunnen*].[78] The Aufbau Publishing House felt obligated to supply a translation all the Yiddish terms in an appendix.) Jurek's forgotten ghetto and camp experiences surfaced in the emotional power of the novel's language or, at least, in the complex of languages that Jurek's evocative, brilliant German represents.

The novel was a success. The reviews were ecstatic, the tone set by Werner Neubert's "official" review in the SED party newspaper *Neues Deutschland*, which praised the novel as "bearing comparison with the best works of our antifascist literature about the horror-filled period of fascism."[79] In the West, Elisabeth Borchers, an editor with Luchterhand Publishers in Neuwied am Rhein, purchased the Western rights. She became Jurek's most aggressive and steadfast Western editor. *Jacob the Liar* was to be the first title in a new and spectacularly successful series, the Luchterhand Collection.[80] By September 1, 1970, 2300 copies had been shipped to bookstores across the Federal Republic of Germany (FRG), and the positive reaction in the West began.[81]

Rave reviews appeared in the West German press. Perhaps the most striking was by another Polish-Jewish intellectual who was remaking himself as one of the literary arbiters of West German literature at the time, Marcel Reich-Ranicki, a survivor of the Warsaw ghetto. He praised the novel as allegorical and described Becker as a "sad humorist," but avoided seeing him as standing in any literary tradition but a German one.[82] Reich-Ranicki's knew where Jurek fit in the spectrum of contemporary German letters, recognizing the extraordinary quality of the novel and its unique treatment of the Shoah. He did not confuse it with the powerful Yiddish literary tradition, with which Jurek was only marginally familiar.

Jurek was uncomfortable with Reich-Ranicki's allegorical reading, as he notes to the West German writer Wolfdietrich Schnurre in a letter thanking him for his comments on the novel.[83] Schnurre had addressed Jurek as the author of a "wonderful and moving" novel, which he compared to the recently published *Last of the Just*, by the Franco-Jewish novelist André Schwarz-Bart. Schnurre's proof of his own philo-Semitism was the fact that his "chief reading for the past ten years has been the Talmud" in preparation for writing a novel with a Jewish protagonist.[84] To this remark, Jurek kindly did not reply. Schnurre read the novel as a self-consciously Jewish testament to a Jewish past, as Schwarz-Bart's novel was clearly intended to be.

The popular as well as the critical response in the FRG reinforced the idea that *Jacob the Liar* was a Jewish book by a Jewish author. It was exotic (read: authentic) and that contributed to its success. A West German reader wrote to the Luchterhand publishing house asking whether the book was written in German or was a translation from Yiddish or Polish.[85] The letter was quietly forwarded to the Aufbau editor in East Berlin to be answered or ignored.

Jurek became pigeonholed as a professional "Jew" in the West as well as in the East. He was asked to review Max Fürst's *Gefilte Fisch* (1973), an account of his childhood in Konigsberg, for the leading West German newsmagazine, *Der Spiegel*, in October 1973. He disliked the narrative pretensions of the book but recognized that in being asked to review it, he had become "a specialist in things Semitic." "My *Jacob* was not programmatic," he wrote, "but a story that occurred to me more or less accidentally."[86] Jurek struggled with the claim (or accusation) that only a Jew could deal authentically with the world of the Jews.

After the publication of *Jacob the Liar*, Jurek received the Heinrich Mann Prize of the Academy of Arts of the GDR (1971) and, in the same year, a Swiss award, the Charles Veillon Prize. The former caused something of a sensation in the official circles of the GDR. Not only was it a first novel to be so honored, but it was a novel by a screenwriter! It was suggested that Jurek be awarded 12,000 marks, the largest amount ever for the prize. Alexander Abusch, however, then minister of culture, abruptly combined Jurek's award with prizes for the work of two much older and more conservative GDR authors, Herbert Otto and Erik Neutsch, and cut Jurek's prize money.[87] Jurek's international success was to be acknowledged but put into a GDR context.

When Jurek accepted the prize, he spoke of his conviction that literature can play only a marginal role in the great historical process of any society.[88] But he also maintained that it played a greater role in a socialist state than elsewhere. He acknowledged the greater availability of literature of all types in the FRG than in the GDR but noted that availability in no way promises impact. At the close of his unpublished speech, he imagined a world from which all writers had vanished. Would it be a poorer world? Yes, it would, for the loss of certain writers would rob the world of richness and beauty. This conservative speech by a young writer contained a set of themes that would become central for Jurek. While exhibiting the necessary modesty of a young writer thrust into the limelight with two much more established writers, yet insisting that only certain writers can move their audiences and can change the way they feel about the world, Jurek expressed his new sense of privilege in the literary world of the GDR. For he was clearly among the elite that could move the world.

When the editor Elisabeth Borchers moved in 1971 to West Germany's most important literary publishing house, Suhrkamp in Frankfurt, Jurek's sense of his own importance as a writer was enhanced. He wrote to Otto F. Walter, the head of Luchterhand, informing him that in spite of the great service Luchterhand had rendered him by publishing *Jacob the Liar* in the West, he felt obligated to go to Suhrkamp with Elisabeth Borchers.[89] At that point, in October 1971, 13,000 copies of *Jacob the Liar* had been printed. Though obviously disappointed, Walter acknowledged the importance of the close relationship between the author and his editor. Borchers remained Jurek's editor for the rest of his career and continued to have a major impact on his work. *Jacob the Liar* later appeared in a Suhrkamp edition.

In October 1972, Werner Alberg informed Jurek that he had been elected a member of the PEN-Club of the GDR. This was a major honor, for the PEN clubs were the international standard for writers who were taken seriously both in their own national literature and around the world.[90] Now Jurek was an author, not merely a scriptwriter. *Jacob the Liar*'s critical success coincided with Jurek's growing sense of alienation from the Ulbricht state. He was asked to do a book signing in October 1969 at a book fair in the Karl Marx Allee. When asked by some visitors from abroad to sign his name and country of origin, Jurek wrote "Jurek Becker, Germany."[91] Germany, not the GDR, was a cultural entity for him. It was the place, including both East and West, where his novel was read.

A fan of Miles Davis and the Beatles, Jurek was seen as an East German hippie, only marginally acceptable. His appearance on the popular GDR-TV program *Actual Camera* was not broadcast because his hair was too long. Jurek ended his letter of complaint to the moderator, Erich Selbmann (who had created the program in 1954) with the comment that he would be willing to cut his hair just to appear on camera. "But I really should inform you that I am of Jewish descent. I would like to mention this potential cause of problems right now so that we don't have complications later."[92] Being seen with long hair, he imagined, was just as stereotyping as being "seen" as Jewish. In denying any "Jewish" visibility, Jurek placed himself both within a German image of the Jew and beyond it. Jurek ironically acknowledged the visibility of difference, quite aware that no one could officially "complain" about his looking "too Jewish" on screen, as they did about his looking too much like a hippie.

Before the publication of *Jacob the Liar*, Jurek had written popular film scripts, principally light comedies. Many of these were for television.

Yet he also worked in darker genres, such as docudrama. In 1969 he attempted to mix these two worlds in a way that was clearly controversial, if not unique. Films in the GDR after the attack on the "Rabbit" films continued to provide a "serious" image of German history (meaning the Nazi period) as seen through the lens of Soviet antifascism. In his film *My Zero Hour* (*Meine Stunde Null*, directed and coauthored by Joachim Hasler), Jurek for the first time used a "comic" approach to the history of antifascism in the Third Reich. Based on the autobiography of Karl Krug and starring Manfred Krug (no relation), it recounts the adventures of Corporal Hartung, a prisoner of war in the Soviet Union who goes behind the German lines on the Eastern front in 1943 to kidnap his commanding officer. At the beginning of the film, this officer, portrayed as vicious and mean, orders Hartung to carry off an unexploded bomb that has been dropped close to his headquarters. When he hears the bomb explode in the distance, he dismisses Hartung, who he assumes has died carrying the bomb, as "not a good German." Indeed, this label is used for all the other Germans in the film. Hartung, in his collaboration with the Soviets (and their German political officers) comes to represent the "good Germans." Having begun as a rather apolitical working-class corporal in the Wehrmacht, Hartung is converted to the humanity of communism and then volunteers to kidnap the abusive officer so as to help the Soviet cause. He rises from being a "little man" to a hero.

The opening voice-over, read by Manfred Krug, emphasizes that war stories of this kind are usually serious or tragic. His war story will be comic. This tale is set on the Eastern front without any mention or even hint of the murder of the Jews. Jurek's initial screenplay for *Jacob the Liar* had indicated the importance of the Eastern front for a confrontation between fascism and communism by having Jacob Heym hear on the radio the location of the Soviet army as it moved toward the West. In both that early screenplay and the novel, *Jacob the Liar* works against all the expectations of the heroic genre. Jacob Heym can never become a hero because he can never be master of his fate. It is not conviction but the press of events that moves him to action. The comic element in *Jacob the Liar* resides in the qualities ascribed to the little man *in extremis* who can act only to ameliorate the suffering about him but cannot alter the randomness of events. Corporal Hartung, on the other hand, can and does act to change the course of the war and defeat fascism.

What delighted readers of *Jacob the Liar* simply mystified viewers of *My Zero Hour*. The humorous retelling of antifascist history puzzled reviewers. "The film is a real attempt to present with humor things and events that have usually been represented seriously. This film tends toward black humor, which could be destructive to young minds."[93] The film "does not do justice to its important theme."[94] But it also caused at least one critic to mention the complexity in representing the past. "Life in war is always many-sided . . . Many German soldiers were seduced, committed no crimes. And, what is more important, why should it not be possible today to look with humor at the past?"[95] In private discussions, the question arose how Jurek could possibly have written such a thing. One Stasi operative "was overwhelmed by the material he [Jurek] was able to master in spite of his less than positive relationship to the state."[96] The film was widely distributed; it was even shown in Moscow. Along with Elisabeth Borchers, Jurek thought the film showed "that heroic times lend themselves to other than monumental representations," something he recognized in the writing and rewriting of *Jacob*.[97] In *My Zero Hour*, however, it is a simple, working-class German soldier (who also marginally appears in *Jacob*) who is converted into a comic hero.

It was the comic that was the problem. What works in connection with a novel depicting Jews is not quite acceptable when it comes to Germans. In the Stasi accounts about the film, Jurek's Jewish background is often repeated. It is explicitly mentioned in a report concerning *My Zero Hour*, though the report falsely states that both Jurek's parents died in the ghetto. But this "fact" is linked to the observation that he had "connections to the black-market circles on Friedrichstraße, whom he meets at the Pressecafé."[98] The associations are ominous, for here being humorous is being Jewish, which is being less than a good citizen. Representing the antifascist struggle in a comic mode is an uncomfortable way of thinking about the past, and it turns out to be a very "Jewish" way of doing so, according to the authorities.

In May 1971, Erich Honecker, who in 1965 had condemned the "Rabbit" films and other manifestations of cultural independence, seized power from Walter Ulbricht. Liberalization in the arts (a "thaw") was part of the new order. On December 16, 1971, Honecker announced a new policy of "art without taboos" (as long as it did not violate the spirit of state socialism). After 1971, it became possible to publish works earlier repressed or seen as "difficult," such as Hermann Kant's novel *The Imprint* (*Das Impressum*). Written in 1968 but published as a book only in 1972, it was loosely based on Kant's experiences editing the student newspaper to which Jurek contributed. The Writer's Union became one of the centers for an internal critique of East German culture in the light of Honecker's reforms. Jurek contended that readers should be educated to see in a work of art the views of the creator, not the pronouncements of the state.⁹⁹ Part of the "official" liberalization of culture was to bring youth into the leadership of the Writers' Union. Contemporaries such as Sarah Kirsch, Volker Braun, and Ulrich Plenzdorf were elected to the leadership along with Jurek. The hidden intention of the SED leaders was equally clear: to rein in Jurek, with whom they had had constant political and ideological difficulties since 1968. With his election to the Writers' Union "he will be more closely bound to the decisions and opinions of the leadership."¹⁰⁰ How little did they suspect the truth.

Misleading the Authorities

In 1970, after Honecker's announcement that there would no longer be any cultural taboos, Jurek began to work on his second novel.¹⁰¹ It was a more difficult one to write. It dealt with the possibilities of living, loving, and functioning as a writer in the GDR. Its title, *Misleading the Authorities* (*Irreführung der Behörden*), was a phrase Jurek had used in screenplays.¹⁰² If *Jacob the Liar* was intended to be read as a historical novel rewritten in contemporary terms, then *Misleading the Authorities* was a contemporary novel about the GDR that was historical in its conception. Both the success of *Jacob the Liar* and the promise of a new cultural politics in the GDR made the theme of this second novel especially relevant. Jurek felt limited in his ability to work through aspects of his "own life, his own experience, his own problems" within an acceptable literary frame.¹⁰³ His readers in the GDR long remembered the audacity and challenge this novel presented to the cultural establishment of the time.¹⁰⁴

At the beginning of the story, in the winter of 1959, the protagonist, Gregor Bienek, is a law student—as Jurek himself was before leaving Humboldt University. Gregor (almost an anagram for Georg; the initials "GB" engraved on a lighter that Gregor's girlfriend gives him as a Christmas present [141] are Jurek's own former initials) wants to be a writer. His sympathetic (and Jewish) law professor has warned him, half in jest, that he should not study law while trying to become a writer, for it is against the law in the GDR to mislead the authorities. Gregor persuades a publishing house to accept his novel after narrating its content to an editor, whom he then seduces. Gregor is a born teller of tales. The main character in his story is a man with a toothache, whose teeth are discovered to be so valuable that the state removes them one by one. This seems to be a metaphor for life in the GDR, as the editor portrayed in the novel notes. Indeed, all of Gregor's stories, like the fairy tale presented in *Jacob the Liar*, have morals.

Jurek set his new novel in the world of Ulbricht's GDR immediately before the invasion that crushed the Prague Spring. Contemporary readers in the GDR also saw it as a commentary on Honecker's GDR after the thaw. It was read as a novel that measured the response of intellectuals to greater "freedom" under Honecker, which simultaneously brought them social and economic status. Jurek selected this world because "I know this environment and its problems especially well, thanks to my own experiences and those of friends. I feel more secure on the terrain than I would be elsewhere even after intensive studies of the milieu."[105] It was an autobiographical fiction but was also clearly historical, as many of his fantasies on contemporary life came to be.

Misleading the Authorities itself consists of two "stories": (1) accounts of Gregor's life and his tales, and (2) a "novel," a schematic presentation of the events in his life from 1960 to 1966. Initially Jurek planned to have the protagonist narrate the first story and an "objective narrator" the second; this idea was reflected in its working title, "Gregor and I."[106] He abandoned this device when he realized that the narrative voice of the protagonist had to reveal his own deepening insight.[107]

The first "story," which makes up the first half of the novel, takes place in 1960 and traces Gregor's decision to become a writer. The second takes place in 1967 and maps the decline of his marriage and the hollowness of his success. The relationship with his girlfriend and future wife, Lola (recall the unfortunate pseudonym that Hermann Kant had inflicted on Jurek as a student), is central to the first story. Lola is pregnant, and Gregor must find the money to pay for an illegal abortion. (Abortions were made legal in the GDR only in 1972.) To raise the money he lies to an old friend, but fails to repay him, though the friend needs the money to supplement his meager state pension. Only in the second "story" does his friend finally confront him. He shames Gregor into giving him the money he owes him, but then never cashes the check. He feels that Gregor needs to show some type of moral responsibility.

Misleading the Authorities is a novel about storytelling and deceit. The first story begins with Lola's own desire to help Gregor shape his tales so as to make them more palatable to the authorities and therefore more salable. He tells her a story about three men who have decided to rob a bank and then discover that their escape plans depend on there being a good road away from the bank. To facilitate their robbery they join in the building of the road, becoming exemplary workers. They rob the bank and find that they have actually stolen less money than they made by working overtime as socialist worker-heroes. Lola, knowing the tone that would be acceptable in the GDR, points out that the story has a flat ending. Gregor should have them abandon the notion of robbing the bank because of the insight they gained as workers into the value of work itself (145–50). (Later in the book, Lola's version is rejected as a film script because of the claim that crime may lead to the improvement of the poor roads in the GDR! [163])

Gregor's relationship with Lola, as with everyone else in the novel, is based on his lies. He lies to everyone about everyone else in order to achieve his notion of success, which he manages to do in the world of filmmaking. The more successful (read: superficial) his films become, the more opportunist and immoral he becomes.

Lola confronts Gregor about his slide into opportunism, noting that the public expects moral responsibility from him, while he leads them astray, "providing stuff that's old hat, which you use your talent to polish up in your studio" (148). The relationship between Lola and Gregor ends with their realization that their very lives have become dependent on Gregor's opportunism. Jurek, in an interview in 1974, noted that "writing is always connected to intent. And that is doubly true of a socialist writer who does not merely want to provide tales for his public. A socialist writer wants to bring his intentions to his public."[108] These "intentions" are never defined, but they seem to reflect Jurek's belief that writers have a special insight into the world and therefore a moral obligation to share this insight with their readers. Jurek did not want to garner any "false" praise from the West as a writer who opposed the official cultural politics. His intention was to "help consolidate socialism in the GDR."[109] His tone, as he wrote about the novel in 1973 to the Jena professor of literature Hans Richter, is almost always polemical.[110] The writer has an obligation to provide readers with a critique of daily life on the way to an ideal socialist world.

Gregor is now successful, as Lola's parents had been at the beginning of the novel. High party functionaries, they enjoyed a wealthy and well-ordered existence at the top of the invisible class pyramid in the GDR. With his success, Gregor believes his marriage has come to an end and asks Lola whether she wants a divorce. She laughs at him and says there's no need to reassure your partner daily that you don't want a divorce. Her laughter is accompanied by her reaching over in the bed and grasping Gregor's arm, "so that I did not try to get away from her, irritated by so much incomprehensible laughter" (249). The end of the novel is ambiguous. Has Gregor learned that success can spoil individual relationships as well as fulfillment of one's obligations to the state and one's public? "I don't think of Gregor Bienek as a lost soul ripe for the junk pile," said Jurek in a 1973 interview, "but I assume he will find a path to other means of interaction. And the first step is recognizing the path."[111] A "positive" reading of the novel's conclusion is provided by an unmistakable metaphor earlier in the novel. Speaking about his producer, Gregor notes that "no one can run around with another nose than his own, not even me" (193). But what is Gregor's real "nose"? Is it a relationship to state and spouse based on moral responsibility? The metaphor itself is odd, because it is the standard reference to the image of the Jew, to that unalterable aspect of Jewish physical difference. The novel contains no reference to anything "Jewish" in the protagonist; yet when Gregor images the inalterable aspect of his world, he uses a metaphor with this strange double meaning. Earlier in the novel he had described the physiognomy of his Jewish professor of criminal law, Gelbach, as asymmetrical, with deep furrows on one side of his face that would allow him to feel at home in a freak show next to the "half-woman." His short legs and extraordinarily large head complete his portrait (51). No image of the Jewish nose is here, but Gelbach is the one, at the very beginning of the novel, who urges Gregor to follow his dream, to write, and not to "mislead the authorities" by claiming to study law. It is a Jew who first leads Gregor to follow his own nose.

If Emmerich's reading of *Jacob the Liar* saw a mark of class in the hierarchy of assimilation in the ghetto, then *Misleading the Authorities* clearly presents a case of class and class envy in the GDR. The vehicle for achieving status was screenplay writing, at least the kind that does not make the viewer reconsider his or her position in society. The notion of becoming a good citizen of the GDR, of giving up all sense of difference, is not treated as something positive in the novel. Success could be read as opportunism in the unspoken class structure of the GDR. The real success, the real "nose," is acknowledging one's role in the state as a writer true to one's own ideals and beliefs.

In 1971, Jurek submitted the finished manuscript of *Misleading the Authorities* to Aufbau, the East German publishing house that had achieved major success with *Jacob the Liar*. The editors solicited a review from Gerd Gericke, who would become the "dramaturge," or script consultant, on the later film of *Jacob*. But they then decided the book was too political (and perhaps not exotic enough) for them,[112] even though they had given Jurek a substantial advance.[113] Disappointed, Jurek submitted it at the beginning of 1972 to the more experimental Hinstorff Publishing house in Rostock, run by Konrad Reich. Jurek wrote to Elisabeth Borchers, who was editing the manuscript for a Suhrkamp edition in the West, that "the book will stir things up among our people. It will be a much bigger seller than *Jacob*."[114] Not that *Jacob* had done poorly, but its

GDR sales were too low, Jurek believed, given its growing international success.

In March 1972, the manuscript for *Misleading the Authorities* received a positive reading from Hans Joachim Bernhard, the reader to whom Hinstorff had sent it. He stressed its difference from the "fascist crimes and antifascist resistance" of *Jacob*. He emphasized that the development of a young, artistically talented individual in "our society" is central to Jurek's project, without noting that Gregor fails. The novel raised new questions about what it means to live a sensual life and the answerability of those leading such a life in "our" society. Even though it dealt with seemingly trivial details, it created exciting relationships that would broaden the spectrum of "our" literature. Bernhard strongly recommended publication.

In the spring of 1973, *Misleading the Authorities* went on the market in both East and West Germany. When the reviews appeared, the opinions on this novel were split along the East-West divide. The Eastern critics, such as Walter Waldmann, hated it, seeing it as "superficial, sometimes too superficial" (especially in contrast to *Jacob*).[115] West German critics, reading it as a critique of the cultural life of the contemporary (rather than the Ulbricht) GDR, loved it. Broadcasting from West Berlin on SFB (Radio Free Berlin), Roland Wiegenstein described the novel as a "history of privilege," written as a "clever, funny, and yet very serious work of self-criticism."[116] After 1968, there had been a strong interest in the West in those GDR authors who were labeled "oppositional."[117] This was especially true when such opposition reflected concern with the same aspects of the German past and present that obsessed younger critics in the West. Writing in a cultural dictatorship (as seen from the West) demanded civil courage and also provided a "real" way of altering the existing society.

Literature mattered, but the literature that mattered to Jurek was self-consciously "literary" rather than socialist. After Heinrich Böll, one of Jurek's literary heroes, won the Nobel Prize in the fall of 1972, Jurek wrote to him, noting the importance of Böll's work for his own idea of fiction.[118] Among other writers Jurek was claiming as his models by the early 1970s were Thomas Mann, Stefan Zweig, and J. D. Salinger.[119] All were novelists whose passions lie above all in the clarity of narrative. All were also writers whose political positions were clearly inscribed in their works. None were "socialist" writers.

Jurek's access to the West expanded greatly after the success of *Jacob the Liar* in the early 1970s. In 1970 he made an extensive trip, giving readings in major West Germany cities and reporting on the trip "through

GDR eyes" for a West German newspaper.[120] "At least we speak the same language," said many of those he would meet, but Jurek was never quite sure what that claim meant. Was his novel read in the FRG in the same way as it was read in the GDR? His contacts with the West increased over time. Between 1973 and 1976 he made fifteen trips to West Berlin, one in February 1974 to the Jewish Community Office to do research for his novel *The Boxer* (1976). In addition, he managed to travel to the Netherlands in March of 1974, and in May 1975 he gave readings from *Jacob* in Belgium and Luxembourg. There he also spoke about the inherently conservative nature of socialist culture and the destructive demands of a state unwilling to tolerate any experimentation.[121] These comments echoed his earlier ones to the Yugoslavian Writers' Congress held in Belgrade in October 1973.[122] Jurek had become part of the international world of German letters, in demand in the West as much as in the Soviet bloc.

On December 16, 1973, Günter Schulz, secretary of the Schröder Foundation, informed Jurek that he had been awarded the 10,000-mark Literary Prize of the City of Bremen in West Germany for *Misleading the Authorities*.[123] Jurek immediately turned to the first secretary of the Writers' Union for advice. What should one do when given a "foreign" literary award? The prize had been given to "Western" writers of the stature of Ilse Aichinger (1955), Ernst Jünger (1956), Ingeborg Bachmann (1957), Paul Celan (1958), and Thomas Bernhard (1965).[124] It had been awarded only once to a writer resident in the GDR; Christa Reinig accepted the award in 1964 and never returned to the GDR. Jurek was the first post-1968 writer from the GDR to receive the prize for a novel deemed, in the West, critical of the socialist system. The Central Committee of the Union of Writers advised that it would "be good if Becker did not accept this prize." But "the final decision remains with him."[125] There was one further problem. Jurek was soon to make his debut as a member of the leadership of the Writers' Union by giving a major speech at its seventh congress. Party authorities feared giving him this visibility after his being awarded a West German prize. His colleagues in the Writer's Union—such as Hermann Kant, who at that point was still actively working for the Stasi—urged him not to accept it.[126] Kurt Hager, however, decided to make a blanket rule against the accepting of this or any other prize from the FRG *in the future*. So Jurek was permitted to go to Bremen to accept the award on January 26, 1974. There he was greeted by a newspaper report that described him as "a Polish writer living in the GDR." This label he strongly rejected, noting that the distinction between being a "GDR author" and an "author living in the GDR" was more than a nuance.[127] In the West he wanted to be seen as a GDR author, not a Polish Jew sojourning in the GDR.

Despite the fears of the party officials, Jurek's address to the Writers' Union congress, "Reality and Truth in Literature" (delivered on November 13, 1974), was well received, at least by the "liberal" writers.[128] It was a programmatic statement of what literature in a truly socialist state had to become. Jurek raised the central question of "internalized censorship" among his colleagues, who knew so well what was not permitted that they were never tempted to cross the line. Jurek dismissed the sudden love of West German critics for oppositional literature in the GDR, literature that they reinterpreted as in opposition to the state. Yet he also saw that there was a necessary tension between a state and its writers. He denied the purely pedagogical role of literature and refused to acknowledge a role for literature in converting individuals to any ideology. He stressed that the appropriate topic and form for literature must be left to authors. He went on to say it was pointless to try to replicate "real" experiences the reader may have had (perhaps a response to the conflation of his forgotten experiences of the Shoah and the writing of *Jacob the Liar*). Literature should not present canned answers but should raise daring questions. This was especially true in the GDR, where it was dealing with the past and trying to prevent a repetition of its problems and mistakes. The worker's movement had always learned more from its mistakes than from anything else.

Ruth Werner, a successful Soviet spy against the Nazis and then against the West, a novelist and biographer, herself of German Jewish origin, and a member of the Stalinist old guard, countered that people were constantly telling her how their reading had changed their lives. Jurek rudely interrupted her: "Is the opinion of a member of the Politburo about the effect of literature the same as the effect itself?" The German Jewish oppositional writer Stefan Heym, who had written his first novel in English during his American exile in the 1940s, sprang to his feet to defend Jurek, declaring that everyone present should remember what he had said about the reality of literature, not its effectiveness. Heym then mentioned Alexander Solzhenitsyn's expulsion from the USSR, which had occurred in 1974 as a result of a crisis in the Soviet leadership created by that author's account of "experiences and facts."[129] The translator Gustav Just, who was sitting next to Heym, applauded. Suddenly the specter of the state's sending a writer into exile because of a state error revealed by that writer became part of the discourse in the Berlin branch of the Writers' Union. There, with Jurek in the leadership, real debates about day-to-day practice in the GDR and the USSR took place. Berlin writers were beginning to see the gap between promise and reality in Honecker's GDR.

Jacob the Liar: The Film

The cultural thaw that occurred—or was thought to occur—after Honecker deposed Walter Ulbricht soon ceased. Jurek's awareness of the new freeze increased with the growing visibility his work. *Jacob the Liar* had by now been translated into a dozen languages and had become a best-seller in both German states. By 1973, Swedish, Czech, Hungarian, Romanian, English, and French rights had been bought; eight other translations (including Polish) had appeared by the early 1980s. *Jacob's* success led DEFA to think about resuming the abandoned project of filming the work with a new screenplay by Jurek and the participation of Frank Beyer. In 1973, after the West German television station ZDF had expressed an interest in filming the novel, Jurek had asked the DEFA officials if they would want to do it.[130] DEFA decided to undertake a joint production with GDR television to keep the project in the GDR. On February 10, 1973, it was agreed that the novel would be filmed.[131] The negotiations were difficult, for Jurek had a substantially higher opinion of the script than DEFA had.[132] The script, the third and final one since 1963, was completed in October 1973, and a new contract was signed.[133]

The third screenplay for *Jacob the Liar* was based on Jurek's extraordinarily successful novel rather than on the earlier screenplays. It abandoned the narrative frame that Jurek had introduced into the novel, replacing it with a single line: "The story of Jacob the Liar never took place as is. Certainly not. Perhaps it did take place like this." Jurek changed other aspects of the novel. He eliminated the entire subplot with Dr. Kirschbaum, which had provided a "heroic" parallel to Jacob and his nonexistent radio. By the 1974 version, Jacob is described as "a man between forty and fifty years old. Unassuming, in no way the type of the movie hero."[134] The Orthodox character Herschel Schtamm is presented as a deeply religious, almost fanatic, figure in contrast to his secularized identical twin brother Roman. The contrast here is important to the representation of the "Jew," for the twins are supposed to be so identical that only Herschel's prayer-locks differentiate them. The difference is the result of individual choice, the casting implies, not any predisposition to a religious identity on the part of Eastern European Jewry. Here the Polonized Jew Roman Schtamm appears as a counter type.

The most important change from the earlier film versions was in the conclusion of the film. The heroic end, with Jacob's despair and the

Russian soldier walking hand in hand with Lina, had been made ambiguous in the novel, where Jurek offered a double ending. Will they survive? Will they die? He rewrote the ending to pick up on the fairy tale inset, which was now to be shot like the flashbacks to Jacob's life in prewar Poland, in brilliant colors. At the conclusion of the film, Jacob, Lina, and the other ghetto dwellers are being shipped in a cattle car to the death camp. Lina asks Jacob about the story he has told her. How was the princess cured by a cloud? Her friends had told her this was impossible. Jacob patiently explains that it was only a symbol for what the Princess needed to believe. Lina turns to Jacob and asks, as the camera pans out of the small window in the cattle car: "But aren't clouds made of cotton?" The last stage direction reads: "The clouds actually look like little cotton balls."[135] The problem of belief becomes a problem of language. What language can we believe?

The language of the Jewish characters is virtually identical to that of the Germans. Very little of the Yiddish coloration remains, and that almost always in the designation of objects such as *gefilte fisch* or *matze*. The German soldiers, as is the entire scene in the ghetto, are "normal" within the abnormality of the Shoah. The film of *Jacob the Liar* clearly understates the horror of the ghetto, as Frank Beyer was well aware: "The images of horror that we know from documentaries about the ghettos and the concentration camps don't appear in our film. We have noticed that the shock has the opposite effect on viewers, closing rather than opening their minds to the thoughts and feelings that the author and director are trying to project."[136] Jurek supported Frank Beyer's vision of the film. He was the author but Beyer was the director. Beyer would regularly meet with Jurek and then get his way "in a democratic manner."[137] Jurek knew it was the director who had the final say.

Beyer eventually persuaded DEFA to shoot the film in color. It is one of the very first DEFA color films. Beyer played with the use of color, using faded colors for the ghetto; bright, almost overwhelming colors for the flashbacks concerning Jacob's life before the ghetto; and pastels for the fairy tale about the sick princess. This was not at all simple, as Beyer had to acquire Kodak film for the scenes that demanded bright greens. The GDR color film did not provide sufficient contrast, and the use of green was central to the movie. There is a total absence of trees in the ghetto. This is highlighted by the trees that appear in the fairy-tale inset (which is also shot in bright color stock) and the final scene, in which the sky, clouds, and trees are viewed through the windows of the boxcar. All are references to the unseen tree that opens Jurek's novel and under which Chana is shot.

The news of the casting of Jacob percolated through the media. Jurek received a telegram from Heinz Rühmann in West Germany requesting a meeting: the actor wanted the role.[138] Rühmann, born in 1902, had been a major German film star. Trained under Max Reinhardt in the 1920s, he was one of the leading actors in Nazi popular films. He became the most popular character actor in postwar West German films, achieving his most notable success in *The Captain from Köpenick*, the 1956 film version of the Jewish exile writer Carl Zuckermeyer's play. Rühmann as Jacob would have brought a completely different set of associations to the role. The notion of one of the most popular actors in West Germany playing in a film based on one of the most popular novels ever published in East Germany was very tempting for Frank Beyer. It would have ensured major box office success in both Germanys. The suggestion moved its way up the hierarchy of the GDR until it eventually landed on Erich Honecker's desk. The head of the government and the party scuttled it, observing that it violated the principle of two essentially different Germanys. A single German culture should not even be hinted at.

Two other actors from beyond the borders of the GDR considered for the role were the French communist actor and singer Yves Montand and his Jewish wife Simone Signoret. The idea of a female Jacob is not that absurd, for Signoret later made the brilliant film *Madame Rosa* (directed by Moshe Mizrahi, 1977), in which she plays an aged survivor of Auschwitz. The local actors considered were Gerry Wolff (because he knew Yiddish folk songs) and Fred Düren.[139] The DEFA star Erwin Geschonneck was cast as the barber Kowalski, Jacob's friend, though he wanted the role of Jacob; and Manuela Simon was cast as Lina. Armin Müller-Stahl appeared in a small role as Roman Schtamm. The cameraman was Günter Marczinkowsky, and Horst Mathuschek was the soundman. Most members of the cast and crew had worked together on Beyer's *Naked among Wolves* a decade before.

Beyer eventually cast the Czech actor Vlastimil Brodsky as Jacob. Having studied in the famous Prague film school, Beyer had known Brodsky when the latter too was studying there; Brodsky, in fact, had starred in Beyer's student film project. Brodsky was to have been cast in the aborted 1966 version of *Jacob the Liar*, and Beyer had already negotiated with him in great detail at that time.[140] He was a mainstay of the Prague theater as well as the film scene. Again in September 1973, Beyer decided to shoot on location in Poland, using at least five Polish actors from Film Polski, the state agency.

Jurek and Beyer traveled to Warsaw on November 5, 1974, to discuss production and casting. The first casting calls took place on November 13,

1974, in the DEFA studios in Babelsberg, near Berlin. Beyer had intended to begin shooting on February 12, 1974, but on January 11 the Polish authorities requested a full translation of the script, contrary to the usual procedures. The translation was sent to Warsaw on January 23. On February 18, the Polish film agency informed DEFA in an unsigned telegram that no Polish actors would be permitted to act in the film. Günter Klein, deputy minister of culture for the GDR and the individual responsible for film, worked actively in its behalf. Polish opposition—which had prevented the original production—was neutralized, and filming began.[141] The exterior shooting was done in Czechoslovakia, in a small town that had been abandoned the year before and was made over as the ghetto.

The official premiere of *Jacob the Liar* took place on black-and-white GDR television on Sunday, December 23, 1974, during a week of anti-imperialist films. The theater premiere was four months later, on April 17, 1975. The film enjoyed immediate success. Jurek, Beyer, and others were awarded the GDR National Prize, Second Class (1975). At the twenty-fifth Berlin Film Festival, on the other side of the wall, the film took the "Silver Bear." It became the only American Academy Award nomination (for best foreign film) of a film from the GDR. This was a clear answer to the complaint, officially stated at the second congress of Film and Television Workers, April 7–8, 1972, about the general decline in movie attendance on the part of GDR citizens. Thanks to *Jacob the Liar*, the film industry in the GDR was suddenly a player in the world market.

At the end of December 1974, Jurek could sit at home and listen to the "Radio in the American Sector" (RIAS) praise the film. It was seen as the work of a ghetto survivor who took his father's tale of a man with a radio and remade it in his own, special way. It was a "timeless parable" of human existence and "the meaning of truth and lies, illusion and reality in our human existence." Dealing with the Jewish past and the German role in it was still difficult, even in West Berlin. Though unable to judge the effect of the color, since he saw the TV broadcast in black and white, the reviewer stressed the technical quality of Beyer's film.[142]

In *Neues Deutschland* at the same moment, a long, very positive review by Klaus Schüler appeared. Beyer's technical ability and Marczinkowsky's camera work also impressed Schüler in their use of the new medium of color. The production values of the film were high by both Eastern and Western standards. Schüler stressed the antinaturalist, antidocumentary nature of the film, and its lack of any attempt to mimic the antifascist "action films" about the war. For him it was a film that combined "the comic and the tragic, the real and the dreamlike, which assures it a rich aesthetic possibility." This type of amalgam "marks the art of the GDR during the past few years, which more and more is presenting a dialectic of reality."[143] The reviews, while always noting Jurek's personal history, tended to move quickly to formal or even aesthetic evaluations. In complex ways, dealing with the past meant dealing with the present. If the readings of the past—which had become the unreflected models by which Germans, West and East, understood the Nazi past—were not simply accepted, then the very present could be called into question. All at once, what had been a unique model for imagining the Shoah in the East revealed a universal truth about human nature. This move to a universal reading meant that it could be enjoyed without fear of disrupting existing models of the past.

Jurek was aware that the film and (by extension) the novel were texts of the late 1960s and early 1970s. In an interview in the GDR weekly *Sonntag,* he commented that a film like *Jacob the Liar* would have been impossible even five years after the war: "Immediately after the war the observer would have seen such a treatment of this theme as blasphemy. I believe that our tale demands a high degree of knowledge. I can approach people with a tale like this only after they have been bombarded with information about that time for twenty or thirty years. In other words, for someone who knows nothing about what happened then, this is an inappropriate text."[144] In 1975, Jurek's sense of the film was that it was a kind of reaction to his childhood experiences, which made it very different from all the earlier films about fascism. Beyer was of like mind. In an interview given before the opening of the film, he too used language that seemed double-edged. The film, while dealing with petit bourgeois figures such as Jacob, still expressed the "great feeling of our Marxist humanism." It was in no way a monument to the "suffering of the Jews under fascism or to the antifascist opposition." Rather, it was a film about "truth and lies in life, about dream and reality."[145] As the reality of the GDR shifted, Jurek's views of the film also changed. On November 17, 1976, at the very moment when Jurek learned about Wolf Biermann's expulsion from the GDR, he labeled the film as "too conventional and too good."[146] The problem of a GDR in which artists may well believe in the ultimate truths of socialism but see them undermined daily by the practices of an ever more rigid state came to be mirrored in Jurek's understanding of *Jacob the Liar.*

When he and Beyer (in 1974) won the nomination for an Academy Award, the state's patience toward any articulate, cultural opposition was already beginning to unravel. It was precisely the "foreign" reception of the work, from the FRG to the USA, that gave Jurek a sense of his own power in relation to the state. He had played with the idea of a film about the Vietnam War as seen from the perspective of the GDR, as well as a biographical film about J. S. Bach between the ages of eighteen and twenty.[147] A script for the latter exists, with the title "The Youth of a Monument," but the film was never made. To write for the films in the GDR, one had to learn to write within concrete as well as implied guidelines for self-censorship. Jurek learned that lesson well.

Jurek had also learned to write fiction, as he later said, in a world in which writing had a "substitute quality," replacing newspapers and radio and film.[148] Novels in the GDR sold out almost as soon as they were published and were read as hiding complex meanings. It was writing from the margin—writing code—a task well suited to someone who never felt quite at home in his language, who always sensed his alienation from the official literature. Jurek's image of the socialist state with its central control of the media (recall that he was trained to write for the media) is that of a state which drove readers into reading books by "deviants."[149] Among the deviants he counted himself. The struggle with the state censor became a game for Jurek, as for many writers of that first generation of GDR citizens who experienced the tensions of the cold war. Proximity to the West created a unique situation, because it was always—even if politically complicated or dangerous—possible to write for German-speaking readers in the FRG. After 1974, when Jurek increasingly confronted the authorities in the GDR, he and they began to see his views as a "problem."[150]

Jurek Becker in the 1990s, a photo taken by his son Nikolaus Becker.

The young Jurek (then called Georg) at eight or nine, having been released from the children's home in Berlin in 1946.

A rather chubby Jurek, or Georg (then nicknamed "Paffi"), in the late 1940s, well fed by his father, thanks to Max's dealings on the black market.

Jurek in grammar school in the late 1940s. His isolation is clearly perceptible as he sits in the very front of the group portrait.

Max Becker and his friend Dora Grosspietsch in the early 1950s.

A rather chubby Jurek, or Georg (then nicknamed "Paffi"), in the late 1940s, well fed by his father, thanks to Max's dealings on the black market.

Jurek in grammar school in the late 1940s. His isolation is clearly perceptible as he sits in the very front of the group portrait.

Max Becker and his friend Dora Grosspietsch in the early 1950s.

The "brothers" Manfred Krug (*left*) and Jurek Becker during their army service in 1956.

Jurek and Rieke on their wedding day in 1961, an event that—for them—overshadowed the building of the Berlin Wall in the same year.

Max Becker and Jurek in the 1960s.

Jurek in the family house in Mahlsdorf in the 1960s.

Jurek (*second from left*) and Frank Beyer (*far right*) on the set of *Jacob the Liar* in 1973.

Jurek and Christine on their wedding day in 1986.

Jurek and his third son, Johnny, in the early 1990s.

Chapter 6

"LIAR" JOINS THE OPPOSITION AND
GOES TO AMERICA, 1974–1978

The Boxer

Following the international success of *Jacob the Liar* as a novel and a film, Jurek Becker became "Liar." This was the pseudonym given him in November 1976 by the Seventh Division in charge of cultural politics, of "Department XX," of the Ministry of State Security (commonly known as the Stasi).[1] He had been of interest to the Stasi from the time he left Humboldt University in 1961, but the intensity and obviousness of the surveillance increased in the mid-1970s. By then he was followed, he was photographed, his phone was tapped, and he knew it. What he did not know was how very many of his friends and acquaintances, like those of so many other GDR intellectuals, were regularly writing reports about their conversations with him. West German intelligence agents were equally interested in Jurek's activities. His political visibility and frequent trips to the West suggested that he was an "unofficial" agent of the Stasi. The West Berlin office of the Verfassungsschutz, the German equivalent of the FBI, kept a detailed file on Jurek at least through 1981.[2]

Germany, as often in its history, was divided into multiple political entities, each with its own espionage service but bound together by a common language and literary culture. East German writers such as Jurek were widely read in the West, and the appearance of his new novel, *The Boxer*, was anticipated both in the GDR and in West Germany, in the FRG. Control over such writers, specifically those who were praised in the West as being part of the cultural opposition in the East, became one of the main activities of the GDR political establishment, up to and including the head of state, Erich Honecker.[3] What had been a "velvet prison" for Jurek, to use Miklos Haraszti's felicitous phrase, was now looking more like a prison from which there could be no escape because it provided the prisoner with the status he needed at home as well as abroad.

Shortly after Max's death, Jurek had begun work on the story of a father and son, both survivors of the Shoah, who came to live in the GDR. The frame of *Jacob the Liar*, which chronicled the life of an adult survivor, was now the focus of the new novel. By October 1974, Jurek had submitted his third novel, *The Boxer*, to Konrad Reich at the Hinstorff publishing house in Rostock.[4] With the publication of books such as *Misleading the Authorities*, Hinstorff had continued to be the most experimental publishing house in the GDR. Jurek wanted to remain part of the literary avant-garde in the GDR, and Reich was delighted to get the novel.

The most autobiographical of all Jurek's novels, *The Boxer* chronicles the life of its protagonist, the Holocaust survivor Aron Blank—who re-names himself Arno—from 1945 to the early 1970s. Jurek acknowledged that he wanted to "work up a meaningful part of his life" after Max's death. "My father died in 1972 when I was thirty-five. It sounds awful, but what really tormented me were the notebooks full of questions that I had never asked him and could not have asked him. I managed to form an image of the relationship between my father and myself only when the relationship was over."[5] The very format of the novel is a gesture to the unanswered questions about his father's life, which remained unanswered precisely because Jurek never asked them. He used the form of an interview to frame his new novel.

The anonymous interviewer notes that by the time the novel takes place he has already filled five little green notebooks with accounts of his conversations with Arno. (Jurek's own habit was to write his early drafts in the little green notebooks used in the schools in the GDR.) These conversations with Arno appear to have an "official" purpose, as the interlocutor plays the role of a social worker and psychotherapist. Ultimately he is a writer trying to capture all of Arno's stories.

The narrator is not always sure whether these stories represent the "truth" or merely Arno's need to maintain the one human connection he has left: "He wants to draw the end of our interviews out. Only he knows how large his store of stories is, still quite small, I think, and he is afraid that he will have to tell me at some point that he has nothing else to tell me" (247). This, of course, is the very opposite of Jurek's experience with Max. Max did not talk to Jurek about his experiences in the Shoah, a situation portrayed in the fictional relationship between Arno and his son Mark in the novel. Nor did Jurek ever ask him what had happened. Indeed, it is never clear in the novel whether we are reading Arno's tales or the narrator's reworking of them into a consistent and clear narrative.

The nature of storytelling in *The Boxer* also reflected Jurek's relationship with his readers in the GDR and, more importantly, the difficult relationship he imagined all writers were having with the leadership of the GDR. The "better" the stories they wrote, the more attention the writers received. But these stories were losing relevance to the needs of the readers. They were supposed to make readers feel their lives were being "changed" by the stories they read. So there was little relationship between the integrity of the story and its acceptance.

The plot of *The Boxer* is a complex version of the stories Max invented when he came to Berlin, stories that Jurek, as he grew up, made part of the permanent record of his father's life. The novel begins with Aron's arrival in Berlin in 1945 and his need for a new identification card. He has his photograph taken, and the face he sees on it looks too Jewish. He then selects a new birth date (exactly six years earlier, the time spent in the camps [20]), and a new place of birth. (18–19) To deny his identity as a Jew, and that means a victim, he transposes two letters and becomes Arno Blank.

The "new" Arno Blank is still too visible as a Jew, as a victim, in his own mind (21). Indeed, his anxiety about his own visibility is reflected in the world in which he lives. When he later meets someone who was in a concentration camp who asks him whether he is a Jew, Arno answers, "Do I look like one?" (67). When confronted by the authorities for some proof of his new identity, he takes out his release papers from the concentration camp. Suddenly, this horrendous experience is the only identity that no one questions. Being a "victim of the fascism" gives him the power to silence even the authorities. No questions can follow.

Aron Blank, according to the narrators' account, was born in Riga, Latvia; taken as a child to Germany; and raised first in Leipzig and then, after 1934, in Berlin. (The inversion of Max's invented autobiography is clear; Max claimed he was born in Germany and raised in Poland.) Aron's life is that of an assimilated German Jew. In 1934, Aron and his non-Jewish wife and three children flee to Prague, and after the German invasion they are sent to a ghetto and then a camp. He survives alone, his wife Lydia having been deported because of her resistance activities. (In Max's account, to the contrary, Chana and Jerzy were deported because of Max's activities.) Two of Aron's children die in his arms, and he is forced to abandon the youngest, just two years old, with a neighbor when he too is deported (28).

After his release from the camps, he finds his third son, Mark, through the Joint (the American Jewish Joint Distribution Organization), as Max found Georg in 1945. A child named Mark Berger is living in a former concentration camp that has been converted to an orphanage. Since Mark is such an unusual first name, it is assumed that some sort of error has crept into the list and transformed Blank to Berger (35). Arno (as he is now called) has no memory of his son's appearance but is still convinced that he has found him. After a long period of commuting to the camp from Berlin, he takes Mark home.

Arno has begun to assemble what seem to be the pieces of a normal life. But when he is given the well-appointed apartment of a former Nazi, he first finds that he can only sleep on the floor in a closet (27ff.). He slowly comes out of his initial trauma and even begins a love affair with Paula Kaplan, the woman from the Joint who helped him find Mark. Arno speaks German with her, sprinkled with Yiddish (*goj, meschugge*). In addition he speaks Russian. Mark speaks German as his primary, if not only, language. No *Lagersprache*, no Yiddish, no Russian intervenes. Yet there is a basic problem in comprehension. Mark's motor and language skills are those of a child some two years younger than his actual age. He is seven but speaks German like a five-year-old (129). When Arno first meets him at the orphanage, he tries to explain that he is Mark's father and Mark is his son. "Son" is a word and a concept that Mark has never heard and at first misuses, but over time learns to use correctly (64–65).

Arno learns that the world of postwar Berlin is different in its values and mores from the world was used to before the war. When he needs to have the photograph taken for his ID, the photographer is unwilling to take it and be paid in money, for money has lost all value. Arno argues with the photographer, insisting that ten times the prewar cost is quite high enough. But when he gets the photograph, he not only pays the photographer but also gives him a pack of cigarettes, the real postwar currency. Arno slides into dealing on the Berlin black market. It is a black market as seen from a Jewish perspective. The interviewer comments that his own accounts of it sound almost as though he were using anti-Semitic clichés. Arno does not like dealing on the black market but has to do it to keep himself and Mark alive. He too sees the black market as "too Jewish," because the Germans associate it with immorality.

Arno eventually becomes a bookkeeper for Tennenbaum, one of the more successful black marketers, after both of them realize that Arno is incapable of the brutality needed to function on the street. He is, in his own self-definition, "a Jew, a black marketer, and someone who has complexes" (145). After finding Mark, he buys children's toys and a bicycle on the black market. The bicycle is for himself (119), so that he can ride from the rail station to the orphanage, but it evokes the bicycle that Max bought for Georg.

More important than anything else he acquires for Mark is a live-in nurse. Paula Kaplan has left Arno, having eventually found her former lover. When Arno brings Mark home, the boy keeps speaking of a nurse, Irma, who was kind to him in the orphanage. Arno meets her and invites her to live with them, and she eventually becomes his lover (181ff.). They establish what looks like a "normal" life. This parallels Max's early relationship with Irma Kautsch and, to a degree, the longer one with "Dorchen" Großpietsch. Both were non-Jewish women; Max's attraction to them reflected his need to be part of a "normal" relationship. In the novel, sexuality signifies the restoration of Arno's "normal" life. He sees this normality in Mark's sexual maturity (260). Yet sexual contact does not automatically lead to social communication, as Jurek shows in the collapse of Arno's relationships. Indeed, it often precludes it. This was certainly not the case with the long, if difficult relationship between Max and Dorchen, which ended only with Max's death.

Arno quits the black market and begins to work for the Russians as a translator, thanks to his language skills. (Max too had left the black market and tried working as a salesman when Jurek entered school.) A normal home seems to be established. Irma, while attentive to the household, begins to give piano lessons. Mark enters school. For Arno, school is a place that may harbor "fascists and perhaps even murderers" (203). When Mark gets beaten up, Arno sees the incident as a "pogrom in the making" (218). Mark refuses to say who beat him, so Arno teaches him to box in self-defense. Boxing becomes a way of providing Mark with the tools to defend himself in a society that Arno sees as inherently anti-Semitic and destructive (223). In this way, sport continues to define the Jewish body (here the survivor's body) as in need of recuperation. As we have seen, both Max and Jurek were obsessed with sports. The sick and defenseless body of a child can be transformed into a healthy body, which will be the body of a citizen of the new state. It will be the body of a German.

While Arno does not want to be seen as a Jew, he sees himself as one. He joins the Jewish Community, and he associates exclusively with Jews. His friends, like him, seem to be frozen in Berlin, unable to move from the city, tied to its slow development after the war. The one exception is the Jewish survivor Kenik, who in 1947 decides to go to Palestine (178).

When Arno insists on seeing him off, Kenik weeps. Having been involved in the black market with Arno, he believes he is the last person to know Arno's real name (194). With Kenik's departure, Arno believes there are no longer any ties to his past, except those within him. But he is wrong. When toward the close of the novel Irma insists that they get married, and Arno cannot understand why they would want to, she leaves, with the words, "I haven't left anything behind, Aron" (267). He is shocked that she knows his secret, for she has never addressed him by his real name before.

According to the interviewer, Arno evinces little interest for socialism, even after the founding of the GDR. (The term "GDR" never appears in the book.) He is aware of the general improvement of society but only as it affects him: "You mean me as a Jew?" "Yes." "Am I a Jew?" (251). Being a Jew does not mean following any religious practice. It means seeing the world through "Jewish" (read: traumatized) eyes. It was the anti-Semites who thus created a Jewish identity. This was Max's view as well as Jurek's, and Jurek articulated it in a series of presentations and fictions from the mid-1970s to the mid-1980s. It was the view popularized after the Shoah by Jean-Paul Sartre in his 1946 essay *Anti-Semite and Jew* and dramatized by Jurek's friend Max Frisch in his 1961 play *Andorra*.[6] That a "Jewish" identity could exist separately from a status as "victim" was perceived by few Jews, and few non-Jews, immediately after the Shoah, even though Jewish thinkers, such as Emil Fackenheim, hotly contested Sartre's position.

The powerful presence of the anti-Semitic past that turned Max into a Jew reappeared each time there was a stressful situation in his life. On June 17, 1953, there was a workers' revolt in East Berlin. This spontaneous reaction to the arbitrary rulings of the Central Committee was as close to a mass uprising as had yet been experienced in the GDR. Yet in the novel, Arno can only understand the agitation on the street "as the beginning of a pogrom." Here the anxiety that haunted Max surfaces in Jurek's text. What made it possible for Max to live in the GDR rather than in Poland was the clear and present control of German anti-Semitism by the military presence of the Soviet forces. Freedom from the threat of anti-Semitism, which Max yearned for, could only be accomplished by repression of the Germans among whom he and Jurek lived. The way he saw it, any uprising against the state augured the resurgence of anti-Semitism.

When he hears about the revolt, Arno runs to the school to "rescue" Mark, hides him in their apartment, and locks the doors (255). He then turns on the radio and listens first to broadcasts from the East and then to

those from the West. One announcer speaks of regrettable errors and calls
for peace and quiet; the other reports a people's rebellion and encourages
further resistance (255). "Eastern" readings of June 17, 1953, recorded
it as a counterrevolutionary putsch, while Western readings commem-
orated the date as a national holiday in remembrance of "our oppressed
bothers and sisters on the other side." Which version can you believe?
Neither, of course. None of the broadcasts spoke of a pogrom, but Arno
knew better. Max's radio, Jacob's radio, became Arno's radio.

Arno's mental instability is mirrored in his physical collapse. He develops massive stomach ulcers and eventually, close to death, is hospitalized.
This sequence reflects Jurek's concern with his father's alcoholism, which
clearly contributed to his death. Max had, in fact, been operated on for a
perforated ulcer in 1954. Jurek never could understand his father's flight
to the bottle. It seemed to him the absolute antithesis of the control over
the details of daily life that marked his own identity. Jurek's own anger,
quick to flare, was always over the inability to control life's unforeseeable
nature. That Max's drinking was his way of dealing with precisely that
same indeterminacy was lost on Jurek.

Mark stops boxing competitively, does reasonably well in school, and
decides to go to university to study mathematics, his weakest subject.
He begins to spend nights away from Arno, presumably with girlfriends,
some of whom he brings home. One day he simply does not return, and
Arno is at a loss. He does not know Mark's friends, is afraid to go the
university to ask about him, and sinks into a depressive, passive state.
Eventually a letter comes from Mark in Hamburg telling his father that
he has fled the GDR. Mark stresses that he has not abandoned his father.
He sees his father's loneliness as rooted in his inability to speak of his
experiences in the Shoah. Mark sees himself "educated to silence." Arno
has never told him anything he really thought or felt (284–85). Jurek, by
blaming the fictional father for lack of communication, was able to free
himself from the guilt he felt after Max's death for not having asked him
about what he had actually experienced.

Mark writes dozens of letters to Arno from all over the world, none
of which Arno answers. Eventually the letters begin to come from Israel,
the last one dated May 1967. Given the silence that follows, Arno believes that Mark has died in the Six Day War between Israel and its Arab
neighbors in June 1967.[7] In the GDR, the war prompted a radicalization
of anti-Zionist rhetoric, especially on the part of the official Jewish organizations. Israel was seen to be a tool of West Germany, since the FRG
had supplied weapons to the Israeli army.[8] An echo of this is to be found
in Arno's puzzlement about how Mark "became a Jew." Arno believes he

has shielded Mark from any sense of his own difference, his own Jewishness. "What made him into a Jew?" Judaism is a religion for Arno and one to which he does not belong. Can't a Catholic child decide not to be Catholic? he asks. Why then can't a Jewish child decide not to be Jewish? Arno can only understand Mark's desire to go to Israel as something he dreamed up, "from nothing." But he rejects the interviewer's desire that he find out what really happened to his son.

Before submitting it to a publisher, Jurek had given the manuscript of *The Boxer* to friends such as Klaus Poche to read.[9] In general their response was positive. The novel had its roots in a reaction to the sort of reportage written in the light of the Bitterfeld movement, the writing about and from the workplace that dominated GDR literature between 1959 and 1964. Jurek's contribution to this movement was a 1963 television documentary about miners and their production quotas titled *Good Morning Means Good Luck* (*Guten Morgen heißt Glückauf*), for which he wrote the voice-over script read by Günter Polensen. Kurt Hager, by that point the ideologue on the Central Committee dealing with cultural questions, formally modified the Bitterfeld movement in March 1972. One feature of this movement was the adaptation of the classic German *Bildungsroman* (novel of education) to the needs of GDR literary culture. The "education" was almost always, as in Dieter Noll's *Adventures of Werner Holt* (1963), from fascism to communism. *The Boxer* fits this mold as it also moves between the worlds of fascism and communism, now seen in the light of Jurek's "victim" status and his ambivalent relationship to the GDR. Nazi victims in the GDR not only were granted material privileges but were exempt from criticism. Jurek saw this as being "frozen out" (*kaltgestellt*) of the society in which he demanded to have a role. Speaking of his father, he once said that when you are isolated as a "victim of the Nazi regime," you are dead before you die. *The Boxer* is as much about the trauma of life *after* the Shoah as about the internalization of the trauma *of* the Shoah.

The political implications of a novel about a father's educating his son to become a citizen of the GDR was clear enough to its readers during the 1970s. Jurek's account of survivors as being permanently in transition, suffering from the total disruption of their lives, should have been paralleled by a healing process in the GDR, by a reintegration of the "victims of fascism" into socialist society. But such a society had no innate ability to "listen" to its members and thus to heal them. *The Boxer* was about the failure of the GDR to serve its most vulnerable citizens. It is not surprising that Mark, a good citizen of the GDR, educated to be internationalist and socialist, flees from the GDR and finds his way to Israel, where he dies as a Jew. Given the powerful anti-Zionism of the time, the conclusion to Mark's education is the strongest possible comment on the failure of education in the world of German socialism.

After *The Boxer* was published, Jurek traveled throughout the GDR giving readings from the novel. In October 1975 in Leipzig, it was received as a "Jewish" book. GDR reviewers registered this immediately. "The author returns to the theme of the Jewish survivor of World War II. This seems to be Jurek Becker's 'true turf': dealing with the history of a people endlessly tested by sorrow, a people that must suffer and be passive."[10] The conclusion of the novel, Jurek's claim that everyone needs to learn about his or her own problems of relating to others and to the state, is ignored. *The Boxer* is seen in the light of the popularity enjoyed by *Jacob the Liar*, both the novel and the film.

Certain Jewish themes, as in one of Jurek's favorite novels of the 1970s, Stefan Heym's *King David's Report* (1972), evoked contemporary politics in the GDR.[11] Heym's account of the court of the biblical David bears a striking resemblance to the "court politics" of "Berlin, the capital of the GDR." Heym himself, however, had not read *Jacob the Liar* as a "political" novel when it first appeared.[12] With *The Boxer*, such a reading was impossible to ignore. When Jurek was asked shortly before its appearance what he intended to accomplish with *The Boxer*, he answered that two of the problems addressed in the novel are the relationship of parents to their children and the demand of older people for tolerance. Tolerance was not, however, to be confused with the absence of criticism.[13] The absence of criticism is precisely something from which "victims of the Nazi regime" suffered. No one criticized them because they were beyond criticism. Jurek once said that exempting Jews from criticism because they are Jews is just as anti-Semitic as attacking them because they are Jews. He himself was never quite sure why his public—or the state—praised him and his work.

The Biermann Affair and Its Consequences

The political pressures being placed on Jurek as a member of the Berlin leadership of the Writers' Union increased immediately after the publication of *The Boxer*. In September 1976, Reiner Kunze's volume *The Wonderful Years* (*Die wunderbaren Jahre*) appeared in West Germany. While not the first of Kunze's books to appear in the West, this book was of a different sort. More than any other single work of the mid-1970s, it marked a shift into radical dissidence for many writers. Kunze, who was married to a Czech woman, had been a strong partisan of the Prague

Spring. In *The Wonderful Years* he attempted to come to terms with the political repression in the GDR, which limited all individual freedoms, especially the freedom of expression. The collapse of faith in the political system among the youth in the GDR he attributed to the march of the Warsaw Pact troops into Czechoslovakia. The problem of a socialist education and its role in creating "good" citizens (that is, passive and weak ones) was his major concern. He concluded the volume with a selection of *samisdat* poetry translated from the Czech, revealing the courage of those now occupied. This was no longer the voice of internal opposition. Kunze's work bore no sign that he believed the GDR capable of reforming itself and achieving its utopian promise. It was clearly a dissident book, as he noted in his own answer to the questions asked by his colleagues in the Writers' Union on October 20, 1976.[14]

The state responded in kind. Kunze was about to publish a book for children, *Leopold the Lion*. All 15,000 copies of the book were immediately destroyed. On October 29, 1976, Kunze was formally expelled from the Writers' Union at a meeting in Weimar. His expulsion—on the grounds that he had not held to the statutes of the Writers' Union about publication beyond the borders of the GDR—was officially announced in *Neues Deutschland* on November 6, 1976. Jurek visited him at his home in Greiz and declared his solidarity with him, condemning his expulsion but making it clear that he did not fully agree with his politics.[15]

On October 29, Jurek had been invited to read from *The Boxer* at the Jewish Community of Greater Berlin on Oranienburger Street. The head of the Jewish Community, the neurologist Peter Kirchner, had read the book and was taken by this "case study" of posttraumatic stress disorder.[16] Jurek therefore framed his reading with a discussion of the "camp syndrome" experienced by victims of the Shoah.[17] About fifty people from the Jewish Community were in the audience. In introducing Jurek, Peter Kirchner appealed to him to address another question before reading from the novel. Would he use the occasion to speak about Reiner Kunze? Jurek stated adamantly that unless Kunze was readmitted to the Writers' Union, he would resign. His pledge was greeted with loud applause. After his reading, Jurek said he was pleased with the response. He observed that he always accepted invitations to the Jewish Community because he was of Jewish descent.[18] *The Boxer* was heard that evening as linking the Jewish experience in the GDR with the oppositional experience, something that Jurek understood well.

Experimental or oppositional literature came under the gun in 1976. Whatever cultural thaw had existed under Honecker was succeeded by the older, Stalinist model. Harry Fauth had replaced Jurek's publisher,

Konrad Reich, as the head of Hinstorff Verlag after the Kunze affair. (Fauth was the Stasi operative "Buch" who reported on Jurek during this period.)[19] Even though he disagreed with Kunze on virtually every matter of substance concerning the possibility of a true socialist culture in an existing socialist state, Jurek opposed Kunze's expulsion as a matter of principle. His own privileged position as an internationally known writer and as one of the leaders of the cultural elite in the GDR provided, he fantasized, a platform from which he could influence such political decision-making. With this hope, Jurek wrote to his fellow leaders of the Writers' Union on November 8, 1976, calling Kunze's expulsion "an attempt to muzzle those writers who think about things in a substantially different way than do members of the leadership of the Writers' Union of the GDR." He added, "I write this letter not so much for Reiner Kunze as for myself."[20] Off the record, in a burst of anger, he again threatened to resign if Kunze was not reinstated.

As a result of the letter and reports about his deep dissatisfaction with the expulsion of Kunze, Jurek was ordered to appear before the Party Committee of the Writers' Union on Monday, November 15, 1976, from 3:00 to 6:00 P.M.—three hours, as he well knew, that would consist of more than a mere interview. Jurek was the only writer required to defend his position, although other leading writers, including Stephan Hermlin, Günter Kunert, and Franz Fühmann, had also protested the expulsion. In this interrogation, Jurek was repeatedly asked whether he had surreptitiously permitted his friend Wolf Biermann to announce Jurek's opposition to Kunze's expulsion. The focus seemed to be more on Jurek's relationship to Biermann than on his support of Kunze. Jurek was puzzled but responded that if he had intended to use an intermediary, he would have "chosen other means."[21] He also made it clear that Biermann had represented his views correctly.[22] Hermann Kant asked Jurek whether he would state for the record that Biermann did not speak for him. Jurek said that he would be happy to do so but would also be compelled to state, for the same public record, that he disagreed with Kunze's expulsion. While action against Jurek was contemplated, he asked the Party Committee to consider his public response to their criticism of his position concerning Kunze. They adjourned until November 22, 1976.

The rush of events precluded any further concern with Reiner Kunze. Kunze's expulsion from the Writers' Union and, hence, his loss of status as an "official writer" gave way to an action similar to the expulsion of Alexander Solzhenitsyn from the Soviet Union. While millions had fled the GDR before 1961, there had been no pattern of expulsion, especially of intellectuals whose interest was reforming state socialism. Those who

wanted to leave were often encouraged to do so, or else they seized op-
portunities to flee. After the building of the Berlin Wall, this freedom
was curtailed. Some dissident writers, like Christa Reinig, left the GDR
when they had the chance; others, like Erich Loest, were quietly exiled
only after they had served time in prison. Oppositional writers such as
Jurek had no interest in leaving the GDR. They were convinced that the
GDR was simply a state in need of reform and that it was a better country
and freer from the fascist past than the FRG.

Biermann had been close to Jurek since they were both students
(though not at the same time) at Humboldt University in the 1950s.
Both had lost a parent in the Nazi camps, Biermann his father, and Jurek
his mother. From 1965 on, Biermann had been condemned to a curious
limbo in the GDR.[23] His tapes and poems circulated, but he was forbidden to perform before the public. This interdiction had been prompted
by the publication of his volume of poems and ballads *The Wire Harp*
(*Die Drahtharfe*) by Klaus Wagenbach in West Berlin during 1965. The
volume was denounced by Klaus Höpcke, then cultural editor of *Neues
Deutschland*, in the crudest manner.[24] Biermann was not only a member
of the literary opposition but also a performer whose songs were accessible to the broadest possible public.[25] His poetry, unlike that of Sarah
Kirsch, Stephan Hermlin, Peter Huchel, or any other poet in the GDR
during the 1960s, was in the tradition of Bertolt Brecht's public performances as a singer in the 1920s.[26] Indeed, his first volume of poetry
included music for the songs. *Neues Deutschland* attacked Biermann as a
tool of Western imperialism and as an "anticommunist" who attacked in
"hateful verses" the "antifascist wall of protection." The West German
media also saw in Biermann (as they saw in other oppositional figures
such as Robert Havemann) a test case by which they could condemn the
impossibility of any freedom of expression, even among those who saw
themselves as presenting a "thoroughly communist critique."[27] Jurek had
been not only Biermann's friend but his public ally. Biermann had long
felt that Jurek and the social theorist Robert Havemann were the only
"real" communists in the GDR in that they wanted state socialism to
succeed in reforming itself.

In October 1965, Biermann was scheduled to appear at one of the
wildly popular "jazz and lyric" performances at the Haus der Lehrer
(Teachers' House) in Berlin. Jazz and folk music performances were, until
1965, the GDR's answer to the Beatles and rock and roll. Biermann,
Manfred Krug, Gerry Wolff, and Eva-Maria Hagen all performed under
the sponsorship of the FDJ (Free German Youth) groups. By the fall of
1965, Biermann was officially forbidden to do so, but as a sop he was given

a ticket for the evening show. Security people stopped him when he tried to go backstage to speak to the performers. He mentioned this to Jurek, who then went backstage himself and told Manfred Krug and the other performers about it. They all went down to the lobby, where they found Biermann surrounded by a cordon of Stasi agents in civilian dress. Krug and the others attempted to take Biermann into the auditorium but he was seized by the Stasi and taken to the central police station, where he was questioned. Realizing that the Stasi agents were unprepared, Biermann began to perform in front of them. This was something they were hardly expecting. He sang songs from his poetry collection *With Marx and Engels's Tongues* (*Mit Marx und Engelszunge*, published only in West Berlin in 1968). He also told them they were causing an outcry because the performance would not go on until he appeared. The audience, in which Jurek and his wife Rieke were seated, waited quietly for an hour for the performance to begin. Biermann was released but again forbidden from entering the theater. Finally, the show started, because the performers were threatened with "consequences" if they did not perform. This was Biermann's first direct confrontation with the Stasi in a public arena. His own "performances" thereafter were confined to his apartment and the homes of his friends.

In June 1974, Biermann was awarded the Jacques Offenbach Prize of the city of Cologne. Jurek, having accepted the Bremen Prize without overt intervention on the part of the state, had become an expert on Western prizes among the oppositional writers in the GDR. He attempted to intercede with Kurt Hager on Biermann's behalf to allow him to go to Cologne and receive the prize.[28] Jurek indicated that he was not an "advocate" of Biermann's political position but because of their personal friendship felt it was necessary to make the case for him.[29] Biermann's mentality, according to Jurek, predisposed him to acting in ways that would counter his own best interests as well as those of the state. The argument Jurek had used in *The Boxer*, of the impact of trauma on the citizens of the GDR, was now applied to oppositional writers. Repression creates trauma, and acting out creates further repression. The "healthy" response of the state would be to allow its citizens to act as if they were in control of their own lives.

When Biermann was approached by a spokesperson for the government on this matter, it was the first time he had spoken to any official for nine years. According to Kurt Löffler, state secretary in the Ministry of Culture, Biermann was forbidden to go to Cologne because "we don't let enemies of the GDR leave the GDR." Löffler added ominously that if Biermann "wanted to leave without permission to return, everything would be quickly arranged." Biermann replied that the official could "kiss his ass."[30] He would remain in the GDR. Needless to say, he was not permitted to go to Cologne. The official response to Jurek's plea on behalf of his friend was that no one wanted to deal with Wolf Biermann. The official concern was to "protect Jurek Becker from harm" because of his advocacy of Biermann.[31]

The consequences for Jurek were swift. At Kurt Hager's urging, Jurek had met with the renowned Swiss novelist Max Frisch in West Berlin in April 1973 and had invited him to read at the Writers' Union.[32] Frisch reciprocated by inviting Jurek to visit him in Switzerland. But Jurek's application in June 1974 to travel to Switzerland with his family in July was refused. Hager had put him on the list (*Sperrkartei*) of those permitted foreign travel only with his personal approval.[33] Jurek became one of the writers perceived as dangerous to the state. His "victim" status and his international reputation seemed to recede in importance.

After being banned from public performance for eleven years, Biermann appeared on September 11, 1976, in the Nikolai Church in Prenzlau. (He later claimed that his visit was tolerated because the Stasi confused him with a pastor there of the same name.) The Lutheran churches had become places where some opposition to the state could be tolerated, and the good atheist Wolf Biermann found his first audience since 1965 there.[34] Following this performance, the ruling party (the SED) bowed to enormous popular pressure from the IG Metall, the West German metal workers' union, to allow Biermann to go to West Germany in November 1976. On November 13, 1976, Biermann gave a concert in the *Sporthalle* in Cologne, which was broadcast on West German television and, of course, seen surreptitiously in East Berlin. His concert was the overt act that enabled the "rotten old men" (his words in a song) of the SED to banish him. The power of his performance was linked to the oppositional message. Poetry read by the elite is much less dangerous than songs or films that reach the masses. The leadership of the SED announced that because Biermann was born in Hamburg (that is, in the FRG), his permission for him to remain in the GDR had been rescinded. Truly scurrilous accounts of his sexual life began to circulate to the media.

In September, Jurek had accepted an invitation to speak and read at a number of venues in the university town of Jena in November.[35] On November 16, just one day after his interrogation by the Writer's Union Party Committee, he traveled to Jena to read from *The Boxer* at one of the major bookstores in the city.[36] He began to read at 7:30 P.M., and in the break received a call from Rieke: she had seen on Western TV that Biermann's citizenship had been revoked while he was in Cologne. At first Jurek didn't believe it. Shaken, Jurek returned to his audience and told them of Biermann's banishment; he said that "a vast barrel has been tapped."[37] He did not close an eye that night, struggling with the question of how he should respond to the expulsion of a friend he had known since 1957.[38]

The next day he was to give two further readings in Jena, at the Carl Zeiss optics factory and at the Peoples' Bookstore at the Holzmarkt. At Zeiss he discussed *The Boxer* with twenty-four people, mainly technical workers.[39] The authorities were much more worried about the larger public reading. It was abruptly moved from the bookstore to a small room, which was quickly packed, with people standing outside in the hall. The bookstore windows, full of copies of Jurek's novel, were emptied just as quickly. Jurek informed his audience that he had been ordered to read only from *The Boxer* or else the event would be stopped. He went on, however, to tell the crowd that Stephan Hermlin had called him at his hotel that morning, asking for his support for a letter to be sent to the party leadership, protesting Biermann's expulsion. It was signed by eleven major literary figures in addition to Jurek: Volker Braun, Christa Wolf, Sarah Kirsch, Stefan Heym, Franz Fühmann, Stephan Hermlin, Gerhard Wolf, Heiner Müller, Rolf Schneider, Erich Arendt, and Günter Kunert. The letter demanded that Biermann, "an uncomfortable writer," be permitted to return to the GDR on grounds of Marxist openness to self-criticism. He should be allowed to return even though the signatories to the letter might not agree with Biermann's "every word and every action" or the West's use of the affair to undermine the GDR.[40] Jurek's position was clear to the audience.

A student jumped to his feet and told Jurek that many present in the audience applauded Biermann's expulsion. Taken aback, Jurek responded ironically that even though he disagreed with her, he would not demand that she be expelled from the GDR because of her advocacy of Biermann's expulsion. This reply garnered boos from the audience. Jurek then read from *The Boxer*. After the reading a young man asked a question concerning what seemed to him the central theme of the novel—the education of the youth of the GDR. Had not Reiner Kunze addressed this topic in a book that was available only in the FRG? Jurek made a careful distinction between his own project and Kunze's. He saw Kunze's project as one-sided and not completely accurate. Yet he stood behind Kunze's right to write and publish his work in the GDR. The response of his listeners was that Jurek's and Kunze's projects were similar because both were attempts to understand the passivity of East German youth vis-à-vis the Warsaw Pact invasion that had destroyed the Prague Spring.[41] Sitting in the audience was a Colonel Lehmann of the Stasi in Jena, who sent an internal telegram summarizing Jurek's statements to Erich Mielke, chief of the Stasi in Berlin.[42] Jurek was a major figure in the cultural world of the GDR. The Academy Award nomination for the film of *Jacob the Liar* meant that Jurek's support of Biermann (and Kunze) would have international echoes beyond West Germany.

Jurek did not want to be heard as a dissident voice. That same day he decided he would attempt a mediating role and might actually have Biermann readmitted. (Stefan Heym viewed this as a pipe dream.[43]) He still believed strongly that the state might make wrong decisions but was not inherently corrupt. He informed the leadership of the Writers' Union that he was prepared to call Biermann in Cologne.[44] He would tell him that no one wanted his expulsion and that if Biermann himself declared his desire to return to the GDR, he would make it possible for the leadership of the GDR to rethink his case. Jurek did call Biermann a number of times in Cologne, but Biermann's sole response was that he was pleased with the support from his friends in the GDR. Jurek's offer to serve as an official mediator was totally unacceptable to the SED; he was simply not trusted to be an honest broker.[45] When he returned to Berlin that evening, he began to call a number of left-wing writers and intellectuals in the FRG to garner support for Biermann. He failed to realize that the authorities had absolutely no interest in doing anything but punish those they viewed as opposing the GDR's goals.

On November 23, 1976, 130 members of the Berlin Writers' Union met to condemn the action of the signatories to the letter in support of Biermann. The official charge was that the signatories had released the letter to the Western media against the interests of the government of the GDR. Jurek was viewed by some of those present as the angriest and most aggressive advocate for any type of action.[46] Arguing that there had to be a unified response of all writers in support of Biermann, he was seen as the ringleader of the group. In response to a question, he referred to his own response to Biermann when Biermann had asked him what he would do if Biermann were not readmitted to the GDR after his appearance in Cologne. Jurek had said, "You have to be kidding. If that actually happens, I'll stand on my head." Jurek regarded his signature as publicly "standing on his head."[47] According to "Adler," an IM (or unofficial Stasi agent), the "politically naive Hermlin managed to shield himself from any repercussions and passed the buck to Jurek Becker."[48] Jurek was seen as moving away from the party line even more sharply than Hermlin, who had been considered the ringleader of the pro-Biermann group.[49]

On November 26, the party organization of the Writers' Union met once again. Jurek kept interrupting the meeting. He disrupted the speech by Gerhard Branstner condemning the letter, calling him a liar. At the end of the evening he again interrupted the concluding remarks of Konrad Naumann, first secretary of the Berlin party organization. At the meeting, Roland Bauer commented that Jurek seemed more flexible and less angry in private, and it is true that Jurek felt there was a space, in private, for compromise.[50] The public meeting, no doubt, reminded him of a show trial. Unlike Slansky and Merker, who remained quiet during their trials, Jurek was certainly not going to do so.

At the end of the evening, the vote was 107 in favor of condemning Biermann's supporters and 6, including Jurek's, against.[51] Not only did the state act in its own vested interest, but its "intellectuals" rubber-stamped its action. Stefan Heym was prescient. The Writers' Union repeated the actions of Soviet writers after Alexander Solzhenitsyn's expulsion. On the same day Robert Havemann, the leading oppositional intellectual, was sentenced to house arrest for his published protest of Biermann's expulsion in the West German magazine *Der Spiegel*.

Biermann's fate had been decided at the highest levels of the SED leadership, by Erich Honecker himself. The letter of support for Biermann bore close to one hundred signatures by November 19, 1976. This powerful lobby quickly crumbled as the signatories, informed that their support would hamper their careers, began to withdraw their advocacy or to modify their positions in print. Honecker must have been delighted. The discussion of the letter about Biermann in the Berlin Writers' Union had gone exactly as he had hoped. He saw the situation as better than expected, given the number of major writers opposed to expulsion. However, in the account presented to him, only one writer was labeled "arrogant and exaggerated" and that was Jurek. Honecker himself suggested that Jurek "be expelled from the Writers' Union, which should be done democratically." "Democratically" in this case meant by the organization in the form of a public trial, all too reminiscent of the anti-Semitic trials that had marked the opening decade of the cold war in the Eastern bloc. Jurek was to be given a chance to publicly "confess" before being expelled.[52]

As Manfred Krug shows in his notes to the transcription of the secret tapes he made before his own more or less voluntary exile from the GDR, Jurek was beginning to take a unique position on the margins of both the GDR hierarchy and oppositional society.[53] He was the most vocal proponent of a position that required the GDR to change so as to fit his own notion of a socialist state. His view was radical and demanded a public discussion of aspects of the Biermann affair that most other oppositional writers, and certainly the representatives of the state authorities, viewed as a private matter within the cultural and political elite. During the secretly recorded session with Werner Lamberz, head of the division for agitation and propaganda in the Central Committee, at Manfred Krug's home on November 20, Jurek unequivocally demanded that Biermann be allowed to return to the GDR, contending that no compromise was possible.[54] He reasoned that Biermann must be permitted to return for the good of the state.

Jurek's position was becoming ever more isolated. Max Frisch, who came from West Berlin to visit Jurek on December 3, was concerned but seemed strangely distant from the turmoil that was taking place in Jurek's life. Stefan Heym joined them and began to explain what had happened to up to that point. Frisch made it clear that he and other writers and intellectuals in the West could offer good will but little more. His sense of his own impotence made his visit rather sad. Jurek, Heym, and later Krug and Beyer, who joined them after Frisch left, sensed that the opposition in the GDR was quite alone.[55]

On December 6, 1976, Roland Bauer again confronted Jurek. He asked him directly if he would follow the guidelines of the party and the Writers' Union concerning Biermann. Jurek's answer was equally clear; if he agreed, he would be a hypocrite. Everything he had been saying since November would have been a lie. "If I say yes, you will ask me: 'Then why have you been saying what you've been saying all this while?' " If he said no, he knew he would be expelled from the party. He was acutely aware of the sudden distance between the wishes of the state and his own position.[56] He realized the brutality of the jargon that the state had used to control its writers, for it was now directed at him. Eva-Maria Hagen, Biermann's former girlfriend, described Jurek sitting in Biermann's apartment, thin lipped, mocking himself by mimicking the party jargon.[57] In totalitarian states, language was never free of the infiltration of power, as Viktor Klemperer had shown in the late 1940s.

The next day, December 7, 1976, Jurek defended himself and the other signatories to the letter in a public meeting of the Writers' Union. He stated that he was unwilling to accept the majority decision of the Union. He could not see how releasing the letter to the foreign press had given comfort to the West. To circulate the letter in the GDR would have made no sense as Biermann's expulsion had already been announced in the official organ, *Neues Deutschland*. What else was there to do? Jurek understood that his political stance was consistent with his calling: "The inherent wish to present opinions and convictions to the public is what moved me to become a writer."[58] His position was fixed. He could not change his mind on political issues without abandoning the role of writer that now defined him.

The initial proposal on the floor of the meeting had been that Jurek, Stephan Hermlin, and Christa Wolf only be condemned for their actions rather than expelled from the party as was recommended for others. Honecker's intent to expel Jurek was modified through the mediation of Klaus Höpcke, now the deputy minister of culture and (since 1973) the chief censor in the GDR, as well as that of his boss Kurt Hager, the ideological arbiter in the Politburo. Höpcke, who was in charge of publishing, liked to call himself the "minister for books." The plan was to allow Jurek to admit his guilt; he would then have his wrist slapped by being "condemned," but he could continue to write and publish in the GDR. It was Jurek's "megalomania, exaggerated sense of self, and stupidity" (according to the official account) that dominated the evening.[59] His vociferous, caustic, and aggressive defense of Gerhard Wolf led him to be expelled, as Wolf was. Before he stood up to speak, he whispered to Wolf, "Just wait," implying that they would throw him out too.[60] He spoke passionately about how he felt a public airing of the Biermann affair was needed so that the nation itself could heal, and how relevant this issue was to his belief that the role of the writer had to be a public one. Among the more than one hundred members present, only eight votes opposed Jurek's expulsion, including (one assumes) his own. He returned home exhausted, deep rings around his eyes, but convinced that any compromise would have destroyed his own moral position.[61] His anxiety was not unfounded. On December 8, the poet Frank Schöne had been sentenced to two and a half years in prison for actions against the state.

Two weeks later, Jurek was removed from the leadership of the Berlin chapter of the Writers' Union. This action infuriated him because he believed he could only be removed by not being reelected at the end of his term. The rule of law had been flouted. Things were going from bad to worse. In February 1977, at a meeting of the party leadership of the Writers' Union, he was accused (in his absence) of being a "counterrevolutionary."[62] On March 31, 1977, rather than wait for the official notice of his expulsion, Jurek sent a letter of resignation to the Writers' Union. Given the election of a new leadership that would clearly not act to change the expulsion of the six members who had supported Biermann, he had no choice but to resign.[63] The results of becoming a "nonperson in the GDR" were clear: he would be a pariah.

Jurek felt victimized. By not playing by the established rules, the GDR was acting like the Nazis. The attitude toward him he perceived as proof of German anti-Semitism. As early as April 1977, Jurek began to label the entire set of events around Biermann as a pogrom. He was recorded as complaining that in "the GDR at present a great anti-Semitic campaign was taking place." His new book, *The Boxer*, "would show how there were anti-Semitic tendencies in the GDR. These also existed in the People's Republic of Poland"[64] (as Jurek was well aware, because of the various Polish responses to the attempts to film *Jacob the Liar*). And herein was the irony: even though every single biographical document in the official account noted Jurek's Jewish heritage and his history as a "victim of the Nazi regime," none of the official or even unofficial statements about his past during the Biermann affair echoed the pernicious anti-Semitism present in the earlier material. Only when there was talk of Jurek's leaving the GDR in August 1977 was it assumed that he would immigrate to Israel because he was a "Jew"[65] (the word is in quotation marks in the Stasi report). That Jews were seen as dangerous because of their "international connections" was something of which many Jewish writers in the GDR, such as Stephan Hermlin and Stefan Heym, were well aware.[66] Jurek had simply become a "Liar" (as the Stasi dubbed him) to the authorities. He had become one of the dissidents, like Havemann or Biermann, and that identity trumped his "Jewish" identity.

At the same time that Jurek was struggling with his role in the intellectual and political world of the GDR, his private world was falling apart. His wife, Rieke, and his sons, Nicki and Lonni, were becoming alienated from him as he focused on his career and his political activities. At thirty-nine, he was entering into what he had described in *Misleading the Authorities* as the uncomfortable period of early success and midlife discontent. His home was still full of artists, actors, and writers, and his family shared his political views. He watched Western television and read Western newsmagazines that often featured him. His home was also clearly middle-class. The economic success of his novels abroad allowed him to buy in stores open only to those with Western currency. And he bought not only cigarettes, alcohol, candy, and the like but also appliances such as a lawnmower and an electric hedge clipper.[67] Middle-class culture became a sign of dissident activity in the GDR. Jurek bought Western popular records and posters for Nicki, whose tenth grade school report mentions these acquisitions as a sign that he was beginning to follow in his father's footsteps.[68] Indeed, Nicki seemed to have "outbreaks of temper" against fellow students even though he was active in the FDJ and well liked. (This description reminds us of the young Georg as a schoolchild.)

Nicki attended the Alexander von Humboldt high school in Köpenick, where he was a friend of Stefan Heym's son. As Nicki recalls it, both boys rather enjoyed being the target of their teachers. After Biermann was denied readmittance into the GDR, the children of those who supported him received intense Stasi attention. "Stefan Heym's son is at the Humboldt High School Köpenick. He has stated that his father signed the petition to the government. The students took no position. He was not hostile to us. No pressure was applied to him. In this school there is also Niklas [Nikolaus] Becker, the son of Georg Jurek [Becker], as well as Katharina Schneider, the daughter of Rolf Schneider. Both children are factual and politically correct in their conversations."[69] As Nicki's views grew increasingly critical, however, his teachers suspected Jurek's influence. The family was simply not trusted. When one of Nicki's teachers came to the Beckers' home to speak with Jurek and Rieke about their son, she spied a Western book on antiauthoritarian education on Jurek's desk. Jurek asked her if she wanted to borrow it; she said yes, and so he lent it to her. A few days later, when he was summoned to the party secretary of the Writers' Union, his book was lying on the secretary's desk. The teacher had immediately turned it over to him. Jurek was accused of distributing Western books to the detriment of the state.

The frequent arguments between Jurek and Rieke focused on Jurek's inability to listen, to understand, or to tolerate anything that he did not see as right. On the floor of the Writers' Union these qualities seemed very positive; at home they became more and more destructive. Twice Rieke demanded that things change or else she would divorce him. Jurek could not see why she was so angry. During the extreme tension that Jurek was experiencing professionally at the beginning of 1977, another fight broke out between Rieke and Jurek. For the third time, Rieke threatened divorce. Jurek, at a loss, agreed to a divorce. Although Rieke was taken aback, and initially objected, the couple filed for divorce in the midst of Jurek's involvement in the Biermann affair.

The divorce was granted on April 4, 1977, on grounds of mutual incompatibility. Rieke retained custody of both minor children.[70] Jurek accepted financial responsibility for his sons; the GDR had no provision for alimony or child support. The impact of the divorce on the family was recorded immediately. Nicki was reported to be "difficult in relation to his fellow students." He had been "raised by his parents" to be critical and "self-aware."[71] These traits were seen as character flaws.

Jurek wanted to move out of the family house as early as April 19, 1977, into an apartment owned by the actress Marita Böhme and used by her as a pied-à-terre when she was in Berlin. It was not until September, however, that he finally moved into the apartment, still leaving most of his things at home. His relationship with Rieke and his sons had not changed substantially, except that his absences meant less friction. Yet in November he happily celebrated his fortieth birthday at the family home, surrounded by friends, family, and the Stasi.[72] Many of his acquaintances at the time thought his political bellicosity was linked to his personal situation.[73] The GDR, and especially the officers of the Stasi, saw "egocentrism, curiosity, and self-esteem" as negative qualities that violated the notion of what a true citizen of the GDR should be.[74] The close connection seen between Jurek's private and his public experiences, it was rumored, was prompting Jurek to leave the GDR after his divorce.[75] Jurek stated more than once, however, that the real reason for his departure was the refusal of the authorities in the GDR to publish his next book.

Sleepless Days

During the previous year, Jurek had been writing his fourth novel, provisionally entitled "Living in the Air." Eventually published on March 1, 1978, as *Sleepless Days* (*Schlaflose Tage*), it was Jurek's first book not published in the GDR. This work's fate reflects the final stage of Jurek's relationship to the GDR. The novel recounts the life of Simrock, a high school teacher of German. Jurek ironically borrows the name of the early-nineteenth-century scholar and poet Karl Simrock, whose works formed a self-consciously apolitical (even antipolitical) answer to the writings of pre-1848 revolutionaries. Among such revolutionaries was the critic Georg Herwegh, whose poetry was widely taught in the schools of the GDR.

At the opening of the novel, shortly after his thirty-sixth birthday, Simrock believes he is having a heart attack. His illness, as he well knows, is a reflection of his unhappiness: "health . . . was not nearly so important for happiness as illness was for unhappiness, and he was unhappy" (4).[76] He is unhappy with his family, with his wife, Ruth, and his daughter, Leonie. He is unhappy with his job teaching high school literature. But there is more. "He was often seized by a discontent that he considered unproductive because, instead of making him face up to its causes, it inevitably turned into self-pity" (7). He feels compelled to deal with his relationship with Ruth. His life with her has subsided into bourgeois comfort. At the beginning of their marriage they all lived in one room; now they have a comfortable apartment. But this is part of the problem. "My marriage is an accomplished fact, my profession laid down. When I look at both my marriage and my teaching career, I have the feeling that both follow rules established without my having been consulted"

(19). Simrock realizes that he has to change his life. He seeks solace first in alcohol, getting drunk every evening. Eventually he asks Ruth for a separation, and a divorce follows. Then he meets a young divorcee, Antonia Kramm, at a dance, and he moves into her apartment.

At school, things are not going well. The principal informs him that he is in trouble because he has told the students that they can choose whether or not to go to the May Day demonstration. Simrock says that this is the official school policy. But the principal knows that Simrock is well aware that all students have to go to all demonstrations. It is an involuntary form of voluntarism. Simrock responds that he will inform the students that their participation is obligatory and that if they have any questions they should take them to the principal. "Like hell you will," answers the principal (44).

Simrock sees his failure as a teacher as the refusal to engage his students and make them question authority, even his own (46–47). He demands autonomy to teach what he believes is right "when his opinions diverge from those that the curriculum requires him to present" (47). He requests that the school free him of all duties over the summer, and he looks for a "real" job (62–63). He finds one at a bakery, where he first has to work shoveling coal (although the ovens are heated by gas) for no reason other than the brutal foreman's resentment of an intellectual. He is eventually rescued by a young driver, Boris, whose "dream was to see Liverpool" (75) and who appoints him his "helper" even though he does not need one. Simrock begins to realize that the society he is in does not want people to do their jobs well, only to act according to their job descriptions.

After a month at the bakery, Simrock leaves with Antonia for vacation in Hungary. He takes with him Max Frisch's *Sketchbook* ("smuggled through customs by his Heidelberg cousin" [86]) and Hermann Kant's *Impressum*, another work that had earlier discomfited the authorities in the GDR. Communist Hungary seems to parody the GDR, as in a fun-house mirror. Simrock recounts two incidents. In the first, a German tourist tries to withdraw money from his German bank account. The check is in his wife's name, and the clerk at the Hungarian bank refuses to cash it. She then advises him to forge his wife's signature, and compares his various attempts to see which is close enough before giving him the money (84–85). In the second incident, Simrock finds himself seated at a table in a restaurant with two elderly Hungarian women who take him for a West German. He begins to act out in this role, claiming that "the Jews and gypsies were beginning to make themselves heard again" (87). Rather than object, they look with some pride on this young man "who at last had the courage to speak his mind" (87). Hungary is not a workers' paradise; it is a corrupt and fascist state disguised as "real existing socialism."

On a whim, Antonia uses the trip to Hungary to attempt an escape to Austria. Standing at the border, she thinks she can simply walk over to Austria. She is captured because, to her amazement, the border guards do not shoot but, instead, outrun her. Simrock suddenly realizes that she has acted on her own, not trusting him with the knowledge of her desire to flee (91). After she is returned under guard to the GDR, Simrock follows her. His carefully smuggled copy of Frisch's book is seized as he crosses the border. Antonia is sentenced to one year and seven months in prison. Her actions make Simrock rethink his own passivity.

In the autumn, a further complaint is lodged against Simrock at school. He has had the temerity to teach Bertolt Brecht's poem "In Praise of Doubt." (Brecht was, of course, the most important contemporary writer in the literary canon of the GDR.) One of the parents has complained that he wants his son to be taught to believe, not to doubt, even though the poem is by a famous GDR poet (97). On another occasion, a young army lieutenant who has come to give a recruiting talk is given the third degree by Simrock, who questions him about his obligations, the limitations on his freedom of actions, and his individual beliefs (116–17). Simrock is suspended from teaching and reapplies for his job at the bakery as Boris's helper, an unnecessary job but one for which he now seems best suited. Eventually the superintendent of schools offers him a deal: he can return to teaching if he agrees to teach only what is on the official syllabus, with no changes whatever. "Simrock sipped his coffee and felt that once again a decision had been made for him" (129). He refuses, demanding an apology from the school system for dismissing him. As he returns to the waiting delivery truck, Simrock spies an ambulance, which reminds him of the heart attack he thought he was having at the beginning of the novel. It is not a happy ending but, rather, the promise that the pain in Simrock's heart, an existential pain of knowing that he does not fit the world he lives in, can be ameliorated by an awareness of the daily compromises that have corrupted him. What causes the pain is not Sartre's sense of the existential nature of human life as incorporated in a feeling of nausea, but the brutal reality of the quotidian life of the GDR.

In employing the schoolroom as a metaphor for the problems of obedience and creativity in the GDR, Jurek was using some of the material that he had already explored in early 1970s.[77] Frank Beyer had then approached him with the idea of writing a screenplay based on Alfred Wellm's novel *Recess for Wanzka* (*Pause für Wanzka*, 1968).

Wellm's novel tells the story of a headstrong mathematics teacher, Gustav Wanzka, who returns to the classroom after years of administrative work. He discovers that the rules he helped make are now inhibiting his teaching. His own innovative instruction in mathematics causes trouble with the other teachers, as his students spend more and more time on his subject and less and less on theirs. The novel is a clear criticism of the existing school system in the GDR. Although Beyer and Jurek completed the screenplay, the film was never approved because Margot Honecker— Erich Honecker's wife, who had been the minister for public education in the GDR since 1963—hated the novel and managed to prevent its being filmed. But Wellm's image of a teacher out to reform education as the key to remaking the socialist state remained with Jurek.

With *Sleepless Nights*, a new pattern appeared in Jurek's fiction. On the surface, his narratives seem to alternate between his two set themes: a Jewish one about life after the Shoah, and a socialist one about life in an existing socialist state. As we have already seen, the themes constantly merge. The relationship of parents to children, of husbands to wives, of citizens to the power of the state, are present in all Jurek's work. His Jewish novels and short stories, which form the most important set of literary texts on the Shoah written by a survivor-author in German, are as much concerned with the socialist state and its promises as are his "GDR" novels. Even in his final novel, *Amanda Heartless* (*Amanda Herzlos*, 1992), the "private sphere" of marriage and personal relationships and the "public sphere" of politics and history overlap each other and structure the novel. Writing "Jewish" texts amounts to writing about a world of private relationships in a complex political context. Here Jurek is a model for other German Jewish writers of the 1980s and 1990s, such as Barbara Honigmann, the daughter of Jurek's former boss at the Thistle and DEFA, who left the GDR for France to find a Jewish community, or the working-class novelist Esther Dischereit, who was born and remained in the West. In very different ways, these writers use the situation of the Jews after the Shoah as case studies for the "human condition." Jews' writing in German about Jews became relatively common, but nearly all these texts are about the impact of the Shoah on the non-Jewish world that the Jewish characters inhabit.

Sleepless Days, like *Misleading the Authorities*, creates an analogy between the breakdown of a marriage and the state of living in the GDR. When he had finished *Sleepless Days*, Jurek thought the novel, with its potentially "happy ending," was flawed because he had compromised.[78] After *Sleepless Days* had circulated, other works using this metaphor appeared, to the disapproval of the state. Armin Müller-Stahl starred in

Frank Beyer's film *Closed Society* (*Geschlossene Gesellschaft*) in 1978. Written by Jurek's old collaborator Klaus Poche (half of the writing team of "Georg Nikolaus"), it was made for GDR television.[79] Unlike *Sleepless Days*, whose publication was suppressed, *Closed Society* was actually shown in the GDR, though only once, in 1978. Broadcast at the crack of dawn to preclude the charge of censorship, it then disappeared into the vaults of the TV studio, resurfacing in 1990. The film describes the collapse of a marriage because of growing isolation, distrust, and inability to communicate. The action takes place as the family is on vacation in an isolated cabin. The couple's young son is drawn into the conflict. The political implications of Klaus Poche's script were transparent to the officials of GDR television.

Jurek discussed his completed manuscript of *Sleepless Days* with Horst Simon, the new editor-in-chief at Hinstorff, on June 13, 1977. (The final title was decided in September, after considerable discussion about the publishability of the manuscript.) Jurek made it clear to Simon that he was willing to make minor stylistic adjustments but no substantial alterations. He saw the novel as a litmus test for his future role in the culture of the GDR, and he was proved right. He wanted a first edition of between 50,000 and 70,000 copies, the same as for the most recent novels of Christa Wolf and Hermann Kant.[80] On the day he met Simon, he also gave a copy of the manuscript to his schoolfriend Helge Braune to send to Elisabeth Borchers at Suhrkamp, in the West. Calling Borchers to check whether it had arrived, Jurek told her that Hinstorff had four weeks to make up its mind. If it rejected the book, he would sign a contract with Suhrkamp.[81] Suhrkamp did eventually publish the novel in March 1978.

On June 16, 1977, Jurek was asked to substitute for Stefan Heym, who had been invited by a pastor, Dr. Schulze, to read at his church in Berlin-Bohnsdorf. Jurek apologized to his audience, who had expected Heym, invoking Columbus, who had expected India and discovered America. He then read three chapters from the manuscript of *Sleepless Days* to about 180 listeners, most of whom were under forty and identified strongly with Simrock. The questions they asked focused on the role of the teacher and the writer as interchangeable categories in the GDR. Jurek confessed that in the past he was "just as opportunistic and dishonest as most of today's writers and skipped past the real difficulties" in his earlier novels.[82] His comments were received with much applause. Later the local city council made a formal complaint to the church that the event was a "counterrevolutionary action." Jurek, according to the complaint, was "well known as someone working against the best interests of the

GDR." In the future, it was strongly advised, the church had better check with the appropriate authority before inviting such speakers.[83]

The manuscript submitted to Hinstorff took a new, though not surprising, path, given Jurek's new status as a dissident. In June 1977, the Stasi received a "reading" of Jurek's manuscript from Käthe Krieg, writing under the pseudonym "Monika." It was a police report on a novel. Krieg saw Simrock as having his head full of antisocialist clichés. She said the novel claimed that socialism suppressed the free development of a personality and created a "schizophrenic" response "in both thought and reactions." There was a total rejection of the structure of socialist society. While the style and narrative stance reminded Krieg of *Misleading the Authorities*, this new book was a more political. Jurek, she alleged, had transparently used the school system as an example of the failure of the state. It was depicted as a system "in which no person can be honest."[84] Needless to say, the general sense of her report was that the manuscript should never be published in the GDR.

In all the discussions concerning the novel, Jurek emphasized that he wanted to be published in the GDR.[85] He wanted to remain a socialist author, and the only way to do so was to be published in the GDR. On July 8, 1977, Klaus Höpcke, Jurek's contact person in the government, talked to Kurt Hager, the literary arbiter in the Politburo, about *Sleepless Days*. Hinstorff, following the Stasi reports, now thought it impossible to publish the work because the entire source of the character's malaise was attributed to his experiences in the socialist state. Publication within the GDR would support the dissident claims of the past few months that opposition played an integral and permanent role in the state. Jurek's threat to publish in the West was a form of blackmail against Hinstorff since a rejection would be used by the West for an "anti-GDR campaign."[86] Only revision of the manuscript would make it acceptable to the GDR, said Höpcke. The revision would have to eliminate any suggestion that the state represses its writers by coercing them or by seducing them into avoiding confrontation with the burning issues of day-to-day life in the GDR.

By the middle of July the "official" recommendations for Hinstorff had arrived in Rostock. On the one hand, the GDR author Gerhard Branstner, whom Jurek had called a "liar" in the meeting that got him expelled from the Writers' Union, stressed the "clumsy language" and "superficiality of thought" as well as the "superficial problem" of teachers. He strongly urged rejection of the manuscript. (Branstner was the Stasi operative "Friedrich" who also reported on Jurek's activities.)[87] On the other hand,

Professor Dieter Schlenstedt of Humboldt University saw the book as containing a "series of complex questions" with the "clear intention to intervene in the public sphere." He too found the writing "not well done," "but the quality of the form reflects the problem in the text." Like most of the readers at this stage, he saw the manuscript as a variant of the central problem in *Misleading the Authorities*. There was an "autobiographical moment of self-criticism," but Schlenstedt also recognized that there had been a "radicalization since 1973." While the text read "more like the first draft of a book," he argued that the publishing house should "allow it to be published, since it would appear anyway."[88] The readers' reports were sent to Höpcke, who discussed them on July 19, 1977, with the representatives of Hinstorff, including Harry Fauth. Fauth would see Jurek the next day, but many other events were simultaneously taking place.

Jurek had agreed to meet with reporters from the major West German newsmagazine, *Der Spiegel*, in early July. On July 18, 1977, the interview was published. Discussing the wide spectrum of events in East Berlin, Jurek stated rather boldly that the government's actions were clearly repressive in case of Biermann, but that these actions resulted from misjudgment. There were writers, he noted, for whom the usual mechanism of repression had become impossible to deal with. "I am one of them," he said. One could no longer provide rationales for the party's actions. "In my country," he commented, "there is not a press, radio, or TV that is free in the Western sense." Everyone, he said somewhat later, knew that "life in the GDR is full of fictions, on both private and state levels. For example, the authorities in the GDR assume that the inhabitants of the GDR are sufficiently informed by the GDR television, radio, and press. They act as if they were sole arbiters of public opinion; they act as if the GDR public oriented themselves through them. Those paradoxes are real. When the press announces something in the GDR that has already been announced in the West, they act as if that information had simply not been available before."[89] Jurek also deplored the fact that in the GDR there was no uncensored literature. Literature, he declared, "is of much greater importance in terms of content than the media." The work of the writer is to tell the ultimate truth.[90]

Many people were now raising the question whether Jurek would remain in the GDR. On July 19, 1977, the GDR novelist Joachim Seyppel wrote an open letter to Jurek in the West German *Frankfurter Rundschau* asking him to remain in the GDR. Seyppel felt that he could approach Jurek only by using the Western media. This was risky, as he knew that the supporters of Wolf Biermann had been condemned for publishing their letter in the West.[91] Seyppel had attempted to have his letter published in East Berlin (as he had attempted to receive some official explanation for Biermann's expulsion) but to no avail. Clearly his words had more power coming from the West than they would have done in a personal letter. He noted that Jurek seemed unable to publish his most recent novel in the GDR, but concluded that "this land would be poorer if you left it." Seyppel lamented that Jurek had been forced out of the Writers' Union and that rumors had him already emigrating to Israel or to the FRG.

Günter Kunert answered Seyppel's "open letter" in the conservative West German newspaper *Die Welt.* Kunert had survived in hiding from the Nazis as a child and was one of the "victims of Nazi persecution" who had chosen to leave the GDR during the Biermann affair. He observed that the official labeling of Jurek as "counterrevolutionary" showed how much the language of power in the GDR had deformed the medium of the writer.[92] Jurek had become the focus of interest. Unlike many of the writers involved in the Biermann affair, Jurek's personal history and the massive success of his work meant that Jurek himself had become a cause célèbre. In complicated ways Jurek's success reinforced his own sense of privilege. Seyppel's open letter to Jurek, however, signals two things: first that the role Jurek was playing was assumed to be leading to his departure from the GDR, and second that Jurek's Jewish identity, so very clear to Seyppel, remained a factor in his public image in the GDR. That Seyppel would have heard a rumor about Jurek's emigrating to Israel showed that this personal history was closely connected to the fantasy of the Jew (read: Zionist) as counterrevolutionary in the GDR.

On July 20, 1977, during the heightened discussion about his status in the GDR, Jurek met with Harry Fauth of Hinstorff to discuss the reader's reports. Fauth promised him that Hinstorff would publish the novel if changes were made. Turning the manuscript down, he knew, would only add fuel to the author's anger and help Suhrkamp to sell the novel as a censored book.[93] A list of specifics, which had been drawn up by Höpcke and Fauth, might, if followed, make the novel publishable in the GDR. Jurek had to revise this manuscript in light of the government's political suggestions. He had to omit all mention of the wall and the border. He had to drop his call for change in the actual structure of the state. According to Fauth, the publisher believed the story to be "aesthetically weak." On the basis of this meeting, Jurek agreed to go to Rostock on August 9–10, after returning from vacation with his family in Zingst, to discuss the manuscript. Fauth also suggested an initial print run of 15,000 copies; Jurek wanted 30,000 in the first year. He was beginning to believe that

a compromise on the nuances of the content was possible. He therefore
promised that on his proposed reading tour in the FRG he would read
only from his published books.[94]

On August 8, 1977, Jurek met with Deputy Minister Höpcke concerning the *Spiegel* interview. The minister intimated that he was pleased
with the position that Jurek took with respect to the public discussion of
the Biermann affair in the context of a West German publication. Again
on the basis of what seemed to Jurek a positive meeting with the highest
level of state authority, he met with Hinstorff representatives on August 9
to negotiate contractual arrangements. According to Ingrid Prignitz, his
editor at Hinstorff, Jurek understood this meeting as an agreement to
publish *Sleepless Days* with minor changes.

Jurek thought he had won. He accepted one change, that it be made
clear that the "regime" he wanted replaced was that of the school, not
the state. He refused to budge on the other suggestions.[95] Following this
"final" meeting, Höpcke sent him a handwritten letter urging him to let
other people read the novel and to listen to them.[96] The signals seemed
to be mixed, at least from Jurek's perspective. From the standpoint of
the state they were clear: make all the required changes, or the work
will not be published. By August there were regular discussions of the
unpublished, but certainly not unread, novel in the West German press.
Reviewers saw the characters as expressing an "anxiety that their lives
can no longer to be connected to socialism," an anxiety that "has gripped
an entire generation."[97] This burst of interest guaranteed that Jurek was
regarded in the West as the spokesperson for his entire generation of
writers.

The "Liar" was permitted to go to West Germany on a prearranged
reading tour from August 22 to September 10. On September 6, 1977,
six weeks after the *Spiegel* interview in the family home in East Berlin,
Jurek met with reporters from the *Frankfurter Rundschau* in Frankfurt
and again discussed the post-Biermann situation in the GDR. His comments on the political realities had become sharper than in the earlier
interview in the GDR. But he was not about to abandon the GDR and
move west, as the poet Sarah Kirsch had just done. For him it was an
"existential question," for "living with illusions is better than admitted
hopelessness." When people leave the GDR, he said, what can those left
behind do? The only cure for the desperation that he and others felt was
for "the party to give up its stiff-necked approach to artists." And then
he attacked the very nature of the post-Ulbricht party. "The party must
decide if we still should live in those circumstances defined by wartime
communism. The people should be given the same freedom as artists

demand for themselves."⁹⁸ His contention that Honecker's GDR was as rigidly Stalinist as Ulbricht's had been, and that some writers and artists actually remained privileged because they had no wish to speak out, was totally unacceptable to the authorities of the GDR. And yet he stated in the interview that his controversial novel *Sleepless Days* would definitively appear with Hinstorff.

When he returned to Berlin, Jurek found a nine-page letter from Höpcke dated September 9, listing what needed to be done to improve the manuscript. Four days later, he met face-to-face with Höpcke, who berated Jurek about his attitude during his West German trip. He rebuked Jurek for his interview with Wolfram Schütte in the *Frankfurter Rundschau*, with its comments on the collapse of values in the GDR and the absence of true socialism there. He contrasted this appeal in the FRG to the more moderate tone of Jurek's *Spiegel* interview. He accused Jurek of insulting socialism. Taken aback by Höpcke's brusqueness, Jurek replied that he was merely practicing "public criticism." The reason authors wanted to leave the GDR was the repressiveness of the state. Jurek warned that court cases raging against certain dissidents would prompt even more writers to leave the GDR. He eventually brought the discussion back to his novel, noting that he had indeed been working on the manuscript of the novel with the help of Elisabeth Borchers of Suhrkamp (with whom he had met on June 26, 1977). He would give it to Hinstorff at the end of the week. At the close of the meeting, Höpcke demanded that Jurek give no more interviews to Western media. Jurek promised he would not. Höpcke then "suggested" that Jurek should come to discuss the book with him at the end of September if he wanted to remain a writer in the GDR.⁹⁹ The lever that Höpcke used to manipulate his author was Jurek's own desire to have his novel published in the GDR, which would allow him to remain a part of the establishment while critiquing it. Jurek called this "interfering" (*einmischen*); it was a sign of belonging to this society. What Höpcke wanted was that any criticism be internal and therefore controlled.

That same day, Höpcke informed his boss, Kurt Hager, of his ultimatum to Jurek.¹⁰⁰ On September 19, Höpcke received a cool letter from Jurek, retracting his commitment not to give any Western interviews and contending that the GDR was in "error" concerning its cultural politics. He felt himself threatened by the tone of Höpcke's letter to him, as it accused him of "libelous activities against our state and its organs."¹⁰¹ In Höpcke's response of September 25, 1977, he expressed "great sorrow" about a writer whose works he cared for. Should Jurek not do something himself to prevent the "collision" between him and the state?¹⁰²

In the meantime, on September 15, Hager had informed Erich Honecker of Jurek's attitude. On September 22, Kurt Hager went public with the state's discomfort with Jurek's position, attacking his interview in the *Frankfurter Rundschau* in a speech at the ninth conference of the GDR's Cultural League (Kulturbund der DDR). He dismissed Jurek (and others) as "having lost their direction." Now all the putative care and interest on the part of individuals such as Höpcke was of no avail. Jurek had become persona non grata. His capitulation in the face of the double-edged praise for his work and the clear threat of the state had placed him in an untenable position.

Hager's public condemnation marked the end of any consideration of *Sleepless Days* for publication in the GDR. On September 26, discussions with Hinstorff finally broke down. Harry Fauth and Horst Simon rejected the revised manuscript on the grounds that Jurek had not changed his criticism of existing socialism, as expressed in Antonia's attempt to flee the East and the objections to stopping her. Fauth and Simon mentioned the Western interviews and Jurek's refusal to define his position as a socialist author. Jurek, having already cut his ties to the GDR with his letter to Höpcke, rejected both the criticism and the warning that publishing in the West would be unlawful without going through the copyright bureau of the GDR.[103] Höpcke sounded the final note on September 28, when he reported to Hager that he had tried unsuccessfully to get Jurek to compromise. The book would appear at the Frankfurt book fair in 1977 "with the accompanying propaganda."[104] Jurek had now become an agent of Western propaganda, and his work disappeared from the cultural scene of the GDR as quickly as *The Boxer* had disappeared from the windows of the Jena bookstore the morning after Biermann lost his citizenship.

Jurek never wanted to cut his ties to the culture of the GDR. Even after he had left the GDR in 1977, Hinstorff published those of his later works that were deemed to be acceptable to the readership of the socialist state.[105] The objections to *Sleepless Days*, it seemed, had more to do with Jurek's political stance than with its content. If Jurek had agreed to withdraw his name from the petition supporting Biermann and to stop giving Western interviews, the objections to the novel could well have been lifted. Its publication in Rostock, as Dieter Schlenstedt noted in his evaluation, would have shown the liberality of self-criticism in the GDR.

The reality was quite different. Jurek's work was now seen as one with his politics. In August 1976, Frank Beyer had directed a film whose screenplay would be Jurek's last for DEFA. *The Hideout* (*Das Versteck*), a comedy with Manfred Krug as the lead, was one of only two DEFA films that Jurek made with Manfred Krug.[106] This actor played an architect, Max Brink, who attempts to win back his ex-wife Wanda (Jutta Hoffmann) by acting as if he were being sought by the police. He seeks sanctuary in her apartment in order to show her that he has changed from the work-obsessed, macho male he had been during their marriage. In "hiding," he cooks supper for her, quits smoking (a theme in many of Jurek's GDR films that focus on daily life), and is for the first time truly attentive to her needs and desires. But he still cannot rebuild their marriage, because Wanda has learned to live without him. According to Jurek's script, the couple, like writers in the GDR, are reduced to talking only of unimportant things and being polite to each other. Indeed, the divorce trial, presented as a flashback, is so amicable that the judge ends it by saying that they both seem quite prepared to make their next marriages a success. Through "hiding out" in her apartment, Max finally understands Wanda's development as an autonomous being. The final scene has Max crashing his car and realizing that every disaster, including divorce, can help you learn something.

The screenplay uses comedy to present a theme that haunted the avant-garde of the GDR: how very much like a bad marriage the relationship between the artist and the state had become. Begun before the Biermann affair, the bulk of the actual filming took place "under extreme stress" after the letter defending Biermann was published. Jurek, Beyer, Krug, and Hoffmann had all signed it. They all met daily in the dressing rooms to discuss their chances for success in getting the state to alter its action. Krug described the film as an attempt to revivify a *kaputt* marriage filmed by four "dissidents." On April 20, 1977, the film received its official internal screening at DEFA. Everyone present, including Armin Müller-Stahl, called it a fine film, though they knew full well that it might never be released.

Manfred Krug left for West Berlin in June 1977. In September, during his discussions with Höpcke, Jurek wrote to Horst Pehnert, the deputy at the Ministry of Culture, asking what had happened to the film.[107] Pehnert answered after a considerable delay, and merely offered to meet with Jurek.[108] In Jurek's mid-September interview in *Der Spiegel*, the film was discussed. The interviewer noted that "there is a film in the safe by Jurek Becker and Manfred Krug, who left for the West in June as the star. Will it be shown?" Jurek: "I don't know whether the film will be shown or not. I'm afraid it won't." Interviewer: "Why not?" Jurek: Why not? "My God! Because the premiere, measured by what are now the norms in our state, would seem rather unusual." Interviewer: "To put it bluntly, because Krug stars in it." Jurek's response puts his own persona at the very center of any interest in suppressing the film: "Don't forget me. When Krug left, there was a small note in the papers saying that he had not taken advantage of all of the possibilities to develop in an artistic manner. It wasn't true. Why do they do this? Because the party always has to be right! That's why they do it. I believe there's now a real doubt whether the party always is in the right."[109] Jurek now saw the failure of the party to acknowledge the demands of the dissidents in the Biermann affair as a failure of faith. He no longer believed in the system as it existed in the GDR.

On September 25, 1977, Frank Beyer had sent a nine-page open letter to Hans Dieter Mäde, head of DEFA, in defense of a new socialist art film.[110] Beyer wanted to film Jurek's unpublishable *Sleepless Days*. The idea was dismissed by Mäde because of the antisocialist tendencies of the book. Beyer stressed the need to have more films that dealt with current problems in the GDR. A recent resurgence of films of this kind included Heiner Carow's *The Legend of Paul and Paula* (*Die Legende von Paul und Paula*, 1973), based on a script by Ulrich Plenzdorf; Konrad Wolf's *The Naked Man at the Sports Field* (*Der nackte Mann auf dem Sportplatz*, 1974); and *Solo Sonny* (1980), as well as Beyer and Jurek's own film *The Hideout*. Beyer detailed a history of the suppression of such films about contemporary events, including, of course, the scandal around his own *Trace of Stones*. He concluded that the division of things into "useful" or "destructive" (*schädlich*) was not helpful to the furtherance of a meaningful film culture in the GDR. *The Hideout* was to be put into very limited release on October 19, 1977. Armin Müller-Stahl rearranged his trip to the West to be present.[111] At the last minute, however, the premiere was canceled.

On October 28, 1977, there was a closed discussion about *The Hideout* in the Academy of the Arts among a number of the leading cultural figures, including the director Konrad Wolf, the actor Erwin Geschonneck, and Jurek, Frank Beyer, and Jutta Hoffmann as guests. Jurek was doubtful that such a discussion would have any effect, as the power to release the film lay elsewhere. Censorship, he noted, can never be justified.[112] In the name of the Academy, Konrad Wolf wrote to the minister of culture, expressing the hope that the film would be released, and Hans-Joachim Hoffmann replied that it certainly would be in good time.[113] Jurek associated censorship of the film with the impossibility of having *Sleepless Days* appear in any form in the GDR. He was no longer to be tolerated in public.[114] When *The Hideout* actually premiered at the Colosseum movie theater in East Berlin on November 7, 1978, Jurek, by then living in West Berlin and wondering whether the prodigal son could ever return, saw it as a sign of "normalization."[115] The film got very few showings in the

GDR and quickly vanished from the theaters, but it received very good reviews.[116]

Since Jurek had no other course than to leave the GDR, the only question was how to do it. On April 16, 1977, Manfred Krug had requested official permission to leave the GDR permanently. He noted that promised roles had been withdrawn, that his records were not released, and that his concert tour to the FRG had been canceled after the Biermann affair. He left his house to the state and his weekend house to the local community.[117] Like a number of other leading oppositional figures, Krug decided he could no longer live in the GDR. Jurek was much more cautious. He still imagined that the state could reform itself. On November 7, 1977, he wrote to Höpcke applying for a visa for two years (until 1979) to write in the West as well as to go abroad. When the visa expired, he would discuss with Höpcke what should then take place.[118] On November 8, the GDR granted Jurek a two-year visa. This made news in both the West and the East.[119]

Before requesting the visa, Jurek had had a series of talks with his family. Although they were divorced and Rieke had custody of their minor sons Nicki and Lonni, Jurek suggested that he apply for a visa for all of them. But the problems of relocating in the West seemed overwhelming to Rieke. She would be forced to rely on Jurek for financial support, and she would be robbed of her personal and social support network. She decided, with the acquiescence of the two boys, to remain in the family house in East Berlin.

Staying in the GDR, however, had its consequences for the family. Rieke had been extensively shadowed by the Stasi during the entire Biermann affair. For Lonni the situation was immediately problematic. His father's visibility in the debates about Biermann and very public decision to leave the GDR marked Lonnie for special attention. He was arrested in the Friedrichstraße train station on November 4, 1978, on his way to a soccer game, for insulting a policeman. He was accused of wanting to cause trouble at the game. The police were more than usually interested in him because his father was "at present abroad in West Berlin," according to the official account of the "crime."[120] In November 1979, Lonni wrote a paper for his history class on the thirtieth anniversary of the GDR; in it he criticized the system for its arbitrariness and self-satisfaction. The paper was sent by the school to the local party office and became one more item in Lonni's Stasi file.[121] The school authorities stressed that Rieke seemed to have lost control over her son, an ironic comment, since Rieke's political views had also been documented by the Stasi. In 1982, Lonni began an apprenticeship to a cabinetmaker who was also a teacher at Lonni's vocational school. In an altercation between the two one day, the cabinetmaker snapped that Lonni was nothing but a "Jewish brat (*Judenbengel*) who should have been gassed." Rieke's official complaint to the school authorities forced an apology and the removal of the teacher. While this incident was the only overtly anti-Semitic one that the family experienced, it was clear that Jurek's visibility as a Nazi victim was understood as a sign of his Jewish identity and marked his children also.

Nicki had no similar experience, but he too felt that his position in school had been affected by his father's decision to leave for the West. Suddenly his teachers made no mention of Jurek, who had been seen as a local celebrity. It was as if he had simply vanished. But when Nicki, supported by Rieke, refused to take the required course in military training (*Wehrerziehung*), which had been introduced in 1978, his attitude was taken as a sign of both parents' bad influence.[122] In 1981 he was labeled "the son of Jurek Becker."[123] By the twelfth grade he was in frequent conflict with his mother, exacerbated by his father's weekly trips to see the two boys. Jurek brought them things like cameras and stereos that were simply not available in the GDR. Nicki identified so strongly with his father that there was some speculation at his school that he wanted to join his father in West Berlin. He remained in East Berlin, however, though Rieke despaired at what he would do with his life.[124]

Jurek was now forty. He was free of all of the obligations that had weighed upon him for the past few years. He took two suitcases of clothes, a box of records, and his typewriter to West Berlin on December 2, 1977, and moved in with his school friend Helge Braune at 74 Brandenburgische Street on December 18. Manfred Krug had temporarily lived with Braune after he left the GDR, and Jurek slipped easily into the space abandoned by his friend in Braune's small apartment.

Jurek thought of himself as only in transit through West Berlin. But there, as in East Berlin, he was a major media sensation. His name and face were everywhere. He held a news conference for foreign journalists on February 2, 1978, declaring that the arts in the GDR were "healthy" and the conflicts were a "normal development of a new, growing society that had led to some misunderstandings."[125] On the following day he was interviewed by a West Berlin literature professor, Peter Wapnewski, on the SFB television channel in Berlin.[126] There he claimed to be only an "internal" critic. He took a number of questions from the audience, some very hostile. His position was that he had high aesthetic goals and that these could also have been fulfilled in the GDR. When asked whether he would support those persons who were banned from certain types of employment (*Berufsverbot*) in West Germany because of their political views, he tried to avoid answering. He claimed that any negative answer about the practice would only support those advocating it. He was also trying to avoid any questions about his loyalty to the GDR as well as to what could well become his "new" country, the FRG.

In early February, he gave a further interview to the *Frankfurter Rundschau* in which he expressed, if indirectly, his anxiety about leaving the GDR.[127] He saw his move to the West as temporary, and when asked why he was not stripped of his citizenship and expelled, like Wolf Biermann, he noted that he could not read the stars but that he was happy about the outcome. This interview, more than any other, reflected Jurek's ambivalence. It was full of second thoughts. He stressed that he could make a career in the West as a writer and that conflicts between writer and society were not the sole prerogative of the GDR. Yet he also noted that every time there was a conflict within the GDR, Western media saw it as inherent opposition to the socialist state. He denied that there was any organized dissidence in the GDR or that he would be part of it if there were.

Jurek remained a member of the loyal opposition. Indeed, he had returned to East Berlin on January 11, 1978, before the TV interview, and had casually "mentioned" to Erika Hinkel, personal assistant to Kurt Hager, that he would avoid any provocative statements on the SFB program. Jurek also told her (and she told Hager) that he "saw a possibility of returning to the GDR to work as a writer." He intended "to offer his next book manuscript to Hinstorff."[128] If it too were rejected, he might well change his mind about returning. This member of the loyal opposition tried to keep the door to the East open while on his way even farther West.

Western Intermezzo

In his East Berlin interview with *Der Spiegel,* Jurek noted that "If I have to shut my mouth, then I would rather shut my mouth in the Bahamas."[129] He did not make it to those islands. He had, however, been approached much earlier by Richard Zipser, a young specialist in the literature of the GDR, to succeed the West German "worker-writer" Max von der Grün as the annual Max Kade Writer-in-Residence in the German Department at Oberlin College, in Ohio, in 1978. Gerhard Wolf, who had taught at Oberlin with his wife Christa Wolf in 1974, had suggested to Zipser that Jurek might be a good choice. Zipser had spent extensive time in the GDR during the mid-1970s interviewing a wide range of writers. As a result, the Stasi believed him to be an agent of the CIA.[130]

Oberlin was founded in 1833 in northeast Ohio as a religious college with a serious political mission. Women and African Americans were among the students admitted to the college from the beginning. It was named after the Alsatian pastor Johann Friedrich Oberlin, who figures in the life story of the Storm and Stress dramatist J. M. R. Lenz and in Georg Büchner's nineteenth-century account of Lenz's final days. By the 1960s, Oberlin College was one of the hotbeds of radical thinking in the United States. Its students and faculty were heavily involved in both the Civil Rights movement and the crusade against the Vietnam War. "Flower power," which had begun to fade elsewhere in America, was still firmly entrenched at Oberlin in the late 1970s.

Zipser initially wrote Jurek from Vienna in October 1975, requesting that they meet that fall. The two met five times in September and October 1976. In October, Zipser sent Jurek a postcard telling him that Oberlin wished to know whether he would be interested in coming for the spring term in 1978.[131] When Zipser received a positive answer from Jurek during a trip to East Berlin, he requested that an official letter be sent to him. On October 19, 1977, Jurek received a letter from the dean at Oberlin, Robert M. Longworth, inviting him to come to the college as Max Kade Writer-in-Residence from mid-February to mid-May 1978. His remuneration would be $5,500. Thus, during most of his discussions with the authorities in Berlin, Jurek had this invitation in his pocket, a fact of which they were well aware.

Before leaving Berlin, Jurek had one major obligation to complete. In August 1977, the West German critic and commentator Hans Jürgen Schulz had asked him to contribute to a series of essays on Jewish identity to be broadcast on the South German Radio in Stuttgart in the first part of 1978.[132] Among the other Jewish writers and thinkers invited were Schalom Ben-Chorin, Günther Anders, Jean Améry, and Hilde Domin, all a generation older than Jurek. Only Yehuda Amichai, the great Hebrew poet, born in 1924 in Germany, was close to Jurek's generation. Jurek's essay, due February 1, 1978, reflected his earlier struggle with the meaning of a Jewish identity in the GDR, which he had expressed in *The Boxer*. Titled *My Jewry (Mein Judentum)*,[133] the series (and Jurek's talk) provided Jurek with a chance to encapsulate his own thoughts about a Jewish identity in the GDR. Jurek's talk was extraordinary in its combination of naïveté and self-revelation.

At its core was the view that the external forces of history that had shaped his identity were connected with his parents' being Jewish, rather than himself,. He was merely an incidental victim. He seemed torn between his ambivalence toward "Jewishness" (not Judaism as a ritual practice) and a strong belief in the political rhetoric of anti-Zionism that had disguised anti-Semitism in the GDR. He attacked the state of Israel as a racist, aggressor state. Here he followed the rhetoric of the United Nation's General Assembly Resolution 3379 of November 10, 1975, which declared that "Zionism is a form of racism and racial discrimination." Using the GDR rhetoric, he dismissed the Zionist project as Nazi-like and therefore criminal.[134] He withdrew this comment twenty years later as "exaggerated and false."[135] Only then did he come to understand that in this specific context anti-Zionism was anti-Semitism, for it did not permit the identification of oneself as a Jew in the public sphere of the GDR. In his 1978 talk, Jurek echoed Arno's long monologue in *The Boxer*. Jurek, now at the point where he was to leave the GDR, was forced to stop and think about what his Jewish identity meant. He articulated it within the acceptable rhetoric of the GDR, whose loyal citizen he desired to remain. With that ambivalence he left Europe for the United States.

When he arrived in New York on February 7, 1978, Jurek felt he had entered a land teeming with Jews. Staying at the Grammarcy Park Hotel, he wrote a mock diary—a series of sketches based on his first impressions of New York and his subsequent trip to the Midwest. Jurek was overwhelmed by the notion that this was a country where Jews were actually visible as Jews.[136] He worked these impressions into a set of images of America, which, he remarked, stemmed from his East German film and TV image of American capitalism. At Kennedy airport he was asked by the immigration official whether he intended to remain in the United States. His unspoken answer was "Who knows?" The customs officer asked him what books he had with him, a question seemingly more appropriate to the German-German border and one to which Jurek's initial response, again unspoken, was "None of your business." Jurek showed the customs officer his manuscripts and the paperback volume of the *Talmud* that he had brought "as reading for America." The officer smiled at him. "Perhaps he's a Jew?" thought Jurek. Perhaps reading the *Talmud* was an appropriate way of understanding "America" and its Jews, people whose religious identity is Jewish, not those who, like Jurek, merely acknowledged their parents as Jewish.

Jurek's image of New York, as seen through the lens of the GDR, was that of American multiculturalism. The Jews were a part of that kaleidoscope of peoples, and Jurek realized that in New York he too was a part of it. He went with a group of tourists to Harlem and visited a black Baptist church. There, along with everyone else, he introduced himself to the congregation. "Where are you from?" "I am from Germany," he answered, even though "I don't know what the word means, but I use it anyway" (155). Not a Berliner, not a citizen of the GDR, not a German (odd as that word sounded to him), Jurek was, simply, foreign. There were real advantages to being foreign. One could shed the mantle of the "German" with all its historical ramifications; one was no longer a victim or a Jew—but one was different nevertheless. As a foreigner he could talk in his broken English. Not speaking the language of the dominant culture well was not a matter of shameful visibility in New York City, as it had been for Jurek's father in Berlin.

New York was the city he prepared for by reading the Talmud; in his fantasy it was the most Jewish city. (Recall that Wolfdietrich Schnurre, in complementing *Jacob the Liar*, told Jurek that he had read the Talmud to prepare for his own novel about the Jews.) Following the model of the GDR, Jurek defined being Jewish in religious rather than in ethnic or political terms. Yet he found his way to Forty-seventh Street, "Diamond Way," the center of the diamond trade carried out mainly by Orthodox Jews. The names on all the shops were Jewish. There he sought out a kosher restaurant, but it had closed years before. "I wanted to eat for the first time in my life what my father had told me about" (150). Instead, he ate a piece of apple pie at a diner, for the most Jewish of cities is also the most American of cities. Apple pie was something he knew of only from the movies. It was as much a part of the American myth as the *latkes*, the potato pancakes that Jacob Heym used to sell in his tiny restaurant before the Germans put him in the ghetto, were part of the Jewish myth.

America also meant sports. Jurek's obsession with sports found fulfillment in New York. He saw the Harlem Globetrotters play their special brand of basketball at Madison Square Garden. He went to a New York Rangers hockey game. He was a foreigner, a Jew, someone speaking with an accent, a sports fan, someone who fitted and yet did not fit his fantasy of America. New York, he wrote, did not excite him, for although it welcomed him, it was a place that made no demands on him.

On February 15, 1978, Jurek traveled to Oberlin. He moved into one of the undergraduate dormitories and began to teach a colloquium on German literature one evening a week. He ate in the German-Russian House, where he met the students. At first he was quite taken aback as they regaled him with tales of Max von der Grün and his extraordinary participation in their lives. They struck him as immature, rather childlike, not serious.[137] Nor did the students take Jurek very seriously at first. After the intense exposure to media and politics in Berlin, he became a virtual nobody at Oberlin.

Jurek quickly decided to outdo his predecessor. He bought a used Ford Pinto and began to hang out with the undergraduates. Among them was a freshman, Hannah Zinn, a student who showed up regularly at the Russian discussion table in the German-Russian house. Raised in a relatively sheltered manner in California, she was now eighteen (she was born May 19, 1959) and away from home for the first time. She had come to Oberlin to do a pre-medical course but also to study the flute at Oberlin's famed conservatory. By March, Jurek and she had begun an intense relationship. They drove in his jalopy to Lake Erie on their first date. He gave her Vladimir Nabokov's *Lolita* to read.

Beautiful, adoring, Hannah was on top of everything Jewish. Her father, an Orthodox, second-generation Eastern Jew, spoke Yiddish. Her family was also very middle class: her father was a dentist in Hayward, California, a suburb of San Francisco. Hannah was the first Jewish woman with whom Jurek formed a strong emotional attachment since the death of his mother. She bore his mother's name, and, as it turned out, her father, like Max, was an alcoholic.

Jurek's media presence in West Germany was heightened by his sudden departure to rural Ohio. When the midwinter snows vanished, *Stern* magazine sent one of its reporters, Eva Windmoeller, with a photographer to Oberlin.[138] The German TV channel ZDF sent its correspondent Dirk Sager to interview Jurek for his program *Kennzeichen D*. Jurek was now receiving attention from all sides.

In mid-April, the German Department at Oberlin held a series of major public events around Jurek's presence on campus. During these, he gave two lectures in English, read from his published and unpublished work, and was present when *Jacob the Liar* was screened. In the reading, he presented his new story "No Parking" ("Parkverbot") which deals with order and belief in a police state.[139] The tale is haunted by the constant presence of the police and the assumption that they must represent what is right. The theme of "misleading the authorities" seemed the best card for his Oberlin audience. But he also announced, to the horror of his hosts, that Israel was the last place in the world that he would want to go to. By the end of his stay he had become an Oberlin legend, eclipsing Max von der Grün. The students called him "Jurek the Terrible."

The semester drew to a close. Jurek had suggested to Hannah Zinn that she accompany him back to Germany. Since he was unemployed and had no place to live, it may well have seemed an unreal hope on his part. In the meantime, Jurek and Hannah arranged to meet in San Francisco, but not until Jurek had seen more of the country, which he wanted to explore on his own. He had already done some traveling, having attended a symposium on GDR literature at Michigan State University in East Lansing, where, very much off the record, he warned one of the speakers not to wash the GDR's dirty laundry in front of an American audience.[140]

Having sold his car, Jurek flew to New Orleans. In the early evening of June 9, 1978, he was in the French Quarter, where he saw two policemen trying to arrest a white tourist who was clearly drunk. The tourist resisted, and the policemen started to beat him. Jurek was incensed. Carefully formulating his sentences in his still rather unpolished English, he shouted: "Now I know journalists in Europe who will write about where the Nazis from Germany went: they became cops in New Orleans!" Needless to say, the police turned their attention to him. They arrested him for "interfering with the police" and made him post a fifty-dollar bond. He skipped out on the bond and headed for the West Coast and Hannah Zinn.[141]

Jurek showed up at the Zinns' house in Hayward. Long-haired and bearded, he fulfilled their expectations of the hippie professor. Hannah's mother, Cynthia, was taken aback by his being a German, but she welcomed him into her home. Hannah's father didn't think that Jurek was Jewish enough for his daughter because he didn't go to synagogue. Her five siblings, especially her seven-year-old brother Jeremy, thought him "cool." Leaving the bustle of the Zinn family, Jurek and Hannah rented a car and drove to the mountain resort of Lake Tahoe, spending an idyllic "honeymoon" there. They went on to Reno and Las Vegas. They watched baseball on TV, took long walks, and grew closer emotionally. Jurek was forty, Hannah eighteen. Each found in the other what they needed. She was very different from any woman Jurek had ever been with. For him, she was exotic: American, Jewish, talented, and young enough to be formed by him.

The summer almost over, Jurek had to decide what to do. Should he remain in the United States? He had left that question open when he arrived in New York City. In the USA he would be isolated from the one thing that he knew provided him with the status and the power he needed to live: his command of the German language and the celebrity attached to it. Uwe Johnson, another major author from the GDR, had spent two years (1966–68) in New York but had returned to West Berlin and to his own language rather than choosing to live in exile. That choice became integral to Johnson's fiction in the following years. Jurek's anxiety about his "new" language, about the German he had so painfully acquired, meant that America was not an option. He wrote to his friend Willi Moese, the caricaturist, in East Berlin: "My English has become so good that people don't recognize that I come from Germany. I am still identified as a European (from the continent, not Great Britain)!"[142] On July 18,

1978, Jurek returned to a new German-speaking world, leaving Hannah behind for the time being.

Jurek again moved in with his friend Helge Braune in West Berlin. It was in that remarkable city that he felt most at home. Neither West nor East Germany, it was an "island city" because of the continued four-power occupation. West Berlin was an artificial construct of the cold war. Jurek was one of those first-generation GDR citizens, raised exclusively within the conscious model of real-existing socialism, who chose to leave the GDR in the 1970s but who did not abandon its socialist ideals. Between 1945 and 1989, West Germany had become the new home for more than four million Germans from the Soviet zone and the GDR. Ideologically, most who fled were not committed to state socialism, having come of age under the Weimar Republic or Nazi Germany. Jurek, raised in the GDR, was committed to an idealized notion of what state socialism could be in Germany. The standards to which he held the GDR were those that the founders of the GDR had themselves established. But from the invasion of Czechoslovakia in 1968 to the expulsion of Wolf Biermann in 1977, it was clear that these ideals were honored in the breach. Jurek's return to West Berlin meant critiquing the system but not becoming a tool of capitalism in its attack on the qualities he still believed socialism to possess. Could he succeed?

Chapter 7

JUREK BECKER IN WEST BERLIN,
1978-1989

Moving West

Jurek returned to West Berlin from the United States in mid-July 1978. On his desk he found a long "personal" letter from Klaus Höpcke, the self-designated "minister for books," dated the day before Jurek had left Oberlin. Höpcke listed in detail all the "errors" in various interviews Jurek had given since the beginning of the year. He offered his own list of corrections (including a refutation of Jurek's claim that his books had been withdrawn from the market in the GDR) and warned Jurek, not too subtly, against presenting such errors to the Western media.[1] Jurek took this admonition quite seriously. He had been trying to tread the fine line between strenuous internal opposition, even though using the "foreign" (that is, West German) media, and outright dissidence.

Jurek's insecurity about his relationship to the GDR was evident to all, including the authorities. He desperately wanted the support of his old circle of friends in the East. How could he be in the middle of things if he were no longer sure where the middle was supposed to be? Crossing to East Berlin to visit Rieke and his sons on July 20, he also saw Willi Moese, Armin Müller-Stahl, Günter Kunert, and Stefan Heym. The next day he tried to reach Erika Hinkel in Kurt Hager's office to discuss his situation in the Politburo, but she was on vacation.[2] He returned to West Berlin on July 24 but planned to return to East Berlin within a few days.

Once again lodging with his friend Helge Braune, Jurek soon met a young American woman who was living in a cooperative, and he struck up a close relationship with her. Irene Dische was born in New York City in 1952. She was of Jewish descent, though raised as a Roman Catholic. Her mother was a German Catholic physician of German Jewish background. Her father was a well-known biochemist. As German was spoken in the family home, Irene spoke it fluently. She had come to Berlin in 1978 and was working as a freelance journalist for the *Nation* and other American periodicals. She had been commissioned to write a piece on young German writers from the East, and she met Jurek in November 1979 after an initial interview with his fellow exile Thomas Brasch. Their short but intense affair ended because Jurek, according to Ottlie Krug (Manfred's wife), was still head-over-heels in love with Hannah Zinn.

Hannah had spent the summer in Hayward and returned that September to begin her sophomore year at Oberlin. Jurek telephoned her regularly at home in California as well as at Oberlin, as he began to explore life as a bachelor in West Berlin. Hannah was someone he thought he could build a new life around. In the meantime he became obsessed with pinball. He spent hours playing the game, needing to win just as he needed to win at table tennis. Control was everything for him, and the less control he felt in his life, the more obsessed he became with sports.

Jurek was in no way isolated in West Berlin. He had never truly been out of the eye of the West German public, and he again became the media's darling in West Berlin. The scandal still swirling about *Sleepless Days* meant created a demand to see him and to hear him read from the novel. On September 21, he gave a reading in Cassel. But he avoided virtually all of its controversial parts, at least those that the officials in the GDR had constantly pointed out to him. In the discussion following the reading he stressed that he was "happy to be citizen of the GDR." When asked, he stated forthrightly that he was also opposed to the arrest on August 23 of Rudolf Bahro, the oppositional theorist.[3] The tightrope walk between East and West was difficult, but so far he had managed to avoid falling. Over the next six months or so he would average two trips a week "home" to East Berlin. He told Willi Moese that the litmus test for his return to the GDR would be whether he was published and read there. "I won't return to live in a country where my books are not published!" he said at a party in East Berlin on October 14, 1978.[4] He was living and publishing in the West. Yet when he accepted a position as a writer-in-residence for the fall semester at the University of Essen (in West Germany), a newspaper report had him commuting to Essen "from his home in East Berlin"![5]

The Stasi made sure they knew what was going on in Jurek's life in both East and West. They photographed the apartment house where he lived in West Berlin; they sent "unofficial" spies into Rieke's home with the pretext of visiting long lost friends; they parked themselves in front her house and photographed the "guests" coming and going. Jurek acted as if the heightened surveillance were the "normal" price he had to pay for being a "celebrity." In West Berlin, things were rather different. There he had become a "Jewish" as well as a "dissident" celebrity, and he was uncomfortable in both roles.

Jurek's major complaint about moving to West Berlin was that "I have suddenly found myself forced to feel as a Jew, something that had played almost no role in my life in the GDR. It isn't because of an obvious presence of Judaism. More often than not, I find expressions of anti-Semitism aimed generally in my direction."[6] On November 2, 1978, Marianne Regensburger and Giselher Suhr interviewed Jurek on West Berlin radio about the status of the Jews in the GDR, a subject almost taboo in West Germany. The East Germans were the enemy; Jews were essentially victims. How could there be a "real" Jewish life in East Berlin? Jurek repeated almost word for word his earlier radio statement, decrying the labeling of people as Jews simply because they had Jewish parents. Again he was uncomfortably paralleling Orthodox Jewish and Nazi definitions of the Jew, as both seemed to him to rely on "biology." He denied that there was any anti-Semitism in the GDR, especially in the attitude toward "right wing" polices in Israel. He was more troubled by the philo-Semitic stress in the FRG than by the politics of the GDR toward Israel. Yet whatever Jurek said, it was clear that he was being used as an authentic voice of East German Jewry. His comments were broadcast along with an anonymous interview with a member of the congregation in East Berlin concerning day-to-day religious experiences in 1978.[7]

In spite of his qualms, Jurek continued to function in the West as a specialist on things Jewish in the GDR. When Stefan Heym published his bleak novel *The Wandering Jew* (*Ahasver*) in the fall of 1981, Jurek reviewed it very positively in *Der Spiegel*.[8] The novel critically evoked the disarmament movement in its East German context, disguising it in terms of the biblical Armageddon. Things important in the GDR were read in terms of biblical narrative. The novel spoke to all of Jurek's interests, but the West German public saw the review, as it did so many of Jurek's activities in the late 1970s and 1980s, in terms of his double reputation as expert on things Jewish and East German.

Jurek's ambiguous status as a member of the internal opposition in the GDR was echoed in a reading that he broadcast on November 14, 1978, from Hanover. Being an expert in Jewish matters relieved him of having to speak about contemporary political events in either East or West Germany. So he read from his essay "My Jewishness" as well as from the ever-growing volume of short stories that he had begun before he left for Oberlin and continued to work on after his return to Berlin. This volume, eventually titled *After the First Future*, would contain a number of important works, including his short story about the Shoah, "The Wall" ("Die Mauer"), which was filmed with his screenplay in the 1990s. The emphasis on his Jewish identity, one with which he was increasingly uncomfortable, became a weapon he used to ward off troubling questions about his identity as an East German writer.

Jurek strongly believed that his books were taken seriously in the GDR as *literature,* independently of his experience in the Shoah and the internal opposition. There, he felt, his work had value beyond its association with his own biography. In the West the works became an extension of that "Jurek Becker" who was understood as a Jew or a dissident. In one interview he noted that "something extraordinary has happened in the GDR. When you give literature value and value those who create it, over time it really is valuable."[9] Jurek was "valuable"; he was at the center of attention. As a writer he was able to negate any parochial self-definition as a victim. Consequently, he could write about Jewish topics as a writer for whom style and plot were, according to his evolving views at the time, more important than content.

In the winter of 1978–79, Jurek's sense of displacement continued. Was he a GDR writer in the West? Was he an oppositional or, worse, a dissident writer about to return to the GDR? Was he a Jewish writer or simply a German writer who happened to have had Jewish parents? Was he a victim of the Nazi regime? Was he a father with two growing sons, or was he the lover of a teenager far off in the fantasy land of California? Being displaced meant moving away from the center of attention. Being a celebrity meant having privilege. An incident that occurred on November 22, 1978, convinced Jurek, rightly or wrongly, that his privileged status in the GDR had vanished when he left for the West. He had arranged to attend a 6:00 P.M. film premiere at the DEFA film studio in Babelsberg, near Berlin. He climbed into his newly acquired gray Audi and tried to cross into the GDR at the Drewitz checkpoint. Even though there were no other cars there, his papers were confiscated—for personal revenge, he assumed. When the border guard asked him whether he had declared everything, he retorted, "You can read, can't you?" On finally getting his documents back, he told the border guard she was repugnant (*abscheulich*),[10] at which point her supervisor was called. It turned out that neither the border guard nor her supervisor had any idea who Jurek was; they just thought him unpleasant and rude. What he had read as proof of his new marginality in the East was simply a "normal" occurrence at the border.

Every time Jurek entered East Berlin, he had to pass through the complex, irritating customs and passport control at the border. Leaving West Berlin, an entity still seen as illegitimate by the GDR, meant exposing oneself to border politics. It made no difference whether Jurek was bringing posters, rock records, or sweets for his sons and cosmetics and other things for Rieke, or whether he was on his way to a reception at the American Embassy, as often happened. At one point Stefan Heym told him that as a "victim" he could be freed from the niggling attention of the border guards. Needless to say, this did not work, nor did an appeal to Hager's office.[11] Jurek had become an "outsider," as, indeed, he always had been.

Meanwhile, at Oberlin, Hannah was missing Jurek badly. His regular calls became a fixture in her life. He offered to send her a ticket to Berlin so that she could join him. Toward the end of the fall semester, she announced to her family that she was dropping out of school and accepting Jurek's offer. Her mother, who thought of Germany in terms of Nazis and Volkswagens, was troubled by her daughter's decision but granted that it was Hannah's choice.

Hannah landed at Tegel airport in the snows of winter, afraid that no one would be there to meet her. Jurek was there, however, and took her to their new, furnished apartment at the corner of Kurfüstendamm and Leibnitz Street. (The building was in one of the more upscale sections of West Berlin. Manfred Krug had tried to get Jurek to move into his building, but Jurek said privately that he would rather be twenty miles away from him.)[12] The world Jurek had created for himself when he left the GDR and moved to America reappeared with Hannah.

Jurek now had to integrate both Hannah and himself into life in West Berlin. He saw his "closeness" to the GDR as more than physical proximity. He retained a close relationship to his family as well as to the small circle of friends and acquaintances that defined the essence of the GDR for him.[13] In West Berlin, Jurek and Hannah became part of a lively cultural world. Theater, film, and the traditional bar scene filled their evenings, often in the company of the Krugs as well as Irene Dische and her new husband, the attorney Nicolas Becker. The interaction among Krug, Nicolas Becker, and Jurek would engender Jurek's most important television productions during the next ten years.

Hannah and Jurek went together for the first time to visit Jurek's East Berlin family on January 8, 1979. Jurek insisted that Hannah, who spoke no German, begin to learn the language. He fantasized that she should develop as a writer, since she had done a little creative writing in high school and college. Irene and Hannah became fast friends as Hannah learned German. Jurek's desire to shape Hannah paralleled her own need to develop in terms of her growing relationship with Jurek. Remaking herself by learning a new language and becoming a writer was something that Jurek could easily understand.

A decade later, in 1988, Jurek read Irene Dische's first volume of short stories and edited it heavily according to his sense of what good prose should be. He saw it as a friendly gesture. But he also refused to recommend her work to his or any other publisher. Taking this as a negative comment on her writing, Irene was very hurt. She thought Jurek's competition with her as a writer made it impossible for him to appreciate her work. Only after her volume of short stories, *Pious Lies (Fromme Lügen)*, was published in 1989 was she told that Jurek had wept over the first story, a tale of a young Jewish man who comes to Berlin to claim his father's inheritance. A Catholic, she too became a "Jewish" writer in terms of her literary reception in Germany.

Hannah thought about continuing her pre-medical studies in Germany, but for that she needed at least two years of college. Should she and Jurek return to the United States? Could they go back to the GDR? What would she or—more importantly—he do there? Jurek's world was limited by the importance of German as his literary medium. Having mastered it, he could not imagine learning English to the same degree. Hannah acquired her German in part by attending Jurek's readings and listening to him present his texts over and over again. As their relationship matured, she became more comfortable in the language. Jurek proposed marriage to her, but she felt she was not ready. Jurek reached out to her family, writing to them (in English!) about how much Hannah meant to him, and they, in turn, wrote to him in September 1980 for his birthday, sending love from his "California family."[14] The couple settled into a normal life. He played table tennis with her and she began to be part of his new life in West Berlin.

The political climate in the GDR continued to change radically. In January 1979, the film *Closed Society (Geschlossene Gesellschaft)* made by Frank Beyer and Klaus Poche, two of Jurek's closest professional friends, became a public bone of contention in the GDR. Even though it was given the most limited exposure, the deputy minister of the State Committee for Television, Hans Bentzien, who had advocated its limited showing, was fired. After that no bureaucrat was going to risk giving Jurek a film or TV commission. Poche felt that he himself was under a cloud would never again get a job.[15] Jurek was certainly under *Berufsverbot* in the East. He had already played with the idea in his novel *Sleepless Days*, when his protagonist Simrock is dismissed from his position as a high school teacher because he takes literally what the system demands of him. Earning money in the West was not merely the means to maintain Jurek's comfortable lifestyle. He had a steady income from the ever-expanding success of *Jacob the Liar*—a sign that he was a productive writer. He didn't want to be a one-book author, whose first book would be his best and most successful. Nor did he want to rely on the money he made in the West. He told an interviewer, "I can't imagine living in the GDR from Western earnings. That would give me an illegal, underground, dissident status, which I am not willing to accept."[16] Where you earned your living defined your position in the world of GDR politics.

Earning money from films was something Jurek had thought he had left behind when he left the GDR. The conflict over Frank Beyer's *The Hideout* had left a bitter taste in his mouth. He was reminded of all of the problems he had had when he wrote for DEFA—the need to have his projects approved at every level and the real risk that even approved projects might never be filmed (or distributed). He enjoyed the sense of autonomy and visibility when he began to write "literature." Writing films was being part of a collective; writing books meant that he was an independent member of the literary establishment. Yet screenwriting provided a financial fallback, as it had done in the GDR. Beginning in 1978, Jurek worked on the script for Peter Lilienthal's film *David*. He met Lilienthal (a Jew who was born in Germany in 1929 but raised in Montevideo, Uruguay) when Lilienthal was looking for a screenwriter for Joel König's survivor autobiography.[17] Who could better do this than the author of *Jacob the Liar*? Jurek was confronted with a book that was part autobiography, part popular history. It told the story of a religious young German Jew who was raised in Silesia because his father had become a rabbi there. It chronicled his family's flight to Berlin, his own attempt to become retrained as a farmer for eventual illegal emigration to Palestine, and his life in hiding until he moved in 1944 from Berlin to Budapest and eventually to Palestine. This story was quite unlike anything Jurek had worked with in his books dealing with the Shoah. It was a very "German" book, rather than a book about Germans as perpetrators and Eastern Jews (and their children) as victims. What is more, König's autobiography rests on its author's strong *religious* identity as a Jew—an identity that disappeared in the film script. The modern Orthodox religious school in which König enrolled when he arrived Berlin, is replaced in the film by a vocational school run by the Jewish social service agency ORT. According to the autobiography, religious belief made König's life bearable. Jurek had had no such experience.

The collaboration on "The Star of David" (*Der Davidstern*), the film's working title, was not a success. Lilienthal regarded Jurek's writing as being too tightly limited by the film conventions he had learned from DEFA. He totally reworked Jurek's initial draft for the film. Only traces of Jurek's draft were left in the final production. The opening sequence, in which the father (played by Walter Taub) and David (played by Torsten Henties) engage in a game of table tennis is an addition to the book. It captures the idyllic nature of childhood as remembered by Jurek from his school days in East Berlin and sets the tone of the film even before the opening credits. When *David* appeared, it was well received, winning the "Golden Bear" as the best picture in the twenty-ninth West Berlin Film Festival in 1979.[18] Jurek's first attempt to write a film script in the West was, at least, a learning experience. Lilienthal gave Jurek and Ulla Ziemann coauthor status for the film, even though the final screenplay was largely his own work.

The ability to earn a living, Jurek found, was used as a weapon by the GDR authorities to threaten the opposition. Höpcke had warned Jurek that publishing in the West violated the new GDR laws on copyright. It could now be seen as an economic crime. In the spring of 1979, both Robert Havemann and Stefan Heym, who received West German royalties, were accused of violating the new laws passed to control the monetary flow between East and West. Heym had denounced these new laws in April 1979, when the maximum fine for publishing "abroad" without permission was raised to 10,000 marks. On June 16, Jurek and Klaus Poche drafted a letter to Erich Honecker, which was signed by many leading cultural figures, including Klaus Schlesinger, Adolf Endler, and Erich Loest, complaining that the state was about to muzzle engaged critical writers by "linking censorship and legal punishment."[19] The gesture was futile. Both Heym and Havemann were fined substantially under the new laws at the end of May.[20] The leadership of the Writers' Union, under the presidency of Hermann Kant, then ordered that the local branches of the union deal with the signatories to the letter to Honecker. Since Jurek was no longer a member, the Berlin branch could not do anything to him. But it expelled Stefan Heym, Rolf Schendler, Kurt Bartsch, Adolf Endler, Karl-Heinz Jacobs, Klaus Poche, Klaus Schlesinger, Dieter Schubert, and Joachim Seyppel among others on June 7, 1979. Seyppel, who had begged Jurek to stay in the GDR and not to go to Israel, left Berlin for the West with a three-year visa in June, as did Jurek's collaborator Klaus Poche.[21]

Jurek's international reputation was growing, but he was still regarded primarily as a Jewish writer. After returning from Oberlin, he was again invited abroad, this time to Scotland. In February 1979, Henry Pais, professor of German at the University of Edinburgh, invited Jurek to Scotland to lecture and read from his work. Pais, a Jewish survivor of Buchenwald, felt especially close to Jurek because of their common background. Following Christa Wolf and Reiner Kunze, who had been in Scotland not long before, Jurek was to lecture under the auspices of the Scottish Arts Council. In the course of negotiations, his perceived position as dissident began to concern officials with the council. Might the invitation anger the authorities in the GDR? Pais finally persuaded the university to assume all the financial obligations.[22] Given Pais's own interests, it was hardly surprising that Jurek was hailed as much as a Jewish writer as a GDR writer. On February 26, 1979, he gave an address titled "A Fiddler on the Roof"; and on March 1, one titled "A Writer East and West." On March 2, he held a seminar on *Jacob the Liar,* and finally on March 3 he read from the volume of short stories he was writing at the time. This fine balance between things "Jewish" and things "GDR" were intended to separate the two themes of Jurek's work, but the audience in Edinburgh clearly did not regard them as separate topics. Jurek was asked, for example, about anti-Semitism in the GDR. He denied that it could even exist there, given the tradition of resistance in the GDR, but he acknowledged that anti-Semitism was alive and well in Poland and the USSR. A Stasi agent in the audience carefully noted all the questions and Jurek's answers and forwarded a detailed report to Berlin.

The stories Jurek read from in Edinburgh were ones that he had been working on before and during his stay in the United States. He had completed about half of the volume by the time he returned to Berlin. The twenty-seven stories would constitute *After the First Future* (*Nach der ersten Zukunft*). This volume was to be the new litmus test to show whether it was even possible to return to the GDR and earn a living there as a writer. Jurek told Horst Simon at Hinstorff that he would ignore the fact that *Sleepless Days* had not appeared in the GDR, but if the short stories were not published, he would have to rethink his relationship to the GDR.[23] This statement was naive, for assumed that Jurek was in a position to determine whether he would to the GDR. The futility of such a claim was soon to be evident.

At the beginning of October 1979, Jurek sent two copies of the manuscript to Hinstorff.²⁴ The publisher's immediate response was that some of the stories were fine, especially the ones that seemed to put the USA in a poor light; some were unacceptable, specifically those which either directly or indirectly reflected poorly on the GDR. Jurek set a deadline—November 2, 1979, the day he was supposed to meet with the cultural authorities at the Central Committee—for Hinstorff to reach a decision. He made it clear that his West German publisher, Suhrkamp, would have world rights except for the GDR and the Eastern bloc. And he made it even clearer that his editor at Suhrkamp, Elisabeth Borchers, already had the manuscript and was working on it.

At Hinstorff, the official opinion was mixed. At least three of the stories were clearly unacceptable. The opening story was a dialogue between A and B that drew from the theme that Jurek had been pursuing since 1976 about the role of the author in the GDR. It began with the difficult question: "What should a writer do who is no longer happy with our country?"²⁵ Jurek's discussion of this question begins with Honecker's claim that there would be no taboos for artists in "our land." The reality is quite different. B (= Becker) argues for freedom of expression even if the expression sought is "wrong." The dialogue ends with the claim that the "author writes what he writes. Now he has no further advice. He makes a living from his books, and this must be emphasized, but no one will publish them." After this note of pathos, Jurek wrote in the margin of the manuscript, "Not convincing." The dialogue convinced neither the Eastern nor the Western reader. Both Simon in the GDR and Borchers in the FRG found it "too East German," though for different reasons. Jurek's claim of a special status for the writer was also a claim for the privileged position of himself as a writer. That privilege was eroding. In the final manuscript, Jurek moved a short story about storytelling— "Grandfather" ("Großvater")—to the opening of the book. In that tale a grandfather teaches his grandchildren about the pitfalls of storytelling but never gets around to telling them a story. The echoes of Max's constant recounting of formulaic accounts of the past and his insistence that Jurek learn to tell stories was captured in this tale.

Among other stories deemed difficult to publish was a very short one about penguins and why they cannot survive in the "pure" atmosphere of a zoo. That this was a reference to the difficult life of the writer in the now sterile GDR was clear to anyone in the GDR who read the manuscript. A further bone of contention, clearly intended to challenge his GDR publishers, was the quotation from Wolf Biermann's poem

"Der Aufsteigende" ("One who Ascends") in Jurek's account of a week in New York City. According to Jurek's text, the poem popped into his mind when he was visiting the United Nations in New York and saw a sculpture of the same name by Fritz Cremer. Cremer had been one of the key figures in the campaign to get Biermann's expulsion rescinded, but caved in to government pressure and withdrew his name from the petition. Linking Biermann and Cremer, even in a memoir of his trip to the United States, would have very different associations for the reader in the GDR, who was attuned to reading subtexts into all published work by members of the opposition. (Jurek cut the poem from the final published version of the account.) The final story in the manuscript that seemed to be problematic to the GDR reader was "The Suspect" ("Der Verdächtige"). It appeared "too specifically" tied to a comment on the submissive role of the intellectual in the GDR.[26]

The reader for Hinstorff, Anneliese Löffler, as well as the chief editor, Horst Simon, wanted some further cuts to give the volume a less fragmented feel. After speaking with Jurek, they thought this a not insurmountable problem.[27] Indeed, the opening dialogue and the final story had been equally criticized by Elisabeth Borchers, who wanted Jurek to rewrite the story, making it clear that it was about the GDR and not about the FRG. The other stories in the volume—including Jurek's only first-person account of the "experiences" of a child during the Holocaust, "The Wall" ("Die Mauer")—seemed beyond reproach. Their range was breathtaking. The double perspective of "Jewish" tales and "GDR" tales as mutually exclusive categories remained. Jurek had also incorporated his first story about West Berlin into the manuscript. It was an especially insightful portrait of a "guest worker" ("Romeo") who finds a girlfriend in East Berlin, where his West German money buys a lot more than human warmth. It was as much a study of the seductive power of Western currency on the soul of an East German woman as it was an interior monologue of the experiences of a guest worker in the West Berlin of the 1970s.[28]

On November 9, Jurek met with Harry Fauth and Horst Simon.[29] He agreed to virtually all the changes requested. Everyone was surprised at his willingness to compromise. He only refused to change the last story, either to make it less GDR (as the East Germans wanted) or more GDR (as the West Germans wanted). The shape of the final volume was agreed on by all parties. Löffler's report was the basis for Hinstorff's request on December 12, 1979, that the volume be approved, subject to Jurek's submission of changes by January of 1980. At that time, however, the Ministry of Culture possessed two Stasi reports on the manuscript, each of which labels it either "negative" or "politically impossible."[30] One report was from IM "Schönberg," who was actually Horst Simon. Simon had been supplying the Stasi with reports that often contradicted his "official" reports to the minister of culture.

Jurek ardently hoped that Simon's attempt would bear fruit and that the book would appear in the GDR. If it did, he could return to the GDR and make a living there, other than through his foreign royalties. It would also mean that he was again a member of the literary establishment on his own terms. Unfortunately, the final political decision had been made when Jurek moved west. Permission to publish the volume in the GDR was denied, and only the Suhrkamp edition came out in time for the Frankfurt book fair in the fall of 1980. Jurek attributed the ministry's denial to the March 1980 interview he had given *Der Spiegel* magazine, in which he saw himself again "giving it" to the GDR.[31] But the refusal to publish the book was clearly the result of the government's desire to punish Jurek for his critical stand during and following the Biermann affair.

After the First Future was reviewed widely, for it was the first of his "Western" books after the publication of the suppressed manuscript of *Sleepless Days*. In a radio review on September 25, 1980, Klaus Sauer profiled Jurek before reviewing the book. He repeated the criticism that Jurek had lodged against Western readings of GDR writers in 1973, and discussed the importance of *Sleepless Days*. Then he turned to Jurek's new book, seeing it as a series of texts reprising the "Jewish" novels and the "socialist" novels "in miniature."[32] For a volume of short stories, it sold well; Jurek's Western audience had been primed for his next book.

Jurek needed to find a niche in West Berlin that would bring in immediate revenue. He left the furnished apartment that he and Hannah had occupied, and in 1980 he rented an apartment in Kreuzberg, the rather funky Greenwich Village of West Berlin, on Hagelbergstraße. Jurek brought some of his furniture over from East Berlin to help furnish the newly restored apartment. Expenses continued to mount. Although Jurek was receiving royalties from his earlier novels, he now had bills to pay in both East and West Berlin. It was not the reality of his expenses, but his sense of always living on the edge, of never being secure in his ability to control the world, that haunted him. For him, security lay in his ability to earn a living.

In 1979, Jurek had sold the film rights for *The Boxer* to the West German TV station ZDF for enough money, he claimed, to live for a year. The film was written and directed by the Jewish director Karl Fruchtmann, a survivor of the concentration camps. It was released on March 3, 1980.

Fruchtmann had been commissioned to film the novel specifically because of his earlier films on the Shoah. Shot on location in Berlin, the film was a relatively accurate version of the book, but with much of its ambiguity resolved. Televising what was clearly (for the audience) an autobiographical work would reinforce the notion that Jurek was a "Jewish" writer. To limit this effect, Fruchtmann simplified the narrative situation. Jurek agreed to all the changes in the script. He was often on the set and on location, observing the filming.

Fruchtmann reconstructed Jurek's complex narrative into a straightforward plot. The novelist/reporter (played by Rüdiger Kirchstein) is the ideal listener to the tales told by Aron Blank (played by Norbert Kappen). The account of Aron's life in the film begins chronologically with Aron's search for a place to live in Berlin immediately after the war. It concludes with the discussion that opens the novel, that the account the reporter has written is in fact the reporter's account of Aron's life, not Aron's own.

In reworking *The Boxer* as a film, Fruchtmann eliminated all Jurek's references to the problems of Jewish identity in Germany after the Shoah. Aron's pathetic question of what had made Mark (played by Patrick Estrada-Pox) into a Jew is missing. The story of Mark's life and putative death in Israel is an afterthought at the very close of the film. As with Jurek's comments on the GDR in the West, Fruchtmann believed it inappropriate to talk about such topics in front of *the Germans*, as Max would have put it. Yet the film was reviewed as autobiography, not art. Hartwig Maack restated Jurek's refusal to see the novel (and film) as a "personal dealing with the past," but he concluded that the film "has evident autobiographical features."[33] This in spite of (or because of) the film's much milder presentation of the ambiguities of Jewish identity in the GDR. *The Boxer* was a success in the FRG. Showing it on East German television, something that Jurek had proposed in the winter of 1979, seemed highly unlikely, although the novel was still "officially" being sold in the GDR. Jurek was too visible in his absence.

Jurek's relationship with Hannah was evolving, his ability to move between West and East kept him in touch with his family and friends, and he had established himself in West Berlin. On November 11, 1979, he met once again with Erika Hinkel in Kurt Hager's office. He told her that although he was willing to make some changes to the collected short stories, he would not agree to abide by the new GDR copyright laws or the new limitations on speaking to Western media.[34] Jurek had clearly raised the stakes. Earlier, he had required the GDR to prove, by accepting his next manuscript, that he could still function as a writer. Now he was demanding access to Western funds and a freedom of speech denied to his peers. At this point, any pretense of wanting to return to the GDR vanished. On November 28, Jurek put these thoughts on paper and sent them to Klaus Höpcke: "I have difficulty living here. I have grown in the past two years. New laws will make me into a criminal. If I come back, I will only be able to write about these difficulties."[35] He stressed that he did not want to give up his GDR citizenship and asked for a ten-year extension on his visa. This was unheard-of. His initial visa had already been unprecedented. It had been created for him, the "Jewish" writer, the internationally visible writer, the loyal son of the GDR. Now he was asking for an additional decade abroad!

To the officials, he seemed torn about his decision. He used his new relationship with Hannah as an excuse for his request. Höpcke took Jurek's request up through the party ranks. He asked Hager to ask Erich Honecker whether a three- to ten-year extension of Jurek's visa was even possible.[36] Honecker, however, agreed to give Jurek the visa he requested, and on December 11, 1979, Jurek obtained a visa for multiple exits for the next ten years. It was to end on December 11, 1989—a month after the Berlin Wall fell, as things turned out.

Why Jurek was granted such an extraordinary boon is a matter of contention. Was it a way of undermining his status in the West? Was it because of his status as the GDR's best-known survivor author? Jurek speculated that it was because he kept his mouth shut. He had, according to his own account, sat quietly writing his short stories and appeared undisturbed by the very restrictions that caused him to leave the GDR in the first place. Perhaps, he thought, it was a royalty for silence, a gesture to keep him suspended with very high status between two worlds.[37] Ten years seemed extraordinary to him. Why not a hundred? Both Jurek and the authorities in the GDR expected the deadlock that existed between him and the state to continue for the foreseeable future.

Life in West Berlin and *Everybody's Darling*

The GDR still had a decade to run its course. Since leaving the GDR in 1978, Jurek had become an established cultural figure in West Berlin, but his celebrity was tied either to his function as a Jewish intellectual or his visibility as a GDR dissident. He discussed this in a number of public interviews, each intended to reshape his profile. At the beginning of 1980 he was emphasizing his independence from the standard image of the dissident writer. He stressed that he remained a socialist as well as a citizen of the GDR, that his goal in life was to write books (no word about films), and that he had no intention of getting involved in West German partisan politics. This was an important statement, for the cultural left in the FRG looked at dissident writers from the GDR as natural allies in their struggle against the often oppressive reaction to left-wing terrorism in the late 1960s and early 1970s. Jurek had absolutely no interest, he stated for the record, in getting dragged into such discussions. Nor did he have the least intention of joining a political party in West Berlin.[38] He had not come to the West to "sound off about the GDR," because such a discussion should be among friends. Privately, he said he could not return to the GDR because he was "bound to open his mouth and then they would have to put him in prison."[39] He intended to live a private life in the West as a writer whose books, he hoped, would appear in the East as well as the West.

For Jurek, actually living a quiet life would have robbed him of the centrality he knew that he could now have as an "honest broker" between West and East. Jurek saw the act of writing as a political act, spanning East and West. He wrote every morning for three or four hours after exercising but seemed to produce little of merit. Yet writing fiction, not films, was necessary for his reorientation as a "pan-German" (not a dissident GDR or a Jewish) author. In May 1981, Jurek was invited to speak at the West Berlin Academy of Arts. Together with a number of major West Berlin cultural movers and shakers, such as Günter Grass and the critic Fritz Raddatz, he was to address the question of whether Germany (East and West) was a single cultural entity.[40] (This question was clearly one of West German interest as it posited a nonpolitical unification of both German states in the realm of culture.) Jurek argued that the question was irrelevant for him, as a citizen of the GDR: "I write out of my understanding, and whether it is a national understanding is something I really don't think about. I write as a writer who is obligated to feel and think, and I am in no way forced to write by a sense of national feeling."[41] The sense that writing was a replacement for his identity as an East German author was tempered by his attempt to divide German literature into "left-leaning" and "right-leaning" camps in each of the countries. This supranational set of categories, clearly adapted from the vocabulary of Marxist literary criticism, meant that he could be "closer to some writers in the West" than in the East.[42] Neither ideology nor public action was missing from Jurek's gradual redefinition of himself as an author. He wanted to stay above the pedestrian political struggle in the West, but this was not to be.

Jurek could not keep away from the hot-button issues of the West Berlin political scene. He became involved in an older project established by Western writers during the radicalization of West German society that had occurred in the late 1960s. The confrontation between students (and their ideological allies) and the West German government had been exacerbated by the role of the conservative press, specifically the newspapers owned by Axel Springer. The call of the Springer newspapers, such as *Bild,* for an equally violent reaction to the violence on the left was seen as triggering a number of assassination attempts against student leaders such as Rudi Dutschke, who was murdered in the late 1960s. Group 47, which represented virtually all of the leading West German writers of the time, called for a boycott of all Springer papers. At the end of 1981, the artist Klaus Staeck and his group "Action Call for Democracy" revitalized the earlier attacks against Springer, who had remained the bête noire of the left. Jurek spoke at the group's huge meeting at Berlin's Technical University on November 11, 1981, along with many of West Berlin's major politicians, including the former mayor, Pastor Heinrich Albertz. He also signed the authors' petition that stated, in part, "We don't work for Springer Newspapers because he cheats the reader when he claims to be non-party-affiliated and independent . . . We give no interviews and will not give our work for prepublication."[43] Since GDR authors were banned from giving interviews to Western media without official consent, Jurek's signature bore a tinge of irony. He was now acting like a West Berlin writer.

During the 1980s, perhaps in an attempt to "educate" Hannah and help form her into a young "German" writer, Jurek began a systematic program of intellectual self-improvement. His decision to study philosophy rather than literature at Humboldt University had left him with a sense of inadequacy about his grasp of literature and culture. When asked in the early 1980s by a GDR cultural magazine what he held to be the most interesting new book to have appeared recently in the GDR, he cited, tongue in cheek, the picture book *Always in Solidarity with the Soviet Union (Mit der Sowjetunion für immer fest Verbunden).* When the interview was published, this answer was missing. On inquiring, he was told that the magazine didn't print ironic answers. He thought it remarkable that even official publications did not take their own propaganda seriously.[44] Reading was serious work. Jurek recalled that the students in Oberlin had read little. He had to know much more, for he was receiving many invitations to speak about—and even to teach—German literature abroad.

In January of each year, beginning in 1981 and continuing until 1997, the year of his death, Jurek compiled a list of "required reading." These New Year's resolutions would be his reading for the next twelve months.

Whatever else he read, he systematically checked off the works he had listed in January as he read them. His reading was eclectic but substantial. It encompassed major works of literature, history, and culture. The first book he read was Franz Kafka's *Metamorphosis* in 1981. In 1982 he explored the Third Reich via Thadeusz Borowski's account of the Polish underground during the Shoah as well as Hannah Arendt's *Eichmann in Jerusalem*. He read Heinrich Heine's fragment *The Rabbi of Bacharach* in 1984; Moshe Feldenkrais's work on body awareness, *The Elusive Obvious*, in 1987; Herman Melville's *Moby Dick* in 1991; and Sylvia Plath's *The Bell Jar* in 1995. The very last book on his reading list for 1997, the year he died, was Salman Rushdie's *Midnight's Children*, which remained unread. Twenty-five books a year, every year, year in and out. His reading was humanistic in the best sense of the word, and this at a time when politics in Europe was losing its humanity.

The cold war by the 1980s had entered into the phase of MAD—mutually assured destruction. The balance of power following the Cuban missile crisis in 1962 meant that the members of NATO and those of the Warsaw Pact had huge numbers of atomic weapons aimed at each other. Germany, both East and West, would surely be at the center of any conflict. The various worldwide movements such as the Campaign for Nuclear Disarmament that were struggling for a nuclear-free world presented an often contradictory picture. Some groups were for a total disarmament, others for only nuclear disarmament. Still others used the issue as a means of attacking either the West or the East. In the GDR, a peace movement began in the Evangelical Church. On February 9, 1982, Pastor Rainer Eppelmann's "Berlin Appeal" called for the removal of all nuclear weapons from both German states. It was signed by leading oppositional figures including Robert Havemann. In East Berlin, a "Berlin Meeting to Demand Peace" was called for December 14, 1982, by Stephan Hermlin.[45] Hermlin's oppositional credentials were spotless, and he was able to arrange for left-wing writers such as Günter Grass and Peter Schneider to be invited from West Berlin. Also included were some of the writers, such as Jurek and Thomas Brasch, who had resettled in West Berlin after the Biermann affair. The GDR authorities hoped to use this meeting as a brush with which to tar the West as the sole cause of the nuclear standoff. The official line was that the peace movement in the West was a good thing, but such a movement was not needed in the East, where the national governments represented the interests of the peace movement. At the meeting, the historian Jürgen Kuczynski took what was literally the "party line" and argued that SED party politics were the GDR equivalent of the peace movement. Hardly any of the speakers invited from "abroad" accepted this argument.[46]

Jurek spoke to the crowd and began by distancing himself from the role of a dissident. He observed that in the West he spoke about the GDR only with those interested in changing things within the GDR. The statements about peace he made in the West, however, were still seen in the GDR as a weapon against the West. Each had to be persuaded by the other's true commitment to peace, not merely its intent to use "peace" as a weapon in the cold war. It was too easy for the struggle for peace to be exploited for party purposes. Here Jurek placed himself above the political argument while still being part of it. He sought to be a writer across cultures. "We writers are disseminators. Our opinions are not unimportant to certain people. We can encourage people in our books, at meetings, at readings, in interviews, to struggle against war and armaments." His role was that of a commentator, but he was clearly embodying a new and very Western freedom of speech. He closed his remarks by observing that "the reason why there are demonstrations for peace in the West and none in the East is that they are simply forbidden in the East or that those who might take part fear they would be punished."[47] Jurek's talk had received a positive response when he seemed above politics. But things turned ugly when he referred to the real situation in the GDR. Voices screamed from the crowd "That's not true." He shouted back: "Then tell me what isn't true about it!" Stephan Hermlin sat behind Jurek and muttered words of support. Jurek had a feeling that "something had begun. I don't know what, but something had changed." But little had actually changed. Even on this most pressing of issues, no consensus was possible. The fragmenting of the GDR opposition after the Biermann affair meant that even on this issue no joint statement could be worked out. The organizers tried to have all present sign a communiqué to *both* sides asking for disarmament. Only half were willing to sign.[48]

On Christmas Eve, Jurek was interviewed on RIAS (Radio in the American Sector) about the meeting. He condemned the television coverage in the GDR as extremely biased. Yet he was sure that the meeting in East Berlin strengthened the West German peace movement even though it was "seen by many as a kind of communist propaganda show."[49] At the end of May of 1982, a second meeting of this group was held, this time in the West, at The Hague. Jurek spoke there as well, condemning the military thinking that was present on both sides of the Iron Curtain.[50] Almost a year later, in February 1983, more than a hundred thousand people filled the streets of Dresden in the biggest demonstration for peace in GDR history. In the West it was read as opposition to the GDR regime. At the end of April 1983, a further meeting was organized in West Berlin under the slogan "Declare for Peace." Neither Jurek nor any of the GDR writers in the West were invited to speak, so that the GDR would not be alienated. Indeed, some, such as Wolf Biermann, were not even invited to attend. Although Stefan Heym and Ulrich Plenzdorf came from East Berlin to critique the GDR media account of the peace movement in the GDR, many saw the exclusion of Jurek and others as a "Western" propaganda coup. Everything in the cold war was political, especially what was supposed to be above politics.

The history of Jurek's novel *Sleepless Days* illustrates some of the difficulties encountered by an internal critic of the system. At the close of 1979, Jurek had negotiated a lucrative arrangement for the filming of the novel. He was to get royalties plus a fee for the screenplay. Directed by Diethard Klante for West German television (ARD), the film was shot in Bavaria. It was first broadcast in September 1981 and then again on the Bavarian television channel in August 1982.[51] It was the fourth in a series of problem plays produced to examine the internal discussion of life in the GDR for the West German TV audience. The first had been based on Ulrich Plenzdorf's novel *The New Sufferings of the Young W.* With Hans-Peter Hallwachs as Simrock, *Sleepless Days* was initially presented with the political world of the GDR as background for a personal crisis rather than a specific element of that crisis. The real reason for choosing this "difficult material," according to the producer Harald Müller, was Jurek Becker.[52] For, unlike Plenzdorf or, especially, Hermann Kant, whose *The Lecture Hall (Die Aula)* had been the second in the series, Jurek had a clear media presence because of the continuing success of *Jacob the Liar.* He was not merely a writer; he had become a celebrity. The reception of *Sleepless Days* in the GDR, where it was never actually shown, was complicated.[53] It was noted that the film version did not reflect Jurek's own relationship to the GDR but was, rather, a cold war rewriting of the novel. Enough people had seen the West German broadcasts of this forbidden book to warrant comment.

Jurek had begun working on a new novel, his first to be written in the West. It recycled the name of the protagonist from a fragment of a novel about soccer that he had begun while still in East Berlin. That fragment was to have been an "inside" tale of life in a German soccer team, following the adventures of the player Kilian. (The name was taken from the actor Siegfried Kilian, who starred in Jurek's very first film.) Jurek had abandoned the project when it became clear that he had no sense of what life in professional sports was all about.[54] For his first novel in the

West, he turned Kilian into a figure from the world of journalism. His new book was to be neither shrilly "oppositional" like *Sleepless Days* nor "Jewish" like *The Boxer*. It was to be a pan-German novel.

The publication of *Everybody's Darling* (*Aller Welt Freund*), followed a familiar pattern.[55] Jurek again believed it could appear in the GDR, even though his last two manuscripts had been refused publication. After completing the manuscript in the spring of 1982, he sent it to Hinstorff on May 4 of that year. It was immediately read by one of the editors, Ingrid Prignitz, who was ecstatic about it. Here indeed was a book that could appear in the GDR! "It is a piece of literature written from a humanistic position."[56]

But on October 11, Hinstorff received a very negative report on the manuscript.[57] While noting that "the book is not an attack on the socialist state" because it could be set anywhere, the reader stated that the work "does not present in its content or stylistic form the minimal qualifications for eventual book publication." Nonetheless, according to the reader, its publication might serve a political purpose if it tied Jurek closer to the GDR. Jurek had already sent the manuscript to Elisabeth Bochers at Suhrkamp. He expected, as did Suhrkamp, that his celebrity would turn this novel into a popular success. Jurek therefore wanted to retain the film rights. Given the sales of *The Boxer* and *Sleepless Days* to film and television, he was playing his hand carefully. He also asked Suhrkamp to let him retain all publication rights in the GDR and socialist countries.[58] He still needed to have a work published in the GDR.

The plot of *Everybody's Darling* is both simple and banal. The thirty-year-old journalist Kilian is about to commit suicide by filling his apartment with gas. He accidentally falls and breaks his arm. The comedy of errors continues when his landlady, who was supposed to leave town, returns because the airport is closed because of fog. She calls an ambulance, and he is taken to the hospital. A physician, who dislikes attempted suicides, brutalizes Kilian and eventually abandons him because he wants to save his time for someone who is really sick. Killian is also threatened by an anonymous agent of the state, who may be armed. The agent asks him mysterious questions about whether he is really willing to risk his life and for what purposes.

We learn that Kilian is one of a pair of identical twins that his mother conceived when she was sixteen. The twins were raised by their grandmother, so his mother seemed more like a sister. After two days in the hospital he is released. He returns to his apartment where his landlady has left him a letter asking him to move out as he presents a danger to her as well as to himself. His mother finds him there and tries to discover what drove him to the suicide attempt. She goes with him to meet with his girlfriend Sarah, who knows only that he has broken his arm. Sarah ends their relationship because Kilian is completely unable to engage emotionally with her or anyone else.

A week later, Kilian's brother Manfred appears. A mathematician who wants to be a writer, Manfred is as much at a loss to understand Kilian as everyone else is. The two go out and get drunk. The next day, Kilian returns to his newspaper, where his boss tells him that he has been re-assigned to the sports section. After four years doing the news, he says, people burn out. For some reporters, the editor notes, "every new story [is] internalized like a death in the family" (170). Kilian returns to the tavern where he and Manfred had gotten drunk the night before, hoping for some type of human response on the part of the barmaid, to whom he was attracted. Odder things do happen, he thinks to himself. The novel ends with the realization that Kilian's suicide attempt was his response to the horrors of the world he had experienced as a reporter.

Jurek structures the novel around an issue that had been well explored in novels like Nathaniel West's *Miss Lonelyhearts* (1933). What happens when (in West's case) a columnist begins to internalize the heartache he learns about in the letters to his advice column? Suicide is the only answer. The German model for this type of plot is Erich Kästner's 1931 satire of journalism in Berlin, *Fabian: The Story of a Moralist*. How can journalists write about horror after horror without being destroyed by their own storytelling? What happens when writers internalize the world about them? Jurek in the 1980s faced the same questions: writers like him, if they remained in the GDR, stopped being writers and started becoming figures in the resistance.[59] The only option, Jurek argued, writing now from beyond the system, was to stick to their calling and remain writers. Stylistically that meant using irony as a distancing device. Jurek ironically has Kilian evoke Raymond Chandler's *The Long Good-bye* (1953) and his detective Phillip Marlow in the suicide scene and elsewhere (10–11). Kilian could only long to be "hard boiled" like Marlow. The irony here is heavy-handed, and the use of Chandler was Jurek's attempt to place the novel in a literary world beyond the party politics of either the FRG or the GDR.

The autobiographical fragments incorporated in *Everybody's Darling* are obvious. The twin brother Manfred, who "is an actor to beat the band" (112), is married to Tilly; Jurek's best friend and surrogate brother Manfred Krug was married to Ottlie. Kilian's twin wants and achieves a quick divorce from Tilly, even though he is not quite sure why. Jurek's state of mind during his divorce from Rieke was similar. The entire world of the novel is permeated with crude anti-Semitism. Kilian's editor at the paper is, according to one of the characters, "either Jewish or he had his balls shot off at Leningrad" (166). In the rumors that circulated about the fictional editor, being a circumcised Jew is the equivalent of being castrated, a calumny that evokes the power of circumcision in German culture. All these references, however, are marginal to the focus of the novel. Even the "doubling" of the protagonist through the device of the twin, the figure of Manfred, is clumsy and half-hearted.

Kilian compulsively tells stories throughout the novel. He tells his landlady about his sister, who was once fogged in (18–19); and when the doctor is taking his history, he tells him about his mother's suicide (28–29). But everything is invented; he has no sister, and his mother is in the hospital waiting room as he is telling the story. Kilian tells stories because he can and because they deny the reality of the world. Hannah Zinn once said to Jurek that he told better stories than anyone else—even better than she did and even when he told them in English.[60] The stories Kilian tells are a counterweight to the stories he has to write as a reporter. Too many wars, too much death, too much horror—but too little of it is actually represented in the novel. Only when Kilian returns to work do we learn that he once had to rewrite a wire story about the Iran-Iraq war. By placing the novel seemingly beyond a national literary culture, Jurek strips Kilian's job of its local specificity. Neither internal censorship of the news in the GDR nor capitalist exploitation of the media in the FRG show up as motivating the characters. Kilian's stories are simply stories, told for the sake of telling them. Jurek's novel was intended to be neither a GDR nor a FRG novel but a "German" novel, set in the greater world of "literature." Whatever Jurek had said about the unity of German culture, here he attempted to create a text that would be above national ideology. Yet there are odd moments and language use that betray Jurek's specific experience. Kilian seeks refuge in a doorway during a blinding storm. More and more people gather there: "there is murmuring as during a pause in a meeting" (*Versammlungspause*)—a clear GDR metaphor, referring to the endless, regular "political education" meetings held to kill time during the workday in every factory and shop in the GDR. Jurek remained a GDR writer, even when he strained to avoid such a label.

Everybody's Darling was published by Suhrkamp in 1982 and by Hinstorff in 1983. Hinstorff clearly wished to bring Jurek back into the fold or, at least, to keep him from wandering too far afield. No one in the GDR was going to take umbrage at this novel. Jurek's older novels, still in print, had editions of 10,000 to 15,000 copies, which regularly sold out.

Publishing the new novel was a safe proposition for the GDR. It showed that Jurek could be present on the cultural scene but did not flout the limits placed by the authorities on the political content of literary work.

A New Family: *Bronstein's Children*

Jurek had received his share of literary prizes, but in 1982 he was given the "most original and delightful literary prize" in Germany: he was named the ninth "City Writer of Bergen-Enkheim."[61] For a year he was to have a house in Bergen-Enkheim (a suburb of Frankfurt) and 2,000 marks a month. He succeeded the poet Peter Bichsel and was introduced to his public on September 3, 1982, by the Swiss novelist Adolf Muschg. Bichsel had complained that "more and more the entire nation is falling asleep in front of the TV" because there was no place for real literature in West German culture, and now a screenwriter was coming to Bergen-Enkheim.[62]

When Jurek arrived, he found over two hundred invitations to meet or speak or give readings. He was overwhelmed but saw it as his duty to have a social role as the "city writer" as well as actually doing some writing. Doing both was difficult when he began to commute between Bergen-Enkheim and Berlin, where Hannah was studying at the Free University. She was often in Frankfurt on weekends, or Jurek found himself in Berlin. Yet they seemed to be growing apart. When she went off for almost a month to England in August and did not contact him, Jurek thought she no longer cared for him, while Hannah thought she was establishing herself as an independent person.

On March 28, 1983, Jurek gave a public reading at the German Booksellers' Academy in Seckbach near Frankfurt. A young woman in the audience caught his eye. Christine Harsch-Niemeyer, born on April 17, 1960, was the daughter of a notable publisher of academic books. She was immediately attracted to Jurek. Christine was well educated and sophisticated; and in her own right she was part of a circle of intellectuals. Jurek asked her to hold his woolen jacket, since the room was too warm to wear it. When he reclaimed it after the reading, he asked for her telephone number, mentioning that he had to go to Canada to give some talks and would be back in four weeks. Christine was pleasantly surprised when, a month later, he called. They began a relationship. Jurek was was so much attracted to her that when she went to France on vacation, he called her home daily to ask whether she had returned. Soon afterward she decided to move to Berlin, began to study at the Free University of Berlin, and lived with her best friend, also a student there. As the relationship intensified, Jurek decided to ask Hannah at the end of the summer to leave their apartment in Berlin, so that he and Christine could move in together.

Jurek prepared his reasons carefully and presented them to Hannah on a trip back to Berlin. Hannah was speechless. She had given up her studies, her country, her language, and her family to follow him to Berlin, and now he was throwing her out. But she voluntarily moved out of their apartment in the fall in 1983, and Jurek gave her some temporary financial support to help her to establish a life separate from him. After some initial difficulties she did indeed shape a life for herself in Berlin and completed her medical studies.

Christine moved into the apartment in Kreuzberg that September, and three years later, on March 7, 1986, she and Jurek were married in a civil ceremony. Jurek tried to obtain the permission he needed from the authorities in East Berlin to marry "abroad." His application was ignored until he threatened to marry without permission. Since the walls in their apartment had ears, approval arrived two days later. Two of Jurek's "friends" from East Berlin, Günter Fischer and his wife Petra, appeared on their doorstep, claiming they had been given permission to visit from East Berlin. They were spontaneously invited to attend the wedding party. Fischer had been sent by the Stasi to see who was present and to report what they said.

On the thirty-fifth anniversary of the *Kristallnacht*, November 10, 1983, Jurek was invited to speak at a small church on the outskirts of East Berlin. He refused the invitation for that event but accepted an invitation from the same source to a reading that would mark the close of the "Decade of Peace," later in November 1983. A political rather than a "Jewish" event seemed more appropriate to his unofficial presence in the GDR. While the peace movement remained a standard part of East German party politics, the government was often unable to control church-based events. About four hundred people came to the church at Neuenhagen, near Berlin, to hear Jurek read from his volume of short stories *After the First Future,* which had not yet appeared in the GDR. The event was introduced by the local pastor, Dietmar Linke, who spoke of the older generation's failed promise to disarm, an ironic turn of phrase given the failure of Honecker's generation to fulfill most of the promises of socialism with which Jurek had been raised.

After the reading, Jurek was asked why he had left the GDR. He recounted his version of the Biermann affair of 1976. There was a great deal of emotion in the audience about mistakes on both sides. The audience not only was interested in the question of peace but saw this question as part of a larger critique of the existing socialist state. Jurek therefore was easily moved to comment on the absence of freedom of information in the GDR. But as he argued for a greater freedom of expression, he was once again in danger of the label "dissident" and of the accusation of being paid by the West German media for a role he did not want. In truth he wanted to be neither a "Jew" nor a "dissident," but he had become both in the eyes of his ever growing public. The reading was so successful that it exceeded the official time allotted to it and had to be stopped.[63] Even some of Jurek's old school mates from the Käthe Kollwitz School attended. His media celebrity in the West had made him an even greater star in the East. Everyone watched West German television.

Jurek's fear that he could not have continued as a writer had he remained in the GDR proved correct.[64] Living in West Berlin but not letting himself be used by the Western media in a directed campaign against the GDR and socialism in general meant that he could have his cake and eat it to. He could be primarily a writer but he could also use his celebrity as a writer to address those political issues he saw as important.

During the year 1983, Jurek rethought his loyalties. He finally moved the rest of his goods from Rieke's house to the new apartment, leaving his family behind in East Berlin. He knew that his relationship with his sons had hit rock bottom. In November 1983, he wrote a long, rather sad letter to Lonni, having just visited him in East Berlin, where they had a long talk about Lonni's future. Bringing his sons material goods from the West in no way compensated for the lack of a father.

In letter to Lonni, Jurek speculated what would have happened in their relationship if Rieke and he had not divorced. He was aware that his absence had harmed both his sons, who were now young adults. The letter was signed "A strange father called Jurek."[65] This apology to his sons was also a rethinking of how his conflicts with his own father shaped his sense of direction. Jurek's advice to his sons, which they ignored, much as he had ignored Max's advice, was aimed at shaping their choices. In thinking about his own new set of choices he realized how very limited they were. The goals he set for himself—to be a loyal citizen of the GDR as well as an effective writer who played a role in shaping public sensibilities—did not include his commitment to his own family. The private was always subordinate to the public. And now he was paying the price.

In the early 1980s, Jurek returned to the topic of the Shoah and his memories of his father, related issues as he believed Max's poor fathering and alcoholism had been the direct result of the damage done to him in the Shoah. For Jurek, the past always seemed present in the way he perceived his world. It was in the light of the Nazi book burnings in 1933 that he saw both the refusal to employ left-wing supporters in public service in the FRG and the banishing of critical programing from GDR television.[66] He began to read intensively about Nazi crimes and perused transcripts of the Nazi war crimes trials.[67] As part of his annual list of reading he devoured Joseph Wulf's extraordinary anthology *Theater and Film in the Third Reich* and Philip Roth's rewriting of the story of Anne Frank, *The Ghostwriter*. In 1985 he read Victor Klemperer's *LTI*, an account of the mutilation of the German language during the Third Reich.

Also in the early 1980s, Jurek undertook another film on a "Jewish" topic. This time he joined with his fellow "exile" Thomas Brasch to write *The Passenger: Welcome to Germany (Der Passagier—Welcome to Germany*, also directed by Brasch). Brasch was born in England in 1944. His father was Horst Brasch, a Communist Party functionary who would become deputy minister of culture when he and his wife returned to Germany and settled in the Soviet zone in 1945. By 1968, Thomas Brasch was an active member of the internal GDR opposition, having served one year of a two-year prison sentence for distributing leaflets against the Warsaw Pact invasion of Czechoslovakia. He had been expelled from his film studies and, unlike Jurek, was forced to leave the GDR as a result of the Biermann affair in 1976.

The Passenger: Welcome to Germany was released in 1987 and was premiered at the 1988 Cannes Film Festival. Like *David,* it was intended to be a film about the Third Reich and the Jews but with a more self-reflexive turn.[68] Like Michael Verhoeven's *Nasty Girl* (1990), it was one of the first experimental examinations of the Shoah in the West German cinema of the 1980s. Set in contemporary West Berlin, the film used Tony Curtis, an American actor with a Hungarian Jewish background, in a role that reflected on his own past as well as the problems of creating art to reflect history and identity. Curtis plays Cornfield (the film's working title was "Last Call, Mr. Cornfield"), a successful American director of a TV series about dogs and horses, who goes to Berlin to film a historical movie about the making of a movie during the Third Reich. For this film-in-the-film to have been made in 1942, thirteen Jews were taken from Auschwitz to be used as actors. They were promised that they would be deported to Switzerland after the film was completed, but all but one of them were murdered.

The use of "real" Jews in the film paralleled the use of Jews from the ghettos in Germany in the making of the anti-Semitic quasi-documentary *The Eternal Jew (Der ewige Jude)* by Fritz Hippler in 1940, as well as Leni Riefenstahl's use of gypsies in her unfinished final film, *Tiefland*. It also had an odd personal resonance for Jurek. In reading Joseph Wulf's anthology about Nazi film making, Jurek read about the making of the most infamous of Nazi films, Veit Harlan's *Jew Süss* in 1940.[69] Harlan, according to Wulf's sources, traveled to Poland to "study various Jewish types" that he wanted to use in the film. They were to be played by the German actor Werner Krauss, who undertook multiple "Jewish" roles in the film. Jews, according to a footnote to a Nazi source, were not actually cast in any roles in the film. Wulf reprinted, however, a fascinating review of the opening of the film in Litzmannstadt in January 1941, which stated that "the film was made here in Litzmannstadt, formerly Lodz. The camera was able to capture in the ghetto the various types of Jews that most visibly represented world Jewry." One can imagine Jurek thinking about this in relation to his parents and his own life in the Litzmannstadt ghetto in 1941. Were they in the film, hidden in the background? Had they been given the option to appear? With the promises of what rewards? For Brasch, the film questioned the line between victim and perpetrator; for Jurek, it was potentially part of his lost autobiography.

The Cornfield of *The Passenger* was a young Hungarian, Janko Kornfeld, who was recruited to act in the 1942 Nazi film with his friend Baruch (played by the Turkish-German actor Birol Ünel). Baruch attempted to escape because he was suspicious of the Nazi promise that the Jewish actors would be freed. We discover at the close of the film that Baruch was murdered during the escape because of Cornfield's hesitation. Even the figures in the film that Cornfield is directing recognize that the film is "therapy, not film making," in the words of one of the characters. The therapy was intended, much like that in *The Boxer,* to help "cure" the trauma that resulted from the experiences in the Shoah. The guilt here, however, is Cornfield's, not the SS man who shoots Baruch. Brasch remarked that there was a tendency to speak of victims only "in their role as victims, whether as Jews or Turks or women or homosexuals." That the victim could also be guilty now is inconceivable, even though there was "a struggle between Eastern and Western Jews in the camps, between the rich and the poor."[70] Blaming the victim was, as Jurek well knew, an established means by which the Germans provided an answer to the guilt created by the Shoah.

A powerful thread in the film-in-the-film is the desire of the Nazi director, Körner (played by Matthias Habich), to have "real" Jews play Jews in his film. The question whether only Jews can represent Jews became central to Jurek's later rereading of this film. Cornfield recruits a German actor (actually played by Charles Regnier) rather than a Jewish actor to play the Jewish banker in his "remake" of the historical film. Indeed, the one actor who claims to be Jewish and states that he was one of the thirteen recruited for the Nazi film reveals himself to have been a German bit-player who had been rejected from the original film, but "who had always wanted to be Jewish." Cornfield himself is an anomaly—"a Jew with blue eyes," as one of the characters remarks. The definition of what is "Jewish" in the final film ("Jews are a people without a country") presented a problem for Jurek.

Jurek distanced himself from the final, filmed version. He must have found the overtly Christian images in Brasch's film discomfiting: the image of Baruch as the crucified Jewish Christ; the scene with the Jewish actors as Jesus and his disciples at the Last Supper, staged like Leonardo Da Vinci's painting, with Cornfield as Judas. Jurek's final credit reads that he "helped with the screenplay." On his copy of the penultimate screenplay he wrote that he had little to do with that version; and on the final one he wrote that he had absolutely nothing to do with it. But the importance of this film lay in the material it provided for the final volume of Jurek's great trilogy of novels on the Shoah and its echo in East Germany.

In 1983, Jurek sat down to research the third novel in his trilogy. *Jacob the Liar* had dealt with the murder of the Jews as told in the voice of a GDR survivor. *The Boxer* narrated the life of the adult survivor and his survivor son in the GDR. The third volume would be dedicated to examining the survivors and their children born in the GDR, those "blessed with a late birth," using the phrase coined by Helmut Kohl, then chancellor of the FRG, on a 1984 trip to Israel. Jurek understood Kohl's phrase as meaning "from now on we should be allowed to suppress the past with impunity." This was certainly not what Jurek had intended to do. What might the proper manner of imagining the Holocaust be for those who, like his own sons, were born after it?[71]

In 1983, Jurek was elected to the West German Academy of Language and Literature at Darmstadt. It was a sign that he had become a member of the intellectual elite of the FRG. His acceptance speech stressed how he had had to learn German as a child, but first had to forget his Polish. He was a "real" German writer precisely because he was not "at home" in the German language but was always consciously searching for a home when he used it.[72] Jurek's reputation was now anchored to his being a "German" writer, and that meant a writer located in the intellectual life of the FRG. But his reputation, increasingly international, was still as a Jew, especially in the United States.

In the spring of 1983, I telephoned Jurek and invited him to participate the following spring in a new model of teaching contemporary writers that I had developed at Cornell University. The students in this seminar would read all (or most) of a writer's work before arriving on campus and then read it again with the writer present. The idea was not to correct our readings but to elicit from the writers their sense of where we were "right" or "wrong." Their responses to our readings were crucial to us, and we analyzed them as well as the works themselves. Jurek accepted with the proviso that by the spring of 1984 he had to have finished his new project, the television series *Liebling Kreuzberg*. Of course I agreed, and he arrived in Ithaca for the month of April 1984. He was accompanied by Christine, whose father was a publisher I knew from earlier scholarly projects. That semester, about ten students gathered each week to read all of Jurek's work from *Jacob the Liar* to *Everybody's Darling*. We placed great emphasis on Jurek's "Jewish" texts, which especially interested me, but also considered other interpretive frameworks such as feminism.

Jurek and Christine came to my family's Passover seder. Our sons were quite small, and we had invited another family with young children to join us. Things were mildly chaotic. Jurek was hardly in his element; it was clear to all of us that he was uncomfortable. We all were a bit too Jewish for him, reveling in the intense family experience of celebrating the departure from Egypt. Eastern Jews and their children may be fine as literary subjects, but not as dinner companions.

Jurek told me later that he felt much more at home with our mutual friend Ruth Klüger, whose autobiography *Still Alive* became a best-seller in its original German in the mid-1990s.[73] Their experiences were very similar: a youth that moved from a middle-class milieu to the camps. Ruth was raised in Vienna, survived Theresienstadt and Birkenau-Auschwitz, and moved to the United States in the late 1940s. She became a major literary critic and a significant cultural player in both the United States and the FRG as a German-Jewish survivor. Jurek had much greater difficulty identifying with Eastern Jews, whose Jewish identity was secular as well as religious.

Being made to feel "Jewish" was not limited to Jurek's reception in the United States—that most Jewish of countries, in his perception. On Christine's urging, Jurek and she went to Israel for the first time, from August 29 to September 18, 1984. Jurek traveled incognito for almost a month. In Israel he found it extremely difficult to converse with people. He saw himself as an observer in a land full of Jews. As he met self-identified Jews and saw the wide range of their identities, Jurek realized that being Jewish was a lot more than being a "victim of fascism" or (in the anti-Zionist rhetoric of the GDR) an aggressor; it was a complicated and nuanced identity, which might even incorporate him.

After returning from Ithaca and Israel, Jurek began to write his new novel. He systemically wrote a page and a half a day of his third "Jewish" novel, tentatively called "How I Became a German"[74] and eventually published as *Bronstein's Children*. It continued Jurek's chronicle of Jewish life after the Shoah into the 1970s, presenting the story of a young man born well after the Shoah whose experience of it is only from the perspective of the GDR. Set between August 1973 and August 1974, it describes the life of survivors and their children in the GDR at the time of the illness and death of the former Communist Party boss Walter Ulbricht in East Berlin (10, 217).[75] This period also saw the resignation in 1974 of Willy Brandt as prime minster of West Germany after a Stasi agent, Günter Guillaume, was revealed as working for him (44). In the novel, Ulbricht represents the repudiation of the GDR's responsibility for the Shoah. In contrast, Brandt's falling to his knees on December 9, 1970, at the monument to the Warsaw ghetto uprising made him into a powerful symbol of German acknowledgement of the Shoah. It was between 1973 and 1974 that the promise of change within real existing socialism offered in 1971 by Ulbricht's successor Erich Honecker could have been fulfilled, but this was not to be. At the same time, West German conservative politics were beginning to unravel Brandt's moral legacy. These negative moments receive prominent mention in the novel as historical signposts.

Jurek used the emotional fragments from his own life and that of his sons as building blocks for his characters and their history. If his struggle with Max, as reflected in *The Boxer*, centered on the conflict that attends all fathers and their sons, the specific explanation that Jurek gave himself for Max's failure as a father was "Holocaust trauma." What accounted for his own failure both as a son and as a father went unspoken. In his new novel, Jurek began to explore the world of Nicki and Lonni, a world he imagined as mirroring his own experiences as a son.

Bronstein's Children, centers on the lives of a survivor of the Holocaust, Arno, and his son, Hans. Hans, who completes high school in 1973 (63), is thus slightly older than Nicki. The narrative begins with Hans's discovery that his father and two of his cronies, Gordon Kwart and Rotstein, have tracked down and kidnapped a guard, Arnold Heppner, who had served at the Neuengamme concentration camp (16). While none of the three were incarcerated at the camp, all are survivors. Hans has to look up "Neuengamme" in the encyclopedia to learn about it, so little does he know of his father's history. The kidnapping occurred because Arno and his accomplices "agreed they were living in an inferior country, surrounded by second-rate people who didn't deserve any better" (66). They considered the GDR an untrustworthy place, the world of the murderers, despite the official claims of the state.

Hans overhears his father and the two other men planning what to do with Heppner after they have finished beating him up and interrogating him. They are speaking Yiddish. "It was inconceivable that Father should be able to communicate in that language; I felt that there must be a stranger in there with Father's voice. Not only had he always avoided speaking Yiddish in my presence: he had never so much as indicated that he was able to" (191). Arno's Jewish identity is defined by the very aspects of his character and background that he cannot talk about with his son. Language, as is rarely the case in such an explicit manner in Jurek's fiction, defines identity and history, and serves to distance father and son.

In his attempt to understand the kidnapping, Hans finds himself in conflict with Arno.

"How am I not to treat you?" Father asked.
"Like an enemy."
"But you are my enemy." (157)

Hans is Arno's enemy because he cannot share Arno's experiences. He is a "new" German, a citizen of a state with laws and justice. Hans's task is to try to understand his father in spite of their totally different experiences, but he fails. After Arno shouts at him because he has wasted the monthly food money, Hans mutters, "You're confusing me with your Nazi — why else won't you give me any food. Or: Do you believe that every Jew should go miserably hungry at least once in his life?" (211). Hans sees himself as being forced into the role that his father was forced into by the Germans. What Hans wants is a "normal life," as his girlfriend Martha notes. "The real victims are forever wanting to celebrate memorial days and organize vigils, and you want silence to be kept" (219). Yet Arno too demands that silence.

After a series of confrontations with Hans, Arno shows up drunk one evening at their apartment. He claims it was the news of Ulbricht's death that made him drink. Hans doesn't believe him (232). He senses that Arno is tormented by Heppner, overcome by waves of memories that have been released by his new, inverted role as perpetrator torturing a victim. Hans, torn between his obligation to "justice" and his filial duty to his father, finally buys a couple of files so that he can force open Heppner's handcuffs and free him.

Heppner's neighbors have not missed him. Since he is over sixty-five, they assume he went to the West (225–26). Hans knows that Heppner cannot go to the police, for that would be an admission of his own guilt. Freeing him means freeing his father of his guilt and restoring "order" in his own world. When he reaches the cabin in which Heppner has been held, he finds his father there, dead of a heart attack. Heppner says over and over that he didn't do it, the mantra he had repeated when asked about his deeds at the camp. Hans first tries to file him loose, then reaches into his dead father's pocket to find the key. The key may free Heppner, but Hans is still trapped by his father's life and death.

The novel, told in flashback form, begins a year after Arno's death. Hans is living with the family of his girlfriend, Martha Lepschitz. Hugo Lepschitz is a minor official in the GDR. He and his wife Rahel are de-lighted that their daughter has a Jewish boyfriend. They are Jewish in terms of their private rituals. Hugo, for example, goes regularly to the one store in East Berlin that sells Hungarian matzos, which he consumes every day as a sign of his Jewish identity (3), though the unleavened bread is normally only eaten during the week of Passover. While liv-ing with the Lebschitzes, Hans learns that he has been admitted to the university to study philosophy. Hugo had suggested medicine, which is also what Arno had wanted him to study (5–6). Like Jurek, Hans chooses philosophy against an adult's wishes. Reflecting Jurek's advice to Lonni about having direction in his life, Hans explains: "I have no idea where my studies will lead me, but . . . I am curious to find out; . . . this curiosity, while not limitless, is still greater than the interest I have in any of the other disciplines" (72).

Hans's mother had died giving birth to him, and his nineteen-year-older sister Elle was institutionalized because of trauma suffered from being hidden by a Polish farmer during the Shoah. It seems to Hans that his own birth was an attempt to replace his sister, whose existence was only revealed to him when he was a teenager. He sees her importance to his father even in her absence. He imagines that Arno was in the black market after the war to ensure that Elle could remain in a good hospital (28). These two women, both missing and yet always present in Hans's life, define his way of seeing the world: "Maybe it's because my mother died so young, but the women I tend most often to gape at are between thirty and forty" (121).

Given Jurek's work with Thomas Brasch on *The Passenger: Wel-come to Germany,* one of the most revealing scenes in *Bronstein's Chil-dren* is the one where Hans observes the filming of a movie about the

Resistance in which his Jewish girlfriend is cast in the role of a Jew. This theme is worked out in the novel as a complex answer to the confusion about casting and identity that haunts the final version of Brasch's film. (Who are Jews in Brasch's film? Are they the non-Jewish and Jewish actors playing Jews from the concentration camps in the film-within-the-film, or the contemporary Jews playing Jews, such as Tony Curtis?)

In the course of the novel, Martha develops an interest in acting. She alters her appearance. She starts "using strange words, rolling her eyes, reading different books, using eye shadow from 'the West' " (8). She has become different in language and appearance, much like the "Jews" in *The Passenger: Welcome to Germany*. But as she plays at being a Jew, she becomes less rather than more Jewish. While this is occurring, she is recruited by the director Roland Minge to be in a film titled *The Years before the Beginning* (91) when one of the other actresses drops out. The film is a variant of the 1970s DEFA antifascist film, emphasizing the communist resistance to Nazi domination, but in this case with a Jewish heroine. It is the story of Rahel, a member of a communist resistance group that kidnaps the child of an industrialist to obtain money for the group's underground activities.

Martha's character Rahel has a love affair with another member of the group. Since all the characters in the film represent communists, Hans thinks any "specific" difference should not be important: "consequently it made no difference to Rahel that she was Jewish—at least that's how I took it" (92). But Minge, who is beginning a relationship with Martha, wants a Jewish actress for the part. "She looked the way Mr. Minge imagined a pretty young Jewish girl looked. I could understand his dilemma: young Jewish girls are few and far between, and here Martha suddenly turns up on his doorstep" (94). The dilemma is further complicated by the definition of who "looks" Jewish.

In Brasch's film, Cornfield casts "against" type by using a German actor to play a Jewish banker. Brasch himself, however, while using a Turkish-German actor to play Baruch, also cast the Jewish playwright and actor Georg Tabori to play the Rabbi in the film. More importantly he changed the identity of Tony Curtis's character in the film from Polish to Hungarian to match the actual origin of Curtis's parents. Hans wonders, "Why did Jews in movies have to be played by real Jews? When Martha was offered this part, she should have replied: Only if the SS men are real SS men" (169). This is a central problem in defining who or what a Jew is. Is a Jew merely one who turns his or her Jewish identity into capital? "It left a bitter taste in my mouth to see a Jewish origin or a Jewish face turned into money" (183). This theme reflects Jurek's own problem as "victim" in the GDR and the advantages inherent to that visibility. It also reflects his reading about the Litzmannstadt filming of Veit Harlan's film: did his parents not look "Jewish" enough to be in the film? What does Jewish visibility mean in the light of the Shoah and its resonance in German culture after 1945?

In *Bronstein's Children*, the meaning of Jewish "visibility" is applied to the second generation of Jews in the GDR. In order to graduate from high school, Hans needs to get a B in the infamous swimming test, which, being poor at physical education, he barely manages to pass. Afterward, as he is showering, a "short husky fellow student" challenges him ordering him to take off his swim trunks as the school rules demand. Hans punches him in the face. Suddenly his memory of discovering Heppner and of his father's role in the kidnapping becomes one with his image of the bully in the shower as a Nazi: "He stared at me with respect as well as anger. I liked him better without that camp-guard look" (33). Later, the student approaches Hans and says he understands. Hans imagines that one of the teachers must have told him, "Hans is a Jew." The cause in this fantasy is Hans's implicit visibility without his swim trunks, his circumcision. But Hans, like Jurek's own two sons, was not circumcised—presumably because of Arno's anxiety about Jewish visibility in the GDR after the Shoah.

Arno's view was that "there were no Jews at all. Jews were an invention; whether a good or bad one was debatable" (37). Hans's sense of Arno's, Martha's, and his own identity as Jews seems shaped only by their shared history. There were still traces of the biological fantasies about Jewishness in the GDR. Hans topic in his biology examination is "The Cell as the Transmitter of Hereditary factors" (77). Is not history also a transmitter of "hereditary factors"?

The novel's provisional title, "How I Became a German," sounded like a handbook on how one becomes a German rather than a novel about the confusion of identity. Christine urged Jurek to come up with something quite new. They spent an evening tossing "Jewish" names for the novel back and forth until Christine suggested *Bronstein's Children*, the title under which the novel appeared in both East and West. Jurek dedicated the work to Christine, who had listened and critiqued every word of it during his nightly readings as the novel progressed.

Who, of course, is Bronstein? The name simply does not appear in the novel. There has been considerable speculation, ranging from Trotsky (whose name was Lev Bronstein) to the protagonist of the novel, whose family name is never mentioned. Jurek maintained that he wanted what would sound like a "typical" Jewish name to his German readers (unlike Becker, one could add, which is also a good German name). Both the name "Bronstein" and the title of the novel reflect the problem of identity among Jews who, like Jurek's sons, were born in a society where Jewish identity was not an easy option.

Although the novel is set in the year of Walter Ulbricht's death, Jurek finished it at the moment when the meaning of the Shoah was raised in a new and unique manner in West German public culture. It was published after the West German historian Martin Broszat's 1985 proposal that the history of the Shoah be "normalized," and after the debate in June 1986 over Ernst Nolte's claim that everything the Nazis did had already been done by the Soviets.[76] Jürgen Habermas's answer was that Brozat and Nolte were revising (and therefore relativizing) the German past. The central issue in this debate, the uniqueness of the Holocaust and the role of ideology in the production of memory (or at least history), were both central to Jurek's project. It was Jurek's intent to present this struggle with the past, from both a "German" and a "Jewish" perspective in the FRG and the GDR.

By March 13, 1986, the manuscript of *Bronstein's Children* was in Elisabeth Borchers's hands at Suhrkamp. Jurek already visualized the novel in print and wanted the various levels of the novel (the sister's letters, the flashbacks, the narratives) designated by different typefaces.[77] In the GDR, Sigurd Schmidt and H. J. Bernard of the University of Rostock had read the manuscript for Hinstorff by September 1986.[78] They strongly supported its publication as an example of antifascist literature that was clearly written and easy to read. The more popular tone of the novel was not lost on Horst Simon and his editor Kirsten Thietz, who pointed it out in their letter of application for government approval.[79] They saw this tone as a "reflex of Becker's work for the Western mass media." They mentioned that they had worked with Elisabeth Borchers to strengthen the text and develop the characters more fully. Although Jurek had improved the narrative and had explored the character of Hans's sister Elle in greater detail, the novel still appeared to have some structural problems. But none of this reduced its impact. Because of its historical GDR theme, it seemed suited to East German readers in a time of growing self-awareness of their own history. The trilogy of *Jacob the Liar*, *The Boxer*, and *Bronstein's Children* mapped the life of Jews in Jurek's fictive world of the GDR after the Shoah and the conflicted reconstitution of a Jewish identity in that world, no matter how fragmentary and misunderstood. Jurek's own children had become "good" Germans; the ghost that Jurek saw in their lives was a projection of his own survivor experience, not of their GDR experience.

Liebling Kreuzberg

In September of 1983, Jurek had a meeting with Manfred Krug that changed both of their careers. Krug had left the GDR shortly before Jurek but had not established himself in the West as well as Jurek had. A movie star and popular singer who had made many records in the GDR, Krug never seemed quite suited to the mass media or to the variety world of West Germany.[80] He had landed a continuing role in a soap opera (*Auf Achse*), but little more. In January 1983, Otto Meissner, a West Berlin television producer, ran into Lothar Loewe, the ZDF programmer, at a party celebrating the birthday of the popular playwright Curth Flatow. Meissner was considering a new series set in contemporary Berlin and dealing with the day-to-day life of a lawyer in both his professional and his private life.

It occurred to Loewe that this would be a good slot for Manfred Krug. Meissner approached Krug, suggesting that he might do a pilot of the projected series, and Krug expressed great interest. But they needed to find someone who could write the series in a manner appropriate both for Krug and for West German viewers. Krug suggested his old friend Jurek Becker,[81] and the two met in September to talk it over.

Jurek's apprenticeship in the West German film industry over the past decade with Karl Fruchtmann, Peter Lilienthal, and Thomas Brasch had taught him what would and what would not work in the West and what his strengths and weaknesses were as a screenwriter. He was well aware that he lacked the specialized knowledge to write anything about the practice of law in West Berlin. Jurek was also suspicious of commercial television. Filming his novels for television was one thing, writing an on-going series was quite another. Jurek and Christine joined Krug and Meissner at an Italian restaurant one evening to discuss the series. Christine had reservations; writing for television was beneath her expectations for Jurek. Krug and Jurek worked hard to persuade her the project was worthwhile. Jurek was only willing to do the writing under a pseudonym, as he had for some of his more popular shows on East German television. The public channel SFB had commissioned the series, but they told Meissner they would show it only if Jurek used his real name. They were convinced that having a "real" writer would increase the series' visibility.

By the time the first episode of *Liebling Kreuzberg* (as the series was named) was aired on SFB on February 17, 1986, the commercial channels had begun to siphon off many potential viewers.[82] Jurek was convinced that good popular television could exist independently of the normal market forces that dominate commercial television. In a "German Media Day" speech in October 1994, he bemoaned the gradual erosion of the public media, including radio, in the new Germany.[83] He remembered radio as a source for truth in a confusing world. In the 1980s, public programming still expressed a seriousness of purpose, though Jurek was constantly doing battle with those who wanted him to write only light entertainment. In promoting the new series, SFB gave Jurek's name top billing. It was a claim for quality that, together with Krug's stardom, attracted the initial audiences. The show became an immediate success.

For the first six scripts, Jurek turned to his friend Nicolas Becker (Irene Dische's husband) to remedy his ignorance about the law. Nicolas was a lawyer in the well-known firm of Schily, Becker & Geulen. The senior partner, Otto Schily, was one of the most prominent liberal lawyers during the 1980s. In the late 1990s he became minister of the interior in the first Socialist–Green Party federal government. Nicolas was at the time very much his junior partner. The working relationship between Nicolas and Schily inspired the humorous relationship between Robert Liebling, the fictional lawyer that Jurek created for Manfred Krug, and his associate, Giselmund Arnold (played by Michael Kausch). Nicolas suggested various cases that were appearing in the West Berlin courts for Jurek to visit, so that he could get a feel for the process and, more importantly, the kinds of people involved.[84] Beginning in the fall of 1983, Nicolas read and commented on each script, correcting the technical errors that crept in. Lawyers in Germany were delighted with the accuracy and tone of Jurek's scripts. They had rarely been presented in a better light on German TV.[85]

Although *Bronstein's Children* was completed after Jurek had finished his work on *Liebling Kreuzberg*, the novel appeared at the same time as the series. It demonstrated that Jurek could write both for television and for a serious reading public. At the core of both the novel and the TV series was his conviction that the formal process of law as found in West Berlin (and the FRG) protected the individual against claims of the state. This view of the law was in unspoken contrast to both the GDR and to the Nazi past. Nazi Germany had dispensed with the formal rule of law, relying on the whim of the leader. In *Bronstein's Children*, the captured Nazi guard says to Hans, "These gentlemen refuse to accept that in those days there was a different law." Arno snaps, "Don't ever utter the word 'law' in my presence!" (17). Liebling provides the shield of the law. A lawyer does not ask whether the client is guilty; a lawyer does not seek the "truth";

a lawyer's function is to balance the power of the state. This, of course, became the dilemma for Hans in the novel. Who protects whom against what? At the Nuremberg trials, Nicolas's own father, Heinrich Becker, was one of the defense attorneys for Ernst von Weizsäcker, the state secretary of the Nazi Foreign Ministry. Nicolas did not always approve of his father's position in this matter but saw the need to defend even the most abject client.

Liebling came to be the embodiment of an antiauthoritarian West Berlin. Manfred Krug, remaking himself into a West German television star, borrowed from Hannes Balla, the character he had played in Frank Beyer's *Trace of Stones*. Coarse, badly dressed, aggressive, and always ironic, Liebling represented the West Berlin notion of a nonconformist. Jurek had chosen the name carefully. The German word *Liebling* means "darling," and the title of the show could thus be read as a paean to "Darling Kreuzberg," the section of Berlin where Jurek lived. Liebling's practice is something of a hobby. His father has left him a real estate firm and so he only takes cases that interest him. In an early episode he hires a West German lawyer, Giselmund Arnold, as his associate. Arnold has fled the comfort of his father's law firm in Stuttgart to come to West Berlin, and then to join Liebling.

Liebling's family situation is complicated. He is a divorced father with a divorced daughter who is a single mother. She plays a stronger and stronger role in the series, which frequently deals with single-parent families. The first episode, "The New Man" ("Der neue Mann"), which sets the tone for the series, opens—before the credits—with an odd scene of two elderly people who come to Liebling's office demanding a divorce. They never reappear. This elderly couple, used as a comic device, reinforces the idea that all relationships can be severed. This would come to be a norm in the series.

The Kreuzberg of Liebling (and of Jurek) figures prominently in the series,[86] which presents West Berlin as a self-enclosed city-state. The Kreuzberg district is defined by the world of Berlin corner bars, the "Turkish" market, the run-down apartment blocks with their sunless courtyards. The force that artificially defined Berlin, namely, the wall, is virtually missing in the first series, written in 1983–84. It appears only twice in the first six episodes, and then only in background shots. It first appears in the third episode, "The Protector" ("Der Beschützer"), when Liebling passes by a section of the wall, pats it, and Manfred Krug adlibs, "High-quality German work!" ("Deutsche Wertarbeit!") The second appearance occurs in the final episode of the first season. Liebling directs a long monologue at his associate to explain his philosophy of law. He stresses the formal aspects of law and the absence of any moral or ethical claims for the lawyer. Defending the client is the point, not asking whether the client is innocent or guilty. During this monologue, Liebling and Arnold are strolling through Kreuzberg. At one point Arnold walks up the viewing platform that enabled people to look over the wall. As Liebling discusses the absolute right of all defendants to have counsel, the camera pans across the death strip, focuses on a guard tower, and then, in the distance, shows the television tower in East Berlin. This shot was the invention of Heinz Schirk in what would turn out to be his last show in the series. The combination of shots, the Turkish market in Kreuzberg and the death strip, point to the contrast between the two legal systems. The implicit contrast in Jurek's script was made explicit in the camerawork. No reference to the wall is to be found in the scripts. When Jurek saw this episode, he lost his temper. This unsubtle comment on the lack of justice in the GDR was the last thing he wanted viewers on the other side of the wall to see. They could easily draw the inference themselves.

Liebling Kreuzberg received an almost 50 percent audience share during its first season. Yet Jurek was dismissive of mere popularity: "If television were produced purely on the basis of market research, three of the five channels here in Germany would be showing pornography; one soccer and boxing; and the other war films."[87] The producer loved the series' success, and Jurek did too, once he realized the amount of celebrity and money such a show can generate.

What Jurek was able to capture in *Liebling Kreuzberg* was the poetry of West Berlin and its multicultural and multifaceted inhabitants. By the mid-1980s, a certain normality had been created in West Berlin. The mutual recognition of both Germanys had meant that more West Berliners could travel to the East, and East Berliners, at least those over sixty-five, could even move to the West. The wall remained standing, and twenty-five years after its construction it defined the mentality of the West Berliners as inherently different from other citizens of the FRG. It was in this West Berlin that Jurek felt most at home by the time he came to write the series. West Berlin was not quite the West. "You ask where I am at home: If I have to say it: I feel at home in West Berlin, no other place is closer or more intimate."[88] The new circle of friends and family was defining "home" for Jurek. This sense of intimacy was the most powerful element in the series. *Liebling Kreuzberg* became one of the primary cultural documents showing how West Berlin was imagined in West German culture in the period shortly before and after the tearing down of the wall. Jurek never claimed that it was an "accurate" portrait of the city. Only sport shows are "true and accurate." The show was about "the unassuming, the proletarian, the quotidian."[89] No major legal cases are presented. The episodes deal with the sort of multicultural clientele that Nicolas Becker had as his clients.

Typical for the power and detail of the series is the third episode, "The Protector," in which Liebling is called on to defend a young Turkish man, Ismail Günes, who is accused of having attacked a fellow countryman, Orhan Anday, with an iron bar. It is revealed that the man who was attacked had harassed Ismail's sister, who is studying medicine. The fathers arrange to settle the case out of court, trading a parcel of land in Turkey for the withdrawal of the charges. In a joint celebration of the two families, Liebling is included in the festivities, though he is upset by the decision to settle as he is not convinced his client would have been convicted. Orhan Anday again harasses the young woman, who shoves him away in self-defense. He hits his head, falls, and dies. She leaves the apartment, and her brother is again accused of the crime. As Liebling is leaving, he sees her calmly leaning against a wall outside the apartment, and approaches her. The show stops at this point. Characterization in this episode is complex. There is neither liberal romanticizing of Turkish life nor general condemnation of a "foreign" way of life. The "Turkish" figures run the gamut from the secularized daughter to the older men who hold to the traditional order of things. No easy answers are given to the problems raised, and the plot does not actually resolve, but the problems are defined by brilliant dialogue and striking situations.

Jurek's key to creating *Liebling Kreuzberg* was the "absence of the duplicity ... that is commonplace in most television."[90] Writers, as Jurek passionately argued both in the GDR and in West Berlin, had to be true to what they believed in. This was why writing fiction was easier than making movies. But writing, like making movies, always involved compromises. Sometimes they were overt, like cutting the Biermann reference in his volume of short stories. More often, as he argued in *Misleading the Authorities,* they were subtle, made unconsciously because of the system in which one lived.

Writing for television in the FRG meant once again dealing with overt censorship. The SFB channel would not approve the sixth episode in the first season of *Liebling Kreuzberg* because it dealt with the alleged mishandling of a suspect by a policeman. The station saw the show as too obvious an attempt to insert contemporary "problems" into what is seen as entertainment. Jurek relented, and replaced the script. Likewise, when he tried to introduce a little of the historical past, he was challenged by an editor who saw it as inappropriate in a popular television show.

In the episode, Arnold needs to buy a robe for court, and Liebling asks why he doesn't simply use his father's. Arnold says it is because the stitches holding the Swastika are still visible on the robe.[91] "Entertain, don't preach" was the motto for the show. Jurek managed to do both.

The success of the show during the 1986 season was extraordinary. Not only was the series widely watched across all of the demographic groups, but it also received critical acclaim. In 1987, Jurek, Krug, and the series' director, Heinz Schirk, received the Adolf Grimme Prize in Gold, the German "Emmy," for the episode titled "The Protector." In 1988, they received the Adolf Grimme Prize in Silver for the entire first series of *Liebling Kreuzberg*. Quality commercial television had become familiar to the German viewing public.

Even before the first series had achieved its high ratings, Otto Meissner and Manfred Krug wanted to plan for a second season, to be broadcast in 1987–88. Jurek needed a break in order to write *Bronstein's Children*. Only when the first series as well as the novel was a popular success did he feel he could continue. Jurek hated Heinz Schirk's conception of how the series should look. Schirk, who was best known for his work in advertising and commercials, had created a smooth, almost touristlike image for Jurek's West Berlin. It was at once too pretty and too obviously political. Krug too disliked working with Schirk. So Krug and Jurek persuaded Meissner to replace Schirk by Werner Masten, with whom Krug had worked in West German television before *Liebling Kreuzberg* became a hit.[92] Meissner was initially opposed to Masten, for Masten had visualized a series with even more fragmentary story lines. Meissner believed that the strong "reality" quality of the series was the basis for its success and got Masten to go along with him. As a result, the second series matched or even surpassed that of the first. Thirteen episodes were added to the initial six.

The program now focused on defining the power of the state. Jurek used the figure of the state's attorney (*Staatsanwalt*) to represent a state that was powerful and self-satisfied with its actions against Liebling's clients. The attorneys representing the state are shown watering flowers, feeding their parrots, and evincing little interest in the claims Liebling and his associate make on behalf of their clients. Liebling continues successfully to defend the "little man" against the power of the state. The "little men" were often foreigners, as in the episode "Court of Honor" ("Ehrengericht"), where a Turk is refused welfare payments because he will not work in a slaughterhouse disemboweling pigs. It makes one wonder what Kafka's world would have been like if Josef K. had had a decent lawyer to defend him.

The series continued to earn awards. In 1988, Jurek received the "Golden Gong" of the popular magazine *Gong*. In the same year he received the "Tele-Star" for the script of the series. In 1989 he was honored by the German lawyers' organization with their "Press Prize" for the seventh episode. In 1990, the Bavarian Television Prize was awarded to the series and to Jurek as scriptwriter. A third series, also directed by Masten, which brought the number of episodes up to twenty-seven, ran through the 1989 season. In the final episode of the third series, "All Sorts of Goodbyes" ("Jede Menge Abschied"), broadcast in 1990, Giselmund Arnold, whose wife has left him, decides to leave Robert Liebling's office and set up on his own. A series that began with a comic divorce in 1986 concluded three years later with another divorce. By then, Jurek had just about exhausted the characters and their lives. He seemed to be repeating himself.[93] Besides, he was already beginning to work on ideas for a new novel. The year 1989 brought changes to everyone's life in West Berlin. For the time being, Jurek was no longer involved with *Liebling Kreuzberg*. The series had served its purpose: Krug was now a star of major proportions, and the income from the series guaranteed Jurek and Christine's life style.

Travel had always been one of the major elements of Jurek and Christine's life together. A workaholic who rarely let his seven-day workweek be interrupted by family, Jurek continued this pattern in his second marriage. Yet travel of all sorts provided respite for the couple. In March 1987, Walter Wetzels, chair of the German Department at the University of Texas, Austin, invited Jurek and Christine to spend a fall semester there. The long stay in the American West enabled the pair to deepen their relationship. Jurek thought of America, even Austin, a "Jewish" country. A natural storyteller, he found himself in a state of natural storytellers. One of his colleagues at Austin recalls that Jurek spoke about literary life in the two Germanys, and about his father and his own childhood, with a command that made his stories of ironic happenstance and real horrors personal, yet devoid of pathos or any trace of sentimentality. He had been asked about his concentration camp experience—what he remembered or what his days were like—and he responded, "I have no memories. Every day was the same. Hunger and brutality are monotonous. They erase memory." It was not said bitterly. It was simply an observation, *eine Feststellung.*[94] The newly married Jurek had developed a vocabulary for talking about the past that distanced it from the present and put it beyond even his own storytelling.

In May of 1988, Joachim Preuß of *Der Spiegel* made Jurek a proposal that he could not turn down. Would he attend the Seoul Olympics from

September 11–27, 1988, and write a follow-up article for the magazine at the end of September?[95] Jurek's enthusiasm for sports, which he had shared with Max, increased as he grew older. His essay catalogued his disappointment at the superficiality and commercialization of the games. He wrote about the perils of sport as a panacea for problems that are greater than sports themselves. The piece was gray, the mood depressing, even though he closed it with a joke he ascribed to Max: A man is asleep and is awoken by the doorbell. He is given a telegram informing him that his wife has died, which he reads with tired eyes. He goes back to bed, saying: "My God, what pain I will feel in the morning."[96] The pain that Jurek felt was the false exploitation of a good thing. Preuß received the piece by the deadline but decided not to publish it. Jurek was angry. He was not some journalist who had to turn in stories on a regular basis, but a writer from whom the essay had been commissioned. "How dare you do this to me!"[97] The anger was again not unexpected. He had lost control of the center of his world, his writing.

In March 1986 *Bronstein's Children* had appeared in the West. A year later Hinstorff published the GDR edition.[98] It was a major success in the FRG: by December of that year it was in its third printing, and at the end of the year it was number 13 on *Der Spiegel*'s bestseller list. In 1986, after reconciling with Hinstorff, Jurek proposed a "new" volume of short stories based on *After the First Future,* which had appeared only in the West with Suhrkamp in 1980. This volume too had again strong support from Hinstorff, with a very strong evaluation by Sigurd Schmidt of the University of Rostock, especially of the two "Jewish" stories in the volume, "The Wall" and "The Favorite Family Story."[99] The volume was finally accepted and published under the title *Stories* (*Erzählungen*). What had been seen in 1979 as politically too difficult had become, by 1986, merely interesting, for Jurek had managed to persuade the authorities in the GDR that he was not "dangerous." The negotiations were not easy. He complained to Ingrid Prignitz who attended a reading by Jurek in Bochum in October 1986, how hard it was to work with Hinstorff.[100] *Stories* came out in 1986, before *Bronstein's Children.* Suddenly Jurek was present on the literary market in the GDR with two new books. Appearing in the GDR allowed him to maintain his relationship to the world that had fostered him. But he had to keep his promise (more or less rigidly) that he would not publicly criticize the GDR in the West. Being a critic of the system was all right; being a dissident, even in the West, smacked of ingratitude.

The fine line between opponent and dissident that Jurek saw himself walking was violated by Armin Müller-Stahl in 1987. Müller-Stahl, a member of Jurek's circle of friends when Jurek was working at DEFA, had begun to establish himself on the American scene. In 1987 he was cast in his first major American role, playing opposite Kris Kristofferson in the made-for-TV film *America*, which was about the fictional occupation of the United States by Russian troops. Müller-Stahl was cast as the Russian General Samonov. He was a cardboard figure, the "evil empire" incarnate. When the film was shown, it was denounced in the United States as right-wing propaganda, although the cold war was not yet over. When Jurek saw cuts from the film on West German television, he was appalled. In a letter to Müller-Stahl, he told him he really had tried to understand the problem of Müller-Stahl's involvement in the project. "You have the right," Becker wrote, "to claim that any project that you are involved in is good and honorable and honest. But you will then have to understand when others condemn you for having switched sides for money or out of conviction (which would be no better)."[101] In accepting his role in *America* (which led to his first major Hollywood film, Barry Levison's 1990 *Avalon*), Müller-Stahl was betraying the unspoken agreement that some of those who had left the GDR in the 1970s had internalized: don't switch sides and don't let yourself be exploited by the West in the cold war as a critic of socialism. By 1987 it was clear to Jurek that the GDR was not a place where there could be real democracy.[102] Indeed, he understood that the destruction of the Prague Spring in 1968 had been actively supported by the East German authorities. Still, in creative work, one should not engage in this type of criticism. Müller-Stahl had overstepped the limit.

In 1988, Jurek was living multiple lives. He regarded himself as a socialist writer living in the West. The West German media also saw him as an exemplary survivor-author, a role that made him uncomfortable, especially after the extraordinary success of *Liebling Kreuzberg*. The success of the television series was matched by that of *Bronstein's Children*, which not only was widely read but, like *Jacob the Liar*, quickly became prescribed reading in schools to focus discussion about the Shoah. The scene was set for a public debate in West Germany about Jurek's identity, which prompted even more intense and divisive debates during the 1990s about the role of the Shoah in German (and Jewish) memory.

The End of the Cold War, and Martin Walser

Things were changing at an extraordinary pace. *Glasnost* and *peri-stroika*, openness and reform, were buzzwords in the mid-1980s. Mikhail Gorbachev had been appointed general secretary of the Communist Party of the USSR in March 1985. By 1987 he was *Time* magazine's "Man of the Year." For the East German authorities there seemed to be nothing to worry about. When asked about *peristroika*, Kurt Hager said that just because the neighbors put up new wallpaper, you didn't have to redo your own.[103] On June 9, 1987, a mass demonstration of more than three thousand people marched down Unter den Linden past Honecker's office, chanting "Gorbachev" and calling for the wall to be torn down.

In the summer of 1987, the Bonn government announced that Erich Honecker would visit West Germany in the fall. Jurek, in an article published in July, wondered what the visit would be like. Would Honecker make the sort of demands that Helmut Kohl (or Ronald Reagan) would make on a similar visit to East Berlin? Unemployment in West Germany must be reduced, West German support of apartheid in South Africa must be stopped, West Germans must cease undermining US-Soviet attempts at disarmament. What will really happen, Jurek wrote, is that Kohl will demand that the order to shoot those attempting to flee the GDR be halted, that travel restrictions be eased, that freedom to determine the direction of the state be introduced. Honecker, Jurek noted, won't be able to say what he wants to say because he is afraid of waking "sleeping dogs," but those dogs "have been awake a long time and can hardly wait to attack him."[104] Honecker's trip to the West actually had negligible results. In his speech, Honecker departed from his prepared text and observed that he hoped that the border between the GDR and the FRG would unite rather than separate the two countries, much as the border between the GDR and Poland had done. Jurek was quite right. The path of change was clear, but its extent was unknown. In 1988, Jurek was asked what would happen in two years when his ten-year visa expired; he responded that "Mr. Gorbachev still has a word to say in that matter."[105] That Gorbachev would actually say something that would transform the GDR was something Jurek may have hoped for but hardly believed would happen.

Later in June and into July 1988, Jurek had taken a trip with Christine and her parents to the People's Republic of China, where the drums of *glasnost* and *peristroika* had not yet been heard. On his return to West Berlin, he was again aware that the debates about politics in the present were demanding a radical rereading of the past, of his own past, which was extremely upsetting for him. In the fall of 1988, Martin Walser, one of the great liberal German authors of the 1960s and 1970s, gave a lecture as part of a long series of "Speeches about Our Own Country," sponsored by the Munich Chamber Theater (*Kammerspiele*). The lecture was published on November 4, 1988, in the weekly newspaper *Die Zeit*.[106] Walser bemoaned the state of German morale, how its negative self-image only served the occupying powers and their control over German pride. Harping on negative aspects of the German past, such as the Shoah, functioned only to perpetuate fascism. This phantom fascism, located in the German past, was being used today, according to Walser, to allow an antifascist position, a position that in turn was being used on a daily basis to beat up on the Germans.

At the beginning of his talk, Walser discussed the images we hold of our own childhood. "Images cannot be reeducated. All that I have experienced has not changed my images. When I return to these images today, I don't think they warrant revision." He attacked those who thought it politically correct to see a Nazi in every German: "Those of us who contradict this fashionable tone of political masturbation run the risk of being told we have no sense of humor. If we understand the joke, then we are all Nazis." Today's Germany was fundamentally different from Hitler's Germany, and even that Germany had islands of solace, peace, and quietude. All of us have pasts: "It should be enough to say that what forms us is the past. Every tree that we see refers to an earlier tree." Walser lamented that the insistent talk of Nazi crimes had poisoned the sweetest memories of his childhood in the Third Reich. As in Edgar Reitz's 1984 television film *Heimat*, the Shoah was totally absent from such fantasies of a German childhood. Unlike Walser, Jurek deplored those fantasies. "When people tell me about the *Glück ihrer Heimat* (happiness of their homeland),"[107] he said on another occasion. In Ruth Klüger's memoir of her life in Terezin and Auschwitz, she mentions being befriended, as a fourteen-year-old in a DP camp immediately after the war, by Martin Walser. The difference in their memories of the past must have been obvious to Walser then, young as he was. But his goal was different in 1988. He now argued for a collective identity for a new Germany, combined with a new image of the past. For Walser, potential unification meant highlighting the positive aspects of the German past.

Jurek was incensed by Walser's claim to an unencumbered memory of childhood. Jurek's memories of his own childhood had been destroyed. Indeed, Walser's reference to the trees of his childhood contrast bitterly with the opening of *Jacob the Liar*, where trees are associated with the murder of the narrator's wife during the period and by the very people that Walser was nostalgic for. He openly confronted Walser on the pages of *Die Zeit*. The loss of twenty members of his family in the Shoah through "gassing or beating or starvation" was very different from Walser's "cozy childhood memories."[108] Unlike Jurek, Walser had "real" memories and could express them in the elegant style of his novels. As for the charge that antifascism was a means of keeping fascism alive in the light of neo-Nazi resurgence in West Germany, Jurek derided it. It was like saying that "Jews with their Jewish fussing keep anti-Semitism alive." He told the story of the dog owner who tells the father of a little girl who had just been bitten, "If your daughter had only stood still like a sensible person, this would not have happened" (81). Reading Walser's piece of drivel, Jurek declared, compels you to reread books of his that you had earlier praised. Given the superficiality of Walser's fantasy, you have to suspect the quality of those novels. Jurek challenged Walser's attempt to revive the older notions of family, land, and state (even though he seemed to draw them into question). By the late 1980s, these categories had reappeared in a West German view of a potentially reunified Germany.

This debate was the beginning of a long series of exchanges with Walser, which continued through the 1990s. The juxtaposition of Walser the "German" writer and Jurek the "Jewish" writer helped determine where German and Jewish memory would go after 1989. Jurek was able to counter Walser and his peaceful childhood with recourse to his own childhood—unique among major West German writers in the 1980s—told from a "Jewish" perspective, from the perspective of a Nazi victim."

In 1988, both Jurek and Walser had an eye toward the shaping of a future united Germany. Jurek admitted that no one knew where "the borders of Europe will run" in the near future. For the moment, there were two German states, but the GDR had become remarkably attentive to the debates in the FRG. Extracts from Jurek's attack on Walser as well as extracts from Walser's speech appeared in the GDR in the spring of 1989.[109] This debate had sudden significance for intellectuals in the GDR who realized that any discussion of the German future, no matter how abstract, involved rethinking the German past. No longer could anyone claim that the German past belonged to that "other" Germany. Walser's speech marked the beginning of his role as the major German intellectual commentator on the Shoah from a conservative, "German" perspective.[110] To Jurek's pleasure, Walser's position was roundly condemned by conservative thinkers such as the Polish-Jewish critic, Marcel Reich-Ranicki.[111]

Jurek was invited to deliver the most distinguished literary lectures in the FRG, the Poetic Lectures at the Goethe University in Frankfurt, during the summer semester of 1989.[112] In the three lectures, published in 1990 under the title *A Warning about the Writer*, he bemoaned the decay of writing as an art and as a craft. He opened by examining the state of writing in the FRG and in the GDR. A true writer, he believed, must be uncomfortable in society in order to produce serious literature. Franz Kafka, that potent symbol of a literature of opposition in the Prague

Spring of 1968, remained for Jurek the prime example of a writer who was uncomfortable. Jurek's former colleagues in the GDR were quite comfortable, even those in the opposition. Oppositional writing in the GDR achieved its goals only because there was censorship. Without censorship there would be no audience interested in reading between the lines of those books that appeared in the GDR. Being even marginally forbidden made you attractive. If East German writers chose to publish in the FRG, they were of interest only if they became objects of scandal. Market forces in the FRG used the GDR as a tool for selling; banning a writer's works in the East increased the number of books sold in the West. What censorship was in the GDR, the market was in the FRG. Each land manipulated literature for its own ends.

In his second lecture, Jurek critiqued the West German cultural scene. Homogeneity was the curse of every writer in the West, no matter how well established, for every writer had to fulfill the expectations of the marketplace. Success was measured by sales, and to achieve sales you could not frustrate the expectations of the market. The subject matter could not be political; a work must only entertain. Oppositional East German literature was attractive in the West because of its entertainment value. A critique of the inner workings of the GDR was a form of exoticism for a reader in the FRG, like reading about life on the moon or in the distant past.

The final lecture was itself a literary work: a dialogue between a writer and a friend who had packed the writer's library into cartons and stored them in his basement—an echo of Walter Benjamin's 1931 essay "Unpacking My Library." If Jurek's books, stored in the East until he finally moved to Kreuzberg, served as the model, then both voices in the dialogue are his own. The writer defends literature as essential; his friend sees television as replacing it. In this view, the weaker and the more debilitated a culture becomes, the more its cultural products are themselves weak and shallow. A literature that engaged the audience in the author's struggles is replaced by a form of cheap entertainment. The complexity of the argument draws even the literature/television dichotomy into question. Everything can be looked at in different ways. Jurek evokes the story of the well-trained rat that claims it has programmed the scientist well because every time it touches the bar, the scientist gives it a sugar cube. Literature remains interesting only when it remains subversive, but the writer is never quite sure whether he is truly subversive or only part of the system. Likewise, even television can be part of a critical literature, while thick novels may turn out to be the sugar cubes that are provided for the reader's escape.

Jurek carefully balanced the culture of censorship in the GDR against the culture of commercialism in the FRG. He had experienced both and had successfully used both systems for his own ends. His privileged status as a writer and filmmaker in the GDR and as an author and a television scriptwriter in the FRG has brought him wide success. The very world of West Berlin, that island of capitalism in a communist world, was about to change radically. Jurek had experienced West Berlin from 1978 to 1989. He too had changed, perhaps without being quite aware of how different he had become.

Chapter 8

JUREK BECKER IN A NEW GERMANY,
1989–1997

The End of the GDR and a New Beginning

By the spring of 1989, officials in the GDR were preparing for the state's fortieth anniversary on October 7, 1989. Mikhail Gorbachev was to be the honored guest. When the date arrived, the crowds in East Berlin demonstrated for the same sort of liberalization that was going on in the Soviet Union simply by shouting "Gorbi." Since Gorbachev's leadership of the USSR in 1985, the GDR had remained one of the most rigid communist states ideologically. (Only Albania was more conservative.) The post-Ulbricht thaw had been quickly reversed.

In that same spring, Jurek was formally invited to appear in the GDR for the first time since he left in 1977. His readings in churches in the East had been unofficial. When Heinz Kamnitzer, president of the East German PEN club, asked him to give a reading, Jurek was amazed. He had been criticizing the repressive nature of the GDR everywhere, and now he was invited to return. Shortly after he received the invitation, I met with him, and he told me that he was thinking about what would be appropriate to read. Then it struck him that he was asking the wrong question. He was censoring himself even before returning to the GDR. Without having been asked what he saw as defining the writer in the GDR, and he was already compromising his potential response. It made him very uncomfortable.

On May 9, 1989, he crossed the border to East Berlin. He was very nervous and once again felt hassled by the border guards, whom he

insulted, suggesting that the border did not represent the "true" GDR.[1]
At the PEN Club on Otto-Nuschke Street, he read from *Sleepless Days,*
the novel still banned in the GDR, and from that portion of his Frankfurt lectures in which he had criticized censorship in the GDR. His old
friend Stefan Heym, in the discussion following the reading, supported
Jurek's contention that writers in the GDR needed to have more courage.[2]
In the audience were representatives of the Hinstorff Publishing House
from Rostock. Jurek complained to them that Hinstorff and therefore
the authorities were still making it impossible for him to publish the
Frankfurt lectures with Hinstorff.[3] The editors from that firm knew that
Jurek was a real commodity, and they continued to keep his novels in
print in large numbers; the sixth GDR printing of *The Boxer,* with a run
of 10,000 copies, appeared in December 1989. After the lecture, a young
East German writer, Ina-Kathrin Koutoulas-Schildhauer, approached Jurek and asked whether he would let her reprint the Frankfurter lectures
in her *samisdat* magazine *Bizarre Städte (Bizarre Cities)*. Despite the
comments he had just made to the Hinstorff representatives, he declined
her request.[4] Censorship may be evil, but he was not going to publish
illegally within the GDR.

In June 1989, when I was teaching at the Free University of Berlin,
Jurek met with my seminar. We were reading his trilogy about the Shoah's
impact on the world of the GDR. Although change was happening all
about us, the students appeared to make no connection between the rum-
blings in the Soviet bloc and Jurek's literary representations of life as a
Jew in the GDR. For these West Berlin students, Jurek's careful locat-
ing of this "Jewish" theme as a historical one in the history of the GDR
seemed secondary to their representation of the Shoah in general. The
past had become separated from the present and, therefore, the future.
The students were struck by how engaged Jurek was, perhaps because
they were less interested in what was taking place in the Eastern bloc.
The Holocaust was the past for them; current events were not the subject
of the seminar. When Jurek tried to connect the transformation chronicled in *Bronstein's Children* with the politics of the 1970s, they nodded
sagely, but saw nothing of themselves in that connection.

In the same month, Jurek traveled to Budapest for a meeting of writers.
His sons joined him, as they were allowed to travel to Hungary but not
to the West. After that meeting, to escape from the growing pressures in
central Europe, he spent the first two weeks of September in Scandinavia
on a reading tour for the Goethe Institute. Hungary was seething with
the changes inspired by *glasnost* and had decided to open its border to
Austria. Rumors had reached Berlin by the middle of July that the West

German embassy in Budapest was giving sanctuary to citizens of the GDR. More and more people crowded into the embassy. Pressure was being put on both the West German and Hungarian governments to do something.

In the GDR too, a response was under way to the changes in the Eastern bloc.[5] On September 9, crowds gathered in front of the Nikolai Church in Leipzig, demanding political change. A popular movement for change had begun in the GDR. How powerful it was Jurek could not estimate, but he pointed out that the awakening of Soviet public opinion under Gorbachev demanded a public acknowledgment in the GDR of differences of opinion.[6] In the Soviet Union, Jurek noted, a third of the population would have been arrested had they acted under the laws of the GDR. As portrayed in *Sleepless Days,* the GDR's constitutional guarantees for freedom of speech and demonstration were undermined by the actual political practice. In West Germany, however, antiwar demonstrators were still being prosecuted in court.[7] Jurek was still carefully balancing his views on law and justice so as to criticize the GDR and the FRG equally.

Shortly after midnight on September 11, 1989, thousands of East Germans flooded through the newly opened borders of Hungary to Austria. In three days, more than fifteen thousand would make it to the West. The kind of spontaneous flight that Antonia, in *Sleepless Days,* attempts across the Hungarian border—a flight that fails because she cannot run fast enough—was now occurring in reality. In Jurek's novel, Antonia is amazed that the Hungarian border guards don't shoot at her. That their real counterparts in 1989 now more or less stood aside after an initial confrontation meant that a hole had opened in the Iron Curtain. Jurek read these events in terms of his fiction: "I am convinced," he said, "that many went to Hungary on vacation with no thoughts of fleeing. The hole in the wall was there by chance, and the people forgot themselves and everything else and fled."[8] Jurek understood that there were obvious reasons for them to leave, but his suggestion that the flight to the West was spontaneous was hardly borne out by the flow of those going to Hungary in order to leave the GDR.

That fall, Jurek conceded that GDR citizens had fled because the state had still not undertaken any reform. Though certain that there would eventually be reforms, he believed they would be preceded by "extensive repression and force." Jurek had "tolerated" the authorities long enough: "Why should we continue to play psychiatrist to the dysfunctional Politburo and continue to put them on the couch looking for motives for their strange behavior?"[9] The officials of the Politburo, of course, had done precisely that to him and had thereby manipulated him. His "privileged" status (and he used this phrase in the late 1980s) was their means of controlling him. It worked only as long as he believed *he* was controlling *them*.

On October 9, 1989, the authorities in Leipzig refused to turn the armed militias against about twelve thousand demonstrators who were chanting, "We are the people—no violence." Jurek tried to understand their motivation. Many on the left stated bluntly that all these people wanted was a physical improvement in their standard of living. Jurek acknowledged the attractiveness of the material goods of the West for those demonstrating in the GDR and beyond. For him and others, the opening of a McDonald's in Moscow symbolized the collapse of communism. Was the ideological basis of his commitment to socialism a mistake, an error of his own education as an East German? Or was the "fact" that the demonstrators seemed to be motivated by material desires proof of the inherently utopian nature of socialism? Was socialism a theory impossible to realize? For Jurek, any *future* socialism could no longer ignore the material difficulties of the present and simply blame its problems on the past. For true socialists, "that is a task that can not truly be resolved. But that is nothing new for them."¹⁰ Socialism became more and more a utopian ideal for Jurek as the GDR began to slip into what he feared would become chaos.

Jurek wanted to understand the inner lives of those citizens of the GDR who were fleeing to the West. He saw them as reacting to the image of their fathers, who were "ugly, broken, unsympathetic, bitter," from the repression of their innermost desires.¹¹ Whether this repression resulted from loyalty or cowardliness made no difference. The fathers had made "little careers" for themselves and held their tongues to do so. Their children certainly did not want to end up the same way. But who were the fathers who failed? Were they the builders of the GDR, like Ulbricht and Honecker, or were they the real fathers who failed their own sons, like Jurek? For Jurek in 1989 it was the state that failed him. He saw the short time left on his visa as "masking a divorce. You don't want to say that the relationship is at an end, that you can't sleep together."¹² Yet even if the father failed, the blood relationship to his children remained. Divorce, that public metaphor for the collapse of faith in the GDR, had been his experience with Rieke. It was a personal failing, linked to his awareness of his failing as a father. He had never felt himself at fault. It was Max who had set him a poor example as a father; it was Rieke who could not deal with him. Nicki and Lonni were quite aware of his failures as a father, even though he regularly drove to East Berlin to see them. Material goods, the product of Jurek's successful career in the West, did not a father make. Nor did they seem to be an appropriate basis for a new political order.

As he began a massive rethinking of what the GDR really meant, Jurek wrote a detailed letter to Klaus Höpcke, deputy minister of culture, on October 2, 1989, requesting another long extension of his visa.[13] He had mentioned this to Höpcke six months earlier but had received no response. He requested that the trips he and Christine made to the GDR and within it be simplified. He asked for visas for his sons, who had not been able to visit him in the West since he had left twelve years before. He believed his two young adult sons should also be granted some privileges because of their father's status.

Reform groups such as "Democracy Now" and "New Forum" began to organize the opponents to the existing government in the GDR. After it became clear that the government no longer had control of the organs of repression, Erich Honecker was deposed on October 18, 1989, by his "crown prince," Egon Krenz. In announcing his resignation, Honecker urged the Politburo to support Krenz as his successor, which branded Krenz, quite correctly, as just one more party hack. The new head of government was quite aware of his very precarious position.

In the meantime there had been a major change in Jurek's obligations as a father. In late October of 1989 Christine told Jurek that she was pregnant. She had long wanted a child, but Jurek had resisted, thinking he was done with his role as parent. What would Jurek's legacy be to this child they were now expecting?

By December of 1989, the slogan heard on the streets in Leipzig and Berlin had changed to "We are one people." The implosion of the GDR, accompanied by a popular movement toward German unification, had begun. The reformers gathered in ever larger numbers. The draw seemed indeed to be greater economic opportunity and the freedom to travel, rather than any reform of socialism.

In early November 1989, Jurek was granted a four-year visa, starting January 1, 1990, and Nicki and Lonni were granted unlimited travel to the West, a privilege they would—as things turned out—have acquired on their own.[14] Höpcke suggested a meeting with his staff on November 17, 1989, to work out the details, but this meeting, thanks to the major events that intervened, never took place.

On November 3, 1989, many of the old leaders, including Erich Mielke, head of the Stasi, and Kurt Hager, Jurek's former teacher and full-time nemesis, were dismissed from the Politburo. Hager lost all semblance of power when he was unceremoniously expelled from his government offices on November 17.

On November 4, 1989, leading artists and writers organized a demonstration in East Berlin. Stefan Heym, Christoph Hein, and Christa Wolf were among the more than two dozen speakers who addressed a rally of about a million people at the Alexanderplatz in Berlin, calling for a reform of the system and the need to listen to the people's demand for change. Christa Wolf began her speech with the remarkable comment that "every revolution frees the language." What the people wanted, however, was not just poetic freedom but the removal of all of the limits inherent in the socialist state.

On November 7, 1989, Jurek appeared on the West German television news show *Panorama* as an expert on what was happening in the GDR. He saw it as a complete failure of the government, which seemed unable to know how to act. Yet Jurek was also convinced that the SED would never willingly give up power. It would remain in power until enough people abandoned the GDR and the state simply collapsed, as it had been in danger of doing in 1961 when the wall was built. No one who listened to the intellectuals that week, either in East Berlin or on West German television, could ignore the sense that the population in the GDR simply wanted their state to vanish. Forty years of oppression and lies, the evident moral failure of the system and its leadership, were all too evident. Freedom of expression came to be the tool for dismantling the state, not an end in itself. Jurek's had predicated his estimation of the leadership's tenacity on his own experience with it during the 1970s and 1980s. By 1989 he was simply wrong. With Gorbachev, everything had changed.

The new leadership of the GDR knew that some type of regulated travel to the West was immediately necessary as a safety valve. On November 8, 1989, the tenth meeting of the Central Committee of the SED began in East Berlin with the complete elimination of the remnants of the older ruling cadre. The reform wing of the SED under Hans Modrow suddenly had a majority. The next evening, around seven o'clock, Günter Schabowski, minister of information, announced the opening of the border crossings to West Germany and West Berlin. Jurek and Christine were in Rieke's living room in East Berlin and saw the announcement on television. They simply did not understand what it meant. Returning to West Berlin before midnight, they were startled by the line of East German cars at the border crossing point but did not register what was occurring. They went home, went to bed, and fell asleep. That same night, thousands of people crossed over into West Berlin. The border between East and West Berlin was open to free transit. The wall had crumbled.

Nicki had been at Schabowski's press conference and had heard a West German journalist ask when East Germans were going to be allowed to go to the West. Schabowski answered, "Immediately." Nicki entered West Berlin with the first wave of East Berliners. At three or four o'clock in the morning, he chanced to meet his mother and brother on the Kurfürstendamm. The three of them decided to buy warm rolls and surprise Jurek and Christine. At the official exchange rate of one West German mark to five East German marks, they were the most expensive rolls they had ever bought. They paid their thirty marks and went on their way to Kreuzberg.

Very early in the morning of November 10, 1989, the doorbell at Christine and Jurek's apartment rang repeatedly. Jurek, startled out of his sleep, went to the door and found Rieke, Nicki, and Lonni standing there with a bag of warm rolls. Jurek's first response was shock. How did they get there? How long were they going to stay? That day a hundred thousand East Berliners joined the Beckers in visiting West Berlin. All at once there was a new world, the possibility of change. Indeed, it was during breakfast that Jurek and Christine told their guests about the baby they were expecting.

On November 13, the new government under the Leipzig politician Hans Modrow as prime minister, with Egon Krenz still as the state president, tried to establish a reform movement within the SED. It seemed to have little mass support. Decades earlier, Modrow had led the "student" raid that destroyed the club where Jurek and Krug met. To rally support among the intellectuals for a new GDR, government leaders tried to use the history of cultural suppression to create new credentials as reformers. On October 26, the newly elected members of the East German PEN club demanded the restructuring of the state as well as other areas of society, including culture. Heinz Kamnitzer, the club president, who had invited Jurek to speak a few months before in a gesture of liberalization, was forced to resign. On November 16, Robert Havemann and the philosopher Ernst Bloch were posthumously readmitted to the Academy of Science, from which they had been expelled for their political views decades earlier.

On November 23, 1989, the government decided to screen Frank Beyer's *Trace of Stones* at the International Cinema in East Berlin, with Krenz present.[15] Beyer invited the cast members now living in the West, including Manfred Krug. Jurek and Christine joined them. A clearly political act, the screening was intended to be a gesture of reconciliation to those who in the 1960s and 1970s, like Jurek and Krug, had struggled to critique the GDR. Krug agreed to come as long as the event did not decay into a paean to the new regime. He was horrified when he was photographed together with Egon Krenz, whose presence had been kept from him. He and the other exiles who attended the premiere were aware of the implications if they were seen to support the new authorities.

Before the premiere, the poet Volker Braun burst into Beyer's apartment. He had just come from a meeting of the Writers' Union, and he cried out to those who had been expelled in 1979, "You have all been readmitted." Jurek said quietly, "Not me. I resigned, I wasn't expelled." For Jurek, the fateful meeting on June 7, 1979, in which Heym, Klaus Poche, and Joachim Seyppel, among others, were expelled following the debate about foreign funds, was "legal," if immoral, and its decisions could be reversed. Jurek had been dismissed from his position in the leadership of the Writers' Union two years before. He then had resigned from the union over that clearly illegal act. His outrage at the GDR's flouting of its own rules in order to expel him continued even after the collapse of the GDR. As a state that violated the rule of law, the GDR was irredeemable. Jurek could not be "readmitted" because he never was expelled. He had quit of his own accord.

Jurek, as we have seen, had been a persistent internal critic of the policies of the East German regime. He had also been a strong opponent of those in the East who allowed themselves be used by the West to attack the GDR. As the possibility of a thaw became an avalanche of change in the GDR, Jurek had a momentary sense that there could be a new type of socialist state. In the fall of 1989, however, he kept a relatively low political profile. In 1981 at the University of Southern California in Los Angeles, he had given a reading, after which one of the students asked the meaning of the word "Western action" (*Westeinsatz*) in his novel *Misleading the Authorities*. He explained that before the Berlin Wall was built, students from Humboldt University in East Berlin were sent to distribute pamphlets and discuss politics with the citizens of West Berlin. One of the professors then asked him: "Mr. Becker, are you sure that you are not taking part in exactly that sort of 'Western action' right now?"[16] Eight years later, in 1989, the tightrope walk between East and West was no longer possible. Jurek admitted he was confused. He had never found it more difficult to reach any conclusions. He listened to everyone, and in the end found that everyone was right.[17]

On November 29, a number of intellectuals in the GDR, including Volker Braun, Stefan Heym, and Christa Wolf, were joined by Krenz and Modrow in a call to maintain "our land: to preserve the independence of the GDR." The general sense that the GDR regime no longer represented anyone had made a defense of the GDR necessary. The momentum was toward the dissolution of the GDR and the unification Germany. The intellectuals argued that a separate GDR could develop a society that was truly in solidarity with the aspirations of the citizens. The alternative would be for the citizens of the GDR to be exposed to Western economic pressures and experience a moral collapse.[18] For a brief moment it seemed that the writers and intellectuals who had opposed the repressive society in the GDR would become the political leaders of a new, reformed state. Indeed, there was even a whisper that Christa Wolf would be its first president. As usual in the GDR, however, prominent and privileged intellectuals were very far from the actual sensibilities of the population and much too close to the desires of the political leadership.[19]

On the day after the wall opened, Jurek received a call from Jürgen Keil, director of the Goethe Institute in Tel Aviv, to confirm his participation in a conference on "Germany after 1945."[20] After November 10, 1989, this topic changed radically from what it had involved when first proposed in February. Jurek arrived in Israel on November 26, 1989—his first trip to Israel since 1984, when he had spent almost a month more or less incognito there. On this new trip he was a public figure and lectured in both Jerusalem and Tel Aviv. His subject matter was the literary problem of language and language confusion. His Israeli audience, however, was anxious to hear about German unification. Jurek had castigated the Israeli government in 1977 as Jewish "supermen" who had thievery in their hearts in their relationship with the Palestinians. In Israel a decade later, he was equally blunt about Germany. He saw only an emotional basis for unification, not a rational one. He was asked whether his relationship to the GDR was ideological or emotional. "Purely ideological" he answered. He had no nostalgia for the landscape of the GDR. This attitude, he noted, contrasted with that of the Israelis, who love their land but detest their (conservative) government.[21] Jurek's position was that the GDR was a political system rather than an emotional symbol, and systems could be changed.

In 1977, Jurek had moved to West Berlin, leaving his two sons on the other side of the wall. He did not think of himself as being in exile but created a new self-image for himself as a celebrity writer living in West Berlin. In his mind, he never truly left the GDR. "I left the GDR in 1977 and have lived since then in West Berlin; I can be described as well integrated. Even today, after sixteen years in the West," he wrote in 1993, "none of my books deals with the West. Even today, all my published writings are set in a country that no longer exists, the GDR. That seems unusual to me, a case for a psychiatrist, and you can be certain that I have tried to do something about it. But all my attempts to make this strange new home (*Heimat*) the subject of my books have been in vain."[22] West Berlin is a construct, a world invented by the shapers of the cold war as a "window into freedom." Jurek felt at home there precisely because it was so artificial. "If I spend longer than a week in other German cities, I tend to grow bored. Whatever the reason, and certainly the East-West constellation is part of it, Berlin is livelier than other cities. One is aware of things here that in other places are only sensed."[23] By the late 1980s, his memory and experience of the GDR too had become an invented world, which never lived up to its promise because of the failings of its leadership. For Jurek, the GDR was already a fantasy by the time it began to unravel in 1989. It was the world that had promised to create an answer to the absence he felt—the loss of language, of parents, of place. By the late 1980s, the reality had become very different the promise. The GDR had failed to create a world without hate and without conflict.

On December 16, 1989, Klaus Höpcke followed up his earlier letter about an extension of Jurek's visa with a personal note. He wrote, "It is in both of our best interests that you don't become a normal West German or West Berlin citizen."[24] The world had changed. Everyone was about to become a West German citizen. This irony was not lost on Jurek. Jurek commented, "I thought that either I would have my visa extended or I would make the GDR disappear. You know what my decision was."[25] Honecker's GDR did indeed disappear before the visa ran out. Höpcke managed to continue in office until the GDR itself dissolved.[26]

The division of Germany had seemed a natural one for Jurek, for the GDR had existed for him since he had had any political consciousness. Also, it was the place where his father had found security.[27] For this reason alone, the disappearance of the GDR was problematic for Jurek.[28] He now saw the legacy of the GDR not in its reality but in its promise—a promise that would never be fulfilled once the GDR accepted the material goods (hence the waste) and the freedom of thought (accompanied by unwillingness to think) that defined the West. He was convinced that the East Germans would accept the goods and the freedom with the intensity of converts, destroying any hope of the promise of socialism. But he was equally convinced that this promise was no longer realizable.

The cry from those who wanted to maintain the GDR in some form was that the desire for material goods alone—for "bananas," as they put it—was moving the population toward union with the FRG. There had to be reform, if just of the leadership. The new GDR leadership saw itself as transitional, even while drafting a new constitution. On March 18, 1990, the first truly free election was held in the GDR, but continuation of the state was doomed by strong popular support for unification. Otto Schily, in a gesture that Robert Liebling would have understood, held up a banana in front of the TV cameras when asked to comment on the meaning of the election.[29]

A new Germany was suddenly emerging. In a newly unified Berlin, Jurek watched the wall being torn down. On both sides of the border, people with pickaxes had already made holes in it on November 11, 1989. Fragments of it were on sale in the streets as souvenirs; entrepreneurs were renting hammers and chisels to those who wanted to go into business for themselves. The market forces of the West that Christa Wolf had warned about were already at play. Souvenirs of the wall became a metaphor for the dissolution of the GDR. What had defined West Berlin was also disappearing.

Jurek's fantasy of a multicultural space under the rule of law, his West Berlin, was ceasing to exist. He had quit work on the TV program *Liebling Kreuzberg* before the wall came down because he wanted to work on a new novel. Well after the broadcast of Jurek's last episode in 1989, the program continued to garner awards. In 1990, Jurek received the Bavarian Television Prize for the series. The success of *Liebling Kreuzberg* and Krug's growing fame demanded that the program be continued even after last episode Jurek wrote, in which Liebling's law practice was closed.

Otto Meissner first asked Jurek's friend Kurt Bartsch, one of the writers expelled from the DDR in 1979, to take over the series. What he produced was hardly usable, even though Meissner suggested that Jurek look at the prospectus and encourage Bartsch to persevere.[30] With Krug's help, Meissner recruited Jurek's old DEFA colleague, Ulrich Plenzdorf, who not only moved the series to Prenzlauer Berg—East Berlin's equivalent to Kreuzberg—but also destroyed the program's subtlety and humor with heavy-handed moralization. Nicolas Becker continued to advise on the scripts but with less and less pleasure. The thirteen episodes of the fourth season, broadcast in 1992–93 and directed by Werner Masten, were generally seen as much less successful than the episodes that Jurek had written. They attempted to deal with the newly merged city of Berlin, but reduced the ironic figure of Liebling to a mouthpiece for partisan political preaching. The program was now subjected to the heavy-handed DEFA scriptwriting that Jurek had had to unlearn before writing the first episodes.

After the final episode of the third season of *Liebling Kreuzberg*, Jurek, Manfred Krug, and Werner Masten decided to replicate their original television success on the big screen. While Krug had had a major film career with DEFA, the fact that he always essentially played himself limited the roles he could take. Jurek was aware of this but also thought it could create a market for the film: "Sure Krug's possibilities are limited. But so are Masten's and mine. The problem is to see these limitations in a realistic light. With *Liebling Kreuzberg* we learned much that can benefit this film."[31] Krug and Masten joined Jurek and the producer Otto Meissner in 1990 in Jurek's first post–Berlin Wall work, the film *Neuner.*

A draft of *Neuner* had been completed before the collapse of the GDR. In the few days after November 9, 1989, the film seemed to have aged years. Jurek, Masten, Krug, and Meissner discussed how it might be rescued. The film was supposed to be a comedy with political meaning, as *Liebling Kreuzberg* was.[32] Jurek felt that the comic form of the work should come from conflicts in the plot. This had been the key to the success of *Jacob the Liar* both as novel and film.

The core of *Neuner,* however, remained as conceived in the draft. It was a comedy about the collapse of a marriage, one of Jurek's older political themes. It was now transformed into a clumsy sex farce recording the infidelities of an aging couple. The film opens with Theo Neuner (played by Krug), a wealthy businessman, attending the funeral of his much younger mistress, Irma Lindner. His wife (played by Claudia Wedekind) has discovered his infidelity, having found a video of the pair's vacation trip. At the funeral, Neuner is introduced to Irma's younger sister, whom he hopes to meet again when he goes to Berlin. The trip to Berlin from the small town where the Neuners live comes to be a catalyst in their relationship. Their young adult son lives there with his girlfriend. Son and father do not get along. The son spends most of the film trying to get money from his father for some unstated purpose. Neuner's wife walks out on the marriage when she believes Irma's sister is beginning a relationship with her husband. The sister, however, has no such interest. Back home, the wife grabs a gun and tries to shoot Neuner, but the gun is not cocked and doesn't go off. Neuner takes it away from her and walks away, muttering that all he needs is a crazy wife.

The plot only hints at how truly unpleasant all the characters are. Neuner is defined by his adolescent sexuality. His wife moves from despair to a sexual relationship with Neuner's best friend in Berlin. Their son is willing to betray his mother's confidence for 2,000 marks. The film is largely concerned with private life, despite a few "political" references.

Neuner goes to Berlin for two reasons. The first is to cheat a friend out of half of their jointly owned apartment building because he believes that the price of apartments will climb sharply with the opening of the wall. Neuner wants the building as a hidden source of income in case of a divorce. That the friend is dying of cancer seems to make little difference.

This part of the film takes place self-consciously in West Berlin. The Kaiser-Wilhelm-Memorial Church can clearly be seen through the window of the couple's room at the Bristol Hotel. The wall functions in one shot to define the space of West Berlin.

Neuner's second reason for going to Berlin is to discuss a joint venture with an East Berlin street-paving company. Here the film emphasizes the chronic neglect of the people in East Germany and its impact on the mentality of its citizens. We see Neuner and the director of the company together inspecting the company's dilapidated plant. They walk through a crowd of West German land speculators looking to buy anything in the East. The building they go into is literally falling apart. When Neuner opens a door, it falls off its hinges; when he touches a pipe, it bursts, gushing water all over his East Berlin host. Afterward, in the East German's car, Neuner gives a long sermon on the need to acknowledge the weakness of the system and to accept the "natural law" of competition.

In *Neuner*, a veneer of political correctness is placed over the tale of a failed marriage, a theme now robbed of any political significance. The story is reminiscent of Jurek's pallid script for *Guests in the House* (*Gäste im Haus*, directed by Fred Mahr), which he wrote for GDR television back in 1963.[33] In that film, an actor, Leopold Berg (Emil Stöhr), seduces the much younger schoolteacher Marianne (Ingeborg Schumacher) while shooting a film on location. When Marianne tracks him down to his rather staid, middle-class home, his wife Therese (Ingrid Rentsch) is appalled. Both women agree to teach him a lesson and use the sexual interest of Leopold's best friend (Eberhard Mellies) in Therese as their vehicle. In that rather slight film, GDR society is a place of sexual exchange where all ends well. In *Neuner*, sex as well as politics has turned sour. The new GDR is a place where pessimism and lethargy seem to rule. Human relations in West Germany are equally corrupt. In the end, both societies are shown to have no values.

Neuner was a critical disaster, even though in 1991 it won both the Bavarian Film Price and the *Bundesfilmpreis* awarded by the FRG's Ministry of the Interior.[34] The totally unsympathetic cast of characters and the pasted-on critique of both West German avarice and East German incompetence seemed unacceptable even to the least sophisticated audience.[35] Few were ready to accept his vision of the present or the future of the GDR.

Jurek stayed on the periphery of the debates about the new Germany. He took part in a mass meeting, a "German-German Writers' Meeting," in West Berlin, February 22–25, 1990. (It was the continuation of a long series of such meetings that had begun in the early 1980s as part of the disarmament movement. The GDR officials, especially Herman Kant, had tried to keep Jurek well away from them.)³⁶ Held at the Literary Colloquium, the former home of Group 47, the meeting brought together writers ranging from Sascha Anderson, who later turned out to have been the Stasi spy who betrayed Wolf Biermann, to Jurek's bête noire Martin Walser. Jurek was only a shadow at that meeting. Which "German" in the "German-German" meeting was he? In the spring of 1990, he again left Germany during one of the most tumultuous periods of change. The movement toward unification seemed unstoppable. The governments of the GDR and the FRG were actively seeking the means to dissolve the GDR.

Instead of becoming involved, Jurek returned for a week (March 15–23, 1990) to Washington University, St. Louis, where he had read from *Bronstein's Children* in the fall of 1987. Paul Michael (Mike) Lützeler had invited him to come as a Max Kade Writer-in-Residence for the spring of 1990, but Christine's pregnancy prevented this. Lützeler again extended an invitation to Jurek to speak at a conference on the literature of the 1980s. The Frankfurt lectures had set the stage for his first clear break with the GDR, but it was in St. Louis that he spoke on "the unification of German literature." He contended that the literature in the GDR had led a particularly sheltered life. It had received the sort of attention it did not deserve, and it would therefore vanish and its writers would transform themselves as quickly as their readers into "German" writers. Because it was central to the cultural life of the GDR, the literature of the GDR was condemned to oblivion.³⁷ Jurek concluded with an ironic version of the admonition that West German politicians had been giving to their Western audiences: "The world need not fear the unification of both German literatures." Jurek's sense of his own position in this new literature had already been fixed. He was a "German" writer in the new Germany.

Jurek was now seen as part of the new majority rather than part of the old, now discredited GDR tradition. His side had won. As early as 1990, there was a massive attack on what Karl Heinz Bohrer called "loyalty kitsch" (*Gesinnungskitsch*), or what Ulrich Greiner called "loyalty aesthetics" (*Gesinnungsästhetik*) in the literature of the GDR. This attack rejected all aspects of writing in the GDR as corrupted by the system. In the Frankfurt lectures, Jurek had already accused this type of "party" writing, as well as the "oppositional" literature produced within the confines of the aesthetic claims of GDR literature, of an "absence of meaning" (*Meinungslosigkeit*). He had, of course, balanced that criticism with his contempt for the market-driven literature of the FRG. All that was left now was the second kind.

While not convinced of the desirability of unification, Jurek became one of its first chroniclers. He had placed himself in a neutral position. According to Christa Wolf, Jurek was hardly to be seen in any public manner in East Berlin during the fall and winter of 1989–90.[38] The conservative thinkers in the FRG wanted to rescue Jurek from the taint of any association with the failed ideology of the GDR.[39] His work was to be defined retrospectively as part of a collective German literature that would be respected because of its command of form and style. Since *Jacob the Liar* had been absorbed into the literary culture of the FRG as one of the primary texts about the Shoah, this was a leap quite easily made.

Jurek had been approached a number of times about refilming *Jacob the Liar*. In 1990, the Franco-Hungarian director Peter Kassovitz, along with the French producer Gouze Renal, developed an idea for a new version of the material. Kassovitz and the French scriptwriter Didier Decoin wrote a new screenplay based on the French translation of the novel, which Jurek read in an early draft. In October 1997, Robin Williams's production company, Blue Wolf Productions, began to film this version of the film. Robin Williams played Jacob Heym; Alan Arkin, the actor Frankfurter; and Armin Müller-Stahl, Dr. Kirschbaum. (Müller-Stahl was the only actor from Frank Beyer's film to reappear in the new version.) The film eventually premiered on September 24, 1999, well after the success of Roberto Benigni's tragicomedy *Life Is Beautiful* (*La Vita e Bella*, 1998). Kassovitz had turned Jurek's novel into an account of a brave man who (almost) had a radio. The film did what Jurek had managed to *un*do in his revision of his first scripts. It stressed the heroic nature of the Jewish resistance and did so in a manner that so violated Jurek's concept of Jacob's character that the entire film failed. It disappeared into the video stores in a matter of weeks,[40] dismissed as a poor version of Benigni's comic reading of the Shoah. This fate was ironic, since Benigni's film was a very poor imitation of *Jacob the Liar*. Jurek had nothing to do with the screenplay of the remake, and was no longer living when it was released.

In November 1990, Jurek was awarded the Hans Fallada Prize of the city of Neumünster. Worth 10,000 marks, it was one of West Germany's most lucrative literary awards.[41] After the prize had been announced, he received a telegram of congratulations from Klaus Höpcke.[42] The irony was not lost on Jurek. Earlier that year, Höpcke had sent him a note when Jurek was elected to the West Berlin Academy of Arts.[43] Written on PDS stationary (Partei des Demokratischen Sozialismus, "Party of Democratic Socialism," was the new name for the SED, now a democratic party in a unified Germany), it expressed Höpcke's warm feelings toward Jurek in spite of personal and public differences.[44] The world had changed. Jurek was now in a position to give Höpcke a hand, though it is highly unlikely he would have done so.

Old opponents reappeared regularly. On November 16, Jurek confronted Martin Walser at the Literary Colloquium.[45] His published attack on Walser attack a few years earlier was fresh in everyone's memory. Walser had become increasingly a spokesperson for the German nationalist right. In a debate moderated by Volker Hage, a literary critic from *Die Zeit*, Walser spoke of the economic pressures on the citizens in the GDR. One should not, he remarked, be dismissive of the desire of GDR citizens for material goods. Their desire was for a good life, and that should not simply be equated with material goods. Westerners who already had everything and Easterners who were privileged and could travel to the West should not place themselves above those in the East who now wished to improve their lot. This was a not too subtle swipe at Jurek, who responded by observing how difficult it was for those in the GDR who sought a middle ground to be heard today. The excitement of unification created a euphoria that masked its potential problems. The small pleasures we have, said Jurek in closing, were always the result of those small misfortunes. The job of intellectuals was to make that clear to everyone in the society. Jurek took his job as a German author seriously. His rebuttal to Walser was not that of a citizen of the GDR but that of a "German" writer who could view the world from beyond the ideological limits of either West German nationalism or the failures of the socialist system.

On June 23, 1990, Christine gave birth to a son, Jonathan Samuel. Before he was born, his parents had called him "Johnny," a sign of their fascination with America. Jurek's first son, Nicki, had been born when the wall was being built. By his own account, he provided his father with an excuse for not becoming more involved with the politics of the 1960s. Johnny was born as the wall tumbled. He provided Jurek with a similar excuse in 1990. To welcome his new son, Jurek threw a huge party, with Jewish food. He saw this as a kind of substitute for circumcision, but eventually the baby was circumcised like his father. Johnny was born in the very last days of the old West Berlin that his father and mother had known so very well. He would be a new citizen of a new Germany.

On July 1, 1990, the day Johnny should have been circumcised by Jewish ritual, the two German states established a monetary union. The shouts of "one for one," one Eastern mark for one Western mark, echoed through the streets of East Berlin as the economies merged. On October 3, 1990, with the agreement of the four occupying powers, the FRG, and the GDR, unification became a reality. The FRG, in fact, absorbed the GDR as the New Federal States. The result was "inferiority on one side, smugness on the other."[46] Jurek sought a third position, a position structured by his being perceived as a Jewish writer in Germany.

In October, Jurek attended the first of what became an annual German-Israeli Writers' conference. He became a mainstay of these meetings, as did other Jewish writers in Germany, including Katja Behrens and many non-Jewish writers as well. It became a venue for major writers (such as Amos Oz and Hans Magnus Enzensberger) to discuss literature as well as politics. Jurek was one of the "German" writers at this meeting. Yet the line between "German" and "Israeli" was almost as blurry as that between "German" and "German." Jurek was a German author born in Poland; yet Aharon Appelfeld and Yehuda Amichai, both born in Germany, were Israeli writers. All were Jews, however they defined the concept. Only their nationality and their languages were different.

Jurek's role as a "Jewish" filmmaker was also marked by his relationship with Artur Brauner, one of the great postwar German film producers. Brauner was a Polish Jew who had survived the Shoah. His film *Morituri* (1947), based on his own experiences in the Lodz ghetto, was anything but a critical success when it was first shown. Nonetheless, he continued to make films about the Shoah and other Jewish topics as well as very successful popular films. In the 1980s, he approached Frank Beyer to do a film based on the strange story of Shlomo ("Sally") Perel, who survived the Holocaust disguised as a member of the Hitler Youth. Beyer turned to Jurek for the screenplay and also to provide a further Jewish legitimization for his doing the story.[47] Jurek refused, however, because he did not think the material convincing. In 1991, Agnieszka Holland, a Polish-Jewish filmmaker, turned it into a very successful film titled *Europa, Europa* (*Hitlerjunge Salomon*). Also in 1991, Brauner again turned to Jurek when looking for someone to write a screenplay based on the Golem legend of medieval Jewish Prague.[48] Being Jewish remained part of the mix defining Jurek in the new Germany.

Jurek's Jewish presence was ever more powerfully represented in the German media at this time. Jerzy Kawalerowicz's film of *Bronstein's Children* appeared in the theaters on June 26, 1992. He had begun filming in the 1990s, shortly after the wall opened. Jurek was credited only with the dialogue, most of which was taken from the novel. Yet it was clearly on his reputation that the film rested. Kawalerowicz destroyed the subtle flashback structure so necessary for the irony of the novel. The film begins with Arno's funeral in the overgrown Jewish cemetery at Weißensee in East Berlin. The novel never describes Arno's funeral in the cemetery where Max Becker was actually buried in 1972, a year before the action in Jurek's novel takes place. By placing the funeral at the opening of the film, Kawalerowicz—himself a Polish Jew and a survivor—stresses the pathetic nature of Jewish existence in the GDR.

The film becomes a complaint about the confusion of Jewish identity under communism. The film-within-the-film (the making of a film about the Nazis in the GDR) loses its critical function. Kawalerowicz uses it as a moment of visual irony. When Hans (played by Matthias Paul) is told by his father that he cannot imagine what it was like in the camps, we cut to a scene of men and women wearing yellow stars being forced into a truck. It turns out to be a scene for the film-within-the-film rather than an evocation of the actual experience of the Shoah, which Arno says is unimaginable.

The conclusion of the novel, with its open structure, is substantially changed. When Arno (played by Armin Müller-Stahl) dies, Hans does not look through his pockets for the key to free the camp guard. The film ends with Hans filing away at the handcuffs. It is a portrait of complete futility.

The critics hated the film. It was dismissed as a "sweaty slide lecture" or a "potpourri of opinions and positions."[49] The moving performance by Rolf Hoppe as the camp guard Arnold Heppner so overwhelmed the status of Arno and his friends as the original victims that they were simply turned into perpetrators. The film simplified Jurek's complex question of what makes a German by asking it only of Hans, not of his father, his sister, or the camp guard. When the film was shown on ZDF on May 9, 1993, it was received more positively. Jurek's status as a Jewish writer was undiminished by the weakness of the film.

A New History and a New House

Immediately after unification, the GDR was redefined as a world in which most of its citizens had been "victims"—of the Stasi, of the Soviets, of the leadership. For Jurek, being a "victim" was not all bad. In 1992, at a reading in the Literary Colloquium in Berlin-Wannsee that I attended, he was asked about his "victimization by the Stasi." He maintained that he had never been "a victim of the SED regime." He added, "The more I opened my mouth, it seemed, the greater the advantages I had."[50] Jurek had always believed that he could manipulate the system because of his victim status and international visibility. The reality was much more complicated, but after the disappearance of the GDR it was impolitic to stress the ambiguity of his position, if indeed he even comprehended it.

As the extent of the secret surveillance of GDR inhabitants became known, the Stasi was identified as the perpetrator. In July, Jurek wrote an essay from his double perspective of one who had experienced both the Third Reich and the Stasi.[51] For him, the Nazi period was the necessary point of departure for understanding the nature of the GDR. The Germans in the Third Reich identified more strongly with the Nazis than the East Germans did with the Communist system. "I cannot imagine that in free elections after 1945 the National Socialist Party would have been as badly beaten as the SED was just recently."[52] To free themselves from responsibility after 1945, the Germans simply blamed everything on their leadership. "It is wonderful absolution to make Hitler responsible for everything, for what the Germans did in the war, in the six years before the war, for every denunciation, for every violation of the law, for every shot to the back of the neck."[53] This pattern continued after unification, and the leadership of the GDR and their agents in the Stasi were regarded as the sole cause of all of the problems in the GDR.

In Jurek's view, the East Germans, like the Germans during the Third Reich, were willing participants in a system of oppression. They recognized this and expressed their frustration with anger. But it was not always honest anger. The glee with which the Stasi was blamed for everything evil in the East was symptomatic of the subjugation that the citizens of the GDR had willingly accepted. Jurek made up two stories by way of illustration. According to the first, he had met a school friend in the 1960s who he heard had joined the Stasi. They went out for a drink, and his friend talked about the advantages of his job, a good salary, and a new apartment. Getting a bit drunk, he thought he sensed Jurek's unspoken antipathy, and shouted that these people needed to be watched. If he had any sympathy for them he would quit his job. "We control, and they let themselves be controlled. Spying on someone takes two." This view of the Germans was very much in line with Jurek's reflection of Max's view in *The Boxer* and *Bronstein's Children*. Because of the Nazi past, the Germans needed to be (and felt the need to be) controlled from above. Jurek's second story concerns an author who wrote a novel that clearly could not be published in the GDR. Jurek read it for him in the 1970s and suggested that he send it to a publisher in West Germany. There never seemed to be an opportune time to publish it. The writer's daughter was graduating from high school and needed to get into college; the writer was buying a home or wanted to take a trip to Egypt. In every case he postponed submitting the novel. After the wall came down, he sent it to a Western publisher, but no one was interested in it anymore. Opportunism was the way intellectuals, even those in the putative opposition, defined their relationship to the power of the state.

Jurek came to view East Germany through the lens of a collective German experience. He used the image of a hypothetical Germany that had been divided after 1945 by a north-south boundary. Would the Stasi have been different in Bavaria, or would the Swabians have called a general strike when the wall was built?[54] Jurek knew they would not. The GDR experience was an accident of history, and the role of the writer in the GDR a reflex of that accident. Jurek separated himself from the two models of East German writer that had been acceptable in the West: the de facto supporters of the state who called themselves oppositional, and those whose opposition had been limited to writing for the desk drawer. He himself wrote about things he believed in, while remaining constantly aware of the way his beliefs were shaped by the world about him. He thus placed himself in a unique position. He considered his own anger healthy because it was inherently different from the anger generated by repression. He was dismissive of colleagues like Wolf Biermann who were furious when they discovered that their "friends" had betrayed them to the Stasi. Since one of the crimes of the GDR was that it turned friend against friend, Jurek pointed out, there was no reason publicly to brand those who spied with the mark of their infamy.[55] Jurek saw his own anger at the state as honest anger, not merely resentment, because it was expressed in private and did not serve to ingratiate him with the new West German power structure. But, of course, he also saw himself as part of that new pan-German cultural world.

In 1990, Christa Wolf published *Was bleibt* (*What Remains*), her account of her own experience in 1979 with the Stasi.[56] All at once, Jurek's anecdote about the writer who postponed publication of his novel until an opportune time became a test case for the nature of all writing in the GDR. Christa Wolf had not published the account of her confrontation with the regime while the GDR existed. Was her hesitancy motivated by self-preservation, and did she publish it now to give herself a new victim status? Her role as the icon of a new direction for the literature of the former GDR was further damaged when it was discovered that between 1959 and 1962 she had had at least informal ties to the Stasi. Similar accusations surfaced about the best-known oppositional dramatist in the GDR, Heiner Müller. Jurek remained silent about these scandals. "I don't like people who curse their former spouse after a divorce,"[57] he explained. The metaphor of divorce continued to represent the curious link between Jurek's politics and his private life. Jurek was already a victim, first of the Nazis and then of the GDR. Although he had no need to claim this role, victim status made life easier and more uncomfortable. He knew the downside of being a victim.

After Johnny's birth, Jurek was surprised how hard it was to settle down and start writing again. He had put off doing much more than taking notes toward his next novel—notes that go back to 1986—until after Johnny was born. After Johnny's birth, Jurek buried himself in work. "When I write a book, I lock myself in a room for two years. I have to be convinced that what I am doing would be a loss for humanity if I did not do it. In lucid moments, I know that is megalomania. But I think this type of overstatement is vital to the creative process."[58] While this may have been his pattern, he also engaged in regular arguments with Christine about his desire to interact with their new baby only on his own schedule. He seemed to be repeating all the mistakes he had made in raising Nicki and Lonni. Christine withdrew from him as he abdicated his role as father and husband to that of writer.

Jurek remained one of the "talking heads" for West German television about what was happening in the East, though he tried to remain relatively neutral, now taking a pan-German perspective.[59] But his public life increasingly interfered with his writing and impinged on what little time was left for his new family. During Christine's pregnancy the idea of "escaping" from West Berlin to a country house acquired urgency. During the early 1970s, psychiatrists in West Berlin had described "wall sickness," the oppressive sense of being trapped by the wall.[60] Jurek and Christine drove through the GDR toward Hamburg looking for a place to find solitude. Three weeks after the birth of his third son, Jurek purchased a house in the tiny town of Sieseby on the Baltic coast. It was as far away from the former GDR as was possible in the new Germany. Jurek's friend Max Neumann, the painter, was later encouraged to buy a house in the same neighborhood. In the isolation of Schleswig-Holstein, Jurek began to reconstitute the circle of friends he had enjoyed in Berlin. And his strained relationship with Christine and their new son began to mend.

After the wall fell, reasons to flee the GDR changed. If escape seemed necessary before 1989, after unification the new Berlin, at least for the moment, became stultifying as it lost its status as an island city. Jurek was "convinced that Berlin is at present the most provincial city in Germany."[61] After 1991, when the parliament decided to move the seat of government from Bonn back to Berlin, a physically united West and East Berlin became the capital of the new "Berlin Republic." The transition made Berlin a city without self-definition.

The Sieseby house became Jurek's refuge, where he could escape with his family from the spiraling political and commercial pressures of Berlin for weeks at a time. It also symbolized Jurek's acknowledgement of his place in the West German bourgeois world. A weekend house in rural northern Germany was as powerful a sign of "belonging" to the establishment as was the house in Mecklenburg that Jurek and Manfred Krug had planned to buy in the late 1960s. Jurek's friend Irene Dische recognized this when she created the Countess of Sieseby in her comic novel *Sad Strains of a Gay Waltz*. In contrast to this "real" member of the nobility, Dische has one of the other characters say to the Countess: "When I was at primary school my parents took me to a little town on the Ostsee called Sieseby. When I got home, I wrote a school essay about Sieseby. So in a sense we're related."[62] Much in the same way, Jurek was related to the rural world of Schleswig-Holstein. The protagonist of his new novel *Amanda Heartless* (1992) labels his weekend house a "paradise for the petite bourgeoisie," but he still enjoys it.[63] By 1992, Jurek could say "I only live a part of the year in Berlin. I live just as much in Schleswig-Holstein." But he added in the same breath, "I believe the GDR will exist as long as its former citizens exists, as long as we live. The GDR is the memory of the GDR."[64] The world of privilege in the FRG is a sign of belonging to the new society, of becoming a German. This identity was formally acknowledged when the new German government awarded him the prestigious Order of Merit (*Bundesverdienstorden*) in August 1992,[65] given to individuals seen to have made major contributions to the cultural life of the Republic. He was one of the few "East Germans" to receive it.

Amanda Heartless

In 1984 at my seminar at Cornell, Jurek was confronted by one of the best students, Sabine Gölz, who by 1990 was teaching at the University of Iowa. She had published a paper she had written in the seminar—on the missing wife in Jurek's short story "No Parking" (*Parkverbot*)—and had deliberately sent a copy to Christine rather than to Jurek.[66] Jurek's story represents in Kafkaesque terms a type of mindless acceptance of authority in the GDR. It begins with a man taking his wife shopping. Since there are no parking places, he parks in a "no parking" zone. The wife then "vanishes" for the rest of the story, while a confrontation takes place between the husband and a man who attempts to hide in his car. The theme goes back to a scene in one of Jurek's early, very slight film comedies, *Come with Me to Montevideo* (1963). The protagonist Siegmund Markgraf (played by Rolf Herricht) is ordered to the Ministry of Foreign Trade. There he learns that he has three weeks to get married so that he can take a new post in Uruguay. He has parked illegally in front of the ministry and is faced with a meter maid when he returns. When he tries to ask her out on a date (as he is looking for a wife), his fine is tripled. The question of where "the wife" is in this early film has an obvious answer: she is the unseen neighbor (played by Brigitte Krause) who pines for Markgraf while he struggles to find a mate.[67]

Jurek saw Sabine Gölz's essay as raising the question of whether the missing character had to be a woman. In looking back at his own work, he became aware of the pattern of the missing woman in his fiction. Gölz's feminist reading led him to rethink some of his basic premises. Christine suggested that he read a few of the classic studies of German feminist theory, such as the work of Alice Schwarzer, and works on feminist language and linguistics, such as that by Luise Pusch.[68] Before Johnny's birth he began to sketch a novel that would focus on the way men imagine women. He wrote for fifteen months to finish the first draft, a further three months for the second, and then three more months for the final draft.[69] It was intended to be, as most of his novels were, a novel in and of the GDR, now more than ever a historical setting. The action takes place in that final decade in the history of the GDR, which Jurek had spent in West Berlin. It ends at five minutes to midnight, in January 1989, a time when there was still a possibility that the GDR would continue to exist. Christine read it chapter for chapter and critiqued it.

Amanda Heartless (*Amanda Herzlos*), which appeared in July 1992, illustrates Jurek's brilliance in writing dialogue. It consists of three sections in different voices, each written by one of the three men in East Berlin who, during the 1980s, figure in the life of the title character Amanda Zobel. Amanda appears only in the narratives of these men. Jurek shows how she actually disappears in their need to make her into an extension of themselves. From these accounts, readers are able to see aspects of Amanda that exist separately from the portrait drawn by her three lovers.

The first of Amanda's lovers, Ludwig Weniger, who becomes her husband, is a version of Georg Bienek at the close of Jurek's 1973 novel *Misleading the Authorities*. He is a relatively unsuccessful sports reporter who is extremely "loyal" to the GDR. His section, titled "The Divorce," is a monologue directed at his lawyer explaining himself and defining Amanda. It begins with the sort of negotiations that Jurek had undertaken with Rieke during their divorce. Who gets what? Who gives up what? Central to these negotiations is Weniger's insistence that he does not want custody of their son Sebastian (12). He wants the decree to look as if he does, but he is unwilling actually to take responsibility for the child. He would much prefer to keep the family car. Amanda can keep their weekend house.

From Weniger we learn a good deal about Amanda's family, her dentist father, Thilo, and her mother, Violetta, who is an SED functionary. Bits of Hannah's biography show up in the occupation of Amanda's father. We also learn that Amanda, according to her father, was sexually abused by an uncle when she was a child (106). Weniger says he wanted a wife who was beautiful and bright (25), but having an intelligent wife is dangerous in a state like the GDR. For one must be smart enough to keep one's mouth shut. After Weniger's marriage to Amanda, he is approached by the Stasi officer assigned to report on the activities at Weniger's newspaper (80). The Stasi agent informs him that Amanda has developed contacts to a Western publishing house. In addition, like Stefan Heym in 1979, she has violated the laws of the GDR by accepting a publisher's advance payment and keeping it in the West. (91) Weniger actually invites the agent to have dinner with them in hopes of both scaring Amanda and impressing the agent, but neither happens (86). After a violent fight with his wife, in which she knocks him unconscious, Amanda leaves him for Fritz Hetmann, a well-known older dissident writer. The violence of Amanda's response reflects Jurek's intense arguments with Rieke's at the end of their marriage, during which she bombarded Jurek with numerous objects.

The second section of the novel consists of Fritz Hetmann's attempt to recount his relationship with Amanda by reconstructing his unpublished novel titled "The Feminist." ("Der Feminist" was also Jurek's working title for *Amanda Heartless*.) Hetmann believes Sebastian has deliberately erased the work from Hetmann's computer (113). Being some twenty years older than Amanda, he is especially aware of his age, his appearance, and his physical condition. He has had a somewhat successful career as a writer in the GDR. His books were published and praised until he stopped paying attention to what the publishing houses wanted from him. When he can no longer expect to be published in the GDR, he sends a manuscript to a publishing house in Munich. It is intercepted, he is called before the Writers' Union, and his work is banned in the GDR (170–71). Hetmann thus becomes a "famous" writer because he is a banned writer (182). He uses censorship to increase his fame abroad and, hence, at home too (181–82). Being a dissident is hard work for Hetmann. In one incident Amanda accompanies him to a reading in a church, where he purposely reads the least political sections of his published novel, which has in the meantime appeared in the West (230–31) In Jurek's novel this refusal to engage in political discourse has more to do with the personal than the political choices Hetmann makes about his life.

Amanda and Hetmann first meet at an underground reading, where he is the star. He pursues Amanda, using his radical difference from her officious husband to seduce her (140). As a further ploy, he offers to read her novel (144). Her writing has little or no other value for him. When Hetmann encourages Amanda to divorce her husband, Weniger tries to blackmail her into giving him some of her Western currency from the advance on her novel (153). Hetmann then arranges for them both to go to the United States, where he has been invited as a "famous" GDR dissident. (185) Amanda does not want to go. Hetmann cannot imagine that she does not want to visit "Niagara Falls, California" (190). Is their relationship at an end? Hetmann (or at least his fictional equivalent in his fictional retelling) wants to have a child with Amanda to secure their relationship (223). Fatherhood is something marginal for both Weniger and Hetmann. As part of his role as a dissident, Hetmann promises to give an interview to Stanislaus Doll, a Western radio reporter from a Hamburg station, if he will bring Amanda a blouse as a birthday present. The third man in Amanda's life is thus introduced.

The final section of the novel consists of diary entries by Stanislaus Doll, beginning in September 1987. Posted to West Berlin to cover the GDR, Doll meets Amanda when he brings her the blouse (260). His perspective is that of a West German in the GDR, who "understands" the system. He makes a bet with a colleague that there are infrared sensors at the border to search out the body warmth of those trying to escape by hiding in cars. In what is without a doubt the funniest scene in the novel, the two journalists load their trunk up with roast chickens before crossing into East Berlin to see whether the chickens register on the monitors. They are waved across the border by a laughing border guard, who tells them that if he is reincarnated he hopes it will be as a newspaperman (271). Life for a Westerner in the GDR is complex. The reporters "know" they are constantly being shadowed by the Stasi. Someone playfully suggests to Doll that he should keep a radio playing all the time to fill up the Stasi's sound-activated tapes (277).

Doll is not much of a reporter, and Amanda begins to write his commentaries for him in ways that are well beyond his own abilities (292). He eventually loses his job, not because of his incompetence, but because his boss in Hamburg, knowing there is now a conservative government in Bonn, wants conservative journalists in the field (295). Compelled to leave Berlin, Doll sees only two ways he can stay with Amanda: by helping her escape, or by marrying her and attempting to leave with her. A third way, by remaining with her in the GDR, never occurs to him, he says (304). Doll and Amanda decide to get married and turn to the Colombiers, an elderly Jewish lawyer and his wife who have re-emigrated to the GDR, for legal advice (326–28, 362, 380; see also chapter 4 above).

For the first time in any of his "political" novels, Jurek presented specifically Jewish characters in the GDR. Colombier seems willing to help them with some of the paperwork, and through his connections he can arrange for Amanda to leave. He is the East German counterpart of Liebling. Based on Wolfgang Vogel, the attorney who negotiated many of the East-West swaps for the GDR, Colombier is an "independent" lawyer who negotiates for those within and beyond the GDR who need to deal with the government.[70] It is not the formal aspects of the law but personal connections that provide help for his clients.

A final hurdle interferes with the couple's departure. The Stasi approach Doll, suggesting that Amanda will be permitted to leave if he is willing to work informally with them (341). He will not have to spy, but merely "help" them. Doll meets with the agent, who is trying to blackmail him and secretly tapes him. He threatens to broadcast the blackmail attempt if Amanda and he are not permitted to leave. Their meeting place is the "Fairy Tale Fountain" in Friedrichshain; Doll is forced to leave his car in a "no parking" area (*Parkverbot*) while he successfully concludes his arrangement. In this way Jurek answers the question posed in Sabine Gölz's article. Here it is the man who momentarily "vanishes" from the illegally parked car in order to give Amanda a chance to leave the GDR.

When everything seems to be arranged, Ludwig Weniger reappears. He threatens to take Sebastian away from Amanda, claiming that he does not want the boy to grow up in the West. His second attempt at blackmail is unsuccessful. Amanda slaps him, and he leaves, thwarted. Doll and Amanda get married at the state office (366). The final diary entry is dated January 3, 1989. The moving van has arrived, and Doll, Amanda, and Sebastian are set to move to the West. The West is not so bad, says Doll; the language is the same, and "you can buy bananas on every corner" (384). The novel ends with the promise of a new life in the West for Amanda. The GDR is at the point of dissolution in 1989 (as readers knew in 1992, when the novel was published). What do we know about Amanda that transcends the limited perspectives of Weniger, Hetmann, and Doll?

Amanda is a writer. According to Weniger, she begins as a journalist who asks hard questions of the kind that were unacceptable in the GDR (23). As a result she gets fewer and fewer freelance assignments. She contacts a West German publishing house (75), whose editor, much like Elisabeth Borchers, meticulously reads and comments on her work. Her early work is about her childhood (77–79) For Weniger those stories are trivial. (78).

Hetmann, who has seen the manuscript of her novel, thinks it hardly worth mentioning (135). According to him, it revealed some originality but lacks verve. "It was one of those books that filled the book shelves and are never actually read" (136). It shows that intelligence is not enough for writing (162). The language is stilted. She thinks the banality of her topics can be overcome by a mass of details (162). Amanda, however, takes Hetmann aback by according little weight to his views.

With Doll, Amanda begins to function as a "real" reporter (292). She uses the perfect metaphors when writing about the GDR. For example, she writes that it is impossible to produce computers in a society in which "people cannot say that two times two is four" (292). Doll acknowledges the superiority of her reports (312). They are "less vicious and yet more aggressive, she hits the sorest spots, she finds exactly the right words. Perhaps the secret is that she writes better than I do" (313). Amanda's description of the 1988 May Day parade, with tired people on the podium waving at tired people in the audience, vividly evokes the end of the GDR (325). She writes a piece for Doll to broadcast on a failed escape to West Berlin, but notes that more people died when an Iranian aircraft was shot down by the Americans in 1988 than had died in the entire history of the wall (354). Doll's conservative boss in Hamburg scolds him about this report, saying that it is not the business of his reporters to present anti-American propaganda. The last of Doll's diary entries expresses amazement that Amanda is writing another novel. She has half of it on her computer by December 1988 (379).

The image of Amanda as a writer projected something of Jurek's sense that GDR intellectuals needed to become first-rate writers. All else was trivial. In the character of Amanda, Jurek also worked through his complicated relationships with the women he had known, from Rieke to Christine. Some fragments triggered memories in his female readers.[71] Renate Kubitza, who claimed to be an old girlfriend from the 1950s, recognized the dance scenes in the first section of the novel as moments from her meeting with Jurek at the "Melody" dance club in East Berlin.[72] At the core of Jurek's image of Amanda was Irene Dische, with whom he had had an intense intellectual relationship about her writing. Jurek's close editing of Irene's fiction, his view that it was not quite good enough to be recommended to a major German publishing house, and his final opinion that she might have it in her after all reflected on the figure of Amanda.

Amanda was "a woman without success and therefore a rather unfashionable woman," according to Jurek. But his "prejudged image of the woman," which he had held since he conceived the novel, was superseded by the idea of Amanda's role as a writer.[73]

Jurek consciously used autobiographical elements in the novel. Like Hetmann, whose age and status is a parody of Jurek's own in the 1980s, he wove aspects of the private into a world that was only on its surface political. The GDR is superficially present in the submissive character of writers like Weniger, in the prominence of dissidents like Hetmann, in the role that the Stasi and the Writers' Union play in the production of culture. At its heart, however, the novel is about learning to write. The quality of the monologues makes it extraordinarily readable. Jurek had come to terms with his mission as a writer in the New Germany.

The response to *Amanda Heartless* was twofold. The public adored it. It shot to the top of the bestseller lists and stayed there for six months, something none of Jurek's novels had ever done before. The critics, with few exceptions, hated it, including Jurek's most engaged reader, Marcel Reich-Ranicki,[74] who thought the very image of the GDR seemed repressed and softened. It was not grim enough to reflect the realities of life under communism, something Reich-Ranicki knew firsthand from his life in postwar Poland. The end result was a harmless, light, weak novel that seemed to be set anywhere but in the GDR. It presented essentially a private world with a bit of GDR window dressing.[75] Iris Radisch dismissed *Amanda Heartless* as the first of Jurek's novels to cross the boundary to popular fiction.[76] Yet none of these critics got the point. It was possible, Jurek believed, to produce a novel that was popular and well written, that presented moral questions, that could deal deftly with the critical comments of intellectuals such as Sabine Gölz, and that was acceptable to a mass audience. The tone that he struck was intentionally ironic, comic, and entertaining.[77] He had done the same thing on television with *Liebling Kreuzberg,* which Marcel Reich-Ranicki praised, so why not in fiction?

The last thing Jurek wanted was a novel that was read but that would elicit the response, "Nice, but why bother?" He could tolerate "nice" but not "why bother?"[78] Nor did he write the book to come to terms with the GDR. "Literature is the wrong place for the accounting of sins and guilt. I don't write books in order to throw tinder on glowing coals."[79] Attacking the GDR after its demise, even in fictional form, would be an act of cowardice: "If I had let more rage, verve, or anger flow into *Amanda,* it would have been like desecrating a corpse."[80] The novel marked his turn from the political to the private. His "divorce" from the GDR was part of the story of the divorce in the novel. In 1992, he did not think he could add anything to the weights that had already been placed on the scales against the GDR.[81] Was the book too harmless? Certainly Jurek did not share the anger of people like Wolf Biermann toward the GDR, but he was not uncritical. His was a sadness born of true disappointment with the system. By 1992, any nostalgia for the GDR was tempered by the growing reality of the new Germany. He was turning inward in order to deal with the complex human results of the historical process, a factor in virtually all of his fiction since the 1960s.

Neo-Nazis and Martin Walser

The final sentence of *Amanda Heartless*, with its reference to the land of endless bananas, ironically expressed Jurek's ambivalence about a new role for the writer in a reunited Germany. He believed the authors from the GDR would have to change. That they would also have to remain political beings in the new Germany may not have been clear to him in 1990. The burning issue in the new Germany was not whether the legacy of the GDR was a critically aware readership. It was the perceived decline of the New Federal States into racist violence.

One of the perceived changes in German society after the disappearance of the GDR was increased violence against "foreigners" and "asylum seekers." In the eastern city of Hoyerswerda, neo-Nazi thugs laid siege to an apartment block that was housing asylum seekers in 1991. In November 1992, three people were killed and more hurt when right-wing extremists firebombed a house occupied by Turkish immigrants at Möllen, near Hamburg. There had always been a level of violence against those who were perceived as different in both Germanys, but there had been very little reporting of such incidents. With unification, they seemed to multiply. The only thing that seemed to have been keeping East German xenophobia in check—as Arno, in *The Boxer*, perceived—was the massive presence of the state. Former GDR citizens believed that their state had been free of such sentiments. After unification, some Germans charged that it was only in the New Federal States that the hatred of foreigners was being expressed, since it was there that its very existence had been denied for so very long.

With the increase of xenophobic violence, Jews in the new Germany felt themselves again under siege. At first, most of the violence took the form of defacing symbolic Jewish spaces such as cemeteries or monuments. In one particularly grotesque case, the reconstructed "Jewish" barracks used as a museum at the concentration camp at Sachsenhausen was fire-bombed in 1991. Later, violence was aimed at human targets; in July 2000, there was a grenade attack on Jewish immigrants in Düsseldorf. As early as 1992, Ralph Giordano stated that if the state would not protect him, he would begin to carry a weapon to protect himself against the skinheads. Giordano was a German Jewish novelist whose 1988 autobiographical account of a Hamburg family in the Third Reich, *The Bertinis*, was turned into one of the most successful German television programs about the Holocaust. In response to Giordano's anxiety, Jurek felt there had been no meaningful action against right-wing terrorism on the part of the state. The police seemed hesitant to act, and the courts did not take such crimes seriously. "I am afraid," Jurek stated. "I demand to be protected. And if the state denies me protection, then I shall have to live somewhere else."[82]

As a model for combating rightwing violence, Jurek told a story from his own youth. When he was thirteen, there was a bully in his class—large, aggressive, dumb, and frightening. One day Jurek watched, from a hiding place, as the bully beat a fellow student bloody. No one knew that he knew, but Jurek started to hate himself. He felt like an abject coward because he had not intervened. Together, he and the other student might not have got the better of the bully, but at least they could have tried. Jurek compared himself at that time to those who were now standing by when rightwing terror was occurring. The state had to intervene, but it was also necessary for individual citizens to confront the growing tide of violence against people unable to defend themselves.[83]

Jurek denied that xenophobia was solely a product of educational policies in the GDR, which minimized or even ignored the fascist past while claiming that the state was essentially antifascist. In the FRG, forty years of democracy had exerted a "civilizing process," while those in the East "are more easily moved to let their feelings show, like the nationalists in Serbia." East German youth were "quick to use anything that is forbidden," like Nazi slogans and gestures. Jurek recognized that this violence was part of the same youth culture that had earlier used Western music to defy the authorities in the GDR.

Jurek contrasted his own youth with the pessimism and depression in the former GDR during the early 1990s. High unemployment, growing drug use, and the sense that their parents had failed them marked this new generation. "When I was sixteen, the future was positive. I kept this basic view for a very long time. Youth in the East feel that they are superfluous. No one wants them. The future is like a black wall."[84] The failed promises of unification led to the reappearance of Nazi symbols, which had promised a better future in 1933. Once again, it was the fathers who were at fault, not the sons.

Nor was the fault that of Western materialism alone, Jurek conceded. The GDR had constrained its citizens to manners of thinking that robbed them of their humanity, forcing them "to deform themselves, and many appear very ugly today."[85] To criticize them for being "crippled" would be hypocritical. If this mental straitjacketing had been done in the West, the West Germans, now so arrogant, would have acted in the same way. For the Third Reich was the last "all-German" state and set the model for the deformations in present-day Germany.[86] This is certainly the way Jurek's Jewish characters saw things in *The Boxer* and *Bronstein's Children.*

The realization that Germany was gradually being defined abroad by right-wing violence moved the government to action. In 1994, neo-Nazi symbols and hate speech were banned throughout the country. This acknowledgment of the past reinforced Jurek's own perceptions. Yet he still needed to see his own youth, suspended between the Lodz ghetto and his exile from the GDR, as a moment of promise. "When I was nineteen, I lived in a state of trust. No matter how much trouble I had in my world, somehow or other I felt certain that I was on my way to a better future."[87] By 1994 he could blame the failure of that dream on the inherent failures of the communist system. He realized that the GDR was built upon an essential lie from its origin: "Of the ten thousand antifascists in Germany [in 1945], eight million lived in the GDR."[88] The self-image of the GDR had limited its ability to deal with the fascist past. Jurek suddenly saw how many circumstances in the daily life of the GDR reminded him of fascism—"the universal control of the party, the ubiquity of spies, the destruction of the private sphere throughout the state, the constant pressure of hypocrisy." Jurek began to see right-wing violence as a reflex of the division of Germany and the history of the GDR. For a while, he felt as if "the wrong team had won the ball game."[89] The newly unified FRG seemed to have all of the problems of both former states it comprised.

At this point Jurek reopened his public debate with Martin Walser. His memories of his own youth in the GDR were under siege. The world Max had brought him into may not have been so perfect after all. Martin Walser's earlier claims that the demands of remembering the Shoah were impairing the memories of his childhood seemed to have a parallel in Jurek's own utopian memory of the GDR. But being a child in Nazi Germany was entirely different from being a teenager in the GDR. Stories about childhood can mask the political realities of the world in which one was raised, as in Walser's case, or they can reflect the desire to create a healthy world, which was what Jurek found in the GDR. Jurek's memories of the GDR helped explain his fragmented sense of self.

In 1993, Martin Walser claimed that all the neo-Nazi activities of the post-unification period could be attributed to the lack of a strong national identity on the part of all Germans. Had an integrated identity been present, Walser claimed, antiforeigner sentiments would not have surfaced.[90] Jurek, who was now convinced that the difference in the political cultures was at the core of right-wing violence, once again dismissed Walser's views as based on resentment. He noted that Walser returned again and again to *his* role as victim and attempted to measure the world from that position. Walser implied that if the Germans could have been proud of themselves after the war, violence would not have become endemic in either system. Jurek disagreed strongly. The writer's role was to provide a critical distance to the claims of the past, not to promote a specific version of it. Yet his nostalgia for the lost promises of the GDR had something of the same taste as Walser's desire for a new German national identity free of guilt about the past.

Changing Perspectives and New Goals

Jurek had told "Mike" Lützeler that he would return to St. Louis as a Max Kade Writer-in-Residence in the spring of 1993.[91] It would be an important trip for Jurek and for his sense of belonging. America had treated him well since his first trip to Oberlin. American Germanists saw in Jurek the perfect German writer: a Jew, a survivor, a dissident, and an author of successful books and films that crossed national boundaries. For writers like Jurek, a critical reception in America was always quite different from that found in Germany. American scholars had never shown disrespect even when questioning his works with new methodological approaches. Christa Wolf too had experienced this constructive criticism; in the commentary volume to her novel *Cassandra* (1983), she recorded her debt to American feminist critics in the very shaping of that work.[92]

America also meant sports for Jurek. St. Louis was a sports fan's heaven, with strong professional baseball and football. Jurek's letters to Lützeler stressed his wish to spend as much time as possible attending sporting events. On this trip, he was accompanied for the full three months (March 5–May 15) by Christine and two-year-old Johnny. In addition, he invited Rieke, Nicki, and Lonni to travel to America for the first time as his guests. They visited him in St. Louis and spent some time touring the country. In St. Louis, Jurek taught a seminar on the newest fiction dealing with unification, including novels by F. C. Delius, Günter

Grass, and Monika Maron. After spending a good deal of time sketching the political background to these texts, Jurek dismissed them as having no literary value. The star text for the class was clearly his own *Amanda Heartless*, which remained a touchstone for good writing in the seminar.

During that same semester Christine visited my seminar at Cornell University to talk about Joseph Roth, the topic of her thesis. For the very first time, Jurek and Johnny were alone together for a weekend. Jurek began to realize the positive aspects of his second chance at fatherhood. His flight from child and spouse into the writing of *Amanda Heartless* had ended.

Jurek and Christine returned to St. Louis in 1995, this time for a three-week vacation while their friend Peter Schneider, a Berlin author, was there as writer-in-residence.[93] Lützeler arranged for a symposium on multiculturalism during that period, at which Jurek spoke of the difficulties an author encounters when speaking about his own work.[94] Although Jurek saw his comments as distancing himself from the role of critic, they were immediately taken as reflecting his self-conscious role as a writer in the New Germany.

"With the GDR, something within me also collapsed," wrote Jurek; "I did not feel well."[95] By the mid-1990s, Jurek had publicly come to terms with his own understanding of the GDR. He recognized that after 1989 there was nothing more to rescue from the dream of "the better path." His silence after the opening of the wall, he explained, was in part the avoidance of redundancy (everyone else was saying what he wanted to say) and was also due to a sense of loss. But he was not permitted to remain quiet. In the spring of 1993, he was asked by Wolfgang Thierse, a member of the SPD faction in the Bundestag (and, in the late 1990s, Speaker of the House) to speak before a commission investigating the cultural politics of the GDR. Thierse had been one of the leaders of the East German movement that eventually led to the dissolution of the GDR. The inquiry revolved around the question whether the GDR was a good or a bad place for artists and writers. By 1993, it was clearly a bad place. Censorship meant self-censorship, and success meant reducing one's own access to the public. Jurek recounted the decay of the writer's ability to address an audience by telling the commission of his own moves from television to film to fiction in search of an ever more elite audience.[96] Had he remained in the GDR, he would eventually have been forced to become a lyric poet! This dialogue between Thierse, a new member of the political establishment, and Jurek, whose West German celebrity now defined him, continued in a reciprocal interview that focused on memories of childhood. Jurek now evoked memories not of his childhood in the GDR but of the ideal world of the FRG under Willy Brandt, when "artists had a meaning. Right at that point writers had a purpose and felt themselves useful."[97] Thierse reminded him that it was in precisely that period, 1966–69, that the student movement was under way and laws were being made concerning civil unrest (*Notstandsgesetze*). So much for any nostalgia for an ideal FRG past.

How the past affects the present was the theme of one of Jurek's major attempts to capture the German-German tension that existed immediately after unification. He again turned to the *Liebling Kreuzberg* team of Meissner, Becker, and Krug and to television, the medium that had brought him the widest public. His intent was instruction as well as entertainment. He wanted to show the problems of unification through the experiences of two groups confronting each other over the function of television. The catchword would be "opportunism" as a "human right," for people on both sides of the new "wall in the mind" (to use Peter Schneider's phrase). This new wall consisted of the residual differences, both real and imagined, between East and West. Jurek was interested in the ways people used unification for their own purposes. Christine suggested that he should also show how this kind of opportunism was very different from that which turned Germans into Nazis after 1933 or, indeed, into good communists in the GDR.[98]

Jurek expressed his view of a new Germany in the nine-part series *We Are Also One People* (*Wir sind auch nur ein Volk*) in 1994.[99] The title, of course, plays on the Leipzig slogan "We are one people," which precipitated the call for unification and stressed the quotidian effects of unification as "normal" life. Who is at fault? the German phrase asks; "I am only human" (*Ich bin auch nur ein Mensch*). This series, like *Bronstein's Children*, used the making of a film as one of its key elements. The West German celebrity author Anton Steinheim (played by Dietrich Mattausch), preparing to write a television series on the problems of the former GDR, confronts the Grimm family in Berlin–Prenzlauer Berg to do a program on their daily life after unification. This situation provided a structure for Jurek to work out the complex questions of group difference and its reflection in language. While Steinheim and Benno Grimm (Manfred Krug) seem to speak the same language, each believes that his own is the more authentic as it reflects his own experiences of the world. The very title of the series evidences such a conundrum. Jurek had to create a platform from which to critique both the Western media and the new citizens of the former GDR.

Where was Jurek to get his East Germans from? He had left the GDR a generation ago, and his vision of what its citizens were had been frozen in memory—as was made amply clear in the reviews of *Amanda Heartless*. Jurek turned to the families of his married sons in eastern Germany for a touch of authenticity. They immediately became suspicious. "You've never been interested in our activities before,"[100] they said, and they made themselves available with the same sense of being observed as the Grimm family evinces in the series. Jurek had "used" his father in his earlier novels. Now, however, he was the absent father using his sons. There was an echo of the three-part series on grandfathers that he had written in the early 1960s for GDR television. Jurek's literary representation of the GDR returned to shape his image of the New Federal States.

If Max Becker was never an adequate father, then Jurek was no better than he. The relationship between the new and the old, between West and East, was matched by the relationship between Jurek's two families, separated by the Berlin Wall even after its fall. But Jurek knew that no family could offer what the media wanted—a "typical" GDR family in the terms of the Western media. So Jurek wrote a scene in which the Grimms "learn" to be a family by watching a West German soap opera. The series that Steinheim was to have written is canceled even before being filmed, leaving the Grimms in the limbo of their new lives.

The group in eastern Berlin that saw the preview of *We Are Also One People* hated their image as comic and slightly corrupt. They asked why the kitchen in the Grimms' apartment was always dirty when "cleanliness was one of the hallmarks of East Germany." Why had Jurek placed the series in Prenzlauer Berg, with its literary associations of the GDR avant-garde and Plenzdorf's *Liebling Kreuzberg*, rather than in the truly poor areas of East Berlin such as Marzahn, with its high level of neo-Nazi violence?[101] After the program was actually broadcast, it was panned by the critics. It was a "complete failure" in capturing the world of unified Berlin, never mind the difficulties of life in the "new German states." Much the same criticism had been leveled at Gabriele Denecke's remake of *Sleepless Days* as a TV film in 1991.[102] It was unrealistic and bore little or no resemblance to the world of the GDR as experienced by its inhabitants or imagined by those in the West.

Like *Amanda* and *Neuner*, Jurek's sense of the "East" spoke neither to Eastern nor to Western critics. Reinhard Mohr, the television critic of the *Frankfurter Allgemeine Zeitung*, ended his review by quoting a remark made by Sternheim in the show: "I must have been an idiot to get involved with such a stupid TV program!" which he took as an autobiographical statement about Jurek's own involvement.[103] The public agreed, and the audience, small to start with, declined as the series continued.

In 1993, Jurek wrote a much more successful screenplay, based on his novella "The Wall," which had appeared in 1980 in his volume of short stories *After the First Future*.[104] *When All the Germans Are Sleeping* (*Wenn alle Deutschen schlafen*) was made for ZDF and directed by Frank Beyer, who had been responsible for *Jacob the Liar*. As with that film, Jurek's status as a "Jew" made it possible for a "German" director such as Beyer, according to his own account, to make the film. The title change was necessary because by 1994, when the film was broadcast, viewers would take "the wall" to mean the Berlin Wall, not the wall around a concentration camp.

The short story was Jurek's one attempt to describe the Shoah from the perspective of a child, here a five-year-old in a nameless ghetto and later in a concentration camp in eastern Europe. The child's portrayal of the camp lines up with Jurek's own complicated account of his missing memories; each retelling adds a detail, remembered or invented. The talkative narrator says his words "push against my checks from the insides, multiplying at a fantastic rate and hurting my mouth until I have to open it" (76). He is full of stories, one of which we hear in the course of his narrative. He understands that his stories have power. Learning that the shopkeeper Tenzer has a cactus, he blurts out this information to a friend. Eventually Tenzer is deported for having the plant (78–79).

The child and his parents are moved into a camp in middle of the ghetto to prepare them for transportation. Suddenly the rhythm of the day changes. "Every morning there is 'inspection'—that's the first word I learn in the foreign tongue" (80). As Jurek learned the *Lagersprache*, the language of the ghetto and the camp, so too the nameless child in the tale learns German. When Jurek was adapting the story as a screenplay, things were quite different. He and Christine had hired a Polish housekeeper, who babysat with Johnny and spoke to the baby in Polish. When Johnny began to talk, he creatively mixed German and Polish words and forms. Jurek was furious. He forbade the woman to speak any Polish with the child or Johnny would never really learn German.

In Jurek's story, the camp is a tedious place. "By the second day I am bored to death" (81). The child's father points out that "this is not a game" (81). While sneaking about the camp, he is grabbed by someone who thinks he is trying to steal. He is let go because "he's the kid of someone I know" (82). Being a child in the camp means being sheltered and succored by adults.

The child and his friends Julian and Itzig decide to explore the abandoned ghetto to see what they can retrieve. To do so, they must climb over the ghetto wall and avoid the guards. Julian, the oldest and most sophisticated of the three, claims that there are no Germans out at night: "Where do you see any Germans here? Besides they sleep at night" (85). Julian and the narrator creep out of the camp, across the wall, and into the dark ghetto. The narrator looks for his cloth ball and his father's flashlight. On the way back they cannot find a place to get back over the wall. They are stopped by a "giant," a German soldier who speaks some Polish. He threatens to take them to the commandant but then instinctively shields the children when a motorcycle passes. He finally allows them to climb onto his back and over the wall. Acting like a German St. Christopher, this nameless "good" German rescues the children. The child is cut on the broken glass embedded on top of the wall, but makes it home, where his parents comfort him and treat his injuries (105). What happens to the children after that is not told. In reality, they would have been deported to the death camps.

Frank Beyer's film shifts the emphasis from the children and their "adventures" to the relationships between parents and children in both the ghetto and the camp. Like *Neuner*, which sought to draw on Jurek's success in *Liebling Kreuzberg*, the new screenplay drew on the continued success of *Jacob the Liar*. When Jurek, in his house on the Baltic coast, sat down to write, he found that the script flowed in ways that he found disconcerting. He "knew" what the apartment occupied by the protagonist's family "looked like" as he wrote. Unlike the tentative and fumbling figures he drew in *Neuner*, the characters in *When All the Germans Are Sleeping* followed an emotional logic that rang true to him and, more importantly, to his viewers. Set in Poland in 1942, the film starred Benjamin Katz as Marek (the narrator), Robin Trumpener as Itzek (one of the friends), and Ilja Smolianski as Julian. It repeats a theme from Beyer's version of *Jacob the Liar*—the survival of children. Here it is not the Jewish surrogate parent, Jacob, but the "good" German that allows them to survive. Unlike Lina, in *Jacob*, the child in *Sleeping* is guaranteed survival. Jurek wrote lines for two narrators—the child Marek, commenting on the events of the moment, and an unseen adult (obviously the survivor Marek, played by Jürgen Hentsch) who provides a retrospective account of the action.

Appearing in the wake of Steven Spielberg's film *Schindler's List*, Beyer and Jurek's version of "The Wall" is a film without overt violence: the one shot that is fired is aimed by a German soldier into the air.[105] Jews such as Tenzer (played by Gerry Wolf, who was one of the actors considered for the part of Jacob in Beyer's 1974 film) die offscreen. The parents (played by Christiane Hagedorn and Mario Grünewald) may have some power over each other, but none in the world of the camps. At the beginning of the film, while still in the ghetto, Marek wonders how powerful his mother is, because even his father, who is clearly the stronger, always listens to her. Later we see her powerlessness. When she wakes up in the camp barracks and discovers that Marek has gone, all she can do is scream. The theme of rescue and the central role that adults must play in the survival of children is subordinate to the more general theme of the German rescue of Jews. As a result "The Wall" has become a staple, as has *Jacob the Liar*, of Holocaust education materials.[106]

It is ironic that Jurek's faded memory of the GDR was seen as inadequate for the 1990s but that his nonexistent memories of the Shoah were taken as case material for teaching about the reality of the Holocaust.[107] Jurek's emotional response to the GDR was tied to his own daily experience of life there before 1977, not to his experience in the 1980s and '90s. It was the powerful feelings generated by the Shoah and by his subsequent life as a victim of the Nazi regime in the GDR that made his fictions come alive. To his German-language readers and viewers they certainly seemed more real than his ever more private world of the GDR and of eastern Germany after unification. Jurek offered his German audience a biographical and emotional authenticity in his representation of the Shoah that they found compelling. By the mid-1990s, this was part of his profile as a German writer in the FRG.

Although he did much of his writing at the house at Sieseby, Jurek also needed a quiet place to work when in Berlin. In 1994, he and Christine bought two apartments on the Braillestraße in the middle-class neighborhood of Steglitz. Jurek's work space was in the building in which he lived. Family, child, work—all seemed to fall into place. Jurek was happy with the way these elements of his life fitted together. Yet the old tensions were only slightly below the surface.

Between the weekend house, the apartments, and travel, Jurek struggled with his new role as a conscientious father and husband. In September 1995, Meredid Hopwood invited Jurek to read and lecture at the Centre for Contemporary German Literature at Swansea, Wales. On this trip, made in October of that year, he was accompanied by a German film crew.[108] The image he wanted to project on the resulting TV program was that of a writer and a father. He was shown walking with Johnny on the Baltic Coast, visiting Swansea, and living the kind of life he had sought. The more he withdrew from a life of public scrutiny, the film seemed to say, the better was his private life. Ironically, this privacy was all captured on film to be broadcast.

Klaus Wagenbach, the Berlin publisher of Wolf Biermann in the 1960s and an old friend, had been after Jurek to do a book with his press. He suggested once again that Jurek compile some of his nonfiction writing— his talks, interviews, and public statements—for this purpose. Jurek, who felt obligated to Suhrkamp, took the idea to Siegfried Unseld, who thought it a good one but insisted that Jurek publish it with his house. In the summer of 1995, Jurek put together a selection of texts and sent them to his new editor at Suhrkamp, Reiner Weiss. (Elisabeth Borchers had retired.) Weiss suggested certain cuts, such as the review of Stefan Heym's *The Wandering Jew* that Jurek had presented so favorably in 1981.[109] Interestingly, Jurek's selection began with his first "West Berlin" piece, his 1977 essay on his Jewish identity. None of the theoretical pieces on the role of literature or the definition of the writer that Jurek had written and, in part, published in the GDR was included. It was as if he had never written or said anything as a GDR intellectual. He was a new German in the Berlin Republic.

Final Episodes

Between October 26 and November 19, 1995, Jurek traveled for the Goethe Institute to South America. He visited Chile, Bolivia, Peru, Ecuador, Columbia, Venezuela, Costa Rica, and Mexico. Upon his return, he felt unwell. Just a touch of the normal sickness that haunts all travelers, he thought. He went to his doctor, who ordered tests. On December 28, 1995, he was diagnosed with advanced rectal cancer. On January 7 he underwent surgery, and the surgeon discovered that the cancer had metastasized into the liver.[110] By February he was undergoing a course of chemotherapy that required that he spend five days in the hospital every three weeks. The only person he asked to be with him, besides Christine, was his old friend Helge Braune. Jurek and Helge spent the days chatting and playing backgammon. Cancer of all kinds seemed to be the curse of dwellers in the New Federal States. Esophageal cancer had killed Heiner Müller two days after Jurek was diagnosed.

In the summer of 1995, Jurek had begun work on the fourth series of *Liebling Kreuzberg* at the urging of Otto Meissner. This new series would revitalize Krug's character and return the program to its earlier quality. Jurek now had to complete the final fourteen episodes of the series, firmly set in the new, united Berlin. The first four episodes were written before his trip to South America, the final ones as he struggled with cancer. He was convinced that he would beat the disease or, at least, would have five more years of life. He began to think about further literary projects, including a novel with the working title "The Book Thief."

Jurek moved the TV series back to Kreuzberg, at its poorer end, near the Schlesisches Tor and the Warschauer Bridge. It was the part of Kreuzberg that abutted the former East Berlin. The program was Jurek's final attempt to understand the changes taking place in the new Germany. Krug found Jurek much more difficult to work with in this series than in the earlier ones. He complained that Jurek considered it a one-man show and refused to take any of Krug's suggestions seriously.[111] Jurek, however, was focusing on the new series as an anchor for his battle with cancer and as a pragmatic legacy for his family.

The episodes dealt with a wide range of cases, many of them raised by the disappearance of the wall. One episode, "Among Us Men," ("Unter uns Machos"), is devoted to correcting a lie that pervades someone's Stasi file. In 1992 it became possible, through the offices of a new authority under the leadership of Pastor Joachim Gauck, one of the leaders of the East German opposition, to examine one's Stasi files. The file that the character retrieves contains the statement that he has had an adulterous relationship. When he takes the file home, his wife reads of this affair and promptly asks him for a divorce. Liebling's new associate, Bruno Pelzer (played by Stefan Reck), persuades the former Stasi spy who wrote the report to get in touch with the man's wife and retract the statement, threatening otherwise to reveal to his present employer that he is a former Stasi agent.

Another episode, "Fantasies" ("Hirngespinste"), deals with the exploitation of an elderly Jewish couple that fled to America to escape the Nazis. They return to lay claim to a piece of property in East Berlin expropriated first by the Nazis and then by the communist state. A lawyer has cheated them of their money, and they come to Liebling to file suit against the unprincipled lawyer. As Liebling works on their case, he falls in love with their often-married daughter, who becomes a fixture by the end of the series. The image of the Jew in the final *Liebling Kreuzberg* series reflects a preoccupation with the meaning of the Holocaust in the new "Berlin Republic." A design competition for a Holocaust memorial was finally set in motion in 1995. The public debates about it dragged on until after Jurek's death. The composition as well as the size of the Jewish community had exploded after 1989. With tens of thousands of Jews emigrating from the former Soviet Union, being Jewish in Berlin—whether in a religious, secular, or political sense—had taken on an entirely new meaning by the mid-1990s. The return of Liebling's new girlfriend from San Francisco to Germany in Jurek's plot was part of a reconstitution of a Jewish presence in the city. Her accent-free German marks her as a returnee, belonging to German culture. Jurek remained focused on the Holocaust while a new population of eastern Jews, often speaking German with a heavy accent like Max, were revitalizing the daily reality in Berlin.

Yet Jurek continued to project Berlin in the private rather than the public sphere. Liebling's cases deal only peripherally with the "big" questions of unification. Even the reclaiming of seized property is transformed into a case of legal malfeasance. The cast of characters remains multicultural—Jews, Russians, Africans, Poles, Turks—and the episodes, unlike the earlier ones, were shot all over Berlin, East and West. The image of the East is gray, but for every slum shown in the East, a parallel one is shown in the West. The hip Berlin of the mid-1990s is missing in the series. The wrapping of the *Reichstag* in 1995 by Christo and Jeanne-Claude, a major cultural event that heralded the Berlin Republic's rethinking of its public image, was not quite the Berlin Jurek wanted to evoke.

Liebling's personal life and that of his new associate, Bruno Pelzer, merge when Bruno becomes engaged to Liebling's divorced daughter. In the final episode, she walks away from the altar, leaving him standing there. No happy ending is promised in Liebling's life. In this final series, each episode is self-contained and each "solves" the problems presented in it. The episodes are more conservative in their structure than in the earlier series. Liebling's character does not develop; he remains sardonically distant and yet engaged in his world, much as Jurek became in the 1990s.

Jurek continued to write episode after episode, often dictating notes to Christine from his hospital bed. Everyone involved knew that the series would draw to an end. The experience with Plenzdorf had made it clear that it Jurek's scripts were crucial.[112] The final series of *Liebling Kreuzberg* began to play on October 7, 1997, and again achieved tremendous popularity.[113]

By October 1996 it was clear that Jurek's cancer demanded more aggressive treatment. Jurek was in hospital for one day each week. The second course of chemotherapy had exhausted him, but he decided to throw a party for his friends. He made cholent for them, the Sabbath dish most typical of eastern European Jews, and told stories until dawn. It was his farewell, and most of those present knew it.

The chemotherapy was having only a negative effect on Jurek, as became apparent in early 1997. The tumors multiplied. Jurek's physician decided to "call an intermission," telling Christine privately that any further therapy would be pointless. He concealed his pessimism from Jurek, however, not wanting to rob him of hope.

Jurek's sense of humor never flagged. He wrote dozens of postcards to Christine after his illness was diagnosed, a tradition he had established with the Krugs decades before. He imagined how he would write a final episode of *Liebling Kreuzberg* in which Liebling is diagnosed with cancer and beats it, or he commented on the rhetoric of politics in the light of his limited ability to digest because of the cancer. "I have been concerned for days with a fundamental question, the answer to which has almost existential meaning. We all know: 'Whoever's bread I eat, that is whose song I sing.' That's correct, that's Marxism . . . Now I've not been able to eat bread for a while. No bread, what now? 'Whoever's noodle soup I eat, that is whose song I sing' sounds absurd."[114] Jurek's ability to joke about his disease made it possible for him as well as his friends and family to endure it.

In February, Jurek gave his final interview. A freelance journalist, Herlinde Koebl, requested permission to photograph him in the apartment in Berlin.[115] She engaged him in a discussion that was published after his death. In it he provided a candid account of how he had become a German and what that meant. He recognized that *Jacob the Liar* would be his principal legacy, but he saw both the strengths and the weaknesses of the book that had made his reputation as a writer. As to what he had inherited from his experience in the camps, he mentioned his aggressiveness and his obsessive desire to reconstruct the past. He had rethought what his Jewishness really meant for his life; he now saw it as an intrinsic part of what he was and did. He affirmed the new importance of family and regretted his earlier neglect of his sons for the sake of his writing. He imagined an ideal GDR past where anti-Semitism was unimaginable and life was positive, at least until 1968. He did not mourn the post-1968 GDR. He defined himself as a new German—one with a multicultural past as foreigner, Jew, survivor, socialist, dissident, East German, West Berliner, and now German. He saw his own life as a set of contradictory experiences of the sort that might be a model for the multiculturalism of the new Berlin Republic.[116] The new Germany, his Berlin, became the antithesis of all that was provincial and small-minded. And Jurek himself was evidence of that openness.

Jurek had one further obligation. In early February, he returned to the German Booksellers' Academy at Seckbach for a final reading. It was there that he had meet Christine in 1983. The two of them decided to leave Berlin in late February and go to their country house. Six months before his death, as the chemotherapy ceased to work, Jurek looked at his emaciated body and said, in English, "Back to the roots." He had begun to look like the photos of concentration camp victims. That was the world he had survived and chronicled, and its memories were etched on his body.

On March 14, 1997, Jurek died in the country house at Sieseby. He was buried in the cemetery of the Lutheran church there. A small group of friends and family were present. The poet Joachim Sartorius spoke at the graveside. Manfred Krug read from *Jacob the Liar*. Today, small stones, a symbol of remembrance in the Jewish tradition, are heaped on the gravestone. The stone reads simply, "Jurek Becker, 1937–1997."

Notes

Introduction

1. Jurek Becker, "Der Tausendfüßler," in *Schrieben zwischen den Kulturen*, ed. Paul Michael Lützeler (Frankfurt am Main: Fischer Taschenbuch Verlag, 1996), 55–64; reprinted in Jurek Becker, *Ende des Grössen Wahns* (Frankfurt am Main: Suhrkamp, 1996), 216–330; quotation from Suhrkamp edition at 221–22.

2. Heinz Ludwig Arnold, "Aus den Stasi-Akten über Jurek Becker," *Text + Kritik* 120 (1993): 16.

3. See my "Bertolt Brecht and the F.B.I.," *Nation* 210 (1974): 560–62.

4. Richard A. Zipser, "Jurek Becker: A Writer with a Cause," *Dimension* 11 (1978): 402–23.

5. Becker, *Ende des Grössen Wahns*, 213–43.

6. See my "An Interview with Isaac Bashevis Singer," *Diacritics* 4 (1974): 30–33.

7. Wladamir Kaminer, *Russen Disko* (Berlin: Manhattan, 2000).

Chapter One

1. The refashioning of identity both by the father and the son, by Mieczyslaw and Jerzy, is a central part of this story. The dates of birth are inconsistent. According to the earliest records of Jerzy that we have from the ghetto, he was born on September 10, 1937. But when, on October 10, 1952, his father noted his birth in official documents, his birth date became September 30, 1937. Becker Papers, Akademie der Künste, Berlin (hereafter cited as Becker Papers).

2. There are a number of good histories of Lodz. Yet the best Jewish account from the 1930s of the city and its struggles in the modern world remains Israel Joshua Singer's magisterial novel of 1936, *The Brothers Ashkenazi* [*De brider Ashkenaz*], trans. Maurice Samuels (New York: Grosset & Dunlap, 1967); quotation at p. 614. By 1937, middle-class Polish-Jewish life in Lodz had already become mythologized, as Singer shows in his novel. The Jews of Lodz were not sentimentalized *Ostjuden* with their *peyes* (side locks) and klezmer music; these were members of a forgotten Jewish middle class—closer in their social and cultural relationships to their Polish neighbors than to the ultra-Orthodox Jews depicted in the autobiography of Isaac Bashevis Singer (I. J. Singer's brother), *Mayn tatn's beys-din shtub* (1956), translated as *In My Father's Court* (New York: Farrar, Straus and Giroux, 1976).

3. "Anmeldung: Der Aelteste der Juden in Litzmannstadt-Ghetto," February 1, 1940, Becker Papers.

4. "Aufnahmeantrag: Humboldt Universität" (July 17, 1957), Becker Papers; reprinted in Holger Jens Karlson, "Jurek Becker: Bausteine zu einer

Schiftstellerbiographie," *Berliner Hefte zur Geschichte des literarischen Lebens* 3 (2000): 5–80; see esp. 72–74. I am grateful to Karlson for making his thesis available to me before it was published. See also Angela Schmidt, "Jurek Becker: Annäherungen an eine Biographie" (Diplomarbeit, Humboldt University, Berlin, 1987).

5. Lillian Kranitz-Sanders, ed., *Twelve Who Survived: An Oral History of the Jews of Lodz, Poland, 1930–1954* (New York: Irvington, 1984), 145. A model for dealing with the childhood narratives is given by Henryk Grynberg in *The Children of Zion,* trans. Jacqueline Mitchell (Evanston, IL: Northwestern University Press, 1997), which puts together the autobiographical accounts of hundreds of Jewish children from Poland in a continuous narrative. In many ways that volume served as the basis for the opening chapters of the present biography. Grynberg gives a general picture, using particular accounts in a mosaic of voices. As Jurek Becker left no accounts of his childhood, I am trying to capture both the general and the particulars of his experience.

6. Kranitz-Sanders, *Twelve Who Survived,* 129.

7. According to the ghetto records "Mordeha" was born on November 9, 1900, in Lodz. According to "Max's" form, which was filled out when he joined the Jewish community in Berlin on January 8, 1946, he was born on March 11, 1906, in Fürth, Bavaria. The spelling of the family name also changed from the Polish spelling of Bekker to Beker and then to Becker. "Chana" was born on March 28, 1902, according to the ghetto records. Her death certificate at Ravensbrück gives "Hania's" birth date as April 30, 1902.

8. *Kinder des Holocaust sprechen... : Lebensberichte,* trans. Roswitha Matwin-Buschmann (Leipzig: Reclam, 1995), 66–67.

9. *Kinder des Holocaust,* 109.

10. Marianna D. Birnbaum, "An Interview with Jurek Becker," *Cross Currents* 8 (1989): 155.

11. Becker, *Ende des Grössen Wahns,* 12.

12. Kranitz-Sanders, *Twelve Who Survived,* 130.

13. The street name was changed to ul. Wieckowskiego. The Poznanski palace, now an art museum, was at no. 36.

14. Kranitz-Sanders, *Twelve Who Survived,* 134.

15. Jurek Becker, *Nach der ersten Zukunft* (Frankfurt am Main: Suhrkamp, 1980), 40–61. Reprinted in Jurek Becker, *Die beliebteste Familiengeschichte und andere Erzählungen* (Frankfurt am Main: Insel, 1995). All references are to the Suhrkamp edition.

16. Singer, *The Brothers Ashkenazi,* 59.

17. See François Guesnet, *Lodzer Juden im 19. Jahrhundert: Ihr Ort in einer multikulturen Stadtgesellschaft* (Leipzig: Simon-Dubnow-Insitut, 1997), as well as his *Polnische Juden im 19. Jahrhundert: Lebensbedingungen, Rechtsnormen und Organisation im Wandel* (Cologne: Böhlau ,1998). See also Jürgen Hensel, ed., *Polen, Deutsche und Juden in Lodz 1820–1939: Eine schwierige Nachbarschaft* (Osnabrück: Fibre, 1999).

18. Singer, *The Brothers Ashkenazi,* 227.

19. Ibid., 570.

20. Kranitz-Sanders, *Twelve Who Survived,* 143.

21. Singer, *The Brothers Ashkenazi,* 474.

22. Pawel Korzec, "Antisemitism in Poland as an Intellectual, Social and Political Movement," in *Studies on Polish Jewry 1919–1939,* ed. Joshua A. Fishman (New York: YIVO, 1974), 12–104.

23. Ibid., 83.

24. Kranitz-Sanders, *Twelve Who Survived,* 125.

25. American Jewish Congress Report, January 13, 1937, YIVO Archives, New York City.

26. *Les "bancs de ghetto" dans les universités de Pologne: Appel aux universitaires polonais* (Paris: Races et racisme, Groupement d'étude et d'information, 1938), 5.

27. Becker, *Ende des Grössen Wahns,* 217.

28. Ibid., 56.

Chapter Two

1. Becker, *Ende des Grössen Wahns,* 12. Jurek collected (and edited) his various nonfiction writings for that volume. I am quoting from that source as it is the most accessible and reflects which versions of his life he wanted to see as holding together.

2. *Kinder des Holocaust sprechen,* 31.

3. After 1930 Litzmann was an early member of the NSDAP (Nationalsozialistische Deutsche Arbeiterpartei, the Nazi party), and from 1932 to his death he was the senior member of the German parliament.

4. Kranitz-Sanders, *Twelve Who Survived,* 140 (translation modified). Compare the discussion in Zohar Shavit, "Aus Kindermund: Historisches Bewußtsein und nationaler Diskurs in Deutschland nach 1945," *Neue Sammlung* 36 (1996): 355–74.

5. Record books of the ghetto in Yad Vashem (Jerusalem) and the *Ummeldung* form for Jerzy Becker of November 13, 1940, Becker papers.

6. After World War I it was renamed ul. W. Bytomskiej.; see "Aufnahmeantrag: Humboldt Universität," February 25, 1955, Becker Papers.

7. Good accounts of the reception of Rumkowski and his reputation appear in Shmuel Huppert, "King of the Ghetto: Mordecai Haim Rumkowski, the Elder of the Lodz Ghetto," *Yad Vashem Studies* 15 (1983): 125–57, and Lucille Eichengreen, *Rumkowski and the Orphans of Lodz* (San Francisco: Mercury House, 2000).

8. Tamar Bermann, *Produktivierungsmythen und Antisemitismus: Eine soziologische Studie* (Vienna: Europa, 1973), and Derek J. Penslar, *Shylock's Children: Economics and Jewish Identity in Modern Europe* (Berkeley and Los Angeles: University of California Press, 2001). See also the discussion in Christopher R. Browning, *Nazi Policy, Jewish Wrokers, German Killers* (Cambridge: Cambridge University Press, 2000), 58–88, for the best evaluation of the question of work in the Polish ghettos.

9. Debórah Dwork, *Children with a Star: Jewish Youth in Nazi Europe* (New Haven: Yale University Press, 1991), 191; see also George Eisen, *Children and Play in the Holocaust: Games among the Shadows* (Amherst: University of Massachusetts Press, 1988); Maria Hochberg-Marianska, and Noe Gruss, eds., *The Children Accuse,* trans. Bill Johnston (Portland, OR: Vallentine Mitchell, 1996); Judith Kestenberg, and Charlotte Kahn, eds., *Children Surviving Persecution: An International Study of Trauma and Healing* (Westport, CT: Praeger, 1998); Wiktoria Sliwowska, ed., *The Last*

Eyewitnesses: Children of the Holocaust Speak, trans. Julian Fay Bussgang (Evanston, IL: Northwestern University Press, 1998).

10. Dwork, *Children with a Star,* 204.

11. Janusz Gumkowski, Adam Rutkowski and Arnfrid Astel, eds., *Briefe aus Litzmannstadt,* trans. Peter Lachmann and Arnfrid Astel (Cologne: Friedrich Middlehauve Verlag, 1967), 126.

12. *Spuren aus dem Getto Lodz: Dokumente der Sammlung Wolfgang Haney, Berlin* (Berlin: Haus der Wannsee-Konferenz, 2000), 55.

13. Gumkowski et al., *Briefe aus Litzmannstadt,* 32.

14. Becker, *Ende des Grössen Wahns,* 116.

15. Irene Hauser, *"Nicht einmal zum Sterben habe ich Protektion..."* Frankfurter Lern- und Dokumentationszentrum des Holocaust, Materialien Nr. 2 (Frankfurt am Main: Fritz Bauer Institut, n.d. [1995]), [7].

16. Oskar Rosenfeld, *Wozu noch Welt: Auszeichnungen aus dem Getto Lodz,* ed. Hanno Loewy (Berlin: Neue Kritik, 1994), 23.

17. Lucjan Dobroszycki, ed., *Chronicle of the Lodz Ghetto, 1941–1944* (New Haven: Yale University Press, 1984), 250–51. Additional studies and texts from Lodz that I have drawn on for this chapter are Hanno Loewy and Andrzej Bodek, eds., *"Les Vrais Riches"—Notizen am Rand: Ein Tagebuch aus dem Ghetto Lodz (Mai bis August 1944)* (Leipzig: Reclam, 1997); Martin Gilbert, *The Holocaust: A History of the Jews of Europe during the Second World War* (New York: Henry Holt, 1970), 430–40; Sarah Bick Berkowitz, *Where Are My Brothers? From the Ghetto (Lodz) to the Gas Chambers* (New York: Helios, 1965). A central text is Hanno Loewy and Gerhard Schoenberner, eds., *"Unser einziger Weg ist Arbeit": Das Getto in Lodz, 1940–1944* (Vienna: Loecker, 1990), which contains Jurek Becker's commentary "Die unsichtbare Stadt," 10–11.

18. Josef Wulf, *Lodz: Das letzte Ghetto auf polnischem Boden* (Bonn: Bundeszentrale für Heimatdienst, 1961), 29.

19. Isaiah Kuperstein, "Rumors: A Social-Historical Phenomenon in the Ghetto of Lodz," *Polish Review* 18 (1973): 63–83. See also Wolfgang Sofsky, *Die Ordnung des Terrors: Das Konzentrationslager* (Frankfurt am Main: Fischer, 1993), 109–12.

20. From a manuscript report from the Litzmannstadt ghetto by the pseudonymous "Leon Hurwitz," cited in Kuperstein, "Rumors," 50.

21. Tamotsu Shibutai, *Improvised News: A Sociological Study of Rumor* (Indianapolis: Bobbs-Merrill, 1966), 40.

22. Gumkowski et al., *Briefe aus Litzmannstadt,* 18–19.

23. Isaiah Trunk, *Ghetto Lodz* (New York: YIVO, 1962), 392.

24. Ibid., 293.

25. Stefan Korbónski, *Warsaw in Chains* (New York: Macmillan, 1959), 110.

26. Gumkowski et al., *Briefe aus Litzmannstadt,* 30, 58, and elsewhere.

27. Dobroszycki, *Chronicle of the Lodz Ghetto,* 504.

28. Laurel Holliday, ed., *Children in the Holocaust and World War II: Their Secret Diaries* (New York: Pocket Books, 1995), 397–98 (translation modified).

29. The radio and oral propaganda are mentioned in the form that Mordeha/Max completed for the Berlin Jewish Community on August 1, 1946. The tale of the radio

is echoed in Jurek Becker's two autobiographical statements of February 13, 1955, and February 9, 1957, reprinted in Holger Jens Karlson, "Jurek Becker: Bausteine zu einer Schiftstellerbiographie," *Berliner Hefte zur Geschichte des literarischen Lebens* 3 (2000): 5–80, esp. 72–74. Also in the Becker papers.

30. Here again we have a multiple set of potential answers. In his statement of 1946, Mordeha states that he was released from the Sachsenhausen concentration camp in 1945. In Jurek Becker's 1955 autobiographical statement, he notes that he later learned that his father had been sent to KZ (Konzentrationslager) Oranienburg near Berlin and then was freed from a concentration camp near Schwerin. In a 1978 interview, he stated that his father had been liberated from Auschwitz. Richard A. Zipser, "Jurek Becker: A Writer with a Cause," *Dimension* 11 (1978): 407. One indication that Mordeha was in Auschwitz was a letter written by Herbert Rosenberg from the Auschwitz Committee in the GDR on March 16, 1950, stating that he personally knew that Mordeha had been released from Sachsenhausen (Becker Papers). Mordeha may have been on a transport from Auschwitz to Sachsenhausen, where he was released, though Rosenberg does not say so. See letter of March 18, 1950, 10.14.4, as well as the pension form, A.30. 626, in the Stasi Files (in the Becker Papers).

31. Dates and places remain clouded. In his 1955 and 1957 autobiographical statements for Humboldt University, Jurek Becker provides more or less identical information to that which Max had given the Berlin Jewish Community in 1946 concerning his release from Sachsenhausen and his son's release from Ravensbrück. According to these statements, Chana and Jerzy were shipped to Ravensbrück in 1943. In the list of the special trains from Litzmannstadt, however, Manja Becker (born July 26, 1920) and Jerzy Becker (born October 30, 1937) were on train number 111 on October 22, 1944 Ravensbrück. Following their names are the words "political" and "Jew," which could be accounted for by the fact that they were associated with Mordeha's having been found with a radio. According to a letter I received from the archive at Ravensbrück, July 18, 1998, this information might pertain to another family with the same last name; there are no earlier records of a mother and son "Becker" on the trains to Ravensbrück from Litzmannstadt. In addition, there is a single mention of the camp at Königswusterhausen in the Becker Papers: "Aufnahmeantrag: Humboldt Universität" (February 25, 1955), following the mention of Ravensbrück and Sachsenhausen. It is possible that Jurek was there for medical treatment at some point late in 1945.

32. *"Dies Kind soll leben": Die Aufzeichnungen der Helene Holzmann, 1941–1944*, ed. Reinhard Kaiser and Margarete Holzmann (Frankfurt am Main: Schöffling, 2000); on the Lodz ghetto, see 315–20, esp. 320 n. 1.

33. Lotte Adolphs, *Kinder in Ketten: Kinderschicksale in Ghettos und onzentrationslagern* (Duisburg: Walter Braun, 1984), 48–49.

34. Jurek Becker, *Warnung vor dem Schriftsteller* (Frankfurt am Main: Suhrkamp, 1989), 10.

35. Dwork, *Children with a Star*, 240.

36. *Kinder des Holocaust sprechen*, 244–45.

37. Kiryl Sosnowski, *The Tragedy of Children under Nazi Rule* (Poznan: Western Press Agency, 1962), 99.

38. Simone Erpel, "Kriegsende und Befreiung," in *Forschungsschwerpunkt Ravensbrück: Beiträge zur Geschichte des Frauen-Konzentrationslager*, ed. Sigrid Jacobeit and Grit Philipp (Berlin: Hentrich, 1997), 47–59.

39. Death certificate issued by the Gemeinde Sachsenhausen, dated April 29, 1968, Becker Papers.

40. 1988 interview with Marianna Birnbaum, reprinted in *Jurek Becker*, ed. Irene Heidelberger-Leonard (Frankfurt am Main: Suhrkamp, 1992), 96.

41. Becker, *Ende des Grössen Wahns*, 57.

42. "Werkstattgespräche mit Jurek Becker," in *Jurek Becker: Werkheft Literatur*, ed. Karin Graf and Ulrich Konietzny (Munich: Iudicium, 1991), 57; and "Ein Mann, der sich nicht in Schablonen packen lässt: Interview mit Günter Gaus," in Günter Gaus, *Zur Person* (Berlin: Ost, 1988), 14.

43. Becker, *Ende des Grössen Wahns*, 114.

44. As Sabine Gölz has elegantly shown in "Where Did the Wife Go? Reading Jurek Becker's 'Parkverbot,'" *Germanic Review* 62 (1987):10–19. See also Ricarda Schmidt, " 'The Gender of Thought': Recollection, Imagination, and Eroticism in Fictional Conceptions of East and West German Identity," in *'Whose Story?': Continuities in Contemporary German-Language Literature*, ed. Arthur Williams Stuart Parkes and Julian Preece (Bern: Peter Lang, 1998), 219–47.

45. Heinz Ludwig Arnold, "Gespräche mit Jurek Becker," *Text und Kritik: Jurek Becker* 116 (1992): 4.

Chapter Three

1. Yehuda Bauer, *Out of the Ashes: The Impact of American Jews on Post-Holocaust European Jews* (Oxford: Oxford University Press, 1989), 36.

2. Erica Burgauer, *Zwischen Erinnerung und Verdrängung: Juden in Deutschland nach 1945* (Hamburg: Rowohlt, 1993), 19.

3. Wolfgang Jacobmeyer, "Jüdische Überlebende als "Displaced Persons," *Geschichte und Gesellschaft* 3 (1983): 421–52.

4. Michael Brenner, *After the Holocaust: Rebuilding Jewish Lives in Postwar Germany*, trans. Barbara Harshav (Princeton: Princeton University Press, 1997), 11–12.

5. Yehuda Bauer, *Flight and Rescue: Brichah* (New York: Random House, 1970).

6. Application for a pension 13-194-BY, June 3, 1953, and application for acceptance at the Humboldt University in 1955, Becker Papers.

7. I am indebted to Angelika Königseder, *Flucht nach Berlin: Jüdische Displaced Persons, 1945–1948* (Berlin: Metropol, 1998), for much of the detail on this question.

8. Ibid., 154.

9. Zipser, "Jurek Becker" (see chap. 2, n. 32), 407.

10. Brenner, *After the Holocaust*, 22.

11. From the Magistrat der Stadt Berlin, December 28, 1945, Becker Papers.

12. Certified Statement of Max Becker and Georg Becker, October 19, 1952, Becker Papers.

13. Brenner, *After the Holocaust*, 45.

14. "Werkstattgespräche mit Jurek Becker," In *Jurek Becker: Werkheft Literatur*, ed. Karin Graf and Ulrich Konietzny (Munich: Iudicium, 1991), 62.

15. "Was heißt hier Liebling? Portrait Jurek Becker" (Inez Jacob, 1996), WDR (Westdeutsche Rundfunk), Becker Papers.

16. Burgauer, *Zwischen Erinnerung und Verdrängung*, 20. The figures for Berlin are less clear. Bauer, *Out of the Ashes*, 56, claims that there were about 7,000 Jews in Berlin in 1945, of whom about 1,600 had returned from the camps. Frank Stern, *Im Anfang war Auschwitz: Antisemitismus und Philosemitismus im deutschen Nachkrieg* (Gerlingen: Bleicher, 1991), 73, cites a much lower figure of about 5,000, of whom about 1,000 had returned from the camps.

17. Zipser, "Jurek Becker," 407.

18. Television discussion on the cable channel *arte* in January, 1995, quoted from Michael Wildt, "Unüberbrückbare Erinnerungen," *Werkstatte Geschichte* 13 (1996): 53.

19. Becker, *Ende des Grössen Wahns*, 11–12.

20. Jan Tomasz Gross, *Sasiedzi: historia zaglady zydowskiego miasteczka* (Sejny: Pogranicze, 2000); translated as *Neighbors: The Destruction of the Jewish Community in Jedwabne, Poland* (Princeton: Princeton University Press, 2001). See also Adam Michnick, "Poles and the Jews: How Deep the Guilt?" *New York Times*, March 17, 2001, and the answer by Leon Wieseltier, "Righteous," *New Republic*, April 9, 2001.

21. Königseder, *Flucht nach Berlin*, 36.

22. Susann Heenen-Wolff, *Im Haus des Henkers: Gespräche in Deutschland* (Frankfurt am Main: Dvorah-Verlag, 1992), 267.

23. "Was heißt hier Liebling?"

24. Königseder, *Flucht nach Berlin*, 49.

25. Ibid., 189.

26. Ibid.

27. Stern, *Im Anfang war Auschwitz*, 110.

28. Becker, *Ende des Grössen Wahns*, 50.

29. "Werkstattgespräche mit Jurek Becker," 57.

30. Ibid.

31. 1988 interview with Marianna Birnbaum (see chap. 2, n. 40), 105.

32. "Lebenslauf," February 13, 1955, Becker Papers; reprinted in Holger Jens Karlson, "Jurek Becker: Bausteine zu einer Schiftstellerbiographie," *Berliner Hefte zur Geschichte des literarischen Lebens* 3 (2000): 72–73.

33. Brenner, *After the Holocaust*, 49.

34. Becker, *Ende des Grössen Wahns*, 98.

35. Viktor Klemperer, *LTI: Notizbuch eines Philologen* (Berlin, Aufbau-Verlag, 1947). See also Karl-Heinz Hartmann, "Das Dritte Reich in der DDR-Literatur: Stationen erzählter Vergangenheit," in Gegenwartsliteratur und Drittes Reich, ed. Hans Wagner (Stuttgart: Reclam, 1977), 306–28; Cathy Gelbin, "Die NS-'Vergangenheitsbewältigung' in der DDR und ihre Widerspiegelung im narrativen Prozeß," *Menora* (1998): 224–44.

36. Becker, *Ende des Grössen Wahns*, 205–6. A longer version appeared in *Der Spiegel*, January 9, 1995.

37. "Rede und Gegenrede" written for the *Westdeutsche Rundfunk* (no date), Becker Papers.

38. Jurek Becker, *Warnung vor dem Schriftsteller* (Frankfurt am Main: Suhrkamp, 1989), 12.

39. See Sander Gilman, *Jewish Self-Hatred: Anti-Semitism and the Hidden Language of the Jews* (Baltimore: Johns Hopkins University Press, 1987).

40. Hellmut Pfeiffer, *Deutsche Autoren heute: Jurek Becker und Günter Kunert werden in Gespräch und Lesung vorgestellt* (Bonn: Internationes, 1984), 6–7.

41. Becker, *Warnung vor dem Schriftsteller*, 12.

42. Jurek Becker, "Wäre ich hinterher klüger? Mein Judentum," *Frankfurter Allgemeine Zeitung*, May 13, 1978, Beilage: Bilder und Zeiten, p. iv.

43. Zipser, "Jurek Becker," 409.

44. Volker Hage, "Jurek Becker: Hinter dem Rücken des Vaters: Interview," in *Deutsche Literatur 1986*, ed. Volker Hage and Adolf Fink (Stuttgart: Ditzingen, 1987), 340.

45. Copies of the letter of March 18, 1950, 10.14.4, and the pension form, A.30. 626, Stasi Files.

46. Compare Malgorzata Dubrowska, " 'Überleben heißt errinnern,': Erinnerung als Weg zur Selbstfindung ostdeutscher Autoren jüdischer Herkunft," in *Nationale Indentität aus germanistischer Perspektive*, ed. Maria Katarzyna Lasatowicz and Jürgen Joachimsthaler (Opole: Wydawnictwo Uniwersytetu Opolskicgo, 1998), 271–79.

47. Becker, *Ende des Grössen Wahns*, 63.

48. Brenner, *After the Holocaust*, 24.

49. Ibid., 12–13.

Chapter Four

1. "Lebenslauf," February 9, 1957, Humboldt University Archive, 7, Becker Papers; reprinted in Karlson, "Jurek Becker" (see chap. 3, n. 32), 73–74.

2. Frauke Meyer-Gosau, "Fortschritte kann auch in Ernüchterung bestehen" (1992), in Heidelberger-Leonard, *Jurek Becker*, 109.

3. Burgauer, *Zwischen Erinnerung und* Verdrängung, 153.

4. Volker Hage, "Jurek Becker: Hinter dem Rücken des Vaters; Interview," in *Deutsche Literatur 1986*, ed. Volker Hage and Adolf Fink (Stuttgart: Ditzingen, 1987), 336.

5. Käthe Kollwitz Schule: Zeugnis für Jurek Becker, Klasse 11b2, Schuljahr 1953–54, Humboldt University Archive, 22, Becker papers.

6. "Begrundung der Berufswahl," February 9, 1957, Becker Papers; reprinted in Karlson, "Jurek Becker," 75–77.

7. "Lebenslauf," February 13, 1955, Becker Papers; reprinted in Karlson, "Jurek Becker," 72–73.

8. On Jewish life and the image of the Jews in the GDR, see Mario Keßler, *Die SED und die Juden: Zwischen Repression und Toleranz—politische Entwicklung bis 1967* (Berlin: Akademie Verlag, 1995); Lothar Mertens, *Davidstern unter Hammer und Zirkel: Die jüdischen Gemeinden in der SBZ/DDR und ihre Behandlung durch Partei und Staat 1945–1990* (Hildesheim; New York: Olms, 1997); Ulrike Offenberg, *Seid vorsichtig gegen die Machthaber: Die jüdischen Gemeinden in der SBZ und der DDR 1945–1990* (Berlin: Aufbau-Verlag, 1998).

9. Angelika Timm, *Hammer, Zirkel, Davidstern: Das gestörte Verhältnis der DDR zu Zionismus und Staat Israel* (Bonn: Bouvier, 1997), argues that the official anti-Zionism in the GDR practiced from the 1950s enabled hidden anti-Semites to express anti-Jewish prejudices under the pretense of political protest. The proclaimed attitude of the SED government toward Zionism, the Jewish question, and Israel enabled the continued existence of a latent anti-Semitism.

10. Leonid Luks, ed., *Der Spätstalinismus und die "jüdische Frage": Zur anti-semitischen Wendung des Kommunismus* (Cologne: Böhlau, 1998), and *Stalin's Secret Pogrom: The Postwar Inquisition of the Jewish Anti-Fascist Committee,* ed. and introd. Joshua Rubenstein and Vladimir P. Naumov (New Haven: Yale University Press, 2001).

11. See Jeffrey Herf, *Divided Memory: The Nazi Past in the Two Germanys* (Cambridge, MA: Harvard University Press, 1997), 106–62.

12. Eric D. Weitz, *Creating German Communism 1890–1990* (Princeton: Princeton University Press, 1997).

13. Keßler, *Die SED und die Juden,* 105. For interviews with East Berlin Jews see *Überleben heißt Erinnern: Lebensgeschichten deutscher Juden,* ed. Wolfgang Herzberg (Berlin: Ausfbua, 1990); Vincent von Wroblewsky, *Zwischen Thora und Trabant: Juden in der DDR* (Berlin: Aufbau, 1993), and its sequel *Eine unheimliche Liebe: Juden und die DDR* (Berlin: Philo, 2001); *Sojourners: The Return of German Jews and the Question of Identity,* ed. John Borneman and Jeffrey M. Peck (Lincoln: University of Nebraska Press, 1995); Robin Ostow, *Juden aus der DDR und die deutsche Wiedervereinigung: Elf Gespräche* (Berlin: Wichern, 1996). A strange mix of fact and fancy about the Jews in the GDR is to be found in the conservative German Jewish historian Michael Wolffsohn, *Die Deutschland Akte: Deutsche und Juden in Ost und West–Tatsache und Legenden* (Munich: Ferenczy, 1995).

14. Karl Corino, *"Aussen Marmor, innen Gips": Die Legenden Stephan Hermlin* (Düsseldorf: Econ, 1996), 6, 68, 88–94.

15. Keßler, *Die SED und die Juden,* 106.

16. Becker, *Ende des Grössen Wahns,* 19. That impression was shared by other secular Jews in the GDR such as Fred Wander, *Das gute Leben* (1996; Frankfurt am Main: Fischer, 1999), 122, where he claims that in all the decades he spent in the GDR he never heard an anti-Semitic comment.

17. "Lebenslauf," 1955, 16–17, Becker Papers; reprinted in Karlson, "Jurek Becker," 72–73.

18. "Lebenslauf," 1957, 7, Becker Papers; reprinted in Karlson, "Jurek Becker," 73–74.

19. "Käthe-Kollwitz-Schule: Beurteilung des Abiturienten Georg Becker Klasse 12b2 vom 22. Februar 1955," University Archive, 24, Becker Papers.

20. Compare Sonja Miltenberg, "Kommunist-Deutscher-Jude: Eine politische Biographie," in *Archiv der Erinnerung: Interviews mit Überlebenden der Shoah,* ed. Cathy Gelbin and others (Potsdam: Verlag für Berlin-Brandenburg, 1998), 213–64.

21. "Ermittlungsbericht," February 2, 1961, Stasi Files II/4-C.

22. Becker, *Ende des Grössen Wahns,* 180.

23. Ibid.

24. Jurek Becker, *Jacob the Liar,* trans. Leila Vennewitz (New York: Arcade, 1990), 64–65. First published in Berlin by Aufbau in 1969.

25. Jurek Becker, *Amanda Herzlos* (Frankfurt am Main: Suhrkamp, 1992), 326–27.

26. When Jurek gave me a copy of the prepublication version of this, his last novel, over breakfast at a café on the Kufürstendamm, he winked and said, "You'll even find something in it to interest you!" And, indeed, this aspect of his work did and does interest me, for I believe it serves as the key to all his other work as well as to the way he shaped his sense of self.

27. Diary from trip to Portugal, 1986, Becker Papers. This is the only diary Becker kept. It was begun as he was reading Franz Kafka's diaries while on vacation in Portugal and consists of about fifteen pages in a school notebook.

28. Becker, *Ende des Grössen Wahns,* 13–14.

29. Sigmund Freud, *Standard Edition of the Complete Psychological Works of Sigmund Freud,* ed. and trans., J. Strachey, A. Freud, A. Strachey, and A. Tyson (London: Hogarth, 1955–74), 20: 274.

30. "Was heißt hier Liebling?" (see chap. 3, n. 15).

31. Herlinde Koebl, "Das ist wie ein Gewitter," *Der Spiegel* 13 (1997): 215.

32. "Aufnahmeantrag für die Humboldt Universität," Berlin, February 25, 1955, 3, Becker Papers.

33. "Lebenslauf," 1955, 17, Becker Papers.

34. "Lebenslauf," 1957, 8, Becker Papers.

35. "Auskunft über die im Operative-Vorgang 16939/60," October 26, 1970, 4, Stasi Files.

36. Zipser, "Jurek Becker" (see chap. 2, n. 32), 409.

37. "Parteiorganization beim ZK der SED. Betr.: Aufnahme des Universitätsstudiums im September 1957 durch den Gen. Becker," University Archive, 9, Becker Papers.

38. "Lebenslauf," 1957, 8, Becker Papers; reprinted in Karlson, "Jurek Becker," 73–74.

39. Wilhelm Schwarz, *Protokolle: Gespräche mit Schriftstellern* (Frankfurt am Main: Lang, 1990), 115–16. From an interview in 1977.

40. "Ermittlungsbericht," February 2, 1961, Stasi Files II/4-C.

41. Jurek Becker, "Betroffen sein aus Liebe: Max Frisch zu seinem 70. Geburtstag," *Der Tagesspiegel,* May 15, 1981.

42. From the 1988 interview with Marianna Birnbaum, reprinted in Heidelberger-Leonard, *Jurek Becker,* 102.

43. Kafka's role as a cultural icon in the Prague Spring of 1968 could not be ignored in East Berlin after the GDR's eager participation in the invasion that destroyed the Prague Spring. Becker, *Ende des Grössen Wahns,* 37.

44. Joachim Köhler and Sven Michaelsen, "Das Fernsehen ist außer Kontrolle," *Stern,* December 19, 1994, 210.

45. Manfred Krug, *Jurek Beckers Neuigkeiten an Manfred Krug und Otti* (Düsseldorf: Econ, 1997), 11.

46. Jurek Becker, *Sleepless Days*, trans. Leila Vennewitz (New York: Harcourt Brace Jovanovich, 1979), 57. Published in German by Suhrkamp in 1978.

47. A detailed Stasi account of their social life there is preserved in "Ermittlungs-bericht," March 1, 1961, Stasi Files II/4-C.

48. "Ermittlungsbericht," February 2, 1961, Stasi Files II/4-C.

49. Becker, *Ende des Grössen Wahns*, 110.

50. Sander L. Gilman, conversation with Wolf Biermann, July 3, 1998.

51. Zipser, "Jurek Becker," 409.

52. Ibid., 410.

53. Becker Papers: "Mit welchen Methoden kann die Produktion von Mehrwert im Kapitalismus gesteigert werden?" (7 pp.); "Der marxistische Begriff der Kausalität und das Determinismus" (15 pp.); "Marx über die Bedeutung der hegelschen Recht-sphilosophie" (5 pp.); Untitled paper on Cartesianism, 2 semester, second year (12 pp.); "Das Wesen des physikalischen Idealismus" (23 pp.); "Der reaktionäre Gehalt der platonischen Staatstheorie" (10 pp.).

54. See the interview with one of Georg's fellow students recorded in Karlson, "Jurek Becker," 31–32, n. 137.

55. Jurek Becker, *Irreführung der Behörden* (Frankfurt am Main: Suhrkamp, 1982), 51. First published by Hinsdorff in Rostock, 1973.

56. In a folder marked "Kabarett Texte" Becker collected the following sketches: "Affenkundig" (2 pp.); "Der Kabarettplan" (a satire of what Kabarett meant in the GDR, 14 pp.); "Sonntagsidee" (2pp.); "Zu spät" (verse, 3 pp.); "Et jibt..." (dialect verse, 5 pp.); "Umweg zum Erfolg" (4 pp.); "Happy end" (3 pp.); "Un-dank" (4 pp.); "Tendenz fallend" (5 pp.); "Schluß damit" (2 pp.); "Bundesratssitzung morgen" (4 pp.); "Die aktuelle Umfrage" (5 pp.); "Garnituren" (5 pp.); "Vorder-ansicht eines Versicherungspalalastes" (3 pp.); "Erziehung mit Gefühl" (3 pp.); "Begegnung im All" (1 p.); "Männer machen Mist: Expose" (6 pp.); "Opfer für die Sicherheit" (5 pp.)" See Schmidt, "Jurek Becker" (see chap. 1, n. 4), 20–23.

57. Hermann Kant, *Abspann: Erinnerung an meine Gegenwart* (Berlin: Aufbau, 1991), 433. See also Karl Corino, ed., *Die Akte Kant: IM "Martin," die Stasi und die Literatur in Ost und West* (Reinbek bei Hamburg: Rowohlt, 1995).

58. Zipser, "Jurek Becker," 410.

59. Becker, *Irreführung der Behörden*, 30–35.

60. Lola Ramon [pseud.], "Groll mit nichts im Magen," *Tua res* 3 (1959): 39–41). He also wrote "Prädikantenlogik," ibid., 7–8, and "Die Schlacht von Zelluloiden," ibid., 5.

61. "Groll mit nichts im Magen," 5.

62. Eduard Stapel, "Interview mit Jurek Becker," *Der neue Weg* (Halle), January 26, 1976.

63. See Schmidt, "Jurek Becker," 10, who describes Becker as having been the subject of five different party censures. Georg's account of this one event is fixed in his "Der Tatbestand und wie ich heute darüber denke," University Archive, 42–43, Becker Papers; reprinted in Karlson, "Jurek Becker," 78.

64. Meyer-Gosau, "Fortschritte kann auch in Ernüchterung bestehen" 110.

65. "Welche Überlegungen veranlassen einen Einzelbauer zum Eintritt in die LPG?" (17 pp.), Becker Papers.

66. "Protokoll der Delegiertenkonferenz vom 19./20. April 1958," Stiftung Archiv und Massenorganisationen im Bundesarchiv (henceforth SAPMO) BPA IV 4/12-6; also cited by Karlson, "Jurek Becker," 40, n.187.

67. Letter from Dr. Pracht, July 2, 1960, Becker Papers.

68. University Records, 47, Becker Papers; reprinted in Karlson, "Jurek Becker," 75.

69. Birnbaum (see this chap., n. 42), 408.

Chapter Five

1. Letter from Georg Becker headed "Exmatrikulationsantrag," June 3, 1960, with note signed Pracht, June 29, 1960, Becker Papers.

2. Letter from Dr. Pracht, deputy director of the Institute for Philosophy, July 2, 1960, Becker Papers.

3. Carl Paschek, ed., *Jurek Becker: Begleitheft zur Ausstellung der Stadt- und Universitätsbibliothek Frankfurt am Main (24. Mai bis 30. Juni 1989)* (Frankfurt am Main: Stadt- und Universitätsbibliothek, 1989), 8; "Jurek Becker über sich," *Wochenpost*, April 27, 1973, 15.

4. Günter Kunert, *Erwachsenenspiele: Erinnerungen* (Munich: Hanser, 1997), 358ff. On the idea of the opposition see Ehrhart Neubert, *Geschichte der Opposition in der DDR, 1949–1989* (Bonn: Bundeszentrale für politische Bildung, 1997); Alison Lewis, "Power, Opposition, and Subcultures: The Prenzlauer Berg 'Scene' in East Berlin and the Stasi," *UTS Review: Cultural Studies and New Writing* 3 (1997): 122–41; Stefan Wolle, *Die heile Welt der Diktatur : Alltag und Herrschaft in der DDR, 1971–1989* (Berlin: Ch. Links, 1998); *Widerstand und Opposition in der DDR*. Schriften des Hannah-Arendt-Instituts für Totalitarismusforschung, vol. 9 (Cologne: Böhlau, 1999).

5. Sybille Eberlein, "Ein Filmmann, der Romane schreibt," *Wochenpost*, April 27, 1973, p. 15.

6. "Autor Jurek Becker über Liebling-Kreuzberg," *Programm extra: Erstes Deutsches Fernsehen/ARD*, September 1988.

7. From the 1988 interview with Marianna Birnbaum, in Heidelberger-Leonard, *Jurek Becker*, 67.

8. From an interview from 1977, in Schwarz, *Protokolle*, 120. .

9. Birnbaum, in Heidelberger-Leonard, *Jurek Becker*, 67.

10. "Jurek Becker über sich," 15.

11. Hage, "Jurek Becker" (see chap. 4, n. 4), 133.

12. Honigmann, a dedicated communist who had returned with his wife from Britain after the war, had written for DEFA and had edited the *Berliner Zeitung*. He resigned from the Berlin Jewish Community under pressure from the party. His daughter Barbara left the GDR with her husband Peter in 1984 for Strasbourg in order to live an Orthodox Jewish life. By the 1980s a religious identity became an alternative model for Jews in the GDR. Barbara Honigmann's novel *Alles, alles Liebe* (Yours, yours truly) (Munich: Hanser, 2000) provides a complex reconstruction of being Jewish in the GDR during the mid-1970s.

13. Günter Schulz, *Produktionsgruppe Stacheltier im Studio für Wochenschau und Dokumentarfilme 1953–54 und Studio für Spielfilme 1955–1964: Filmographie* (Berlin: Bundesarchiv-Filmarchiv / DEFA-Stiftung, 2000), 158–59. See also Gisela Lieven, "Gezähmter Igel," *Der Tagesspiegel,* August 25, 1991.

14. "Also sprach das Stacheltier: Filmspiegel—Cohn," Becker papers.

15. Letter from Voigt, February 22, 2001, Bundesarchiv: Filmarchiv.

16. "Ermittlungsbericht," February 2, 1961, Stasi Files II/4-C.

17. See Sonia Combe, *Une société sous surveillance: Les intellectuels et la Stasi* (Paris: Albin Michel, 2000), 40, 84, 88, 181; and Siegfried Mampel, *Das Ministerium für Staatssicherheit der ehemaligen DDR als Ideologiepolizei* (Berlin: Duncker & Humblot, 1996).

18. April 24, 1961, Stasi Files VIII/I/164/3199/61.

19. "Information vom 16.5.1962" in: JAIZJA 6364, on sex 36/164, Stasi Files.

20. Bstu 000133, Stasi Files.

21. Heinrich Küntzel, "Der Faschismus: Seine Theorie, seine Darstellung in der Literatur," in *Die Literatur der DDR. Hansers Sozialgeschichte der deutschen Literatur 11,* ed. Hans-Jürgen Schmitt (Munich: Carl Hanser, 1983), 435–67.

22. Max Thomas Mehr, "Eine nicht ganz vollzogene Scheidung," *Tageszeitung* (Berlin), *TAZ Magazin,* September 25, 1989.

23. Testimony before the Deutscher Bundestag. in *Aufarbeitung von Geschichte und Folgen der SED-Diktatur in Deutschland am 4. Mai 1993: Kunst und Kultur in der DDR,* sec. 35, p. 135.

24. See Edgar Hilsenrath, *Zibulsky oder Antenne im Bauch* (Düsseldorf: Claasen, 1983), 11–12.

25. Stasi-files: II/4 209.

26. Heinz Kahlau, "Verteidigung eines Vaters: Über Jurek Becker," in *Liebes- und andere Erklärungen,* ed. Annie Voigtländer (Berlin / Weimar: Aufbau, 1972), 17.

27. 1961: *Mit der NATO durch die Wand* (directed by Peter Ulbrich; Stacheltier); 1962: *Wenn ein Marquis schon Pläne macht* (directed by Peter Hagen; GDR-TV); 1962: *Komm mit nach Montevideo* (directed by Fred Mahr; GDR-TV), and *Guten Morgen heißt Glückauf* (directed by Hugo Hartmann; GDR-TV); 1963: *Gäste im Haus* (directed by Fred Mahr; GDR-TV); 1963–64: *Zu viele Kreuze* (directed by Ralph J. Boettner; GDR-TV); 1964–65: *Ohne Paß im fremden Betten* (directed by Vladimir Brebera; DEFA); 1967: *Immer um den März herum* (pseud., Georg Nikolaus; directed by Fred Mahr; GDR-TV), and *Mit 70 hat man noch Träume* (pseud.,: Georg Nikolaus; directed by Fred Mahr; GDR-TV); 1967–68: *Urlaub* (pseud., Georg Nikolaus; directed by Manfred Mosblech; GDR-TV); 1968: *Jungfer, Sie gefällt mir* (directed by Günter Reisch, DEFA); 1969–70: *Meine Stunde Null* (directed by Joachim Hasler, DEFA); 1974: *Jakob der Lügner* (directed by Frank Beyer, DEFA /GDR-TV); 1976–77: *Das Versteck* (directed by Frank Beyer, DEFA).

28. *Fernsehdienst: Information des Deutschen Fernsehfunks für die 34. Sendewoche vom 20. August bis 26. August 1967* (Berlin: n.p., 1967), 2.

29. Margot Franz, "Immer um den März herum," *Freiheit,* August 25, 1967.

30. Helmut Ullrich, "Ein Riesenrad spielt Zufall," *Neue Zeit,* November 16, 1965.

31. "Information der Bezirksleitung Berlin an das ZK der SED über einige ideologische Erscheinungen im künstlerischen Bereich vom 19. November 1965,"

Lesemappe des 11. Plenum vom 15.–18. Dezember 1965, Stiftung Archiv und Massenorganisationen im Bundesarchiv (henceforth SAPMO), ZPA IV/2/1/188.

32. Constanze Pollatschek, "Ein Besuch bei Autor Jurek Becker," *Filmspiegel* 9 (1970): 9.

33. "Kleist—sträflich frei verwendet," *National-Zeitung,* March 18, 1969.

34. Günter Sobe, "Kleist als Klamotte," *Berliner Zeitung,* March 25, 1969.

35. The reviews were mixed. Most critics stressed the superficial representation of the private world of the miners. "Zu viele Kreuze," *Neue Zeit,* March 12, 1964; "Mahnung," *Volksstimme Magdeburg,* March 12, 1964; "Zu viele Kreuze," *Filmspiegel,* April 5, 1964.

36. *Fernsehdienst: Information des Deutschen Fernsehfunks für die 11. Sendewoche vom 8. Bis 14. März 1964* (Berlin: n.p., 1967), 12–13.

37. Paschek, *Jurek Becker,* 50

38. Helen L. Cafferty, "Survival under Fascism: Deception in Apitz' *Nackt unter Wolfen,* Becker's *Jakob der Lügner,* and Kohlhaase's 'Erfindung einer Sprache,' " *West Virginia University Philological Papers* 30 (1984): 90–96.

39. Stephen Lewis, *Art out of Agony,* CBC Radio Series, May 30–June 3, 1983 (Montréal: CBC Enterprises, 1984), 92.

40. Compare Jurek's statements at a conference in Toronto concerning the relationship of the novel to history, "Answering Questions about *Jakob der Lügner,*" *Seminar* 19 (1983): 288–92.

41. Files of the Ministry of Culture / DEFA: DR 117: exp. 39, Bundesarchiv. On the film and its variants see Thomas Jung, " 'Widerstandskämpfer oder Schriftsteller sein…' " *Jurek Becker—Schreiben zwischen Sozialismus und Judentum* (Frankfurt am Main: Peter Lang, 1998), 89–180.

42. Ralf Schenk, ed., *Regie: Frank Beyer* (Berlin: Hentrich, 1995), 72.

43. Files of the Ministry of Culture / DEFA: I 811, Bundesarchiv. See also Frank Beyer, *Wenn der Wind sich dreht: Meine Filme, mein Leben* (Munich: Econ, 2001), 183.

44. Files of the Ministry of Culture / DEFA: DR 117 2998: Letter from Maaß, Bundesarchiv.

45. Files of the Ministry of Culture / DEFA DR 1 - 4266: Report of Jahrow, February 3, 1966, Bundesarchiv.

46. Ibid., February 21, 1966.

47. Files of the Ministry of Culture / DEFA: DR 1 - 4266: Plot summary, February 4, 1966 sent to Maaß. Bundesarchiv.

48. Eleven films were censored by the shift in policy. Two of these, *Der Frühling braucht Zeit* (Günter Stahnke, 1965) and *Spur der Steine* (Frank Beyer, 1966), had premieres before being banned. At least one other film, *Denk bloss nicht ich heule* (Frank Vogel, 1965), was shown to test audiences. The remaining films at the time of their production were screened only within the studio or before officials. Postproduction work on many was left uncompleted. These films and their directors included *Berlin um die Ecke* (Gerhard Klein, 1966); *Denk bloss nicht ich heule* (Frank Vogel, 1965); *Jahrgang '45* (Jürgen Böttcher, 1966); *Das Kaninchen bin ich* (Kurt Maetzig, 1965); *Karla* (Hermann Zschoche, 1966); *Der verlorene Engel* (Ralf Kirsten, 1966); *Wenn du groß bist, lieber Adam* (Egon Günther, 1966); *Fräulein Schmetterling* (Kurt

Barthel, 1966); *Hände hoch, oder ich schiesse* (Hans-Joachim Kasprzik, 1966). See Joshua Feinstein, "The Triumph of the Ordinary: Depictions of Ordinary Life in the East German Cinema, 1956–1966" (PhD diss., Stanford University, 1995).

49. Wolfgang Jacobsen, Anton Kaes, and Hans Helmut Prinzler, eds., *Geschichte des deutschen Films* (Stuttgart: Metzler, 1993), 344–57. See also "Gespräch mit Frank Beyer," interview by Ralf Schenk, in Schenk, *Regie*, 8–105, esp. 52–61; and VEB Berliner Filmtheater, Abt. Filmeinsatz/Presse/Werbung, June 29, 1966, and Abt. Kultur, "Aktennotiz," July 14, 1966, both Stiftung Archiv und Massenorganisationen im Bundesarchiv DY30/IV2/2024/36 (Büro Hager).

50. Becker, *Sleepless Days*, 24–25. For firsthand accounts see Stefan Heym, *Der Winter unsers Mißvergnügens: Aus den Aufzeichnungen des OV Diversant* (Munich: Goldmann, 1996), 67; and Beyer, *Wenn der Wind sich dreht*, 126–53.

51. The question of how individuals respond to trauma has been much debated over the past decades. To no small degree this interest, at least recently, has been spurred by the consequences of the Shoah and subsequent mass traumatic events. Some individuals are able to deal with the effects of trauma, including that of the Shaoh; others become fixated on the trauma. There are also those who become fixated on avoiding any evocation of the trauma except in structures, and writing is one of those structures in which they feel they have control. Bessel A. van der Kolk has provided an overview of the earlier literature. He points out that contradictory responses to trauma such as hyperarousal versus numbing may take place. The need to repeat trauma (as Sigmund Freud saw it) in order to control it seems to be paralleled in some individuals with a true withdrawal from emotional response (anhedonia). Dissociation is often the result, but a growing inability to modulate aggression also occurs. Many trauma victims feel that their inability to modulate anger is their major symptom. This is not to say that all anger is traumatic, but a pattern of anger in which the sense of lack of control is the central trigger seems to be a result of trauma. In discussing Jurek Becker's anger, I have no desire to reduce it to a (or the) symptom of the trauma he suffered as a child, and yet it is clear that anger plays a substantial role in the shaping of his adult personality and in his literary work. See Bessel A. van der Kolk, *Psychological Trauma* (Washington, DC: American Psychiatric Press, 1987); and *Traumatic Stress*, ed. Bessel A. van der Kolk, Alexander C. McFarlane, and Lars Weisaeth (New York: Guilford Press, 1996).

52. Schwarz, *Protokolle*, 114.

53. Files of the Ministry of Culture / DEFA: DR 1 - 4266: Letter of transmittal by Bruk (DEFA) to Maaß: August 2, 1966 with a detailed account of the chronology of discussion with the Polish authorities and film studio, Bundesarchiv.

54. Schenk, *Regie*, 62.

55. Irma Zimm, "Vom kleinen Helden Jakob," *Berlin Zeitung am Abend*, May 19, 1969.

56. "Jurek Becker: Politisches Verhalten ist optimistisches Verhalten," *Post-Gewerkschaft*, March 20, 1983.

57. On the text see Martin Kane, "Tales and the Telling: The Novels of Jurek Becker," in *Socialism and the Literary Imagination: Essays on East German Writers*, ed. Martin Kane (New York: Berg, 1991), 163–78; Jürgen Egyptien, "Die Riten des Erzählens und das Stigma der Identität: Anmerkungen zum Verhaltnis von

Poetologie und Judentum in Erzählungen Jurek Beckers," in Heidelberger-Leonard, *Jurek Becker*, 279–87; Robert Clinton Rockwell, "Jurek Becker's Three Character Types: The Schlemiel, Picaro, and Willenloser" (PhD diss., Washington University, 1998); Claudia Mauelshagen, "Zur Erzählkonzeption in Texten Jurek Beckers," *Literatur für Leser* 22 (1999): 73–91; Hans-Joachim Neubauer, *The Rumour: A Cultural History*, trans. Christian Braun (London: Free Association Books, 1999).

58. Marianne Wambutt and Ehrentraud Novotny, "Ich habe die Absicht..." *Berliner Zeitung*, March 7, 1974.

59. "Was heißt hier Liebling?" (see chap. 3, n. 15).

60. Becker, *Jacob the Liar* (see chap. 4, n. 24), 2. All references are to the Vennevitz translation.

61. Karl Corino, "Deprimiriend ist für mich kein Schreibmotiv," *Deutsche Zeitung*, March 15, 1974, 13. The account is not of his father's bravery but of a neutral "hero."

62. Graf and Konietzny, *Jurek Becker*, 59

63. Heinz Ludwig Arnold, "Gespräche mit Jurek Becker," *Text + Kritik* 116 (1992): 9.

64. August 26, 1968, Stasi Files XX/R16.

65. Bärbel Dalichow, ed. *Sandmann auf Reisen* (Berlin: VISTAS Verlag, 1993).

66. "Betr.: Vorstand des Schriftstellervebandes," August 31, 1968, Stasi Files XX/1

67. "Operative Information 908/68"; Hauptabteilung XX/R16; Au XX/1; HAXX/5; XX/1, August 3, 1968; Stasi Files XX/1. See Stephan Hermlin, *In den Kämpfen dieser Zeit* (Berlin: Klaus Wagenbach, 1995); Stephan Hermlin, "Was wissen die Jüngeren von unseren schweren Kämpfen? Ein ZEIT-Gespräch von Fritz J. Raddatz," *Die Zeit*, April 21, 1995, 14. On the problem of Hermlin's repression of his "Jewish" identity, which confronted him as a returnee, see Henryk M. Broder, "Im Dickicht der Lügen," *Der Spiegel*, November 11, 1996, 196, 199; and Heinrich Detering, " 'Die Stimme im Dornbusch': Jüdische Motive und Traditionen in den Exilgedichten Stephan Hermlins," in *Deutsch-jüdische Exil- und Emigrationsliteratur im 20. Jahrhundert*, ed. Itta Shedletzky and Hans Otto Horch (Tübingen: Max Niemeyer, 1993), 253–69. After the war, Hermlin "invented" a 1934 incarceration in Sachsenhausen to provide himself with additional status as a "victim of fascism." Karl Corino, *Aussen Marmor, innen Gips: Die Legenden des Stephan Hermlin* (Düsseldorf: ECON, 1996).

68. Paschek, *Jurek Becker*, 49.

69. Stadtbezirkgericht Lichtenberg: 510 S 403.73/221-415-73-17 dated August 15/16, 1973, Becker Papers.

70. Stasi Files XX/7: Li 1335 / 73.

71. Jurek Becker, "Fajngold und drei ganz Kilometer," in *Neue Texte 68: Almanach für deutschsprachige Literatur*, ed. Lektorat zeitgenössische deutsche Literatur (Berlin und Weimar: Aufbau, 1968), 44–56.

72. In the summer of 1969, I was in West Berlin and asked a friend at the (East) Akademie der Wissenschaften to suggest some of the new books for me to read. He told me of a wonderful new translation from the Polish that had just appeared—and I bought and read Jurek Becker's first novel. Not only was it *not* a "translation" from the Polish, but it was one of the most authentic German voices I had ever read

on the Jewish experience in the Shoah. I was hooked on Becker's voice and on his gift as a storyteller. It was also the first self-consciously Jewish voice I had read in the GDR about the Shoah, and the very first comic text. The survivor-author Edgar Hilsenrath's satirical novel of the Shoah, *The Nazi and the Barber* (*Der Nazi und der Friseur*) appeared first in English, translated by Andrew White (New York: Doubleday, 1971). It was published in German in a bowdlerized version for the German reader in 1977. Leslie Epstein's extraordinary novel of the Lodz ghetto, *King of the Jews* (New York: Coward, McCann and Geoghegan, 1979) is the first comic novel about the Shoah written in English.

73. Becker, *Ende des Grössen Wahns*, 147.

74. Richard A. Zipser, *DDR-Literatur im Tauwetter* (Frankfurt am Main: Peter Lang, 1985), 3: 125.

75. Wolfgang Werth, "Das imaginäre Radio," *Der Monat* 268 (January 1971): 32–35. Fritz J. Raddatz picks up on this theme even though he uses the novel to introduce (in 1972) the newest writing in the GDR. Fritz J. Raddatz, *Traditionen und Tendenzen: Materialien zur Literatur der DDR* (Frankfurt: Suhrkamp, 1972), 372–73. For a critique of the international reception of the work in this context see Thomas Taterka, *Dante Deutsch: Studien zur Lagerliteratur* (Berlin: Erich Schmidt, 1999), 150–51.

76. See Klaus Schlegel, "Tewje und seine Schwiegersöhne: Zur Analyse von zwei Szenen des Musicals *Der Fiedler auf dem Dach* in der Inszenierung von Walter Felsenstein," *Jahrbuch der Komischen Oper* 9 (1971): 65–79.

77. Becker, *Ende des Grössen Wahns*, 21.

78. Fred Wander, *Der siebente Brunnen* (Berlin: Aufbau, 1971); see also his memoir *Das gute Leben* (1996; Frankfurt am Main: Fischer, 1999), 156–58, on *Jacob* see 207.

79. Werner Neubert, "Wahrheitserpichter Lügner," *Neues Deutschland*, May 14, 1969.

80. See the review by Rolf Michaelis, "Der andere Hiob," *Frankfurter Allgemeine Zeitung*, March 30, 1971, which discusses the series.

81. Letter from Bochers to Becker, September 7, 1970, Stasi Files.

82. Marcel Reich-Ranicki, "Das Prinzip Radio," *Die Zeit* (Hamburg), November 20, 1970.

83. Letter to Wolfdietrich Schnurre, January 14, 1971, Becker Papers.

84. Letter from Wolfdietrich Schnurre, January 30, 1970, Becker Papers.

85. Letter from Heinz Brieger, January 8, 1972, Archiv des Aufbau Verlags, Staatsbibliothek Berlin, Nr. 1605.

86. Letter to Schröder, October 14, 1973, Becker Papers.

87. etter from Abusch, February 19, 1971 to Helmut Baierl, head of the Sektion Literatur und Sprachpflege, Stiftung Archiv der Akademie der Künste ZAA 1895L.

88. "Dankrede von Jurek Becker," undated, Stiftung Archiv der Akademie der Künste ZAA 1895.

89. Letters from Jurek to Otto F. Walter, September 28, 1971, and from Otto F. Walter to Jurek, October 8, 1971, Becker Papers.

90. Letter from Werner Alberg to Jurek, October 7, 1972, Becker Papers.

91. Operative Information 865/69, December 23, 1969, Stasi Files.

92. Letters to Professor Hans Richter (on Miles Davis and the Beatles), May 15, 1973, and to Selbmann, February 15, 1973, Becker Papers.

93. Renate Holland-Moritz, "Kino-Eule," *Eulenspiegel* 17/25 (1970) 23, p. 6.

94. Klaus Meyer, "Film," *Sonntag* 24 (1970): 12.

95. Christoph Funke, "Der gestohlene Major," *Der Morgen*, May 15, 1970.

96. May 18, 1970, Stasi Files 1569.

97. Letter of Elisabeth Borchers, May 7, 1970, Becker Papers.

98. May 18, 1970, Stasi Files 1569.

99. *Bericht über die Ergebnisse der Gruppengespräche, die im Dezember 1972 und Januar 1973 im Bezirksverband Berlin des Schriftstellerverbandes der DDR durchgeführt worden sind*, SAPMO-Barch, BPA IV C-2/15/687.

100. *Zu einigen Fragen der Partei- und Verbandsarbeit in der Bezirksorganization Berlin des Schriftstellerverbandes der DDR vom 27. Juni 1973*, SAPMO-Barch, BPA IV C-2/15/686.

101. June 28, 1971, signed "Kant," Stasi Files XX/7/II.

102. Jurek Becker, *Irreführung der Behörden* (Rostock: Hinstorff, 1973). All quotations are in my own translation from the Suhrkamp edition (Frankfurt, 1973). The book was reprinted in the GDR in 1989 (Berlin: Volk und Welt). See also Reinhild Köhler-Hausmann, *Literaturbetrieb in der DDR: Schriftsteller und Literaturinstanzen* (Stuttgart: Metzler, 1984), 47–66, for a detailed account of the context and background of the novel.

103. Corino, "Deprimiriend ist für mich kein Schreibmotiv," 13.

104. Neubert, "Wahrheitspichter Lügner," 215.

105. Eberlein, "Ein Filmmann, der Romane schreibt," 15.

106. June 28, 1971, signed "Kant," Stasi File: XX/7/II.

107. Eberlein, "Ein Filmmann, der Romane schreibt," 15.

108. Wambutt and Novotny, "Ich habe die Absicht . . . "

109. Corino, "Deprimiriend ist für mich kein Schreibmotiv."

110. Letter to Professor Hans Richter, May 15, 1973, Becker Papers.

111. Eberlein, "Ein Filmmann, der Romane schreibt," 15.

112. Letter from Gerd Gericke, December 6, 1971, Archiv des Aufbau Verlags, Staatsbibliothek Berlin, Nr. 1605. See Gerd Gericke, "Für Jurek Becker," *Film und Fernsehen* 2 (1997): 50–51, as well as Joachim Seyppel, *Ich bin ein kaputter Typ: Bericht über Autoren in der DDR* (Wiesbaden: Limes, 1982), 54 and 236.

113. Letter from Voigt to Jurek, October 9, 1972, Becker Papers, informing him that the remaining advance for the novel had been repaid from incoming royalties.

114. Letter to Elisabeth Borchers, June 8, 1972, Becker Papers.

115. Walter Waldmann, "Gregor der Lügner," *Ostsee-Zeitung*, October 13–14, 1973. Even Werner Neubert, who had praised Jurek's first novel, praised the quality of the new book, while observing that it had not lived up to its potential. Werner Neubert, "Nachdem sich's 'weggelesen' hat . . . " *Berliner Zeitung*, September 8, 1973.

116. Bundesarchiv: Staatliche Kommittee für Rundfunk, Abteilung Monitor S1-50, 18, January 23, 1974.

117. See Eberhard Lämmert, "Beherrschte Literatur: Vom Elend des Schreibens unter Diktaturen," in *Literature in der Diktatur: Schreiben in Nationalsozialismus und DDR-Sozialismus*, ed. Günther Rühle (Paderborn: Schönigh, 1997), 15–37.

118. Letters to Schnurre, January 14, 1971, and to Böll, October 31, 1972, Becker Papers.

119. Letter to Professor Hans Richter, May 15, 1973, Becker Papers.

120. "Gute zwei Wochen," written for the *Kölner Stadtanzeiger* (November, 1970), Becker Papers.

121. Stasi Files VIII /4. 1388/76.

122. "Rede in Belgrad zum jugoslawischen Schriftstellerkongress, Oktober 1973," Becker Papers.

123. Letter from Günter Schulz, December 16, 1972, Becker Papers.

124. For material on Jurek's prize, but not his speech, see Wolfgang Emmerich, ed., *Der Bremer Literaturpreis 1954–1987* (Bremerhaven: Die Horen, 1988), 77–82.

125. *Information Gerhard Henningers in der Sekretariatssitzung des Schrift-stellerverbandes am 19. 12. 1973*, Protokoll vom 20. Dezember 1973. SAPMA-Barch, BPA IV C-2/15/688.268/55 (1974).

126. February 20, 1974, signed Ponig, Stasi Files XX/7.

127. Frank Beckelmann, "Ich nehme einen ausländischen Literaturpreis an," *Frankfurter Rundschau*, January 25, 1974.

128. Jurek Becker, "Über verschiedene Resonanzen auf unsere Literatur," *Neue deutsche Literatur* 22 (1973): 59–66. See also November 14, 1974, Stasi Files XX/7.

129. Heym's reference is to Solzhenitsyn's 1962 *One Day in the Life of Ivan Denisovich*, which was published in the leading Soviet literary periodical *Novy Mir* (New World) . The more recent event was the publication in 1974 of the first volume of *The Gulag Archipelago*. Solzhenitsyn was immediately attacked in the Soviet press. Despite the intense interest in his fate that was shown in the West, he was arrested and charged with treason on February 12, 1974. He was exiled from the Soviet Union on the following day, and in December he took possession of his 1970 Nobel Prize.

130. Schenk, *Regie*, 72.

131. Letter from Walter Nowjowski to Jurek, February 10, 1972, Becker Papers.

132. Letter from Jurek to Walter Nowojski, February 22, 1972, Becker papers.

133. Files of the Ministry of Culture / DEFA: DR117/RD56, Bundesarchiv.

134. Files of the Ministry of Culture / DEFA: DR117/2998, Bundesarchiv.

135. Shooting version of the script *Jakob der Lügner* (July 7, 1974). In the Library of the Filmhochschule Konrad Wolf (Babelsberg).

136. Frank Beyer, "Traum vom besseren Leben: Zum Film 'Jakob der Lügner,' " *Neues Deutschland*, December 17, 1974.

137. Jurek Becker, "Über die Historie hinaus," *Berliner Zeitung*, December 20, 1974.

138. Telegram from Heinz Rühmann, March 16, 1972, Becker Papers. Compare Beyer's account, *Wenn der Wind sich dreht*, 180–98 and 368, which creates a scenario in which Jurek comments on the Peter Kassovitz remake of the film that appeared after his death.

139. Files of the Ministry of Culture / DEFA: 3192 / 3 (719), Bundesarchiv.

140. Files of the Ministry of Culture / DEFA, Bundesarchiv. See the exchange in DR117/3188/5 (369)

141. Files of the Ministry of Culture / DEFA: DR117/2998, Bundesarchiv.

142. Files of the Ministry of Culture / DEFA: Heinz Kosten, "Jakob der Lügner," RIAS, December 23, 1974 at 16:40, Bundesarchiv.

143. Klaus Schüler, "Unzerstörbar die Würde des Menschen," *Neues Deutschland*, December 24–25, 1974.

144. Jutta Voigt, "Lust auf Leben. 'Jakob der Lügner' eröffnet den Monat des antiimperialistischen Films: Gespräche mit Jurek Becker," *Sonntag*, April 20, 1974, 3. Bundesarchiv.

145. Beyer, *Neues Deutschland*, December 17, 1974.

146. "Information zum auftreten den Schriftsteller Jurek Becker am 16. Und 17. 11. 76 in Jena," p. 3 (Tonbandabschrift, January 20,1976), Stasi Files XX.

147. Irma Zimm, "Vom kleinen Helden Jakob," *Berlin Zeitung am Abend*, May 19, 1969; and Wambutt and Novotny, "Ich habe die Absicht . . . "

148. Becker, *Ende des Grössen Wahns*, 120.

149. Ibid.

150. On the more general case of the cultural politics of the GDR see Richard A. Zipser, ed., "Literary Censorship in the German Democratic Republic, II: The Authors Speak," *Germanic Review* 65 (1990): 118–29; David Bathrick, *The Powers of Speech: The Politics of Culture in the GDR* (Lincoln: University of Nebraska Press, 1995); Wolfgang Jäger, *Die Intellektuellen und die deutsche Einheit* (Freiburg im Breisgau: Rombach, 1997).

Chapter Six

1. Report signed Holm, Stasi Files XX/7: XV/4618/76.

2. "Hinweise aus dem Bereich des gegnerischen Verfassungsschutzes," Stasi Files XX/7/1076/84

3. Roger Woods, *Opposition in the GDR under Honecker, 1971–85: An Introduction and Documentation* (Houndmills, Basingstoke, UK: Macmillan, 1986).

4. All quotations are in my translation from Jurek Becker, *Der Boxer* (Frankfurt am Main: Suhrkamp, 1979. See also Carlotta von Maltzan, "Das Schweigen des Juden als Überlebender: Jurek Beckers Romane *Der Boxer* und *Bronsteins Kinder*," *Acta Germanica: Jahrbuch des Germanistenverbandes im Südlichen Afrika* 23 (1995): 79–91.

5. Hage, "Jurek Becker" (see chap. 4, n. 4), 340.

6. Jean-Paul Sartre, *Réflexions sur la question juive* (Paris: Gallimard, 1954); originally published in 1946 by Paul Morihien ; translated George J. Becker as *Anti-Semite and Jew* (New York: Schocken, 1948); Max Frisch, *Andorra: Stück in 12 Bildern* (Frankfurt am Main: Suhrkamp, 1961).

7. On the reception of the war in the GDR in the memory of a Jewish writer, see Fred Wander, *Das gute Leben* (1996; Frankfurt am Main: Fischer, 1999), 194–96.

8. Erica Burgauer, *Zwischen Erinnerung und Verdrängung—Juden in Deutschland nach 1945* (Hamburg: Rowohlt, 1993), 191–93.

9. Operative Information Nr. 264 1730/74, October 11, 1974, Stasi Files.

10. "Nachdenken über die Opfer," *Leipziger Volkszeitung*, November 26, 1975.

11. Zipser, *DDR-Literatur im Tauwetter*, 3:125 (on Becker); Nancy A. Lauckner, "Stefan Heym's Revolutionary Wandering Jew: A Warning and a Hope for the

Future," in *Studies in GDR Culture and Society, 4: Selected Papers from the Ninth New Hampshire Symposium on the German Democratic Republic*, ed. Margy Gerber (Lanham, MD: University Press of America, 1984), 65–78; and Hannah Liron Frei, "Das Selbstbild des Juden, entwickelt am Beispiel von Stefan Heym und Jurek Becker" (diss., University of Zürich, 1992).

12. Interview with Stefan Heym and Inge Wüste, July 17, 1998. Retrospectively, the question whether this even was a GDR novel has been raised by Jurek's GDR contemporaries such as Fritz-Jochen Kopka, "Von der Unübertrefflichkeit des ersten Buches: Jurek Becker, *Jakob der Lügner*," in *Verrat an der Kunst? Rückblicke auf die DDR-Literatur*, ed. Karl Deirtiz and Hannes Krauss (Berlin: Aufbau, 1993), 156–60.

13. Eduard Stapel, "Sprache als Abenteuer," *Der neue Weg* (Halle), January 28, 1976.

14. Letter from Kunze to the Writers' Union, October 20, 1976, Archiv der Akademie der Künste: SVneu 549. See also Reiner Kunze, *Deckname "Lyrik": eine Dokumentation* (Frankfurt am Main: Fischer-Taschenbuch-Verlag, 1990).

15. Robert von Hallberg, ed., *Literary Intellectuals and the Dissolution of the State: Professionalism and Conformity in the GDR* (Chicago: University of Chicago Press, 1996), 231.

16. Letter from Peter Kirchner to Jurek, October 27, 1976, Becker Papers. See also the interviews with Peter Kirchner in *Überleben heisst Erinnern: Lebensgeschichten deutscher Juden*, ed.Wolfgang Herzberg (Berlin: Aufbau, 1990), 352–424; and *Juden aus der DDR und die deutsche Wiedervereinigung*, ed. Robin Ostow (Berlin: Wichern, 1996), 18–31.

17. April 26, 1977, Stasi Files XX: 321/77.

18. OvD-Bericht of November 6, 1976, 7:50 P.M. (a voluntary report by phone from a member of the Jewish Community, Ernest Engelmann, who worked for the local electric company, BEWAG), Stasi Files; Hauptabteilung 20/7: "Bericht," November 10, 1976, Stasi Files.

19. Jurek had received a partial key to the names from the "Gauck" commission. Becker Papers: Letter signed Iburg, Der Bundesbeauftragte für die Unterlagen des Staatssicherheitsdienst (August 2, 1996).

20. Abschrift, Stasi Files BstU 121.

21. Stasi Files 64/322.

22. November 16,1976, Stasi Files XX/7.

23. See also Roland Berbig et al., eds., *In Sachen Biermann: Protokolle, Berichte und Briefe zu den Folgen einer Ausbürgerung* (Berlin: Christoph Links, 1994); Oliver Schwarzkopf and Beate Rusch, eds., *Wolf Biermann Ausgebürgert* (Berlin: Schwarzkopf und Schwarzkopf, 1996); Hermann-Josef Rupieper and Lothar Tautz, eds., *"Warte nicht auf bessere Zeiten . . . ": Oskar Brüsewitz, Wolf Biermann und die Protestbewegung in der DDR 1976–77* (Halle/Saale: Mitteldeutscher Verlag, 1999); Fritz Pleitgen, ed., *Die Ausbürgerung: Anfang vom Ende der DDR* (Berlin: Ullstein, 2001).

24. Klaus Höpcke, "Der nichts so fürchtet wie Verantwortung," *Neues Deutschland*, December 5, 1965.

25. Conversation with Wolf Biermann, July 3, 1998.

26. John Flores, *Poetry in East Germany: Adjustments, Visions, Provocations, 1945–1970* (New Haven: Yale University Press, 1971). This seminal study appeared during the struggle over Biermann and is dedicated to him.

27. Biermann is quoted in the article "Zum Vorsingen," *Der Spiegel*, December 15, 1965, 144. On the same page a long extract is reproduced from the initial and most devastating critique of Biermann in *Neues Deutschland*.

28. June 4, 1974, Stasi Files XX. See the "Treffbericht" written by Hermann Kant covering this matter, written on June 11, 1974, which presents Jurek's discussions concerning Biermann, in *Die Akte Kant: IM "Martin," die Stasi und die Literatur in Ost und West*, ed. Karl Corino (Reinbeck bei Hamburg: Rowohlt, 1995), 312–15.

29. "Information vom 12. Juni 1974: Parteileitung des Bezirksverbandes des Schriftstellerverbandes der DDR.," Stiftung Archiv und Massenorganisationen im Bundesarchiv (henceforth SAPMO), BPA IV C–2/15/686.

30. "Operative Information," October 11, 1974, Stasi Files.

31. "Information vom 12. Juni 1974."

32. Letters from Gerhard Henninger to Kurt Hager, April 5, 1973, and from Peter Heldt to Hager, April 17, 1973. SAPMO-Barch, BNPA IV B 2/906/63.

33. June 6, 1974; June 10, 1974; July 3, 1974; Stasi Files XX/7.

34. Robert F. Goeckel, *The Legacy of Protestant Opposition in the GDR and the Stasi Revelations* (Washington, DC: American Society of Church History papers, 1992).

35. Letters from Volksbuchhandlung Jena to Jurek, September 17 and September 27, 1976, Becker Papers.

36. See Udo Scheer, *Vision und Wirklichkeit: Die Opposition in Jena in den siebziger und achtziger Jahren* (Berlin: Links, 1999).

37. Stasi Files XV/17.11.76.

38. "Objektdienststelle Zeiss, Jena," November 17, 1976, Stasi Files.

39. Ibid.

40. Copy of a telegram sent to Reuters on Wednesday November 17, 1976, then unsigned by Jurek, Stasi Files. The text reads: "Wolf Biermann war und ist ein unbequemer Dichter—das hat er mit vielen Dichtern der Vergangenheit gemein—Unser sozialistischer Staat ... müsste im Gegensatz zu anachronistischen Gesellschaftsformen eine solche Unbequemlichkeit gelassen nachdenkend ertragen können. Wir identifizieren uns nicht mit jedem Wort und jeder Handlung Biermanns und distanzieren uns von Versuchen, die Vorgänge um Biermann gegen die DDR zu missbrauchen. Biermann selbst hat nie, auch nicht in Köln, Zweifel daran gelassen, für welchen der beiden deutschen Staaten er bei aller Kritik eintrat.—Wir protestieren gegen seine Ausbürgerung und bitten darum, die beschlossene Maßnahme zu überdenken."

41. "Tonbandabschrift," November 11, 1976, and November 20, 1976, Stasi Files XX/Aig 92.

42. (Stamped) November 18, 1976, Stasi Files XX/7/2994/76.

43. Interview with Stefan Heym and Inge Wüste, July 17, 1998.

44. A detailed account of this from the standpoint of Stefan Heym is recorded in Heym, *Der Winter unsers Mißvergnügens: Aus den Aufzeichnungen des OV Diversant* (Munich: Goldmann, 1996). On Biermann and Becker, see 90–95. The

Stasi had a complete list of Jurek's phone calls during this period, which they gave to Roland Bauer, who used them to try to intimidate Jurek.

45. Roland Bauer, taped talk from December 14, 1976, SAPMO-Barch, Tonarchiv, Tonband V 2 C–2/5/240.

46. "Bericht," November 24, 1976, Stasi Files XX/134.

47. Quoted in Berbig et al., *In Sachen Biermann*, 86–90, 93 (Kopfstand).

48. Operative Information, "Parteiversammlung des Berliner Schriftstellerverbandes am 23. 11. 76, gez. Holm," Stasi Files XX/7.

49. "Parteiversammlung des Berliner Schriftsteller," November 24, 1976, signed "Grubitz," Stasi Files XX/7.

50. Stasi Files XX/7: 12.76: 7.

51. "Operative Information Nr./76," November 27, 1976, Stasi Files XX/7.

52. "Aktennotiz über die Berichterstattung im Sekretariat des ZK am 24. November 1976 über die Ergebnisse der Parteiversammlung des Schriftstellerverbandes am 23. November 1976." SAPMO-Barch BPA IV C–2/15/688.

53. Manfred Krug, *Abgehauen: Ein Mitschnitt und ein Tagebuch* (Düsseldorf: ECON, 1996), 30, 38, 42, 45, 60, 82–83, 99, 102. Krug bartered a promise not to release his transcript of this meeting for visas to enable his family to visit relatives in the GDR. Werner Lambertz agreed, and the transcript was published only after the GDR itself vanished. See Beyer, *Wenn der Wind sich dreht*, 373.

54. For Stefan Heym's version, see his *Der Winter unsers Mißvergnügens*, 64–66.

55. Ibid., 125–26.

56. Conversation of Roland Bauer with Jurek Becker, December 6, 1976, Tonbandabschrift. SAPMO-Barch. BPA IV C–2/15/688.

57. Eva-Maria Hagen, *Eva und der Wolf* (Düsseldorf: ECON, 1998), 436.

58. "Stellungnahme vor der Parteiversammlung des Schriftstellerverbandes am 7. Dezember 1976," Becker Papers.

59. "Information: Parteiversammlung des Bezirksverbandes Berlin des DSV am 7.12.1976," December 8,1976, Stasi Files XX/7.

60. "Gerhard Wolf im Gespräch mit Peter Böthig," in *Die Poesie hat immer recht: Gerhard Wolf; ein Almanach zum 70. Geburtstag*, ed. Peter Böthig (Berlin: Janus Press, 1998), 103.

61. Stefan Heym wrote a detailed diary of the events relevant to the Biermann affair, including Jurek's role in it. See *Der Winter unsers Mißvergnügens*, 143–47.

62. Seyppel, *Ich bin ein kaputter Typ*, 146–48.

63. Letter of April 4 1977 to the Schriftstellerverband, Becker Papers.

64. Berlin: "Ergänzung," April 4, 1977, April 7, 1977, "IM Bericht der KD Wss," Stasi Files XX/3.

65. "Information: Haltung des Schriftstellers Jurek Becker zur 'Ausreiseproblematiik,' " August 30, 1977, Stasi Files XX/11: 689 / 77.

66. Interview with Stefan Heym and Inge Wüste, July 17, 1998.

67. "Information," April 21, 1976, 89, Stasi Files.

68. "Abschrift, 76," Stasi Files.

69. "Bericht der Abteilung Volksbildung und Wissenschaften der SED Bezirksabteilung, über die Behandlung von 'Unterzeichnerkindern' in Schulen," quoted in *In Sachen Biermann* (Berlin: Christoph Links Verlag, 1994), 298.

70. "Stadtbezirk Lichtenberg: 554 F 280/77—Verkündet am 4.4.1977," Becker Papers.

71. "Pädagogisches Gutachten für Nikolaus Becker: Abschrift," October 20, 1977, Stasi Files.

72. "Vermerk OV Lügner: Absprache mit Abt. VIII über einzuleitende Beobachtungen am 30.9 und 4.10. 1977," November 28,1977, signed Pahl, Stasi Files XX/7.

73. Interview with Stefan Heym and Inge Wüste, July 17, 1998. Wüste raised this point during our discussion; Heym seemed surprised by it.

74. Charles S. Maier, *Dissolution: The Crisis of Communism and the End of East Germany* (Princeton: Princeton University Press, 1997), 48.

75. Berlin, April 6, 1977, "Ergänzung": April 7, 1977, "IM Bericht der KD Wss," Stasi Files XX/3. Jurek told the pseudonymous informant that he had no desire to remain in the GDR after his divorce and would like to go "over."

76. All quotations from *Sleepless Days* are from the Vennewitz translation (see chap. 4, n. 46).

77. Alfred Wellm, *Pause für Wanzka, oder Die Reise nach Descansar* (Berlin: Aufbau, 1968). See the account, with Jurek's comments, in Corino, *Die Akte Kant*, 330–31.

78. "Über die durchgeführte Lesung des Schriftstellers Jurek Becker am 16. 6. 1977 in der Kirche von Berlin-Bohnsdorf," Stasi Files.

79. Beyer, *Wenn der Wind sich dreht*, 214–78.

80. Letter from Klaus Höpcke to Kurt Hage, "Information über die Behandlung des Manuskriptes 'Leben in der Luft' von Jurek Becker durch des Hinstorff Verlag." July 8, 1977, Stasi Files. The manuscript was picked up at Jurek's home on June 13, 1977.

81. "Information," July 14,1977, Stasi Files XX.

82. "Bericht über eine Schriftstellerlesung mit Fragestellung und Diskussion," June 17, 1977; "Über die durchgeführte Lesung des Schriftstellers Jurek Becker am 16. 6. 1977 in der Kirche von Berlin-Bohnsdorf; Bericht: Buchlesung des Schriftstellers Jurek Becker 21. Juni 1977 (Kreisdienststelle Treptow)"; Stasi Files.

83. Letter from Pettelkau to the Superintendent of the Kirchenskreises Oberspree, July 20, 1977, Becker Papers.

84. Abschrift/AP 30.6. 1977: "Gutachten zu einem Manuskript ohne Titel (169 S.)," signed "Monika," June 29,1977, Stasi Files.

85. "Ich glaube, ich war ein guter Genosse," *Der Spiegel*, July 18, 1977, 128.

86. Letter from Klaus Höpcke to Kurt Hager (see n. 79), Stasi Files.

87. Letter signed "Iburg" from Der Bundesbeauftragte für die Unterlagen des Staatssicherheitsdienst, August 2, 1996, Becker Papers.

88. All the readers' reports are in the archive of the Hinstorff Verlag, Rostock.

89. "Ich fühle micht nicht im Exil," *Lutherische Monatshefte*, March 1981, 133.

90. "Ich glaube, ich war ein guter Genosse," 128–32.

91. Joachim Seyppel, " 'Austritt: Jurek Becker, Bezirksverband Berlin' (DDR)," *Frankfurter Rundschau*, July 19, 1977. See also Seyppel, *Ich bin ein kaputter Typ*, 154–55, for his account.

92. "Mit dem Weggang der Künstler schwindet die moralische Legitimation," *Frankfurter Rundschau*, August 5, 1977.

93. "Information: Rostock, July 18, 1977, signed "Buch," Stasi Files.

94. "Information: Jurek Becker," July 22, 1977, signed Major Regorius, Stasi Files XX.

95. August 30, 1977, Stasi Files XX/7.

96. Berlin, August 26, 1977, "Information über den Schriftsteller JB: Discussion with Klaus Poche," Stasi Files.

97. Heinz Klunker, "Abschiede von der DDR: Verlorene Identität," *Deutsches Allgemeines Sonntagsblatt*, August 7, 1977.

98. Wolfram Schütte, "Die Bevölkerung muß endlich so behandelt werden wie die Künstler: FR-Gespräch mit dem Schiftsteller Jurek Becker (DDR)," *Frankfurter Rundschau*, September 6, 1977.

99. "Vermerk," Meeting with Höpcke on September13, 1977, Stasi Files XX/7.

100. Letter to Jurek, September 13, 1977, Stasi Files.

101. Letter from Jurek to Höpcke, September 19, 1977, Stasi Files.

102. Letter from Höpcke to Jurek, September 25, 1977, Stasi Files.

103. "Aktennotiz: Fauth und Simon," July 26, 1977 signed Fauth, Stasi Files.

104. "Vermerk: Buchprojekt Jurek Beckers beim Hinstorff Verlag Rostock," September 28, 1977, Stasi Files XX/7.

105. Becker, *Ende des Grössen Wahns*, 123.

106. Krug, *Abgehauen*, 127–28; and Beyer, *Wenn der Wind sich dreht*, 209–10.

107. Letter from Kurek, September 19, 1977, Stasi Files.

108. Letter from Pehnert to Jurek, October 5, 1977, Stasi Files.

109. "Ich glaube ich war ein guter Genosse," 132.

110. Beyer, *Wenn der Wind sich dreht*, 399–408.

111. Note, September 26, 1977, Stasi Files.

112. "Bericht und Zusammenfassung zum Gespräch über den Film 'Das Versteck,'" 5.

113. Letters from Wolf to Hoffmann, October 7, 1977, and from Hoffmann to Wolf, January 31,1978, Stiftung Archiv der Akademie der Künste ZAA 1895.

114. Files of the Ministry of Culture / DEFA: DB / 643, Bundesarchiv.

115. Report of IMS 'Günther' about a discussion with Jurek after the showing of the film, November 9, 1978, Stasi Files XX/7.

116. Fred Gehler, "Das Versteck," *Sonntag*, December 3, 1978; and Güter Agde, "Versteckspielen mit Augenzwinkern," *Filmspiegel* 26 (1978).

117. Letter from Krug to the Rat des Stadtbezirks Pankow, April 16, 1977, Becker Papers:.

118. Letter, November 7, 1977, Becker Papers.

119. Wolfgang Werth, "Ein Unbotmäßiger auf Urlaub," *Süddeutsche Zeitung*, December 20, 1997.

120. Police Report, November 4, 1978, on "Becker, Leonard," Stasi Files.

121. Letter from H. Otto, November 20, 1979, to Werner Neugebauer, with a copy of the school assignment and paper, Stasi Files.

122. October 2, 1978, Stasi Files XX.

123. "Einschätzung des Sohnes von Jurek Becker," August 19, 1981, Stasi Files XX/7.

124. "Kurzprotokoll über ein Gespräch mit Frau Becker, Mutter von Nikolaus Becker," undated, Stasi Files.

125. "Information," April 18, 1978, Stasi Files HV A/XI/1404.

126. Jurek Becker: Staatliches Komitee für Rundfunk 2. 582: FS III/SFB 20:15 13.02.78, Stiftung Archiv der Akademie der Künste.

127. "Für Offenheit in der SED," *Frankfurter Rundschau*, February 8, 1978. The question of *Berufsverbot* is addressed by Joachim Seyppel in *Ich bin ein kaputter Typ*, 220–21.

128. "Information" and "Notiz über ein Gespräch mit Jurek Becker am 12.1.1978," signed Hinckel, January 13, 1978, Stasi Files XX/ 13.1.1978.

129. "Ich glaube, ich war ein guter Genosse," 133.

130. Berlin, January 31, 1978, 3, Stasi Files XX/7.

131. Letters from Richard Zipser to Jurek October 14, 1975, and October 11, 1976, Becker Papers.

132. Letter from Schulz, August 15, 1977, Becker Papers.

133. Hans Jürgen Schulz, *Mein Judentum* (Stuttgart: Kreuz Verlag, 1978), 10–18. The West German context of this talk is provided by Stephan Braese, *Die andere Erinnerung: Jüdische Autoren in der westdeutschen Nachkriegsliteratur* (Berlin: Philo, 2001), 485–516, based on Wolfgang Hildesheimer's contribution to the Schulz volume.

134. Becker, *Ende des Grössen Wahns*, 17.

135. Ibid.

136. These are reprinted in his collected short stories: Jurek Becker, *Nach der ersten Zukunft* (Frankfurt am Main: Suhrkamp, 1980), 145–64. All references are to this edition.

137. Letter to his publisher Sigfried Unseld, February 27, 1978, Becker Papers.

138. "Urlaub von der DDR," *Stern Magazin* 31 (July 13, 1978): 116–20.

139. Becker, *Nach der ersten Zukunft*, 165–74.

140. "Zusammentreffen mit Schriftsteller Jurek Becker (Mai 1978)," Stasi Files XX/7/IV/2051/78

141. Letter from Jurek to Rieke, May 2, 1978, Becker Papers.

142. Letter to Willi Moese, March 3, 1978, Becker Papers.

Chapter Seven

1. Letter from Höpcke, July 17, 1978, Stasi Files.

2. "Information," July 29, 1978, Stasi Files XX.

3. Dresden, September 28,1978, Stasi Files XIX.

4. October 17, 1978, Stasi Files XX.

5. M. K., "Autoren aus Ost und West berichten über ihre Arbeit," *Westdeutsche Allgemeine Zeitung*, October 24, 1978.

6. Marcel Reich-Ranicki, "Denk ich an Deutschland in der Nacht: Sieben Schriftsteller, deren Heim die DDR war, beantworten unsere Fragen," *Frankfurter Allgemeine Zeitung*, October 18, 1980.

7. Staatlich. Komitee für Rundfunk: Abteilung Monitor, November 2, 1978, Stasi Files.

8. Jurek Becker, "Ahasver. Der ewige Jude gibt keine Ruhe," *Der Spiegel*, November 2, 1981, 240–46.

9. Jörg Hafkemeyer, "Wenn Literatur zu wichting wird," *Konkret*, September 1979, 36.

10. "Bezirksverwaltung Potsdam: Drewitz," November 22, 1978, Stasi Files XX/2/4065/78.

11. "Sonnenalle Berlin: Fahndungsergebnis," July 30, 1981, Stasi Files HA/BV.

12. October 10, 1978, Stasi Files XX/7.

13. "Ich fühle micht nicht im Exil," *Lutherische Monatshefte*, March 1981, 132.

14. Card from the Zinns, September 22, 1980, Becker Papers.

15. "Operative Information," April 20, 1979, Stasi Files XX/7.

16. Hafkemeyer, "Wenn Literatur zu wichting wird," 37.

17. Joel König, *Den Netzen entronnen* (Göttingen: Vandenhoeck & Ruprecht, 1967); reprinted as *David: Aufzeichnungen eines Überlebenden* (Frankfurt am Main: Fischer, 1979).

18. "*David:* Ein junger Jude will überleben: Filmsensation auf der Berlinale," *Hamburger Abendblatt*, March 1, 1979; Karena Niehoff, "Einer, der übrig bleibt," *Der Tagesspiegel*, April 6, 1979.

19. Letter from Kurt Bartsch, Jurek Becker, et al., to Erich Honecker, May 16, 1975, Archiv der Akademie der Künste: SValt 1255. On the context see *Protokoll eines Tribunals: Die Ausschlüsse aus dem DDR-Schriftstellerverband 1979*, ed. Joachim Walther et al. (Reinbeck: Rowohlt, 1991).

20. Peter Hutchinson, *Stefan Heym: The Perpetual Dissident* (Cambridge: Cambridge University Press, 1992), 185.

21. Seyppel, *Ich bin ein kaputter Typ*, 188–89.

22. February 1, 1979, letter to XX/7 XX/7/414/79 (dated Leipzig, October 8, 1979), Stasi Files XV.

23. "Information," October 2, 1979, Stasi Files.

24. "Aktennotiz," October 4, 1979, Stasi Files.

25. Two versions of the "Protokoll eines Gesprächs, für das sich kein Partner findet," the second with handwritten comments, Becker Papers.

26. Claus Altmayer, " 'Der Mythos von der allgegenwärtigen Kralle': Die Rolle der Stasi in Jurek Beckers Der Verdächtige und Gunter Kunerts Lovestory—made in DDR," *Literatur für Leser* 20 (1997): 196–213.

27. Horst Simon and Andreas Fecker, "Verlagsgutachten: Jurek Becker, Nach der ersten Zukunft" (December 21, 1979), and Anneliese Löffler, "Zum Manuskript von Jurek Becker: Nach der ersten Zukunft" (October 31, 1979), Hinstorff Archive.

28. A film version of this story, *So schnell geht es nach Istanbul* (*One Can Go So Quickly to Istanbul*) was made by Andres Dresen in 1990 and set in the new GDR just as the GDR was about to disappear. It starred Yolcu Yüksel and Janet Mattukat.

29. Harry Fauth and Horst Simon, "Aktennotiz über das Autorengespräch mit Jurek Becker am 9. November 1979," Stasi Files.

30. October 19, 1979, and IM "Schönberg" October 30, 1979 "Einschätzung des vorgelegten Manuskripts von Jurek Becker," Stasi Files XX/7 (name disclosed by Jurek Becker). Jurek had received a partial key to the names from the "Gauck" commission.

Letter signed Iburg, Der Bundesbeauftragte für die Unterlagen des Staatssicherheits-dienst on August 2, 1996, Becker Papers. The others he worked out in his notes to his files.

31. "Jurek Becker und die Politik: Die DDR hat kein Repressions-Monopol," *Fell-bacher Zeitung*, May 29, 1981.

32. Ordner Jurek Becker (no shelf number): Staatliches Komittee für Rundfunk; Monitor: Klaus Sauer DLF; September 25, 1980, Archive der Akademie der Künste.

33. Hartwick Maack, "Selbstzerstörerische Melancholie," *Der Tagesspeigel*, March 2, 1980.

34. "Aktennotiz zu einem Gespräch mit Jurek Becker am 16. 11. 79," Stasi Files.

35. Letter from Jurek to Höpscke, November 28, 1979, Becker Papers.

36. December 1, 1979, Stasi Files XX.

37. Ulrich Schwarz and Rolf Becker, " 'Ja, wenn Stalin ein großer Mann war . . .' : Schriftsteller Jurek Becker über seine Existenz zwischen Ost und West," *Der Spiegel*, March 3, 1980, 205.

38. Reinhard Hübsch, "Politisches Verhalten gehört zu meinem Stoffwechsel," *Stuttgarter Zeitung*, January 15, 1980.

39. "Operative Information: Hinweise auf das Verhalten einiger DDR-Künstler, die zeitweilig im Ausland leben," March 2, 1982, Stasi Files XX/7.

40. Jurek's letters to Raddatz are collected at the Schiller-Nationalmuseum: Deutsches Literaturarchiv in Marbach.

41. June 14, 1981, Stasi Files XX/5.

42. "Ich fühle micht nicht im Exil," 132.

43. "Information 1072/81," November 20,1981, Stasi Files XX/5.

44. "Jurek Becker und die Politik," citing Schwarz and Becker, " 'Ja, wenn Stalin ein großer Mann war . . .' "

45. Ehrhart Neubert, *Geschichte der Opposition in der DDR 1949–1989* (Bonn: Bundeszentrale für politische Bildung, 1997), 419–21.

46. "Jurek Becker am Telefon: Etwas hat sich verändert," *TAZ*, December 17, 1982.

47. Ibid.

48. Ausführung von Jurek Becker während der "Berliner Begegnungen," Decem-ber 14, 1981, Stasi Files.

49. Hanno Kremer, "In diesen Stunden: Gespräch mit Jurek Becker," *RIAS Mag-azin*, December 24, 1981.

50. Photocopy of invitation to the Meeting at The Hague, undated, Becker Papers; "Information," May 26,1982, Stasi Files XX.

51. Letters from Harald Müller to Jurek, January 16, 1980, and September 29, 1981; letter from Peter Hoheisel of the Bayerischer Rundfunk on February 3, 1982; Becker Papers.

52. "Drehspiegel," *Süddeutsche Zeitung*, August 14, 1982.

53. Roman Ritter, "Nächtlicher Herzschmerz," *Unsere Zeit*, December 7, 1982.

54. Manuscript beginning "Der Trainer, außer sich über den Verlauf des Spiels, rief Kilian an den Spielfeldrand," Becker Papers.

55. All references are to Jurek Becker, *Aller Welt Freund* (Frankfurt am Main: Suhrkamp, 1982).

56. "Aktennotiz: Gespräch mit Jurek Becker am 4. 6. 1982 in Berlin," Stasi Files.

57. "Einschätzung des Manuskripts 'Aller Welt Freund' von Jurek Becker," Stasi Files XX/7.

58. Letters to Ritzerfeld at Suhrkamp, June 5, 1982, and from Unseld, June 30, 1982, Becker Papers.

59. "Jurek Becker, Stadtschreiber in Bergen-Enkheim 1982/83," *Forum, Mainzer Texte* 8 (1983): 36.

60. "Ich will Ihnen dazu eine kleine Geschichte erzählen," *Betrifft: Erziehung*, July–August 1983, 98.

61. "Jurek Becker wird der neue Stadtschreiber," *Frankfurter Rundschau*, May 26, 1982.

62. "Jurek Becker: Politisches Verhalten ist optimistisches Verhalten," *Post-Gewerkschaft*, March 20, 1983.

63. From "Werner," "Information: Betr. Lesung und Diskussion mit Jurek Becker in der Dorfkirch Neuenhagen 16.11.1983, and Information zur Lesung mit Jurek Becker im Rahmen der Friedendekade," Stasi Files 8928/91; "Lesung und Diskussion mit Jurek Becker in der Dorfkirche Neuenhagen am 16.11.1983," December 7,1983, Stasi Files XX/7; "Vermerk" (with comments on Kristallnacht), October 18, 1983, Stasi Files XX/4.

64. "Jurek Becker, Stadtschreiber in Bergen-Enkheim 1982/83," 36.

65. Letter to Lonni, November 7, 1983, Becker papers.

66. Jurek Becker, "Rede auf dem Römerberg: Zum 50. Jahrestag der Bücherverbrennung," in *Weiches Wasser bricht den Stein: Widerstandsreden*, ed. Katja Behrens (Frankfurt am Main: Fischer, 1984), 70–71.

67. Letter from Brugel Zeeh at Suhrkamp to Jurek, February 7, 1983, Suhrkamp Archive.

68. See Norbert Otto Eke, "Wahrnehmung im Augen-Schein: Thomas Braschs (und Jurek Beckers) filmische Reflexion über die Kunst nach Auschwitz: 'Der Passagier—Welcome to Germany,'" in *Literatur und Demokratie: Festschrift für Hartmut Steinecke zum 60. Geburtstag*, ed. Alo Allkemper and Norbert Otto Eke (Berlin: Erich Schmidt, 2000), 285–300, and Margrit Frölich, *Between Affluence and Rebellion: The Work of Thomas Brasch in the Interface between East and West* (New York: Peter Lang, 1986).

69. Joseph Wulf, ed., *Theater und Film im Dritten Reich* (Berlin: Ullstein, 1966), 443–58. See also David Welch, *Propaganda and the German Cinema, 1933–45* (Oxford: Clarendon Press, 1983), and Yizhak Ahren, Stig Hornshoj-Moller, and Christoph B. Melchers, *"Der ewige Jude"—wie Goebbels hetzte: Untersuchungen zum nationalsozialistischen Propagandafilm* (Aachen: Alano, 1990).

70. Karsten Witte, *Der Passagier—Das Passagere: Gedanken über Filmarbeit* (Frankfurt am Main: Frankfurter Bund für Volksbildung, 1988), 7.

71. Marianna D. Birnbaum, "An Interview with Jurek Becker," *Cross Currents* 8 (1989): 160.

72. Michael Assmann, ed., *Wie sie sich selber sehen: Antrittsreden der Mitglieder vor dem Kollegium der Deutschen Akademie* (Göttingen: Wallstein, 1999), 257–58.

73. Ruth Klüger, *Weiter leben: Eine Jugend* (Göttingen: Wallstein, 1992); translated as *Still Alive: A Holocaust Girlhood Remembered* (New York: Feminist Press, 2001).

74. Hildegard Nabbe, " 'Wie ich ein Deutscher wurde': Das Problem der Identität in Jurek Beckers *Bronsteins Kinder*," in *Hinter dem schwarzen Vorhang: Die Katastrophe und die epische Tradition*, ed. Friedrich Gaede, et al. (Tübingen: Francke, 1994), 256–67, and Susan G. Figge and Jennifer K. Ward, " '(Sich) Ein genaues Bild machen': Jurek Becker's *Bronsteins Kinder* as Novel and Film," *Germanic Review* 70 (1995): 90–98.

75. Jurek Becker, *Bronsteins Kinder* (Frankfurt am Main: Suhrkamp, 1986). All references here are to the translation by Leila Vennewitz, *Bronstein's Children* (New York: Harcourt Brace Jovanovich, 1988).

76. Wolfgang Wippermann, *Wessen Schuld? Vom Historikerstreit zur Goldhagen-Kontroverse* (Berlin: Elefanten-Press, 1997).

77. Letter from Unseld to Becker, March 13, 1986, Becker Papers.

78. Sigurd Schmidt, "Gutachten zu dem Roman 'Bronsteins Kinder' von Jurek Becker," and H. J. Bernard, "Gutachten Jurek Beckers 'Bronstein's Kinder' " [*sic*], Hinstorff Archive.

79. "Verlagsgutachten: Jurek Becker, Bronsteins Kinder," Hinstorff Archive.

80. Becker, *Ende des Grössen Wahns*, 112.

81. Detailed account by Otto Meissner, sent to Jurek on October 14, 1991, outlining the background of the series, Becker Papers.

82. Knut Hickethier, *Geschichte des deutschen Fernsehens* (Stuttgart: Metzler, 1998), 460–64.

83. Becker, *Ende des Grössen Wahns*, 208–10.

84. Letter from Nicolas Becker to Jurek, January 19, 1984, Becker Papers. See also Nicolas Becker, "Anwalts Liebling: Jurek Becker und die Justiz," *Frankfurter Allgemeine Zeitung*, March 17, 1997.

85. David Rock, "Jurek Becker as TV Scriptwriter: A former Communist engages with Market Forces?" *Literature, Markets, and Media in Germany and Austria Today*, ed. Arthur Williams, Stuart Parkes and Julian Preece (Bern: Peter Lang, 2000), 115–26.

86. See Manfred Durzak, "Erfolge im anderen Medium: Jurek Becker als Fernseh-Autor; Überlegungen zur Fernsehserie *Liebling Kreuzberg*," in *Jurek Becker*, ed. Irene Heidelberger-Leonard (Frankfurt am Main: Suhrkamp, 1992), 312–31, and David Rock, "Jurek Becker as TV Scriptwriter: A Former Communist Engages with Market Forces?" in *Literature, Markets and Media in Germany and Austria Today*, ed. Arthur Williams et al. (Oxford: Peter Lang, 2000), 115–26.

87. Uwe Schmitt, "Vom Schreiben wie man's spricht," *Frankfurter Allgemeine Zeitung*, April 4, 1987.

88. Max Thomas Mehr, "Eine nicht ganz vollzogene Scheidung," *Tageszeitung, TAZ Magazin*, September 25, 1989.

89. Schmitt, "Vom Schreiben wie man's spricht."

90. "Werkstattgespräche mit Jurek Becker," in *Jurek Becker: Werkheft Literatur*, ed. Karin Graf and Ulrich Konietzny (Munich: Iudicium, 1991), 68.

91. Becker, *Ende des Grössen Wahns*, 204.

92. "Bißchen mächtig," *Der Spiegel* 9 (1988): 179.

93. "Geschichte über Geschichten," *Buch Journal* 3 (1992): 20.

94. Janet Swaffer, personal communication, February 5, 2001.

95. Letter from Joachim Preuß to Jurek, May 6, 1988, Becker Papers.

96. First printed in Becker, *Ende des Grössen Wahns*, 63–77.

97. Letter from Jurek to Preuß, October 2, 1988, Becker Papers.

98. It is with this novel that the debate about whether Jurek Becker continues to be a GDR author crystallizes. See Uwe Wittstock, *Von der Stalinallee zum Prenzlauer Berg: Wege der DDR-Literatur 1949–1989* (Munich: Piper, 1989), 185–89.

99. Sigurd Schmidt, "Gutachten der 'Erzählungen' von Jurek Becker," March 19, 1986, and Horst Simon, "Verlagsgutachten: Jurek Becker, Erzählungen," March 26, 1986, Hinstorff Archive.

100. "Jurek Becker Schriftsteller," Stasi Files XX/7.

101. This exchange is summarized in Gabriele Michel, *Armin Müller-Stahl: Die Biographie* (Berlin: List, 2000), 183–85.

102. Jurek Becker, "Ernüchterung," *Die Tageszeitung, TAZ Magazin*, February 20, 1987.

103. Charles S. Maier, *Dissolution: The Crisis of Communism and the End of East Germany* (Princeton: Princeton University Press, 1997), 155.

104. Jurek Becker, "Er kommt," *Die Zeit*, July 24, 1987.

105. Schmitt, "Vom Schreiben wie man's spricht."

106. Martin Walser, "Über Deutschland Reden," *Die Zeit*, November 4, 1988.

107. Marianna D. Birnbaum, "An Interview with Jurek Becker," *Cross Currents* 8 (1989): 157.

108. Jurek Becker, "Gedächtnis verloren—Verstand verloren," *Die Zeit*, November 18, 1988, reprinted in Becker, *Ende des Grössen Wahns*, 78–84, quotation p. 82.

109. Jurek Becker, "Gedächtnis verloren—Verstand verloren," *Neue deutsche Literatur* 35 (1989): 164–70; "Information zur derzeitigen Situation des Schriftstellers Jurek Becker," March 23, 1989, Stasi Files XX/7.

110. Jeffrey Herf, "Old Arguments and New Problems," *Partisan Review* 66 (1999): 375–91; Amir Eshel, "Vom eigenen Gewissen: Die Walser-Bubis-Debatte und der Ort des Nationalsozialismus im Selbstbild der Bundesrepublik," *Deutsche Vierteljahrsschrift für Literaturwissenschaft und Geistesgeschichte* 74 (2000): 333–60.

111. Letter to Marcel Reich-Ranicki, November 29, 1988, Becker Papers.

112. Jurek Becker, *Warnung vor dem Schriftsteller* (Frankfurt am Main: Suhrkamp, 1990). See Rhys W. Williams, "German Literature and Its Discontents: Jurek Becker's *Warnung vor dem Schriftsteller*," in *Jurek Becker*, ed. Colin Riordan (Cardiff: University of Wales Press, 1998), 85–93.

Chapter Eight

1. "Über eine Lesung des Schiftstellers Jurek Becker am 9.5.1989," Stasi Files.

2. Information: "Buchlesung des Schriftstellers Jurek Becker am 9.5.1989 im Club der Kulturschaffenden in Berlin," Stasi Files XX/7/2261/89.

3. "Jurek Becker, Lesung am 9.5.89," signed Klawun, Stasi Files: XX/7.

4. "Über eine Lesung."

5. The two standard histories of the transition are Konrad H. Jarausch, *Die unverhoffte Einheit 1989–1990* (Frankfurt am Main: Suhrkamp, 1995), and Charles S. Maier, *Dissolution: The Crisis of Communism and the End of East Germany* (Princeton: Princeton University Press, 1997).

6. Max Thomas Mehr, "Eine nicht ganz vollzogene Scheidung," *Tageszeitung, TAZ Magazin*, September 25, 1989.

7. Jurek Becker, "Eine Art von Selbstverstümmlung," *Der Spiegel*, February 8, 1988.

8. Mehr, "Eine nicht ganz vollzogene Scheidung."

9. Ibid.

10. Jurek Becker, "Die Suppe ist eingebrockt," *Die Zeit*, October 6, 1989.

11. Julia Hell, *Post-Fascist Fantasies: Psychoanalysis, History, and the Literature of East Germany* (Durham: Duke University Press, 1997), 50ff.

12. Mehr, "Eine nicht ganz vollzogene Scheidung."

13. Letter to Klaus Höpcke, October 2, 1989, Becker Papers.

14. Official Letter from Klaus Höpcke to Jurek (undated), marked III/6 and noted as an answer to Jurek's letter of October 2, 1989, Becker Papers.

15. See Klaus Wischnewski's discussion of the private showing on October 28, 1989, "Spuren eines Films," *Die Weltbühne* 47 (November 21, 1989): 1487–88. See also Beyer, *Wenn der Wind sich dreht*, 341–42.

16. Two version of this tale exist. The first is closer to the date of its actual occurrence and is virtually identical to the second except in detail. The first is a radio broadcast written by Jürgen Werth, ". . . daß Fortschritt auch in Ernüchterung bestehen kann: Über Jurek Becker," WDR, December 7, 1981, 10:30–11:00 P.M., and retold almost verbatim in "Geschichte über Geschichten," *Buch Journal* 3 (1992): 20–24; quotation p. 20.

17. Rainer Traub and Rolf Becker, "Wunsch nach etwas Obsessivem," *Der Spiegel-Spezial* 3 (1992): 107.

18. Christa Wolf, *Reden im Herbst* (Berlin: Aufbau, 1990), 119.

19. See Wolfgang Jäger, *Die Intellektuellen und die deutsche Einheit* (Freiburg im Breisgau: Rombach, 1997); Ursula Bredel, *Erzählen im Umbruch: Studie zur narrativen Verarbeitung der "Wende"* (Tübingen: Stauffenburg, 1999); Stephen M. Brockman, *Literature and German Reunification* (Cambridge: Cambridge University Press, 1999).

20. Letter from Keil to Jurek on February 12, 1989, Becker Papers.

21. Anne Ponger, "Reden übers eigene Land," *Süddeutsche Zeitung*, December 6, 1989.

22. Becker, *Ende des Grössen Wahns*, 173.

23. Mehr, "Eine nicht ganz vollzogene Scheidung."

24. Unofficial letter from Klaus Höpcke to Jurek, December 16, 1989, Becker Papers.

25. Traub and R. Becker, "Wunsch nach etwas Obsessivem," 104.

26. Maier, *Dissolution*, 163. Klaus Höpcke found a life after the GDR as a member of the PDS (Party of Democratic Socialism) for Thuringia. He has written prodigiously to explain his past as well as his present views. See Klaus Höpcke, *Personen-Querelen und Politik-Qualität: Zwölf Reden, drei Briefe, eine Presseerklärung, ein Antrag, zwei mündliche Anfragen an die Landesregierung und ein kulturpolitisches Thesenpapier; Februar–Dezember 1992* (Erfurt: Linke-Liste-PDS-Fraktion, 1992); *Gegensteuern: zur Politikwechsel-Debatte* (Schkeuditz: GNN-Verlag, 1998); *Meinung verpflichtet* (Schkeuditz: GNN-Verlag, 2000).

27. Becker, *Ende des Grössen Wahns*, 183.

28. Jurek Becker, "Über die letzten Tage: Ein kleiner Einspruch gegen die große deutsche Euphorie," *Neue Rundschau* 101 (1990): 90.

29. Jarausch, *Die unverhoffte Einheit 1989–1990*, 206.

30. Letters from Otto Meissner, January 6, 1990, and May 21, 1991, Becker Papers.

31. Wolfgang Brenner, "Comeback des Boxers," *Tipp* 23 (November 1990): 30–35.

32. Ibid.

33. "Gäste im Haus," *Berliner Zeitung*, July 17, 1973; Hans Gärber, "Sommerlich leicht," *Schweriner Volkszeitung*, July 27, 1963.

34. Letter from Flotho for the minister, Wolfgang Schäuble, April 19, 1991, Becker Papers.

35. See the interview with Jurek about the film, "Das ist meine Art von Bankraub," *Brandenburgische Neueste Nachrichten*, November 10–11, 1990, in which he speaks about his tendency to be unkind and sharp-tongued.

36. Karl Corino, ed., *Die Akte Kant: IM "Martin," die Stasi und die Literatur in Ost und West* (Reinbeck bei Hamburg: Rowohlt, 1995), 472–84.

37. First published as Jurek Becker, "Die Wiedervereinigung der deutschen Literatur," in *Spätmoderne und Postmoderne: Beiträge zur deutschsprachigen Gegenwartsliteratur*, ed. Paul Michael Lützeler (Frankfurt am Main: Fischer, 1991), 23–34; reprinted in Becker, *Ende des Grössen Wahns*, 118–35.

38. Personal communication from Gerhard Wolf, February 10, 2001.

39. See Volker Hage, "Die Wahrheit über Jakob Heym," *Die Zeit*, March 15, 1991.

40. See Sander L. Gilman, "Is Life Beautiful? Can the Shoah be Funny? Some Thoughts on Recent and Older Films," *Critical Inquiry* 26 (2000): 279–308.

41. Letter from Dr. Sadek, November 5, 1990, Becker Papers.

42. Telegram from Höpcke to Jurek, November 30, 1990, Becker Papers.

43. Letter from Walter Jens, August 3, 1990, Becker Papers.

44. Letter from Klaus Höpcke August 9, 1990, Becker Papers.

45. Letter from the Literarisches Colloquium, November 5, 1990, Becker Papers; "Meist freundlich, aber auch heftig: Martin Walser und Jurek Becker im Literarischen Colloquium zu Gast," *Der Morgen*, November 17–18, 1990.

46. Maier, *Dissolution*, 165.

47. Beyer, *Wenn der Wind sich dreht*, 314–15.

48. Letter from Artur Brauner, July 29, 1991, Becker Papers.

49. Christiane Peitz, "Bebilderte Podiumsdiskussion," *Tageszeitung, TAZ Magazin*, June 26, 1992; Frank Schnelle, "Viel zu sagen, nichts zu sagen," *Frankfurter Rundschau*, June 26, 1992. See also Thomas Jung, " 'Widerstandskämpfer oder Schriftsteller sein . . .' " *Jurek Becker—Schreiben zwischen Sozialismus und Judentum* (Frankfurt am Main: Peter Lang, 1998), 217–26.

50. DPA wire-service story, July 22, 1992, Becker Papers.

51. Jurek Becker, "Zum bespitzeln gehören zwei," *Die Zeit*, August 3, 1990.

52. Ibid.

53. Ibid.

54. Jurek Becker, "Der Defekt ist der Normalfall," *Der Spiegel* 36 (1993): 86.

55. DPA wire-service story, July 22, 1992, Becker Papers.

56. Christa Wolf, *Was bleibt: Erzählung* (Frankfurt am Main: Luchterhand, 1990). Compare Bernd Wittek, *Der Literaturstreit im sich vereinigenden Deutschland: Eine Analyse des Streits um Christa Wolf und die deutsch-deutsche Gegenwartsliteratur in Zeitungen und Zeitschriften* (Marburg: Tectum-Verlag, 1997).

57. Traub and R. Becker, "Wunsch nach etwas Obsessivem," 107.

58. Brenner, "Comeback."

59. See Becker's interview "Zur deutschen Einheit" on the news program *Dienstag*, HR3, February 19, 1991.

60. Dietfried Müller-Hegemann, *Die Berliner Mauer-Krankheit: Zur Soziogenese psychicher Störungen* (Herford: Nicolai, 1973).

61. Jürgen Leinemann, *Der gemütliche Moloch: Zwei Berlin auf dem Weg zu einer Hauptstadt* (Hamburg: Rasch und Röring, 1991), 75.

62. Irene Dische, *Sad Strains of a Gay Waltz* (New York: Henry Holt, 1993), 193. The novel was first published first in German as *Ein Fremdes Gefühl* (Berlin: Rowohlt, 1993).

63. Jurek Becker, *Amanda Herzlos* (Frankfurt am Main: Suhrkamp, 1992), 305. All references are to this German edition.

64. Klaus Wilke, "Es geht nicht an . . . " *Lausitzer Rundschau*, October 22, 1992.

65. Letter from Meinard Ade, August 14, 1992, Becker Papers.

66. Sabine Gölz, "Where Did the Wife Go? Reading Jurek Becker's 'Parkverbot,' " *Germanic Review* 62 (1987): 10–19.

67. See the very negative review by Hans Gärber, "Komm mit nach Montevideo," *Schweriner Volkszeitung*, January, 19, 1963.

68. Alice Schwarzer, *Der "kleine Unterschied" und seine großen Folgen* (Frankfurt am Main: Fischer, 1977); Luise Pusch, *Das Deutsche als Männersprache: Aufsätze und Glossen zur feministischen Linguistik* (Frankfurt am Main: Suhrkamp, 1984). Jurek also read works by Ursula Scheu, Marilyn French, and Simone de Beauvoir.

69. "Geschichte über Geschichten," 22.

70. Norbert F. Plötzl, *Basar der Spione: Die geheime Missionen des DDR-Unterhändlers Wolfgang Vogel* (Hamburg: Spiegel, 1997).

71. Compare Gunilla-Friederike Budde, "Der Körper der 'sozialistischen Frauenpersönlichkeit' Weiblichkeits-Vorstellung in der SBZ und frühen DDR, " *Geschichte und Gesellschaft* 26 (2000): 602–28.

72. Letter from Renate Kragel, née Kubitza, January 20, 1993, Becker Papers.

73. Geschichte über Geschichten," 24.

74. By the 1990s, Marcel Reich-Ranicki had a unique place in the German cultural sphere. Not only had he been the book reviewer and book review editor of *Die Zeit* and the *Frankfurter Allgemeine Zeitung* for over a decade, but he had also run the most success cultural program on television, *The Literary Quartet*, since 1988. Born in Poland, raised in Berlin, a survivor of the Warsaw ghetto uprising, a communist agent in Great Britain after the war, Reich-Ranicki had led a life similar to Jurek's own. On Jurek, see Marcel Reich-Ranicki, *Mein Leben* (Stuttgart: Deutsche Verlags Anstalt, 1999), 444. While a great supporter of *Jacob the Liar*, he was very cool about Jurek's novels once Jurek moved to the West. There was a very unpleasant moment in 1986 when Jurek accused Reich-Ranicki of having authored an anonymous and almost slanderous review of *Bronstein's Children*. On receiving Jurek's letter, Reich-Ranicki

sent it to Jurek's publisher, denying that he had written the review (Becker papers). Jurek appeared on Reich-Ranicki's television show in 1990 to discuss Umberto Eco's *Foucault's Pendulum*, which he refused to read. Stephan Reichenberger, ed., . . . *und alle Fragen offen: Das Beste aus dem Literarischen Quartett* (Munich: Heyne, 2000), 97–114. All their public and private arguments were marked by profound respect. See Jochen Hieber, ed., *"Lieber Marcel": Briefe an Reich-Ranicki* (Stuttgart: Deutsche Verlags Anstalt, 1995), 13–17 for selected (positive) letters written between 1977 and 1988.

75. Marcel Reich-Ranicki, "Drei Idioten," *Frankfurter Allgemeine Zeitung*, September 19, 1992.

76. Iris Radisch, "Irene trostlos," *Die Zeit*, August 7, 1992.

77. Traub and R. Becker, "Wunsch nach etwas Obsessivem," 111.

78. "Amanda Seltsam," *München Journal*, December, 1992, 81.

79. Sven Michaelsen, "Seufzen aus der Seele," *Stern* 31 (1992): 32.

80. Reich-Raniciki, "Drei Idioten."

81. Traub and R. Becker, "Wunsch nach etwas Obsessivem," 107.

82. Jurek Becker, "Ich verlange, beschützt zu werden," *Süddeutsche Zeitung*, November 28–29, 1992, 19.

83. Becker, *Ende des Grössen Wahns*, 158–62.

84. Ibid.

85. Ibid.

86. Martin Ebel, " 'Der Staat tut seine Pflicht nicht'," *Badische Zeitung*, November 6, 1992.

87. Martin Doerry and Volker Hage, "Zurück auf den Teppich!" *Der Spiegel* 50 (1994): 200. The promise of the good future that existed in his childhood in the GDR was a theme that Jurek used as early as 1981: Werth, ". . . daß Fortschritt auch in Ernüchterung bestehen kann," 5.

88. Doerry and Hage, "Zurück auf den Teppich!"

89. Leinemann, *Der gemütliche Moloch*, 28.

90. Martin Walser, "Deutsche Sorgen," *Der Spiegel* 26 (June 28, 1993): 45–47.

91. Paul Michael Lützeler, "Jurek Becker starb am 14. März 1997: Versuch eines Nachrufs," *GDR Bulletin* 24 (1997): 85–88. See also Gregory Baer's interview with Jurek made during this time, "On Track? Jurek Becker on Reunification and German Literature," *GDR Bulletin* 20 (1994): 18–20.

92. Christa Wolf, *Voraussetzungen einer Erzählung: Kassandra* (Darmstadt: Luchterhand, 1983).

93. See Peter Schneider's posthumous recollections of Jurek in Berlin, "Jurek im Café," in Schneider, *Die Diktatur der Geschwindigkeit* (Berlin: Transit, 2000), 127–32.

94. Jurek Becker, "Der Tausendfüßler," in *Schreiben zwischen den Kulturen*, ed. Paul Michael Lützeler (Frankfurt am Main: Fischer Taschenbuch Verlag, 1996), 55–64; reprinted in Becker, *Ende des Grössen Wahns*, 216–330.

95. In a long television interview with Günter Gaus on January 21, 1993, published in Günter Gaus, *Zur Person* (Berlin: Edition Ost, 1998), 16–17, 23.

96. Testimony before the Deutscher Bundestag, *Aufarbeitung von Geschichte und Folgen der SED-Diktatur in Deutschland am 4. Mai 1993: Kunst und Kultur in der DDR*, sec. 35, pp. 136–37.

97. "Kein Dauergeschwätz," *Wochenpost,* June 19, 1994, 28–29.

98. Mehr, "Eine nicht ganz vollzogene Scheidung."

99. Jurek Becker, *Wir sind auch nur ein Volk,* 3 vols. (Frankfurt am Main: Suhrkamp, 1994). See also Moray McGowan, "Zoo Story? Jurek Becker's Television Script *Wir sind auch nur ein Volk,*" in *Jurek Becker,* ed. Colin Riordan (Cardiff: University of Wales Press, 1998), 94–105.

100. Doerry and Hage, "Zurück auf den Teppich," 197.

101. Klaudia Brunst, "Saubere Küche Ost," *Tageszeitung, TAZ Magazin,* December 17, 1994, 16.

102. Klaus Katzenmeyer, "Einschläfernde DDR—Geschichte," *Volksstimme Magdeburg,* December 30, 1991.

103. Reinhard Mohr, "Welch ein Fluch der Einheit!" *Frankfurter Allgemeine Zeitung,* December 20, 1994, 30.

104. Jurek Becker, *Nach der ersten Zukunft* (Frankfurt am Main: Suhrkamp, 1980), 62–103; quoted from the translation by Leila Vennewitz, "The Wall," *Granta* 6 (1983): 75–106. See Beyer, *Wenn der Wind sich dreht,* 259–60.

105. Uwe Jens Deecke stressed the absence of violence that made this a good family film. "Leben mit der Angst," *Berliner Zeitung,* July 31, 1995.

106. "Woche der Brüderlichkeit," *ZDF-Journal* 3 (1996): 37. The film also appeared in July of 1995 in a French version on the Arte television channel as part of a series on the Shoah.

107. See, for example, Wolfgang Pasche, *Lektürehilfen Jurek Becker Bronsteins Kinder* (Stuttgart: E. Klett Verlag für Wissen und Bildung, 1994).

108. "Was heißt hier Liebling? (see chap. 3, n. 15).

109. Letter from Reiner Weiss, August 23, 1995, Becker Papers.

110. Letter from Dr. D. Huhn, Virchow Krankenhaus, August 22, 1996, Becker Papers.

111. Letter from Manfred Krug, June 12, 1995, Becker Papers.

112. Shortly after Jurek's death, Manfred Krug suffered a minor stroke. In interviews given at the time, Krug reflected on Jurek's final illness, on their work together, and on their friendship. Rolf Rietzler, "Ein Schuß vor den Bug," *Der Spiegel* 34 (August 18, 1997), 188–91; Joachim Wehnelt and Adriano Sack, "Liebling Deutschland," *Die Woche,* September 8, 200, 44–45.

113. Ulf Teichert, "Manfred Krug in Bestform—und *Liebling Kreuzberg* geht zurück zu seine Wurzeln," *Berliner Kurier,* March 4, 1997; "Liebling ist zurück" *Hamburger Morgenpost,* October 7, 1997.

114. Postcard to Christine Becker, January 15, 1997, Becker Papers.

115. Herlinde Koebl, " 'Das ist wie ein Gewitter," *Der Spiegel* 13 (1997): 210–16.

116. Becker, *Ende des Grössen Wahns,* 241–52.

Index